Ted Yu

121168

SCHEDULING CONSTRUCTION PROJECTS

EDWARD M. WILLIS

Department of Engineering Technology
College of Engineering
University of North Carolina at Charlotte

JOHN WILEY & SONS,
NEW YORK • CHICHESTER • BRISBANE • TORONTO • SINGAPORE

Photo credits

Chapter 1: Courtesy the Port Authority of New York and New Jersey. *Chapter 2*: Courtesy The Port Authority of New York and New Jersey. *Chapter 3*: Rhoda Galyn/Photo Researchers. *Chapter 4*: Courtesy Times Square Hotel Company. *Chapter 5*: Courtesy Bethlehem Steel Corporation. *Chapter 6*: Courtesy of Times Square Hotel Corporation. *Chapter 7*: Courtesy Bethlehem Steel Corporation. *Chapter 8*: Courtesy Times Square Hotel Company. *Chapter 9*: Courtesy Bethlehem Steel Corporation. *Chapter 10*: Rohm & Hass Company. *Chapter 11*: Courtesy The Port Authority of New York and New Jersey. *Chapter 12*: Courtesy The Port Authority of New York and New Jersey. *Chapter 13*: Mona Zamdmer. *Chapter 14*: Courtesy The Port Authority of New York and New Jersey. *Chapter 15*: Courtesy Howard J. Rubenstein & Associates. *Chapter 16*: Photo by Michel Legrand. Courtesy Tishman Construction Company.

Book designed by Karin Gerdes Kincheloe cover photo by Mona Zamdmer

Library of Congress Cataloging in Publication Data:

Willis, Edward M.
  Scheduling construction projects.

  1. Construction industry—Management. 2. Scheduling (Management) I. Title.

TH438.W55 1986   624'.068   85-26589
ISBN 0-471-80869-5

Printed in the United States of America

10 9 8 7 6 5 4 3 2 1

To my wife, Joan Brewster Willis, who provided unflagging support while I was writing, as well as assistance in preparing the manuscript

PREFACE

This book describes several project scheduling methods for construction. It enables its readers to prepare schedules based on those methods and demonstrates the uses that can be made of project schedules and of other data derived from those schedules. The methods covered include the Critical Path Method (CPM), the Precedence Method (PM), the Program Evaluation and Review Technique (PERT), and a probabilistic method. Several scheduling-related techniques are also discussed, including activity crashing and project expediting, cash flow projections, and resource leveling and resource-constrained scheduling.

The application of computers, in particular microcomputers, to the solution of scheduling problems is explored. Several chapters have material on computer applications, and one chapter describes the types of commercially available programs that are suitable for use on microcomputers. An appendix (Appendix B) contains computer program listings in the BASIC computer language. These programs can be used to solve most of the scheduling problems presented in the book.

The text describes techniques for preparing schedules and provides numerous practical examples of the kinds of construction problems a scheduler will encounter. Exercises at the ends of most chapters enable readers to apply the information presented in the chapter discussions.

Chapters 1 to 4 are introductory. Chapter 1 describes how scheduling fits into the overall construction process. Chapter 2 covers work breakdown, the subdividing of the total project work into tasks, and the determination of task attributes such as duration and cost. Appendix A, which is a concise summary of a cost estimating technique, is meant to be used in conjunction with this chapter. Chapter 3 covers the construction of Gantt charts (bar charts). Chapter 4 introduces logic diagramming techniques that are applicable to the scheduling methods presented later in Chapters 5 to 10 and enables readers to compare the similarities and the differences of these scheduling methods. Chapters 5 to 10 describe the Critical Path Method (CPM), the Precedence Method (PM), the Program Evaluation Review Technique (PERT), and a probabilistic scheduling method. The first two of these methods are discussed in considerable detail, and the last two are discussed in sufficient detail so that readers can understand their advantages and disadvantages and can use them in solving scheduling problems. Chapters 11 and 12 cover calendar day scheduling and updating the schedule, topics that are extensions of the material presented in Chapters 5 to 10. Chapters 13 to 15 describe project expediting, resource-constrained scheduling, and cash flow projections, which are all applications of the previously presented material. The final chapter, Chapter 16, describes the use of microcomputers in the solution of scheduling problems.

I thank the following instructors who reviewed the manuscript during its development: Dwight Bonner, Columbus Technical Institute; Terry L. Bradbury, Purdue University; William E. Brewer, Bowling Green State University; James Rowings, The University of Kansas.

A solutions manual also accompanies this text.

Edward M. Willis

CONTENTS

CHAPTER 2   TASK DEFINITION: THE FOUNDATION OF A
SCHEDULE   **19**

CHAPTER 3   GANTT CHARTS   **55**

SCHEDULING CONSTRUCTION PROJECTS

INTRODUCTION
TO SCHEDULING

OBJECTIVES

The objectives of this chapter are to examine the reasons for scheduling construction projects and to define certain terms that are used in the following chapters. This chapter also briefly describes the construction industry and how project scheduling fits into the overall construction process. It considers the nature and content of a construction contract.

REQUIREMENTS FOR CONSTRUCTION SCHEDULES

Significance of Costs and Time

The cost to complete a construction project and the time that will be required for its completion are almost always of major significance to the parties who are involved. Project costs are closely related to project duration. Costs will increase if the project must be completed in an unusually brief period and will also increase if the construction is drawn out over an unnecessarily long period. The individual or firm that engages a contractor to complete a project is concerned about the actual construction cost and also about the financial cost resulting from having capital tied up in land. Such an individual or firm may find it preferable to spend more on construction to have the project completed in shorter time.

A construction schedule is a management tool that enables construction managers to direct the accomplishment of construction projects so as to complete them in a timely and cost-effective manner. Occasionally, a construction manager will balk at using a particular scheduling technique, particularly if it is a new technique; however, few construction managers dispute the need for construction project schedules. The type of schedule that is required for a particular project depends upon the nature of the project. A simple bar chart schedule may be appropriate for a project involving only a few tasks that must be accomplished in some specified sequence, even though the project may have a high dollar cost and may require the exercise of advanced construction skills. A more complicated project, one involving the completion of a great many highly interrelated tasks, calls for the use of a sophisticated technique, such as the Critical Path Method (CPM). Use of the sophisticated technique may be appropriate for a complex project, even though the project has a low dollar value. A sophisticated technique may be appropriate simply because the contract documents specify its use.

Sophisticated Versus Simple Scheduling Methods

A construction project can be a very complex operation. There may be dozens of crafts and subcontractors simultaneously working on as many or more different elements of the project. The progress made by one party in this team effort will affect the rate at which other parties can proceed with their work. It may be very difficult for even an experienced construction manager to take into account all the interrelationships between the tasks. Although a bar chart schedule may be prepared that is based on study of the relationships that exist between the elements of project work, the bar chart will not actually depict these relationships. If it should become necessary to revise the sequence in which tasks are performed, the effects of such a revision may not be apparent. Sophisticated scheduling methods are appropriate for complex projects because sophisticated methods allow the scheduler to depict the relationships between tasks. Some of the scheduling methods that are described later in this book enable the scheduler to define these relationships more precisely than does the CPM.

Appropriate Level of Detail for a Schedule

The topic of appropriate level of detail is covered in depth in Chapter 2. A schedule should be prepared in sufficient detail to reflect all the significant relationships that exist between the tasks that make up the project, insofar as these relationships are known or can be predicted.

Scheduling and Uncertainty

There is almost always some uncertainty concerning the factors that will actually govern the rate of progress on a project. Weather conditions and labor and materials availability can only be estimated when the schedule is prepared. This uncertainty is an argument for the preparation of a detailed schedule, rather than an argument for proceeding with a sketchy schedule or no schedule. If the construction manager has prepared a detailed schedule, he or she can immediately determine the impact that some unexpected event will have on the project progress and can take corrective action to minimize such impact. For example, the manager can call for overtime and weekend work to make up for the loss of a week of construction time because of unseasonable heavy rainfall. Although this corrective action may appear obvious, it is not always obvious whether such expediting action is required for all tasks, or just certain tasks.

ESSENTIAL TERMS

Project

A project is a planned undertaking. The scope of a project may range from very broad to very narrow. An example of a project with a very broad scope would be one involving the repair, upgrading, or replacement of all deteriorated or substandard bridges in the Interstate highway system. Such a project would be conceived at a very high level within the nation's executive or legislative branch. After Congress approved the project and provided the funding for its implementation, the project might possibly be divided into subprojects for execution based on such criteria as geographic region and urgency. A project with an intermediate scope might be one in which a private firm develops a commercial and industrial park. Such development might include market studies to determine the optimum location, size, and nature of the park and its facilities, acquiring the land, arranging for short-term and long-term financing, and designing and constructing the buildings and the utility and road systems. An example of a project with a narrow scope would be a project to alter the interior partitioning of an existing building.

Construction Project

The construction process includes planning, designing, and constructing. For the purposes of this book, a construction project is defined as a project to construct a specific facility or group of facilities, such as a building or a group of buildings, and the related utility and road systems. Although a construction project, as defined, has a narrow scope, such an undertaking can be very complex. The construction of a large office or industrial building may require the coordinated efforts of the general contractor and dozens of subcontractors, material fabricators, and vendors.

Construction Project Schedule

A construction schedule is a time-phased plan to perform the work that is necessary to complete a construction project. Hereafter, the contractor will be indicated as the person who prepares the construction schedule. The schedule may actually be prepared by a member of the contractor's staff, the scheduler, who will be assisted by other members of the contractor's staff and, sometimes, by scheduling consultants. The schedule is almost always prepared in a graphic format, in a tabular format, or in both formats. The schedule indicates the planned starting and ending dates for each of the work elements that make up the total amount of construction work to be performed. A subsequent chapter will cover the principles for breaking down the total amount of work to be performed into work elements. In this book, these work elements are called tasks but they may also be called work packages or activities.

The modern art of scheduling began with the development of the bar chart, often called a Gantt chart, about 70 years ago. The bar chart was originally applied to industrial management but was soon adopted by the construction industry. It enables the user to depict graphically the planned sequence of project work activities. The bar chart is still widely used today, either as the primary scheduling tool or as an aid in presenting schedules that have been prepared by using more contemporary techniques. The bar chart schedule is described in detail in Chapter 3.

PARTICIPANTS IN THE CONSTRUCTION PROCESS

Most of the following parties will be participants in a typical construction project. Throughout this book, the term "he" will often be used to refer to an individual. Such usage is meant solely for the sake of brevity. Women now play significant roles in all sectors of the construction industry, and it is expected that their participation in the industry will continue to increase.

The Owner

This is the individual, the firm, or the organization that funds the construction project and will own the completed facilities. The owner, perhaps assisted by consultants, specifies the scope of the construction project. In some instances, the owner may specify the detailed layout of the facility, the type of materials to be used, and so forth. The owner, perhaps assisted by some of the parties described below, and depending on the technical expertise of his or her own staff, may inspect the project work as it is being performed and on its completion. The golden rule in the construction process is: "He who has the gold makes the rules." Because the owner controls the purse strings, he or she dictates the kind of contract that will be used and selects the other parties to the project.

The Designers

They may be employees of the owner, but are more often the employees of an architect–engineer (AE) firm. In addition to designing a facility that meets the expressed needs of the owner and that complies with applicable building codes, the AE may be retained by the owner to act as his or her representative in inspecting the project work, to review and approve materials that the contractor proposes to use in the work, to review and recommend contractor requests for progress payments, and to perform other functions on behalf of the owner.

The Contractor and Subcontractors

These are individuals or firms that undertake to perform required construction work in return for a contract price. Contractors may be categorized as prime contractors and subcontractors. Prime contractors have a contractual relationship with the owner, whereas subcontractors have a contractual relationship with the prime contractor or with another subcontractor. General contractors are prime contractors who contract to perform all of the required work, possibly excluding some specialty items such as electrical and mechanical work that the owners desire to contract directly with the specialty contractors. Subcontractors are sometimes referred to as first-tier subcontractors, second-tier subcontractors, and so on. A first-tier subcontractor has a contractual relationship with a prime contractor. A second-tier subcontractor has a contractual relationship with a first-tier subcontractor, and so forth. A typical construction contractor, regardless of whether a prime contractor or a subcontractor, will perform certain functions, either personally or by use of his staff. These functions include the following:

> **Home Office Functions.** These include the selection of potential projects, estimating the costs of such projects, the preparation of bids or negotiating construction contracts, the procurement of construction materials, the management and maintenance of contractor-owned equipment, and personnel and financial management. The titles of home office contractor staff members might include: estimators, schedulers, procurement specialists, accountants, counsel, project managers, fleet managers, safety officer, quality control officer, and others.

Field Functions. The contractor's principal field function is project management. The contractor may have a project manager, a project superintendent, or both as his field supervisors at the project site. Other contractor field personnel may include office engineers, office clerks, time-keepers, clerks, inspectors, and foremen.

The Construction Manager

He or she is an employee of a professional construction management firm that may be retained by the owner to perform predesign planning, to help select the designer, to help select contractors, and to perform post-contract award functions. The construction management firm may perform all or some of these functions in return for a fee. When capitalized, the term Construction Manager (CM) means an employee of such a firm. The term construction manager can also be applied to many other management level personnel within the construction industry.

The Design—Build Firm

The term is usually reserved for firms that perform both design and construction functions, but such a firm may also perform planning functions.

Fabricators and Vendors

These terms apply to firms that contract with the owner or with the contractor to fabricate and deliver fabricated or off-the-shelf construction materials to be used in the project. The construction contract may call for the contractor to purchase and install all of the material, or it may call for the owner to purchase some of the material for installation by the contractor. Material that has been procured by the owner is termed **owner-furnished material,** or **OFM.** If the owner is the federal government, the material is termed **GFM.**

BASES FOR PREPARATION OF THE CONSTRUCTION PROJECT SCHEDULE

Arbitrary Basis

The owner may dictate that a project must start and end on specified dates and that major elements of the project must also start and end on specified dates.

An arbitrary schedule for a project with a broad scope may serve a useful purpose in that it serves as an outline for preparation of schedules for included subprojects, if it can be realistically met and if it is not so detailed as to prevent effective implementation by the contractors who will actually perform the work. A schedule that has been prepared on an arbitrary basis is in a general form, with the expectation that the contractor will fill in the details of the schedule and will take other management actions necessary to complete the project on schedule. In general, the owner will best attain his or her objectives by telling the contractor ''what to do'' and by restricting directions on ''how to do it'' to matters of real significance.

Intuitive Basis

The contractor, based on his experience and on his ''gut feelings,'' may prepare a schedule without recourse to the use of formal scheduling techniques. This may be a very effective basis for scheduling projects of a type with which the contractor has had extensive experience. Large and complex projects involving unusual construction methods will require more experience and judgement than simpler projects that are similar to previous projects. As the size of a project increases, it will be very difficult for even the most experienced contractor to prepare a realistic schedule purely on the basis of intuition.

Scientific Basis

The contractor analyzes the project, breaks it down into simpler parts, and determines the relationships between the parts. Then, using formal scheduling techniques and his judgement based on experience and intuition, he prepares the schedule. This book will emphasize the scientific method of scheduling, but the reader is cautioned that even the most exhaustive study of scheduling techniques is not a substitute for a thorough understanding of construction procedures and methods.

THE CONTRACT CONSTRUCTION INDUSTRY

The contract construction industry is one of the largest industries in the United States, both in annual dollar volume and in the number of persons it employs. Although some owners, particularly government agencies and public utilities, will perform a large amount of construction using their own employees, the great preponderance of construction work is performed by the hundreds of thousands of construction companies. Individual construction companies range in size from those that have an annual business volume of under $100,000 to those with an annual volume of several billion dollars. There is an increasing tendency for general contractors to subcontract out portions of the work to specialty subcontractors. Some general contractors now subcontract out essentially all of the work, whereas others may subcontract out only a small percentage of the work. The author recently visited a job in which three different specialty subcontractors were engaged: one to erect forms for cylindrical columns, another for flat slabs, and the third for waffle slabs, with the general contractor constructing some other forms with his own employees. This is a typical example of the diversity of subcontracting practices. The principal reason for subcontracting work is that few general contractors can afford to keep specialized craftsmen continuously on the payroll in view of the fluctuations in the quantity and nature of their projects.

THE CONSTRUCTION CONTRACT

Legal Considerations

A contract is an agreement between two or more parties, the terms of which agreement are enforceable by law. The essential elements of a contract are as follows:

> **Mutual Understanding.** The agreement must be based on mutual understanding. Regardless of whether the agreement is oral or in writing, the terms of the agreement must clearly specify the rights and obligations of all parties to the contract. In case of a dispute between the contracting parties, the courts will look at the contract as a whole (the contract forms, the contract plans, and the contract specifications); the courts will interpret the words in the agreement using the ordinary meaning of those words within the local construction industry; and the courts will resolve ambiguities in the agreement against the party who was responsible for inserting the ambiguous words in the contract.
>
> **Legality of the Agreement.** The agreement must be on a lawful matter. An agreement between several contractors in which one or more of the parties agree to refrain from bidding on a construction project would be construed by the courts as an illegal restraint of trade, and such an agreement could not be part of a valid contract.
>
> **Valid Consideration.** The agreement must involve a valid consideration for each of the parties involved. In the legal sense, valid consideration

consists of the exchange, or the promised exchange, of something of value. In a construction contract, the contractor promises to construct a facility, and the owner promises to pay the contractor for doing that work. The consideration need not be adequate, but it must be present. The promise by one party to perform a duty that he is already obligated to perform is not a valid consideration. For example, if an owner is already obligated to pay a contractor a stipulated price for performing specified work and then refuses to pay the contractor that price until the contractor agrees to perform additional work without additional compensation, there has been no valid consideration. Conversely, a contractor may not demand additional compensation to perform a duty that he is already legally obligated to perform, for example, expediting work to complete the project by the contract completion date.

Legal Competence.   The parties to the contract must be legally competent, meaning that they are of sound mind and that they are authorized to make the agreement. A contractor will ordinarily authorize only a few of his employees to commit him contractually. However, a contractor may inadvertently confer such authority on an employee by honoring an unauthorized exercise of such authority.

Possibility of Performance.   The things that are promised must be possible to perform—not necessarily easy, just possible. The courts would find invalid an agreement between a contractor and an owner in which the contractor was required to construct a substantial building in an impossibly brief time. The courts would find valid an agreement in which the contractor was required to construct a building on a site having no satisfactory access road, even though construction of such an access road was not specifically called for in the agreement.

Valid Form.   The agreement must be in a valid form, meaning that some agreements must be in writing, as opposed to being oral. Within the construction industry, it is common that agreements will initially be oral and then later are reduced to written form.

Other books contain detailed coverage of contract law as it pertains to the construction industry. It has been said that ''a man who serves as his own attorney has a fool for a client.'' Although there is some truth in this saying, a construction contractor needs a sound personal working knowledge of contract law.

Types of Construction Contracts

The form that will be used in a particular contract is specified by the owner. The Associated General Contractors of America and the American Institute of

Architects have jointly developed several standard contract forms. Government agencies and large firms have also developed their own standard contract forms. Regardless of who has developed the form, the construction contract is usually of one of the types described below.

Lump Sum or Fixed-Price Contracts. Under this type of contract, the contractor is obligated to perform all the work specified in the contract documents for a specified contract amount. If the actual cost of doing the work is more than the contractor estimated, the contractor is required to absorb the costs without an increase in the contract amount. Conversely, if the actual costs are less than estimated, the contractor will retain the savings as an increase in his profit.

Cost Plus Fixed-Fee Contract. The contractor is again required to perform the work specified in the contract documents. In return, the owner is obligated to reimburse the contractor for costs actually incurred and to pay the contractor an agreed-to-in-advance fee that is meant to include the contractor's general overhead costs and profit. Such contracts often include a maximum cost clause, under which the contractor is required to absorb any costs in excess of some stipulated sum. These maximum cost clauses usually specify that the owner and the contractor will share in any savings if actual costs are less than the stipulated maximum amount.

Cost Plus Percentage Contract. The contractor is entitled to reimbursement of his actual costs plus a percentage of those costs to cover his general overhead costs and a profit. Such contracts can reduce the contractor's motivation for controlling costs; hence, they are not used in federally funded projects.

Unit Price Contracts. The contractor is entitled to payment of an agreed-to-in-advance price for each unit of work (e.g., tons of bituminous concrete placed) that is actually performed. This type of contract is often used for grading and paving projects in which the exact quantity of earth to be excavated and of pavement to be laid can be determined only as the work is performed and as the exact nature of the site conditions is revealed.

Other Variations. A construction contract may contain some of the features of several of the types of contracts described above.

Any of the contracts described above may be modified after they are initially made so as to reflect changes in the project scope desired by the owner, unforeseen site conditions, or errors and omissions by one of the contracting parties in discharging his or her obligations. Such modifications, usually called change orders, may modify the contract price, the contract duration, or the technical nature of the work to be done. In general, both parties must agree to the revision of contract terms. However, most contract documents give the owner at least some authority to unilaterally revise the terms of a contract.

Selection of Contractors

The two bases for award of a construction contract to a particular contractor are negotiation and competitive bidding.

> **Negotiation.** The owner may request that a contractor submit a proposal (an offer) to perform the work. The proposal will contain the contractor's proposed price. The owner may accept the offer or he may negotiate with the contractor for changes in the terms of the offer. If an offer is made and accepted, an agreement has been reached. If an offer has been made by the contractor and if a counter-offer is made by the owner, the contractor may accept that counter-offer, he may submit a revised offer, or he may simply withdraw from the negotiations. In general, receipt of a counter-offer releases the original offerer from his offer.

> **Competitive Bidding.** The owner may advertise a project, requesting submission of bids from all qualified contractors or from specified contractors. In general, the owner will award the contract to the responsible contractor who submits the lowest responsive bid. A responsible contractor is one who possesses appropriate experience in the type of work to be done and who also has adequate financial assets to be able to complete the project. A responsive bid is one that is in accord with the advertised project requirements. A contractor's low bid might be disqualified if the contractor proposed completing the work in more time than was stipulated by the owner.

Federal and other government agencies, as well as government-regulated public utilities, are generally required by law to award contracts on the basis of competitive bidding. These agencies may also be required by law to set aside a certain amount of construction work for award to small business companies or to minority-owned businesses.

Contract Requirements

A construction contract includes the contract forms that are described in the preceding section and other documents including general conditions, special conditions, contract plans, and contract specifications. The contract documents may require that the contractor not only perform the contract work, but that he also submit the following documents.

Bonds

The contractor may be required to submit a bid bond with his proposal. A bid bond is a guarantee to the owner that the contractor will sign a construction contract if his proposal (offer) is accepted by the owner. The guarantee may be in the form of the deposit of cash or other valuable instruments, or it may be in the form of a surety bond issued by an acceptable (to the owner) surety. A surety is a company that agrees to discharge the legal duties of another company or of an individual if that other company or individual fails to discharge the duties. If the contractor is unwilling or unable to sign the contract, the deposit or money from the surety will be used to reimburse the owner for financial losses that he suffers when he must award the contract to another contractor who may have submitted a higher bid. The owner stipulates the amount of the bid bond.

If the owner offers a contract to the contractor, the contractor may then be required to submit payment and performance bonds. These bonds may be in the form of a deposit or in the form of an instrument issued by a surety. The payment bond will be used to pay workmen, vendors, and first-tier subcontractors if the contractor has not made such payment. The performance bond will be used to reimburse the owner for additional costs that he may incur if the contractor is unwilling or unable to perform the work in terms with the contract, and if the owner must have some or all of the work performed by another contractor. These bonds are meant to protect the financial interests of the owner, not of the contractor. If a surety is required to make payment on a bond to the owner, the surety will seek indemnification (repayment) from the contractor. The contractor must pay the premiums for these bonds, the premiums being related to the contractor's financial condition and his track record on previous projects. The cost of the bonds is just another cost for completing a project, and the contractor will consider these premiums when he proposes a contract price.

Insurance

The contractor may be required to purchase insurance policies that will protect the owner from liability for claims by the public for injuries or damages they suffer as a result of the contractor's operations. The contractor may also purchase various forms of insurance that are meant to protect his own interests, for example, losses that he may incur as a result of fires or accidents. The contractor will also be required to pay the premiums for workmen's compensation insurance and for unemployment compensation insurance.

USES OF CONSTRUCTION PROJECT SCHEDULES

The types of persons who use construction schedules and the uses they make of those schedules are as diverse as is the construction industry itself. The owner and his representatives will use the construction project schedule to monitor progress on the project. The contractor's project managers, project superintendents, foremen, and subcontractors will also use the construction schedule.

To Predict Progress

Project Completion Time

The project completion time is the date when a project will be completed. If the project is being performed under the terms of a contract that specifies a contract completion date, there may be financial penalties for late completion. If the schedule indicates that the plan will result in late completion, then the construction manager has been put on notice that he must revise that plan. Perhaps he can employ more craftsmen, mobilize more equipment, work overtime, or perform tasks in a different sequence.

Task Times

Task times are the times that specific tasks or activities will commence or end. With this information, the manager can make arrangements to have material, craftsmen, and equipment on hand when they will be needed. Procurement of material is often a critical task. The manager can schedule the preparation of procurement specifications and shop drawings, the architect's approval of these documents, and the fabrication and delivery of the material. If the schedule does indicate that initiation of critical tasks will be delayed by the lack of some resource, then the manager is alerted to the need to take extraordinary action to obtain that resource in a timely manner.

Conflicts in Work Sequence

Examination of the task times may reveal conflicts that will occur between different trades or subcontractors because of limited work space. It may also reveal that one trade is scheduled to start a task before another trade has done work that must be completed before that task can be started.

Requirements for Financing

The rate of progress on the project determines the rate at which labor, equipment, and material resources will be consumed and costs will be incurred. It also affects the rate at which the contractor will receive progress payments. The difference between costs incurred and paid and payments received represents the contractor's cash flow on a project. During the early stages of a project, the cash flow is negative, meaning that more cash has been paid out than has been taken in. The contractor may need to borrow additional working capital if he doesn't have enough liquid assets to cope with the problem.

Effect of Proposed Changes

Changes in the project scope, in the type of materials to be used, or of any kind may affect the starting and finishing dates of uncompleted tasks. These changes may increase or decrease the overall project cost. If these changes are initiated by the owner and if they result in increased costs to the contractor, then the contractor should request additional compensation. One of the commonest causes for increased project cost is the extension of the project duration. The cost component **project overhead,** or **POH**, is nearly proportional to project duration. POH includes the salary cost for field supervisors, the onsite utility costs, and so on.

To Serve as a Record

Delays in Work

The schedule should be periodically updated to show both scheduled and actual task times. It should show when work was delayed, whether by the contractor's acts or omissions, by acts of God, or by changes in the project scope or design initiated by the owner. If a task actually starts later than its scheduled time, that delay may affect costs incurred on other tasks. If the delay was caused by the owner, the contractor is entitled to a time extension and additional compensation. If the delay was caused by neither the owner nor the contractor, then the contractor may be entitled to a time extension.

The project superintendent should maintain a project diary and should make frequent job photographs. These records, together with the updated schedule, will indicate to the contractor the amount and reasons for delay and increased costs, and will aid him in negotiating fair compensation from the owner. Such records may be valuable if the contractor wishes to defend himself against penalties that the owner intends to assess for late completion. They may also assist the contractor in justifying increased compensation, which is warranted because of changes initiated by the owner.

Actual Versus Scheduled Completion

It is customary in contract construction for the contractor to submit a periodic invoice or request for partial payment as the work progresses. He will receive progress payments that are based on the percentage completion of the project at the time the invoice was submitted. Often, the owner will withhold some percentage of the contractor's earnings until the project is completed. The **retainage** may be 10% of cumulative earnings until the project is 50% completed. Thereafter, if the project is on schedule, the retainage may be reduced to 5%. A detailed schedule, one that has been properly posted with current project status, is one of the most acceptable forms of evidence that the percentage completion claimed by the contractor is accurate.

Historical Cost Data

A properly updated schedule may be a valuable source of cost and scheduling data that estimators and schedulers can use for future projects.

To Satisfy a Contractual Requirement

Often, in contract construction, the owner of the future facilities has a contractual right to be provided with a copy of the contractor's schedule. He may also have a contractual right to direct the contractor to accelerate progress, perhaps by working extended hours, if the schedule reveals that the job will not be finished by the contract completion date. Some owners may specify the form of the schedule that they are to be provided. For example, the U.S. Army Corps of Engineers often specifies, on larger projects, that the contractor submit a Critical Path Method schedule.

EXAMPLES OF USE OF SCHEDULES FOR CONSTRUCTION PROJECTS

The following examples illustrate the use of construction schedules on various real and hypothetical projects.

A Project Completed Before the Advent of Modern Scheduling Methods

Imagine the scene that may have existed at the site of a large construction project in ancient times, perhaps the construction of a pharaoh's pyramids. Assume that work is progressing without the benefit of a schedule. Hundreds of masons stand idle while their foreman inquires about the status of the bricks. At another location, the brickmakers are awaiting delivery of straw. The farmers are planting the hay, having just learned of the huge market for straw to be used in the bricks that are needed for the construction of Cheops' pyramid. Hopefully, such a scene cannot be witnessed at a modern construction site. In fact, it is unlikely that work on even this ancient project was proceeding entirely without the benefit of some form of schedule. Modern owners (and, presumably, such historic owners as the pharaohs) tend to want their projects completed as soon as possible, if not earlier. The owner will insist that the project proceed at a rate that will result in completion by the date specified in the contract. Contemporary owners may fire their project managers, or terminate their contracts with contractors, if progress falters. The fate that may have fallen on one of a pharaoh's incompetent managers can only be a matter of speculation.

A Sequential Project

Many construction projects involve the performance of a few tasks in a sequential manner. Even though the project may have a high dollar cost and may require that the contractor have a high level of construction skill, such a project can be termed a simple project in that there are few options open to the contractor in sequencing the work. A project to construct a long pier out into a body of water might be a project of this kind if the job conditions were such that the only feasible way of driving piles was from a pile driver on a previously erected section of the pier. Road construction, airfield construction, and bridge construction also tend to be sequential projects.

Even sequential projects demand the preparation of a project schedule. The construction manager must forecast the rate at which work will progress so that he can arrange to have labor, equipment, and material on hand when it is needed.

Concurrent Projects

The construction of large, multistory buildings are concurrent projects. They involve the completion of numerous tasks, with the construction manager having many options as to the sequence in which the tasks are performed. Use of sophisticated scheduling techniques to produce detailed schedules are particularly appropriate for such projects.

A Complex Project Involving Great Uncertainty

The author recently observed a project in which the members of a religious congregation constructed a meeting hall in less than 60 hours. All labor was volunteer labor. The project managers could not actually predict how many volunteers would turn out from their own congregation and from nearby congregations. In a project that was to be constructed in such a brief period of time, even a normal seasonal rainstorm could extend through the project duration. In fact, it did rain throughout most of the construction period. A very brief delay in the delivery of materials could, and did, seriously affect the rate of progress.

I observed no use of a schedule, other than the congregation's plan to finish the job by Sunday. They were successful in that they did complete the project on time and they gained a great deal of satisfaction by meeting their goal. This project was unusual in that the expenditure of labor effort, all labor being contributed, was of little importance. From 50 to 250 workers, mostly unskilled but very enthusiastic persons of all ages, labored around the clock and in disregard of the rain. It is estimated that the man-hours of effort committed to this project were double what would have been required if more deliberate procedures had been followed.

Other Projects in Which Speed Is More Important Than Cost

U.S. Army Engineer units train in peacetime to accomplish wartime projects as rapidly as possible. Units located in Germany routinely construct floating bridges across the 1200-foot wide Rhine River in less than four hours. They succeed in these operations because they have a large and versatile force of soldiers and because they move several cranes and dozers to the site even though each item will be needed for only a brief period of time.

TASK DEFINITION: THE FOUNDATION OF A SCHEDULE

2

OBJECTIVE

This chapter discusses task definition, which is the initial step in preparing a construction project schedule. The principles of task definition are presented and illustrated with construction-related examples.

TASK DEFINITION

Task definition includes work breakdown and the determination of task attributes. Several terms will be used in this chapter. **Work activity** means work in general. A **work element** is an aggregation of work activity that will lead to the completion of some identifiable component, or group of components, of a structure, such as the installation of a door frame, or of all the door frames in a building. **Total project work** includes all work activities that are involved in the completion of a project. All scheduling methods require as an initial step that the total amount of work making up a project be broken down into a manageable number of aggregations of work activities. These aggregations of work activity will be termed **tasks** in this book.

The tasks must be defined, meaning that the work they require must be determined and their properties specified. The properties of a task are termed **task attributes.** Two of these task attributes are **estimated task duration** and **estimated task cost.** Other books may use different terms; **work package** and **activity** usually have the same meaning that **task** has in this book. The term

work breakdown structure has the same meaning that **breakdown of total work** has in this book.

Breakdown of Total Project Work

It is not practical to break down the total amount of work that makes up a project into numerous and extremely small elements such as "carpenter bends down," "carpenter grasps board," "carpenter straightens up," "carpenter lays board on supports," "carpenter saws board," and so on. If the tasks were defined in this detail, there would be so many tasks that the resulting schedule would be too long and too complicated to be of use.

Neither is it practical to break the total amount of work down into just a few broadly defined tasks. A list containing only the items "perform preconstruction activities," "construct foundations," "erect structural shell," and "finish building interior" is not a task listing; it is a brief description of the major phases of a construction project. Each of those phases contains numerous tasks, which may have complex relationships with each other and with tasks that are parts of other phases of the project.

If the total project work is broken down into overly broad groupings, it will be difficult or impossible to define the logical relationships that may exist between the work elements included within those groupings. The objective in the work breakdown process is to divide the total amount of work into enough tasks so that the relationships between work activities can be specified.

Task Attributes

There are two kinds of task attributes, quantitative attributes and qualitative attributes. Some task attributes, such as task duration, will be used directly in preparing the schedule; others, such as task cost, will be used in preparing schedule-related documents such as cost reports.

Quantitative Task Attributes

These attributes have units of measure, for example, days and dollars. The quantitative attribute "task duration" has days as a unit of measure. The quantitative attribute "estimated task cost" has dollars as a unit of measure.

Qualitative Task Attributes

These task attributes do not have a unit of measure but may still be of importance for scheduling-related purposes. For example, it may be desired to obtain a computer printout of a schedule with the printout including only those tasks that will be performed by craftsmen who are employed by the contractor. If the attribute "accomplishment by direct hire" were assigned to those tasks where such assignment was appropriate, then a computer program could produce the desired schedule.

Relationship Between Work Breakdown and Attributes

A major criterion for breaking down the total project work is the grouping together as tasks of those work activities that have related attributes. The scheduler should anticipate the uses that will be made of a schedule before commencing the work breakdown procedure. If the sole purpose of the schedule is to obtain a prediction of total project duration and of the dates that various tasks will start and end, then the scheduler will find it necessary to consider only a few of the many possible task attributes. If, however, it is anticipated that the schedule may be used to prepare projections of the rate at which costs are incurred, or if it is anticipated that the schedule will be used to predict the day-by-day requirements for such construction resources as craftsmen and equipment, then additional attributes must be asigned to the tasks that make up the project.

Consider a group of related work activities that will result in the erection of an interior partition constructed of concrete block. Assume that, as the masons lay the blocks, electricians and plumbers will work along with them to install electrical conduit and pipes within the wall. If the scheduler's objective is merely to predict the dates that erection of the wall can be started and finished, then the scheduler can define a single task, "erect block wall," with that task including all the work done by the masons, the electricians, and the plumbers. If the scheduler wishes to produce a schedule that will predict the dates at which each of these three crafts can start and finish their work on the wall and the total day-by-day project requirements for each of these three types of craftsmen, then he will define three tasks: "erect block wall," "install in-wall conduit," and "install in-wall plumbing." Having defined three tasks, rather than one, to encompass all of the work related to the erection of the wall, the scheduler can also assign other attributes, such as "estimated task cost," to each of the tasks. Then, the scheduler can produce a projection of the rate at which costs will be incurred by his own employees, say, the masons, and by the electrical and plumbing subcontractors.

TASK ATTRIBUTES

Examples of quantitative and qualitative task attributes are described below. The descriptions include a discussion of the possible uses of schedules that are produced with the various attributes being considered.

Quantitative Task Attributes

These attributes have a unit of measure. The units are days, dollars, percentage completion, specific task resource requirements such as carpenters or trucks, and so on. Some quantitative attributes are assigned values. For example, the scheduler estimates a task's duration and assigns that value as a task attribute. Other quantitative attributes are derived. For example, the earliest date that a task can be completed is derived during the scheduling process. The value is derived on the basis of the logical relationships between that task and other tasks and the durations of the tasks.

Time-Related Attributes

These attributes have a time value as unit. Time values can represent a point in time or a period of time.

Estimated Task Duration (Days)
The estimated durations of the tasks can be expressed in **workdays** or in **calendar days.** They can also be expressed in hours, weeks, or some other unit of time. This attribute will be used directly when preparing the schedule. It is an assigned value.

Task Times (Work Dates or Calendar Dates)
Task times are derived attributes indicating the earliest and latest dates that tasks can be started and completed. The value of these attributes is determined during the scheduling process. The meaning of work date and calendar date is discussed in following chapters.

Actual Task Start and Finish Dates (Calendar Dates)
If the schedule is to be periodically updated, then each task must be periodically assigned attributes indicating the actual dates they are started and finished. Chapter 12 covers the updating of project schedules.

Percent Completion
If the schedule is to be periodically updated, then, at each update, all tasks that have been started, but not yet completed, must be assigned an attribute specifying the percentage completion as of the date when the update is made.

Cost-Related Attributes

A schedule is an estimation of the rate at which project work will be completed. If cost-related attributes are assigned to the tasks, the schedule can be used to produce a prediction of the rate at which costs will be incurred, expenses will be incurred, earnings will be made, and income will be realized. A **cost** is a financial obligation of the contractor that has been incurred because workmen or subcontractors have done work. An **expense** is the actual payment of money by the contractor to discharge such an obligation. **Earnings** are entitlements to the contractor that he has earned by performing work and are obligations by the owner to the contractor. **Income** is actual money received by a contractor from the owner to discharge the owner's obligations. The difference between a contractor's project income and his project expense is termed the **project cash flow.** A more detailed explanation of these terms is presented in Chapter 15.

Estimated Task Cost ($)

This is the estimated total direct cost for accomplishing a task. Most tasks will have a value for this attribute. Some tasks may have a zero value for the attribute, at least as far as the contractor is concerned. A project may include work to be done by the owner or by another contractor. Such work must be defined as tasks, and the scheduler must take into account the time required to perform these tasks; however, the work will be done at no cost to the contractor. Estimated task cost may be subdivided into the following attributes: estimated materials cost, estimated labor cost, estimated equipment cost, and estimated subcontractor cost.

Declared Task Value ($)

Frequently, the contractor will be required to submit to the owner a list of **declared task values.** The sum of all the declared values on such a list will be equal to the contract amount. Usually, such submission is required very soon after the contract is awarded. Such a listing is meant to be the basis for computing partial payments that will be paid to the contractor as he performs the project work. A task's declared value will be greater than its estimated direct cost because it includes general overhead and profit. The owner will review this listing of values. If he or she agrees with the values, then partial payments, also termed **progress payments,** will be based on periodic (say, monthly) requests for partial payment (invoices) submitted by the contractor to the owner. The owner will not necessarily agree with the contractor's declaration. He may determine that the contractor has "front-loaded" the values, that is, placed a higher than reasonable value on those tasks that will be completed early in the project and a lower than reasonable value on those tasks that will be completed late in the project duration. A contractor might be tempted to **front-load** a project so as to be able to accelerate the rate at which he receives compensation (income) for the work he has done. Each such request will contain the following data:

> *Percent completion of each task* (or of the entire project) as of the invoice date.

Cumulative earnings by the contractor as of the invoice date. This value is equal to the sum of all the task earnings as of the invoice date. The task earnings for a particular task are equal to the product of that task's declared value and its percent completion. Alternatively, the cumulative earnings may be computed as the product of the contract amount and the percentage completion. The earnings will usually include the value of materials that have been purchased and delivered to the project site, even though they have not been installed.

Cumulative amount due the contractor. This cumulative amount due is equal to the cumulative earnings less a **retainage** of 5% or 10% (the retained percentage will be specified in the contract documents). The purpose of this retainage is to protect the owner's financial interest in case the contractor defaults and the owner incurs additional costs to have other contractors complete the project work. Often, the retainage will be reduced if the project is on schedule after it is 50% completed.

Cumulative amount paid to the contractor in previous partial payments.

Amount due the contractor. This is the cumulative amount due, less previous partial payments.

Resource-Related Task Attributes

These are the resources that are required to perform a task. They include materials, labor, and equipment. The units of measure for labor would be masons, welders, laborers, and the like. The units of measure for equipment would be tractors, dump trucks, cranes, and the like. The units of measure for materials might be cubic yards (CY) of concrete, thousands (M) of bricks, and so on. If some of these resources are constrained (available only in a limited quantity or at a limited rate), then the contractor's progress on a project may be **resource-constrained.** Even if the available quantity of a resource is unlimited, the daily requirements for that kind of resource may fluctuate widely, and the scheduler may desire to schedule the project based on **resource-leveling** methods. Chapter 14 covers resource-constrained and resource-leveling scheduling methods.

Qualitative Task Attributes

Qualitative task attributes are assigned values that do not have a unit of measure. Assignment of at least a few qualitative task attributes is essential for the preparation of even a minimum schedule. Assignment of additional attributes may be useful for the preparation of enhanced schedules or for other scheduling-related purposes. For example, it may be desired to obtain a computer printout of a schedule that included only those tasks that would be performed by a specific subcontractor or that included only those tasks that required the use of contractor-owned construction equipment. The assignment of appropriate attributes would permit the production of the desired schedule by a computer.

Essential Qualitative Task Attributes

The following qualitative task attributes must be assigned regardless of the scheduling method being used.

Task Description
This is a concise description of the work included with a task. It will appear in the completed schedule and on bar charts. Regardless of whether the schedule is prepared manually or by a computer, only a limited amount of space will be available for printing task descriptions if the overall dimensions of the schedules and reports are to be kept at a manageable size. Computer printers will typically print 80 to 132 characters on a page that has a width of 8.5 to 13.2 inches. Within this page width must be printed a half dozen or so task attributes. The examples used in this book and the BASIC computer programs listed in Appendix B are based on task descriptions that have a maximum allowable length of 24 characters.

Task Number
This is a unique number that identifies a task. Assignment of task numbers is important for any schedule; it may be essential if the schedule is to be prepared by a computer. Some computer programs use task numbers to depict the logical relationships between tasks. Other computer programs require that additional task attributes be assigned to depict these logical relationships. The chapters that follow will cover the assignment of these attributes.

Other Qualitative Task Attributes

These attributes may be assigned if they are required for schedule-related reports and documents.

Task Cost Codes
These are used to classify tasks in respect to whether work will be done in-house or by subcontractors, by a specific craft or by a specific contractor, and the nature of the work included within the task (masonry, concrete work, carpentry, etc.). Cost codes are used to generate scheduling-related reports and to format the computer-generated schedules. One cost coding system that is frequently used is the Construction Specification Institute (CSI) system. This system has

been endorsed by the Associated General Contractors of America (AGCA) and by the American Institute of Architects (AIA).

Workday Regime Codes

Schedules can be prepared in work date format or in calendar date format. The distinction between the two formats is covered in Chapter 11. One method of preparing calendar date schedules allows the scheduler to assign **workday regime** codes to the various tasks. One such code might indicate that work can proceed on that task 7 days a week, whereas another code might indicate that work can only proceed on weekdays.

WORK BREAKDOWN

It is unlikely that several schedulers who are working independently on the same project, will break the total project work down into identical lists of tasks. There can be many different correct breakdowns of the total work making up a project. However, a useful work breakdown will have the characteristics described below.

Comprehensive Listing

The listing of tasks will be comprehensive, meaning that all of the work that makes up the project is included in one, and in only one, of the defined tasks. A scheduler who is familiar with construction operations (construction project schedulers must be familiar with construction operations) will always consider, in preparing a task listing, those work activities that result in the completion of such structural elements as foundations, slabs, columns, roofs, walls, and electrical and mechanical systems. A scheduler will seldom omit from his listing those tasks that are essential to the construction of these building components. For example, tasks that are related to the construction of a concrete slab include installing forms and reinforcement; placing, finishing, and curing the concrete; and stripping the forms. These work activities may be grouped together as a single task, or they may be listed as separate tasks.

There are, however, several kinds of work activities that are frequently omitted from task listings. A description of some commonly overlooked work activities is given in the discussion that follows. It can be argued that the definition as tasks of the work activities described below is unnecessary, because everyone knows that these activities have to be completed in a timely manner. It could also be argued that it is unnecessary to schedule the construction of foundations, because everyone knows that the foundations must be completed before erection of structures can commence. The best argument for including these time-consuming activities within a defined task is that this inclusion will virtually guarantee that the scheduler consider their impact on the overall project duration.

Engineering Activities

Some of the engineering-type tasks that are listed in the following discussion will be accomplished by the contractor whereas others will be accomplished by the contractor's suppliers and subcontractors. In most instances, the designer will also be involved. Regardless of who performs the work, the tasks require time for accomplishment and should be included in the task listing.

Shop Drawings

Steel reinforcing bars (rebar) for cast-in-place concrete are normally cut to length and bent into the correct shape by a fabricator. Before the fabricator cuts and bends the rebar, he will prepare shop drawings that contain information on the radius of the bends and the length and location of splices. This information will be used to guide the fabricator's employees, and it will be in greater detail than the information that is found on the drawings prepared by the designer. Most contracts require that such shop drawings be reviewed and approved by the designer before fabrication starts. The drawings are submitted to the designer through the contractor and are returned to the fabricator through the contractor with comments. If the designer has found serious flaws in the shop drawings, he may require that they be revised and resubmitted for further review. Preparation and review of shop drawings, together with the actual fabrication process, can require from a few days up to many weeks. Because time is required to complete these activities, the schedule should include one or more tasks within which they are included.

Other kinds of fabricated material for which shop drawings are normally required include structural steel members and connections, steel open-web joists (OWJ), laminated timber components, electrical control systems, and fire protection systems. In general, shop drawings must be submitted for any materials or assemblies of materials that require additional engineering beyond that provided by the designers. The contract specifications will list those materials for which shop drawing approval is required.

It is not good practice to define a single task as "prepare and review all shop drawings." The initiation of work to prepare some shop drawings, for example, rebar for footings, will be much more critical than the work to prepare shop drawings for other components that will be installed later in the construction sequence, such as store fronts or air-conditioning ducts. The contractor should schedule the preparation of shop drawings and the designer's review and approval of those drawings, in view of how soon the material will be installed and in view of the time required for their preparation and review.

Mix Designs

The contractor is frequently required to submit to the designer mix designs for portland cement concrete, asphalt cement concrete, and similar plant mixed material, together with laboratory test reports on the mixtures he plans to use. The preparation of such mix designs and test reports is routine for batch plant operators and their testing laboratory consultants. However, considerable time may be required to test these mixes, perhaps as much as 28 days for testing a portland cement concrete mix. If the scheduler defines as a task the design and testing of such a mix, he is not likely to overlook later the impact of this work activity on the overall schedule.

Site Surveys and Layout

The designer will have made a site survey, and he or she may have placed some survey markers at critical points. Usually, the designer's survey and markers will be inadequate for guidance of the contractor's equipment operators, so the contractor must resurvey the site and set out grade stakes and other markers.

Test Piles

The contract documents may call for piles that have a specified bearing capacity. The length of the piles that must be driven to attain this required capacity may be determined by driving test piles soon after contract award, and then loading those test piles with concrete weights to ensure that settlements are within pre-scribed limits. Only after these test piles have been driven, and after the designer has approved their performance, will the contractor initiate action to procure the required number of steel piles, or to direct the supplier to cast the required number of concrete piles.

Preconstruction Activities

Permits, Bonds, and Insurance

The contractor is usually responsible for securing building permits, for providing performance and payment bonds to protect the financial interests of the owner, and for purchasing public liability and other forms of insurance. All of these actions may have to be completed before work can start on the project.

Erosion Control

One of the first construction tasks that will be started on a typical construction site is the clearing and the grading of the site. The contractor may be required to construct silt fences and sedimentation ponds before grading commences.

Materials Procurement Activities

Samples, Catalog Cuts, and Technical Data

The contract documents may require that samples or descriptive literature be approved by the architect–engineer before certain materials are procured. For example, architects often require that actual samples of face bricks, floor coverings, and other finish materials be submitted for review. The architect may also require that a sample brick wall be constructed so that he and the owner can ensure that its appearance is satisfactory. Many contract plans and specifications call for the use of specific makes and models of plumbing and electrical fixtures or "their equal." This open type of specification is particularly common in publicly funded projects but is also used in privately funded work. The purpose of such open specifications is to create competition among the various vendors and manufacturers, thereby decreasing the cost of materials.

The contractor is responsible to prove to the designer that the material he plans to use actually is equal to the material referenced in the specifications. He does so by submitting **catalog cuts.** A catalog cut is normally a brochure or a photocopy of a manufacturer's catalog. Submission of detailed technical data reports may be required for items such as air-conditioning system components and electrical switch gear. Again, the contract specifications will indicate the items of material for which such approvals are required.

Procurement of Off-the-Shelf Material

Even for standard off-the-shelf kinds of materials, there may be significant delays between the time a purchase order is made and the time that materials can be delivered. Such delays will result if the contractor needs an exceptionally large quantity of material, particularly if the regional or national demand for that kind of material has increased and the manufacturers have not had time to increase their production schedules. Nationwide, or even worldwide, economic and political situations may create drastic shortages of construction materials. Political unrest in the Middle East, followed by the Arab oil embargo, caused a worldwide energy crisis in the 1970s. This energy crisis caused worldwide shortages of many kinds of construction materials, ranging from portland cement to copper wire. Perhaps that crisis could not have been reasonably predicted. However, during part of that decade, an annual strike by the West Coast stevedore and longshoreman unions was very predictable, and contractors who depended on the use of the struck ports quickly learned to take the possibility of such a strike into account when scheduling jobs.

The contractor should always consider that procurement of materials is a potential cause of project delay. If the contractor defines as tasks the delivery of critical materials, and if delays in delivery ensue, the contractor will be able to readily revise his schedule. Even if there is no practical way in which such delays can be made up, the contractor will have credible evidence that lateness in project completion was due to factors beyond his control.

Mobilization Activities

Jobsite Mobilization

The contractor will need some sort of a field office, usually a trailer. He will need a telephone hookup for the office and an electrical hookup for the office and for construction operations. He will need portable toilets and drinking water for his employees. He may have to recruit employees from surrounding regions.

Equipment Delivery, Setup, and Dismantling

Construction equipment, whether owned by the contractor or rented from others, must be transported to the jobsite. Several days may be required for its delivery. Several days may be required to assemble, and eventually to disassemble, equipment items such as pile drivers and tower cranes. An allowance must be made for these activities when estimating the duration of the tasks in which the equipment will be used, or separate tasks must be defined to include them.

Project Closeout Activities

Project Closeout

When the construction work is completed, the contractor must clean the facilities and the site. He must correct deficiencies found at a joint inspection with the owner. He must remove his field office, his equipment, and his leftover material from the jobsite.

As-Built Drawings and Equipment
Operation Instructions

The contractor will usually be required to submit in reproducible form copies of the contract plans that indicate any deviations of the structure as it was actually built compared to how it was designed, even though all such deviations have been approved by the owner's agents. He will be required to submit copies of operating manuals and maintenance manuals for the equipment that he has installed, for example, air-conditioning units and elevators.

Descriptive Title

Each task will have been given a descriptive title. It is good practice to have these titles consist of at least two words, a verb and a noun. If necessary, additional words may be added to make the meaning clear. Examples are "excavate sewer trench'' and ''place slab-on-grade concrete.'' These title should be concise. Otherwise, they will be too long to fit into the available space on bar charts and other scheduling documents, and it may be necessary to truncate them to the point that they are no longer descriptive.

Logical Grouping of Work Activities

The work activities will be logically grouped together to form tasks. It is easier to present an example of an illogical grouping of activities than it is to describe logical grouping. A task that was defined as ''install all steel'' would include work activities such as the installation of steel baseplates, steel columns, steel girders and beams, steel decking, steel stairs and railings, steel door and window frames, and steel hatches. Some of these activities would be accomplished early in the construction sequence whereas others would be accomplished near the end of the project. Several different trades and subcontractors would perform these activities. Installation of the columns must be done before the girders are installed, but no such logical relationship exists between the installation of door frames and roof hatches. The principles for logically grouping of activities together to form tasks are as follows.

Common Constraints

Group together as a task only those work activities that have common constraints to being started and that, as a group, serve as a common constraint to the start of other tasks. As an example of the application of this principle, consider the erection of load-bearing masonry walls and nonload-bearing masonry partitions. Completion of a foundation may be a constraint to starting the erection of a load-bearing wall, whereas completion of a floor slab may be the constraint to starting the erection of nonload-bearing partitions. Completion of a load-bearing wall is a constraint to starting the installation of beams and joists that are supported by that wall, whereas completion of nonload-bearing partitions may not be a constraint to starting such installation. For this example, it would be incorrect to define a task as ''erect masonry walls and partitions.'' It would be correct to define two tasks: ''erect load-bearing walls'' and ''erect partitions.'' It might even be desirable to break each of these two tasks down into smaller groupings of work activity, such as ''erect first floor partitions,'' ''erect second floor partitions,'' and so on. Defining a task that includes the laying of load-bearing walls and nonload-bearing partitions violates the principle that a task should contain only work activity that has common constraints or serves as common constraints.

Continuous Performance

Group together as a task only those work activities that can be accomplished on a continuous basis. Continuous means that they can be completed without being interrupted while a work activity that is included in another task is being performed. As an example of the illogical grouping together of activities that cannot be completed on a continuous basis, consider a task calling for "place floor slab and resilient flooring." The laying of the flooring will be delayed for some time after the slab is poured to allow masons to erect interior partitions. Note that although it should be possible to perform a task on a continuous basis, it does not follow that a task must be completed on a continuous basis. Inclusion of the activities to pour a floor slab and to place the flooring on the slab within a single task violates the principle of defining the tasks so that their included work can be performed continuously.

Predictable Duration

Group together as a task only those work activities which, as a group, have a predictable duration. The task "landscape project site" might include work activities such as spreading top soil, applying fertilizer and lime, spreading grass seed, and planting trees and shrubs. It will usually be desirable to complete the activities required to establish a stand of grass as early as possible. However, planting of trees and shrubs may have to be delayed because of seasonal considerations, because the owner may desire types of trees and shrubs that will be available only at certain times of the year, or for other reasons. The delays may be unpredictable, and the duration of a task covering all of these activities will be unpredictable. The grouping together of work activities leading to the establishment of a lawn with the tree and shrub planting activities violates the principle of defining tasks that have a predictable duration.

Different Attributes

Break down into several tasks a group of related work activities, even though they meet the above criteria for being grouped together, if the resulting tasks will have different attributes. Placement and compaction of select material beneath a concrete floor slab will be done nearly simultaneously with installation of underslab utility lines. However, several different trades and subcontractors (qualitative task attributes) will be required to perform these related work activities. As another example, rough grading, placement and compaction of select base course material, and finish grading for a road will be performed sequentially, with each work activity requiring a predictable time. However, the types of resources (quantitative attributes) required for the tasks are very different. If the schedule will be used to determine the requirements for a scarce resources, say, scrapers, vibratory rollers, and motorized graders, then it will be helpful if these related work activities are broken down into three tasks: "perform rough grading," "place base course," and "perform finish grading."

Long Lead-Time Materials

Break down into three separate tasks the preparation of shop drawings and the procurement and the installation of long lead-time materials. Weeks may be required to prepare the shop drawings for a chiller unit for an air-conditioning system; months may be required to procure it; and only a few days may be required to install it. A delay of several weeks in the shop-drawing phase or the procurement phase cannot be made up during the installation phase, regardless of how many mechanics are assigned to that latter phase. Grouping the three phases together as a single task will obscure the importance of the engineering and the procurement activities.

Appropriate Level of Detail

The tasks will be defined at an appropriate level of detail. Appropriate means suitable for the needs of the person or persons who will use the schedule, as well as being sufficiently detailed so that the logical relationships between tasks can be specified.

Varying Needs of Users

The owner and the contractor will need less detailed information than will the project superintendent, his foremen, and the subcontractors. The owner may be completely indifferent to the scheduled date for completing the installation of a built-up roof, but the superintendent and the painting subcontractor need to know when the building will be **closed in** and ready for interior finish work. This discussion implies that it may be desirable to prepare several different versions of the same schedule, each suitable for the needs of a different class of user. The preparation of different versions can be facilitated if the schedule is computer-generated and if a cost coding system has been used that will permit the automatic grouping together of related tasks as **supertasks.**

Excessively Broad Definition

A great many more schedules are prepared with insufficient detail than are prepared with excessive detail. It is fairly common to find a construction schedule posted at the field offices of major projects that contains only a few dozen tasks. A bar chart schedule may show "electrical work" as extending from very early in the project until the project is nearly complete. Such a broadly defined task might be defined if the electrical subcontractor will be responsible for installing temporary construction wiring as well as the permanent wiring and the installation of the electrical fixtures. Such a broad task definition serves little purpose other than to indicate that some of the electrical subcontractor's men will be present at the project site during most of the project duration.

Basis for Progress Payments

Earlier in this chapter, it was stated that one of the uses of schedules was to serve as the basis for computing progress payments that are due to the contractor. If the schedule shows that completion of a particular task may require many months, the contractor may have difficulty in convincing the owner that he is due payment for completing the major part of the task in the first few months of the project duration. If the broadly defined task "electrical work" was broken down into several tasks, "install underslab conduit," "pull wires," "install rough wiring in partitions," "install lighting fixtures," and so on, and if each of these tasks has been assigned a declared value, the contractor will have reduced the area of potential disagreement with the owner concerning the cumulative value of work accomplished.

ESTIMATED TASK COSTS AND TASK DURATIONS

These two task attributes are so closely related that they will be covered together. If the project has been estimated using the detailed or **scientific** estimating method, then most of the effort required to determine both task costs and task durations will have been completed. See Appendix A for a brief description of the scientific estimating method. Both the cost and the duration for tasks depend on the magnitude and nature of the tasks; on how many resources are committed to the task; on the hourly rates that will be incurred for these resources; on whether the work will be accomplished on a straight-time or an overtime basis; on the productivity of the resources (equipment and labor) that are committed to the tasks; on the level of supervision exercised during task performance; and on unpredictable factors such as weather. Values for most of these factors will themselves be estimates; hence, the reader may properly conclude that it is very unlikely that an estimator or a scheduler will consistently make exact estimates of task cost and task duration. Fortunately, it is not essential that these task estimates be consistently exact. If all the estimates are reasonably accurate, and if they are made without either an excessively optimistic or an excessively pessimistic bias, then the "law of compensating errors" will result in estimates for total project cost and total project duration that will usually be adequate.

Unfortunately, this law will not protect the contractor if there are significant errors on individual projects, even though his or her average cost estimating accuracy and average project duration estimating accuracy for a number of projects has been very good. The contractor will tend to win a high percentage of contract awards where the cost estimates are low and a low percentage for those projects where the cost estimates are high. He will often finish projects late and be assessed liquidated damages for late completion of projects for which he has underestimated project duration, but will less frequently be awarded a bonus for early completion for projects on which he has overestimated project duration. The contractor's goal for estimated total project cost and total project duration should be accuracy on individual projects rather than an average accuracy for all projects estimated.

Cost Estimates

Project cost estimate will include direct costs (sometimes termed **job directs**) and general overhead costs (**job indirects**).

General Overhead Costs

These represent the contractor's home office expenses, and most of them will be incurred whether or not a particular project is awarded to the contractor. They are allocated to particular projects for bidding purposes on the basis of an average general overhead rate or on the basis of the requirements that a particular job will have for home office support.

Direct Costs

These will be incurred only if the contractor is awarded a contract to construct a particular project. These costs are estimated. The project's direct costs are those that will be incurred in the completion of tasks that have a unit of measure (cubic yards, square feet, etc.). If a task covers the erection of masonry partitions, then the unit of measure might be squares (hundreds of square feet, or SQ) of partition. Project overhead costs are those costs that must be incurred to support project progress but that cannot be conveniently broken down and charged against tasks that have a unit of measure. The superintendent's salary, the cost of maintaining an office trailer, and the cost of performance and payment bond premiums are examples of project overhead costs. Both task costs and project overhead costs are time dependent. In general, task costs increase as task duration decreases whereas project overhead costs increase as project duration increases. Both task costs and project overhead costs are made up of one or more of the following components: materials cost, labor cost, equipment cost, and subcontractor cost. Some project overhead costs, for example, premiums for payment and performance bonds, do not clearly fall into any of these four categories. They may be considered either materials costs or subcontractor costs.

Materials Cost

This cost is a function of the quantity of each type of material that is required (including an allowance for waste) and the unit price of the material (including an allowance for delivery costs and sales taxes). The estimator makes a quantity takeoff from the contract plans and specifications determining as exactly as possible the quantity of each type of material that is required. The estimator must include not only those materials that will be incorporated into the completed structure but also those materials that will be consumed during construction (form lumber, form oil, nails, etc.). Then, perhaps assisted by a procurement clerk, the estimator solicits proposals from vendors. Vendors often assist the estimator by making their own quantity takeoffs and by submitting a proposal to provide all of the required material of certain types for a fixed price. The estimator should ensure that these proposals include delivery costs and that they will remain in effect until such time as the material is delivered for installation.

Some vendors will guarantee prices only for a limited period of time. In such cases, the estimator must estimate the rate of inflation, being guided in this effort by his daily scrutiny of financial journals. The estimator will have little difficulty in finding a pundit, or several pundits, who will predict the rate of inflation. The estimator's difficulty rests in selecting which of the often widely different predictions to rely on.

Labor Cost

This is a function of the type and amount of work to be done, the productivity of the craftsmen who will do the work, and the hourly wage rate to be paid the craftsmen. The amount of work to be done can usually be estimated accurately (lay 55,000 face bricks), but the estimator must consider associated work (erect 500 square feet of steel scaffolding and mix 120 cubic yards of mortar). The productivity of craftsmen must be estimated in quantitative terms (masons will lay 100 face bricks per hour). The productivity of craftsmen depends upon their skill, on the effectiveness of the supervision they receive, and on economic and job conditions. Skilled craftsmen will be more readily available during periods when the construction industry is in the doldrums than when it is prosperous. Craftsmen are supervised by a working foreman (a straw boss) who receives a wage supplement for his supervisory role or by a full-time nonworking foreman. Considering that the productivity of craftsmen is influenced by the quality of supervision as much as or more than by any other factor, a contractor should usually employ the best available foremen and he should not saddle them with craft responsibilities to the extent that they cannot exercise effective supervision.

Job conditions include the weather, the degree of site congestion, whether or not the work is being performed under the terms of a collective bargaining contract, and so forth. Hourly wages will depend on inflation and on the level of construction activity in the region, and they should include allowances for such employer-paid fringe costs as premiums for workman's compensation and unemployment compensation insurance, social security, and union pension funds. The estimator's best guide to the determination of accurate values to be used for estimating labor costs is his or her own experience, supported by the tabulations of cost and productivity rates incurred on similar jobs completed in the recent past. Lacking this experience, the contractor may consult one or more of several cost estimating manuals and handbooks. The productivity data contained in these tables may be based on national averages and on average conditions and may not be applicable to the estimator's project.

Equipment Cost
This is a function of the amount of work to be done, the productivity of the equipment items selected to do the work, and the hourly cost of the equipment items. The quantity of work to be done is determined in the quantity takeoff process. The productivity of equipment is affected by some of the same factors that affect labor productivity.

Subcontractor Cost
This cost is usually based on proposals that have been submitted by subcontractors.

Task Durations

As previously stated, task durations depend on the amount of work of various kinds in a task and on the number and the capabilities of the resources that are committed to do that work. There is usually a principal kind of work in a task (laying bricks as opposed to mixing mortar). The number and capacity of the resources (masons and bricks per mason-hour) committed to the accomplishment of that primary kind of work will govern the task duration.

The following examples illustrate the principles discussed in this chapter. The reader will find it helpful to refer to Appendix A while studying them.

Example 1 Work Breakdown

A project involves the construction of a three-story office building to be con-structed of precast, prestressed concrete elements. All precast elements have steel connection plates cast into their surfaces at required connection points. Floor plans, elevations, and sections are shown in Figure 2.1. The structural components and other data are listed below. *Break the project work down into tasks*, applying the principles described in this chapter. As an aid in breaking down the project work, it is suggested that you subdivide the total work into major phases such as preconstruction activities, job mobilization activities, and site preparation activities. It is further suggested that you attempt to limit your task descriptions so that they have a maximum length of 24 characters.

Site Work.   The structure will be erected on a cleared and level site. It will be necessary to remove and dispose of 1000 cubic yards (CY) of ordinary earth from beneath the building site and to replace it with 2000 CY of select fill. Also, 2000 square yards (SY) of asphalt pavement must be placed for parking and for driveways, 400 SY of concrete walks must be constructed, and 20,000 SY of grounds must be fertilized and seeded.

Foundations.   The structure will be supported by cast-in-place concrete piers and by cast-in-place reinforced concrete grade beams around its perimeter. The holes for the piers will be bored to sound soil, or to rock, and will be cleaned and extended to a minimum penetration of 6 inches into that supporting material.

Columns.   Precast, prestressed concrete columns will be welded to baseplates that are anchored to the piers. The columns are three stories in height.

Girders.   Precast, prestressed concrete girders will be welded to the columns around the building's perimeter.

Floors.   Four inches of gravel will be placed over the compacted subgrade soil. The ground floor slab will be poured over this gravel. It will be reinforced with welded-wire fabric. The second floor and the roof will be precast, prestressed concrete double-tee sections that will span the narrow dimension of the building. These double-tee sections will be supported by, and welded to, the perimeter beams along the building's long dimension. A 2 inch thick, welded-wire-fabric-reinforced, lightweight concrete slab will be placed on each of the double-tee section floors.

Exterior Walls.   The exterior walls will be nonload-bearing. They will be made up of an 8 inch thick, reinforced concrete block inner wall and a 4 inch thick, face brick outer wall. There will be a 1 inch thick, foil-faced, rigid foam insulation panel and a ½ inch thick air space between the inner and the outer walls. The block wall will have steel ladder-type reinforcement in alternate horizontal joints, starting at the first joint above the grade beams, and it will be anchored to the

FIGURE 2.1
A SMALL OFFICE BUILDING

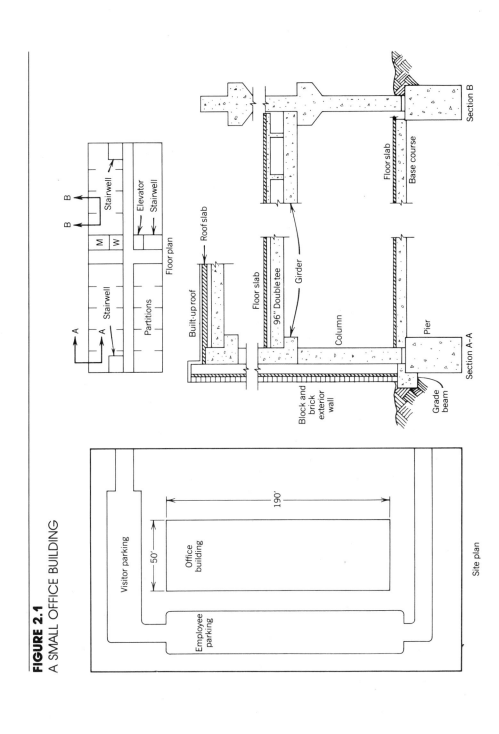

columns and the slabs at 24 inch intervals. No vertical reinforcement is required. The exterior walls will extend 12 inches above the roof slab as a parapet.

Interior Partitions.   The interior partitions are nonload-bearing. Some partitions will be unreinforced, 8 inch thick, lightweight concrete block walls. The remainder will be constructed of steel studs and gypsum wallboard.

Roof.   The roof will be a four-ply built-up roof.

Doors and Windows.   All exterior and interior doors and windows will be preglazed units set in steel frames anchored to the walls and partitions. Steel angles will be used as lintels above exterior doors and windows.

Stairs and Elevators.   The stairs will be made of steel forms filled with concrete. Elevator shafts and stairwells will be constructed of concrete block reinforced with ladder-type reinforcement. The two elevators will be operated by hydraulic cylinders installed in a drilled hole below the elevator shaft.

Interior Finishes.   The interior surfaces of all concrete block will be covered with gypsum wallboard, except in stairwells and elevator shafts. All walls will be painted. Floors in baths will be ceramic tile. Other floors will be sheet vinyl. Ceilings will be acoustical tile supported by a steel grid suspended from the floor above.

Hardware.   There will be panic hardware on exterior doors, and single cylinder locks on all interior doors.

Electrical.   All wiring will be in steel conduit cast into floor slabs or recessed into block walls and partitions; or they will be in the space between the suspended ceiling and the slab above. Lighting fixtures will be recessed into the suspended ceiling.

Mechanical.   Heating and cooling (HVAC) will be by a roof-mounted heat pump with air distribution through ducts above the suspended ceiling.

Solution to Example 1

See Figure 2.2. The total project work has been divided into major phases, and the work making up these phases has been broken down into tasks. The available data permit only the assignment of the attributes "task description" and "task number." There are two versions of the task descriptions. The first version of each task description has a length that often exceeds 24 characters, while the second version has a length of 24 characters or less. There are two reasons for limiting the character length of task descriptions. The first, and most important, reason is that the width of a computer printer page is often limited to 80 characters, with much of that width being required for task attributes other than task description. Similarly, task descriptions must be lettered on logic diagrams. If the task descriptions are too long, then the diagram will be unnecessarily wide. The second reason is that use of brief descriptions will reduce the effort required to enter data into a computer and to letter them on diagrams. In this example,

FIGURE 2.2

TASK LISTING FOR EXAMPLE 1

Task	Task Description	Duration, Workdays	Short Description (24 Characters Maximum)
Preconstruction Phase			
10	Secure building permits	5	Sec bldg permits
20	Secure performance and payment bonds	5	Sec perf/paym't bonds
30	Secure liability and builders risk insurance	5	Sec liab/bldrs rsk insur
40	Prepare and erect project sign	5	Prep/erect proj sign
Engineering Phase			
150	Secure designers approval of concrete mixes	5	Sec app concr mixes
160	Prepare shop drawings—foundation rebar	10	Prep SD found rebar
162	AE review shop drawings—found. rebar	10	Rev SD found rebar
164	Fabricate foundation rebar	15	Fab found rebar
170	Prepare shop drawings—precast concr. mbrs	10	Prep SD PC concr mbrs
172	AE review shop drawings—PC concr. mbrs	10	Rev SD PC concr mbrs
174	Fabricate precast concrete members	30	Fab PC concr mbrs
180	Prepare shop drawings—HVAC ducts	15	Prep SD HVAC ducts
182	AE review shop drawings—HVAC ducts	10	Rev SD HVAC ducts
184	Fabricate HVAC ducts	30	Rev SD HVAC ducts
Procurement Phase			
290	Assemble technical data on heat pumps	15	Ass tec data heat pumps
292	AE review tech data on heat pumps	10	Rev tec data heat pumps
294	Procure heat pumps	90	Proc heat pumps
300	Assemble technical data on HVAC controls	15	Assb tec data HVAC contr
302	AE review technical data on HVAC controls	10	Rev tec data HVAC contrl
304	Procure HVAC controls	20	Proc HVAC controls
310	Assemble samples—vinyl/ceramic flooring	10	Ass samples flooring
312	AE approval—vinyl/ceramic flooring	10	App samples flooring

FIGURE 2.2
(CONTINUED)

Task	Task Description	Duration, Workdays	Short Description (24 Characters Maximum)
314	Procure vinyl/ceramic flooring	20	Proc flooring
320	Assemble catalog data/samples— hardware	15	Ass data/sample hardware
322	AE approval—hardware	10	App hardware
324	Procure hardware	20	Proc hardware
330	Assemble tech data on elevators	20	Ass tec data elevators
332	AE review tech data on elevators	10	Rev tec data elevators
334	Procure elevators	60	Proc elevators
340	Assemble catalog data/samples— plbg fixt	20	Ass dat/sampl plbg fixt
342	AE approval—plumbing fixtures	10	Appr plbg fixtures
344	Procure plumbing fixtures	30	Proc plbg fixtures
350	Assemble catalog data/samples— light fixt	20	Ass dat/samp light fixt
352	AE approval lighting fixtures	10	Appr lighting fixtures
354	Procure lighting fixtures	30	Proc lighting fixtures
360	Assemble face brick samples	10	Assble face brick samples
362	AE selection of face brick	10	Appr face brick samples
364	Lay sample brick wall	10	Lay sample brick wall
366	AE approval of face brick bond/ worksmanship	10	Appr sample brk wall
368	Procure face brick	20	Proc face brick

Job Mobilization Phase

Task	Task Description	Duration, Workdays	Short Description (24 Characters Maximum)
470	Set up project office trailer	5	Set up offc trailer
480	Install temp electric svc for office/ site	5	Instl temp elec svc
490	Erect fence—materials storage area	5	Fence stg area
400	Install temp toilets/wash facilities	5	Instal temp toilets
410	Hook up telephone lines project office	5	Hook up offc telephone

Site Preparation Phase

Task	Task Description	Duration, Workdays	Short Description (24 Characters Maximum)
520	Survey site and set grade stakes	5	Svy and lay out site
530	Install silt fences/sediment pond	10	Inst silt fence/pond
540	Strip/stockpile topsoil	5	Strip/stckpl topsoil
550	Dispose of unsatisfactory soil	5	Dispose unsat soil
560	Grade/compact subgrade	5	Grade/compact subgrade
570	Place/compact select fill	5	Place/comp select fill
580	Install temp site drainage system	5	Inst temp drainage

Foundation Construction Phase

Task	Task Description	Duration, Workdays	Short Description (24 Characters Maximum)
690	Bore pier holes	10	Bore pier holes
692	Pour pier concrete	5	Pour pier concr

FIGURE 2.2
(CONTINUED)

Task	Task Description	Duration, Workdays		Short Description (24 Characters Maximum)
700	Drill and case hole for elevator cylinders	4		Drill/case elev hole
710	Place/compact base course	5		Plc/compact base course
720	Install underslab water lines		5	Inst US water lines
730	Install underslab electric conduit	5		Inst US electr cond
740	Install underslab water lines and drains	5		Inst US water lines/drns
750	Form/reinforce/pour grade beams	10		FRP grade beams
760	Form/reinforce/pour footings for elevators	10		FRP Elev Ftgs
770	Poison soil below grade slab	1		Poison soil
780	Pour/finish/cure grade slab	5		PFC grade slab
Structural Phase				
800	Set baseplates on piers	5		set baseplates
810	Erect structural frame	20		Erect struc frm
820	Install roof drains	5		Inst roof drains
830	Install thru-roof vent sleeves	5		Inst thru-roof sleeves
840	Reinforce & pour topping slab on tee-beams	15		RP topping slab
850	Install thru-slab plumbing/electr sleeves	5		Inst TS plbg/elec slvs
860	Install in-slab electrical conduit	5		Inst IS elec cond
870	Erect stairwell/elevator enclosure walls	10		Erect stwl/elev walls
890	Install/fill steel stair forms	10		Inst/fill stair forms
Closing in the Building Phase				
900	Erect/insulate exterior block/brick walls	28		Erect/insul ext walls
912	Install frames—exterior doors/windows	5		Inst ext dr/wind frms
920	Install insulation/built-up roof/flashing	10		Inst BU roof/flashing
922	Install exterior doors/windows	10		Inst ext drs/wind
930	Erect interior block partitions	20		Erect int blk partns
932	Install interior door frames	10		Inst int dr frms
940	Install exterior security hardware	5		Inst ext secur hdwr
Roughing in Electrical and Mechanical Phase				
1000	Install electric panels	5		Install elec panels
1010	Pull wires/install switches/receptacles	10		Pull wire/inst junc bxes
1020	Install HVAC ducts	10		Inst HVAC ducts

FIGURE 2.2
(CONTINUED)

Task	Task Description	Duration, Workdays	Short Description (24 Characters Maximum)
1030	Set heat pump on roof	5	Set heat pump
1040	Rough in plumbing	15	Rough in plbg
1050	Install elevator pumps, controls, cars	15	Inst elev equip
Interior/Exterior Finish Phase			
1100	Install gypsum wallboard	15	Inst GWB
1110	Install ceramic floor tile	5	Inst cer flr tile
1120	Paint interior walls	15	Paint int walls
1130	Install ceiling grids	15	Inst clg grid
1140	Install recessed luminaires	15	Install luminaires
1150	Install plumbing fixtures/accessories	10	Inst plbg fixt/access
1160	Install vinyl flooring/base	15	Inst vinyl floor tile
1170	Activate/test electrical system	5	Test elect syst
1180	Install HVAC registers	5	Install HVAC regist
1190	Test/balance HVAC system	5	Test/bal HVAC system
1200	Install emergency lights/exit signs	5	Inst emerg lights/signs
1210	Install interior doors/hardware	5	Inst int drs/hdwr
1220	Key locks	5	Key locks
1230	Clean exterior masonry	5	Clean ext masonry
1240	Install toilet cubicle partitions	5	Inst toilet partitions
1250	Install electric switch/receptacle plates	2	Inst swtch/recep plates
1260	Install treads on stairs	2	Inst stair treads
Paving Phase			
1300	Pave walks	5	Pave walks
1310	Pave parking areas/drives	10	Pave drives/pkg areas
1320	Stripe pavements/install signs	5	Stripe/inst signs
Landscaping Phase			
1400	Fertilize, lime, and seed lawns	5	Seed lawns
1410	Plant shrubs and trees	5	Plant shrubs/trees
Project Closeout Phase			
1500	Clean interior	5	Clean interior
1510	Clean grounds/dispose of debris	5	Clean exterior
1520	Prefinal inspection with owner	5	Prefinal inspection
1530	Correct deficiencies	5	Correct defic
1540	Prepare and submit operational manuals	10	Submit opnl manuals
1550	Prepare and submit as-built plans	10	Submit as builts
1560	Remove project office and temp facilities	5	Remove proj facil

insufficient data have been given to compute any quantitative task attributes; however, values have been arbitrarily assigned for the task attribute "task duration." These values are representative of actual task durations for a project of this type and size. The task numbers are assigned in increments of 10, so that additional tasks can be defined and given an appropriate task number. Example 2 will illustrate procedures for the estimation of task durations.

Phases of the Project. The total project work was broken down into the phases described in the following discussion below. Work listed in a particular phase will, in general, be completed in the order shown. However, a task that is assigned to one phase need not necessarily be completed before a task that is assigned to some subsequent phase can be started. The selection of the listed phases is arbitrary. The phases are a framework, or an outline, that will aid the scheduler in defining the tasks. The general approach to defining the phases and the tasks is to mentally construct the building and related facilities from the ground up.

Preconstruction Phase. Tasks assigned to this phase can, and generally should, be initiated as soon as possible after project award. The general and special conditions of the contract will specify certain actions the contractor must take after contract award. Tasks that satisfy these contract requirements belong in this phase.

Engineering Phase. The contract specifications will call for the preparation of shop drawings for certain structural, mechanical, and electrical components. Tasks should be defined for the preparation and review of these shop drawings if there is any possibility that such preparations or reviews may be the critical factors in respect to completing the project on schedule. A concrete mix must be designed and samples must be tested.

Procurement Phase. The procurement of any materials that may possibly be the critical factors in respect to project completion have been assigned to this phase. Tasks have been defined for materials that require AE approval of colors or textures. No tasks have been defined for the procurement of such common off-the-shelf items as nails, paint, form lumber, and so forth.

Job Mobilization Phase. Any activities that are essential to setting up a project office and making the jobsite operational have been assigned to this phase.

Site Preparation Phase. Grading work and similar activities have been assigned to this phase.

Foundation Construction Phase. The piers will be constructed and then the base course for the slab on grade will be placed. All underslab water, electrical, and sewer lines will be installed before the grade beams are constructed, since the grade beams will hinder the operation of trenching and compaction equipment.

Structural Phase. There are three major components in the structural frame, all being precast, prestressed, concrete members. It is not feasible to erect all the columns, then all the girders, and then all the tee-beams, because the members must brace each other during erection. The fabricator of these precast members will also erect them, fastening the members by welding together the connection plates that are cast into the members. He estimates that 20 days will be required to do this work. As soon as the structural frame is erected, the reinforced slabs will be placed on top of the concrete tee-beams, so as to stiffen the structure. The concrete block stairwell and elevator shafts will be constructed after the precast concrete members are placed. Some rough electrical and mechanical work must be done concurrently with the pouring of slabs.

Closing in the Building Phase.   None of the masonry walls or partitions is load-bearing. Erection of the outer walls is more urgent than construction of interior partitions, since completion of those outer walls is essential to closing in the building. The installation of exterior doors and windows and of the built-up roof is also essential to closing in the building. No interior finish work can be initiated until the building is closed in. The block, insulation, face brick, and lintels for the exterior walls will be placed concurrently, so this work may be considered a single task. Erection of the interior partitions is not essential to closing in the building. However, this work has been positioned in this phase because it is of a similar nature to some of the tasks that are essential to closing in.

Roughing in Electrical and Mechanical Phase.   This phase includes installation of electrical and mechanical components that can be done after most of the structural work is complete and before finish work begins.

Interior/Exterior Finish Phase.   The tasks in this phase are listed roughly in the order in which they will be accomplished. For example, the walls will be painted before the ceiling grid is installed, to avoid the need to cut in the wall paint around the grid.

Paving Phase.   This includes paving walks, drives, parking areas, installing signs, and painting stripes on the pavements.

Landscaping Phase.   This includes planting grass, trees, and shrubs and the related work.

Project Closeout Phase.   Although some of these tasks (preparation of as-built drawings and operating manuals and cleaning the site) are shown in the last phase, work would commence earlier in the project.

Task Listing.   The work making up each of these phases has been broken down into tasks. See Figure 2.2 for the task listing.

Discussion of Solution to Example 1

A total of 114 tasks have been defined for this project. Of these, 40 have been for preconstruction, engineering, materials procurement, and mobilization type activities. Note that most tasks were numbered in increments of 10. The ones that are not numbered in increments of 10 were added to the task listing as an afterthought. It is very likely that a scheduler will recognize the need for adding still more tasks when he prepares the logic diagram. Another scheduler would have come up with a somewhat different listing of tasks. He would have combined some of the listed tasks and would have subdivided some of the listed tasks. The combined duration of the listed tasks is over 2000 workdays. There are about 200 workdays in a year. Many of the listed tasks will have to be accomplished concurrently if the total project duration is to be kept down to some reasonable value, say, under 200 workdays.

Example 2   Estimating Task Costs and Task Durations

Determine the duration and the cost for task 900—Erect Brick and Block Exterior Walls—of the project used for Example 1. The installation of the rigid insulation and erection of the brick veneer will proceed concurrently with the erection of the block walls. The cost of the insulation is not included in this example. See Figure 2.1 for the dimensions of the wall.

Solution to Example 2

The "scientific" estimating method that is outlined in Appendix A was used to make this estimate of task cost and task duration. The productivity data and the unit costs that have been used for material, labor, and equipment should be considered as data that the estimator has recorded on previous similar projects.

Materials Cost

A detailed quantity takeoff resulted in the estimation of the materials requirements shown in Table 2.1. All unit costs include delivery to the jobsite. An allowance for waste and for sales tax has been included.

Labor Cost and Task Duration

The number and productivity of masons will govern task duration. The contractor has maintained records indicating the following production rates:

Masons can lay 25 *concrete blocks* per man-hour in walls of this height, including installation of ladder reinforcement and allowing for normal breaks. Mason man-hours to lay blocks are

$$\frac{22{,}550 \ + \ 6764}{25} \ = \ 1172 \ MH$$

TABLE 2.1

MATERIALS TAKEOFF AND COST DATA[a]

Item	UM	Qty Rqd	Waste, %	Qty Buy	Unit Cost, $	Cost, $	Tax, $	Item Cost, $
Concrete block								
8 in. × 8 in. × 16 in. nominal	EA	22,550	1.0	22,776	0.55	12,527	501	13,028
8 in. × 8 in. × 8 in. nominal	EA	6,764	1.0	6,832	0.40	3,734	109	3,843
Concrete brick	M	8.180	1.0	8,262	90.00	744	30	774
Face brick	M	193.9	1.5	196.8	122.00	24,010	960	24,970
Ladder reinforcement	LF	21,533	5.0	22,610	0.22	4,974	199	5,183
Brick anchors	EA	7,390	5.0	7,760	0.025	194	8	202
Lintel angles	LF	384	0.0	384	1.25	480	19	499
Masonry mortar mix	SK	540	10.0	594	6.50	3,861	154	4,015
Mortar sand	CY	88	20.0	106	7.50	795	32	827
Total materials cost								53,341

[a] UM, unit measure; EA, each; M, a thousand; LF, length in feet; SK, sack; CY, cubic yards.

Masons can lay 80 face bricks per mason man-hour in walls of this height, bond, and class of workmanship, allowing for normal breaks. Mason man-hours to lay bricks are

$$\frac{193,900}{80} = 2424 \text{ MH}$$

Total mason man-hours are

$$1172 + 2424 = 3596 \text{ MH}$$

Mason man-days at 8 hours per day are

$$\frac{3596}{8} = 449.5 \text{ MD}$$

On a bricklaying task of this size, it should be feasible to use as many as 20 masons. Assume the average number of masons is 16, so task duration is

$$\frac{449.5}{16} = 28 \text{ days}$$

One helper will be required for each two masons, so required mason helper man-hours are

$$\frac{3596}{2} = 1798 \text{ MH}$$

Two laborers will be required to install *rigid foam insulation*. Four more will be used to set up and move scaffolding. One laborer will be used to operate the mortar mixing machine. Total laborer man-hours will be

$$7 \times 28 \times 8 = 1568 \text{ MH}$$

An equipment operator will be required to operate a forklift to transport materials to the scaffolds. Operator man-hours are

$$28 \times 8 = 224 \text{ MH}$$

A masonry foreman will also be required for 224 MH.

The labor requirements, hourly labor costs (including wages and employer's contributions to FICA, unemployment insurance, and workman's compensation insurance), and total labor costs are as shown in Table 2.2.

Equipment Cost
The contractor owns all of the equipment that will be used on the job. He has established hourly equipment costs for the motorized equipment as indicated (Table 2.3). He has further determined that a charge of 3% of the labor cost

TABLE 2.2

LABOR REQUIREMENTS AND HOURLY RATES

Craft	Rqmt, MH	Avg Wage Rate, $/MH	Craft Cost, $
Masons	3,596	10.50	37,758
Mason helpers	1,798	8.75	15,732
Laborers	1,568	7.75	12,152
Equipment operator	224	9.75	2,184
Foreman	224	12.75	2,856
Total labor cost			$70,682

TABLE 2.3

EQUIPMENT REQUIREMENTS AND COST

Item	Hours	Hourly Cost, $/HR	Delivery and Return, $	Item Cost, $
Mortar mixer	224	5.75	100.00	1,388
Forklift	224	9.75	100.00	2,284
Miscellaneous (0.03 × 70,682)				2,120
Total equipment cost				5,792

will enable him to recover the cost of scaffolds, mortar pans, and other miscellaneous equipment.

Subcontractor Cost
None in this example.

Total Estimated Cost
$129,815.

Estimated Task Duration
Twenty-eight workdays.

EXERCISES

EXERCISE 2.1   Task Definition
Define the tasks in a project having the following scope. Include preconstruction work activities. Perform only the work breakdown phase of task definition.

Construct a two-lane, single-span bridge having a length of 60 feet. See Figure 2.3.

FIGURE 2.3
TWO LANE BRIDGE, EXERCISE 2.1

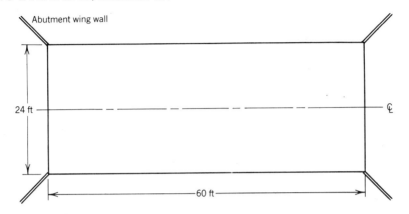

Abutment wing wall

24 ft

60 ft

Plan View

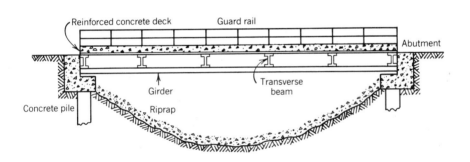

Reinforced concrete deck   Guard rail

Abutment

Girder

Transverse
beam

Concrete pile   Riprap

Longitudinal Section

b

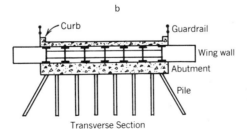

Curb   Guardrail

Wing wall

Abutment

Pile

Transverse Section

The superstructure of the bridge will be supported by designer-specified bearings anchored to cast-in-place concrete abutments. Each abutment will be supported by eight precast concrete piles. The length of the piles will be determined on the basis of the capacity of a test pile to be driven at the site of each abutment.

The superstructure will be made of steel girders supporting steel transverse beams and of required bracing members. The superstructure members will be fabricated in a steel fabricator's shop and will be bolted together in the field. A reinforced concrete deck will be cast in place on reusable forms supported by these beams. Formed curbs will be cast monolithically with the deck.

Steel guard rails will be installed on both sides of the deck. The rails will be of a patented type that has been specified by the designer.

Paint all steel members.

Install speed and weight limit signs and stripe the deck.

Rock riprap will be installed on both banks to prevent erosion.

EXERCISE 2.2   Task Cost and Task Duration
Estimate the task cost and task duration for installing a four-ply built-up roof on a concrete roof slab having dimensions of 60 feet by 200 feet. Use the productivity and cost data provided below.

Required *material quantities* do not include waste nor a 5% sales tax. Unit costs do include delivery. Assume that a 5% waste factor is applicable for all materials:

Four plies of roofing felt are required. A ply of felt costs $3.00/SQ; 1 SQ covers 100 SF, including laps, but not including waste.

The concrete slab will be primed with 1 gallon of cold primer per square costing $2.50/GAL.

Each ply of felt will be rolled into hot asphalt applied at the rate of 3 GAL/SQ (gallons per square) and costing $5.00/GAL. An additional layer of hot asphalt will be applied above the top ply at the rate of 5 GAL/SQ.

Gravel will be spread over the hot asphalt at the rate of 400 pounds per square and costing $12.00/TON.

Metal flashing will be installed at the intersection of the roof and the parapet wall. The materials will cost $45/100 LF, including fasteners and flashing cement.

Labor productivity and *hourly wage rates* are listed below. Productivity rates allow for normal breaks. Hourly wage costs include employer-paid fringe costs. Assume that the crews will work 8 hours per day.

The roofing crew will consist of a foreman ($12/HR), six roofers ($10/HR), and six laborers ($8/HR). The crew can install four-ply built-up roofing at the rate of 6 SQ/HR.

An additional laborer will be required to tend the asphalt kettle and pump.

A roofer and a laborer can install flashing at the rate of 100 LF/HR.

Assume that contractor-owned equipment costs will be 10% of direct labor costs. The general contractor will make available a forklift to lift felt, gravel, rollers, and so forth, to the roof at an hourly rate of $30 including operator. Two hours use of this lift per day is estimated.

GANTT CHARTS

3

OBJECTIVE

The objective of this chapter is to describe the format and the uses of the Gantt chart. The Gantt chart schedule was developed by Henry Gantt about 1900. It is frequently called a bar chart. It enjoys wide use today because its format is readily understandable. The Gantt chart can be the only scheduling tool used for preparing a schedule, or it can be used as a format for the presentation of schedules developed by the use of more sophisticated scheduling techniques. The Gantt chart is a graphic representation of the schedule for a project. An example of such a chart is given in Figure 3.1.

CONTENT OF BAR CHARTS

Content of Simple Bar Chart

The bar chart in Figure 3.1 contains a project title, a brief description of project scope, information on project location and project owner, and data on the 12 tasks that make up the project. Each task has been given a short descriptive title. Time-scaled bars have been drawn to represent the scheduled start and finish dates for each task.

FIGURE 3.1

EXAMPLE OF SIMPLE GANTT (BAR)
CHART

```
Project Title: Rte 22 Bypass Road    Scope:Construct 0.6 miles asphalt road
Contract Nbr: NC-DOT-M-1234-85       Contractor's Job Nbr: 21-85
Location: Pleasant Grove,NC          Owner: NCDOT        Awarded: 5/20/85

                        June 1985                    July 1985
-------------------------------------------------------------------------------
                        000000011111111111222222222230000000001111111111111111
TASK DESCRIPTION        345678901234567890123456789012345678901234567890123456
                        MTWTFSSMTWTFSSMTWTFSSMTWTFSSMTWTFSSMTWTFSSMTWTFSSMTWTF
-------------------------------------------------------------------------------
Survey Route            ---
Clear Right of Way          --------------
Perform Rough Grading           --------------
Install Culverts                    -------------
Compact Subgrade                    ------------------
Place Base Course                           -------------
Compact Base Course                           -------------
Perform Fine Grading                              --------
Lay Pavement                                        -------
Stripe Lanes                                           ------
Install Signs                                          -----
Perform Landscaping                                 -------------
-------------------------------------------------------------------------------
                        SS      SS      SS      SS      SS      SS      SS
```

Scheduled Starting and Finish Dates

The task that is titled "survey route" is scheduled to start on Monday, June 3, 1985, and to end on Wednesday, June 5, 1985. The task titled "clear right-of-way" is scheduled to start on Monday, June 10, 1985, and to end on Friday, June 21, 1985. Note that both a calendar date and a day of the week are given in the heading above the time-scaled bars.

Overlapping Bars

Note that some of the bars overlap. For example, placement of the base course is scheduled to start when about one-half of the subgrade has been compacted.

Construction Logic

The logic that the scheduler used in preparing this bar chart can only be surmised because it is not explicitly stated anywhere on the bar chart schedule. However, if the scheduler's logic was as stated hereafter, then the bar chart shown as Figure 3.1 would have resulted.

Project Start
The project work can start on Monday, June 3, 1985. All the tasks will be worked 5 days a week.

Surveying Is the Initial Task
The first task that can be started, on Monday, June 3, 1985, is the surveying of the right of way. Surveying will require three days and can be completed on June 5, 1985. No other work can start until the surveying is completed.

Clearing Right of Way
Although the surveying will be completed on June 5, 1985, clearing of the right of way is not scheduled to start until Monday, June 10, 1985. This delay of 5 calendar days will allow a cushion in case surveying is delayed by rain, rain being quite likely at this season of the year. Clearing will start at one end of the road. After one-half the length of the road is cleared, the clearing crew will move to the other end of the road to make way for the grading equipment on the section that has been cleared. The clearing operation should be finished by Friday, June 21, 1985.

Rough Grading
This work can commence when one-half the length of the road has been cleared and the clearing crew has moved to the other end of the road. Rough grading will require 5 days' work; however, rain may delay progress, so two weeks have been allowed for rough grading. The task can start about Monday, June 17, 1985, and should be finished by Friday, June 28, 1985.

Culverts
Some of the culverts, the ones that will be beneath a filled section of roadway, should be installed during the rough grading phase. Others can be installed after rough grading is finished. Allowing two weeks to install the six culverts, this task can start on Monday, June 24, 1985, and be completed by Friday, July 5, 1985.

Subgrade
Compaction of the subgrade must commence shortly after the rough grading starts, because compaction will be necessary while fills are being made. Compaction of the subgrade cannot be completed until after all rough grading is finished. The subgrade compaction is scheduled to start on Monday, June 17, 1985, and to be finished on Friday, July 5, 1985. Compaction will be necessary

over the culverts, which will not be completed until Friday, July 5, 1985; but the area to be compacted over the culverts is small, and the culvert installation crew can perform the compaction.

Base Course
The base course will be compacted as it is placed. Start placing and compacting the base course after some of the subgrade is compacted and after some of the culverts are installed, on Monday, July 1, 1985. Complete these two tasks after all subgrade is compacted and after all culverts are installed, say, on Friday, July 12, 1985.

Fine Grading
It is desirable to do the fine grading as soon as practical after the base course is placed and compacted, and to do the paving as soon as possible after the fine grading is done. The fine grading could start about 2 days after base course compaction starts, say, on Wednesday, June 26, 1985. However, it is not practical to perform fine grading while trucks are hauling base course material over the road. Furthermore, the required quantity of asphalt concrete (1800 tons) can be laid in a little less than 5 days by the 400 ton per day paver that will be used. The fine grading and paving cannot be completed until a few days after the base course compaction is completed on Friday, July 12, 1985. If the fine grading and paving start on Wednesday, June 26, 1985, and cannot be completed until about July 15, 1985, then the paver will have to be on the job for over two weeks. The paver is an expensive equipment item, one that will be needed on other projects. Start the fine grading on Thursday, July 11, 1985, and complete it on Wednesday, July 17, 1985. Start the paving on Monday, July 15, 1985, and complete it on Friday, July 19, 1985.

Painting (Striping) and Signs
Painting lane markers on the pavement can start on Monday, July 12, 1985 and can be completed by Friday, July 16, 1985. The installation of traffic signs can be done during the same period.

Landscaping
Fertilizing and seeding of the cleared, but unpaved, right-of-way can start as soon as base course compaction is done, on Monday, July 15, 1985 and can be completed on Friday, July 26, 1985.

Alternatives to Surmised Construction Logic

The previously stated logical considerations are only surmises. The scheduler may have considered other factors that led to the schedule shown in Figure 3.1. For example, the clearing of the right-of-way may have been scheduled to start on June 10, 1985, because the land-clearing equipment was not scheduled to be available until that date.

Content of Minimum Bar Chart

The determination of what data belong on a bar chart is a matter of judgement and preference. The example shown in Figure 3.1 contains little more than a bare minimum of data. An example problem to be found later in this chapter involves preparation of a Gantt chart containing more data. See Figure 3.2 for an outline of a bar chart. As a minimum, a bar chart should contain the following:

Section A. The heading should include the project title.

Section B. This section should include a brief description of each task.

Section C. This section should be ruled off in columns, representing time. Bars, representing the tasks, should be drawn to indicate the period of time during which the tasks are scheduled to be in progress.

Content of More Elaborate Bar Charts

Each of the three sections of a bar chart can contain additional data. Any such additional data will make the bar chart more useful to some users in some respects. However, adding additional data to any of the three sections will increase the required size of the paper on which the bar chart is to be printed or drawn. Furthermore, addition of too much data to a bar chart may make the chart less understandable. Some considerations relating to the amount of data that should be included in a bar chart follow.

Space Limitations

The Gantt chart may be prepared manually, or it may be printed on a computer output device. In either case, there will be some practical limit on how wide a page or sheet can be. Typical computer printers will print 80 to 132 characters

FIGURE 3.2
CONTENTS OF BAR CHART

```
SECTION A - HEADING

SECTION B                          SECTION C
TASK DESCRIPTION AND TASK DATA     TIME SCALED BARS SHOWING THE
                                   PERIOD OF TIME THAT THE TASKS
                                   WILL BE IN PROGRESS
```

on a line. If the amount of information on a scheduler wants to include on a Gantt chart will not fit into a printer line, the chart will have to be printed in sections. Several sections can be taped together to form a chart of virtually any width. If a computer-driven plotter is available, the chart may be of any desired width. If the chart is to be prepared manually, using roll paper, then it may also be of any desired width. The length and height of the wall upon which the chart will be displayed are the only real limits on the overall dimensions of a Gantt chart. However, the chart should not be so large as to make it difficult to handle it or to copy it.

Duplication of Data

It is often a convenience to the scheduler, and to the reader of a schedule, to have a great amount of information listed on the Gantt chart form. Some of the data that might be printed on a Gantt chart may be available on other documents. Schedulers should weigh the advantages of duplicating data on the bar chart against the cost of such duplication, and they should consider who will be reading the chart. As a general rule, do not include data on a chart simply because the data are available. Unless the reader of the chart needs the data to understand the chart, omit them or provide them in a separate report.

Confidential Data

Bar charts are frequently displayed in the project office or at other locations where they can be viewed by casual visitors to the project office. Certain data are confidential and should not be included on a publicly displayed chart. Most cost data fall in this category. The total contract amount, at least on publicly funded projects, is a matter of public knowledge. However, the contractor will usually desire to keep confidential the estimated and actual costs.

Possible Data Elements

The following paragraphs describe the possible data elements to be contained on the Gantt chart.

Section A: Heading
The heading should, as a minimum, contain a short project description in enough detail so that the reader can identify the project. The following data are also often useful:

> **Project Location.**
>
> **Project Owner.** The individual or company for whom the project is being constructed. If the owner is represented by an architect, a construction manager, or an agent, inclusion of this information may be useful.

Contract Number. This is the number assigned by the owner. The contractor may have his own internal job numbering system, and inclusion of that number may be useful.

Contract Amount. This is the lump-sum or fixed-price contract amount, plus information on liquidated damages, early completion bonuses, and the like. Keep in mind that the owner or the contractor may not want to have financial data revealed to outsiders. Therefore, the Gantt chart may not be an appropriate place to list these data.

Award Date. This is the date the contract was awarded. It may also be appropriate to list the date that the owner issued a notice to proceed with construction, the contract completion date, and so on.

Project Status Update. If the schedule will be revised periodically to indicate current status and changes in work sequence, scope of work, and so forth, it is important that the date of the current status update be listed.

Miscellaneous. List the names of the project manager, project superintendent, and other key persons, if desired.

Section B: Task Description

As a minimum, a short description of each task is required. Depending on the project, the following data may be included in this section:

Task Number. A unique number may be assigned to each task to facilitate status reporting.

Task Duration and Status. The estimated duration, the revised estimated duration, and the actual duration of completed tasks can be entered in this section. The current status of partly completed tasks may be included as well as an indication of how actual status differs from the scheduled status.

I-Node and J-Node. If the schedule is based on the CPM Method, it is useful to list the I-node and the J-node numbers of the tasks. The meaning of I-node and J-node numbers is covered in Chapter 4.

Resources. The quantity of critical or limited resources required to accomplish the task may be included. Craftsmen, trucks, and tractors are examples of resources.

Cost Codes. These are numbers that the contractor uses for categorizing different types of costs. Many contractors use the CSI (Construction Specifications Institute) coding system, but others use their own system. The project owner may want to have task costs recorded and reported by a coding system of his or her choice.

Miscellaneous. Include here any other task-related data. Although time values will be displayed by means of time-scaled bars, it is also useful to present time values in numerical form. The scheduled and actual starting and finish dates for tasks can be included in this section as well as the estimated and actual task costs.

Section C: Time-Scaled Bars

The vertical lines in this section may be ruled off in units of months, weeks, days, or workdays. If the project duration is very long and days are the time units, the resulting Gantt chart will be very wide. If this is true, it may be desirable to print the Gantt chart twice. For the first printing, use a time unit of months so that the entire schedule can be shown on a chart of reasonable width. On the second printing, use days as the time unit, but print out only that part of the schedule representing a part (say, 90 days) of the project's entire duration. The task bars are drawn or printed horizontally across the chart to represent the scheduled and actual start and finish times for each task.

If the chart is prepared manually or by a computer-driven plotting device, different colors may be used to distinguish between scheduled and actual data. The same type of distinction can be made by use of the different characters on a printer. The bars are generally shown as straight lines on manually or plotter-generated bar charts. The bars are generally shown as a series of letters, often the letter X, on computer printer-generated charts.

USE OF BAR CHART AS THE ONLY SCHEDULING TOOL

Many schedulers will use the Gantt chart technique as their only scheduling tool. As they draw the task bars, they will mentally adjust the starting time for a bar on the basis of start times and end times of previously plotted tasks. This process was illustrated previously under "Content of Minimum Bar Chart." On a complex job, one in which there are many logical relationships between the tasks, this may be very difficult. There is a tendency to work backward when plotting a Gantt chart. Knowing the project's contract completion date, the scheduler may plot the bar representing the final task so that it ends at that time. He will spread the other bars out so they cover the time available from the start date. If this practice is followed, the result will be a schedule in which task starting and finish times are arbitrarily specified and unrealistic.

USE OF THE BAR CHART AS A FORMAT

The bar chart format is very understandable, more so than tables containing numerical data. Schedulers will often prepare a schedule using a "scientific" scheduling method, such as CPM, and then plot a bar chart using the time values computed by that method. Many commercially available computer programs that are based on the CPM or the Precedence Method contain an option that will produce a bar chart.

Example 1

Prepare a Gantt chart using workday scheduling. This project calls for the contractor to construct a temporary two-span, bypass bridge for use while a permanent bridge is being replaced. Figure 3.3 contains a sketch of the project. The owner has not yet issued a **notice to proceed** with the work, so the contractor does not know the project start date, but he knows that he will have eight weeks (56 calendar days) to complete the project after receiving this notice. He is making a preliminary schedule, based on working 5 days a week, to assure himself that his planned construction procedure will enable him to complete the project within 56 calendar days. There are 5 workdays in a week; hence the contractor will have $8 \times 5 = 40$ workdays to complete the project. He will schedule the project based on workdays.

Scope of Work

The bridge's substructure will include two abutments and a midstream pier. The abutments will be constructed by driving a row of timber piles. Heavy planks will be spiked to the shore side of these piles to act as a retaining wall. A heavy timber will be placed on top of the row of piles as an abutment cap. The pier will be constructed by driving two rows of timber piles. Heavy timbers will be fastened on top of these piles to serve as the pier cap. The superstructure will consist of steel beams supported by the abutment and pier caps. Timber decking will be secured to the steel beams to serve as the roadway. Miscellaneous bracing, curbs, and guard rails will be installed to complete the bridge. It will be necessary to construct an asphalt concrete access road at both ends of the temporary bridge and to demolish that access road once the bypass bridge is removed. The scope of this project does not include removal of the bypass bridge or its access roads.

Planned Work Sequence

Only one pile-driving rig is available. It is not possible to drive this rig across the existing bridge, and it is not feasible to detour around the bridge; therefore, all piles must be driven from one side of the stream. All other equipment needed for construction can cross over the existing bridge. Work will start with the construction of the access road to the east bank pier. This access road will not be paved until pile driving is completed. Next, the piles will be driven for the east bank abutment, and the east bank abutment will be completed. Then, the

FIGURE 3.3
CONSTRUCTION OF TEMPORARY
BYPASS BRIDGE

Guard rail

Curb
Asphalt pavement
Timber decking

Cross bracing

Steel beams

Timber caps

Timber piles

Center pier

Timber end dam

West abutment

Temporary bypass bridge

West access road

East access road

Barricade

Existing bridge

Site plan

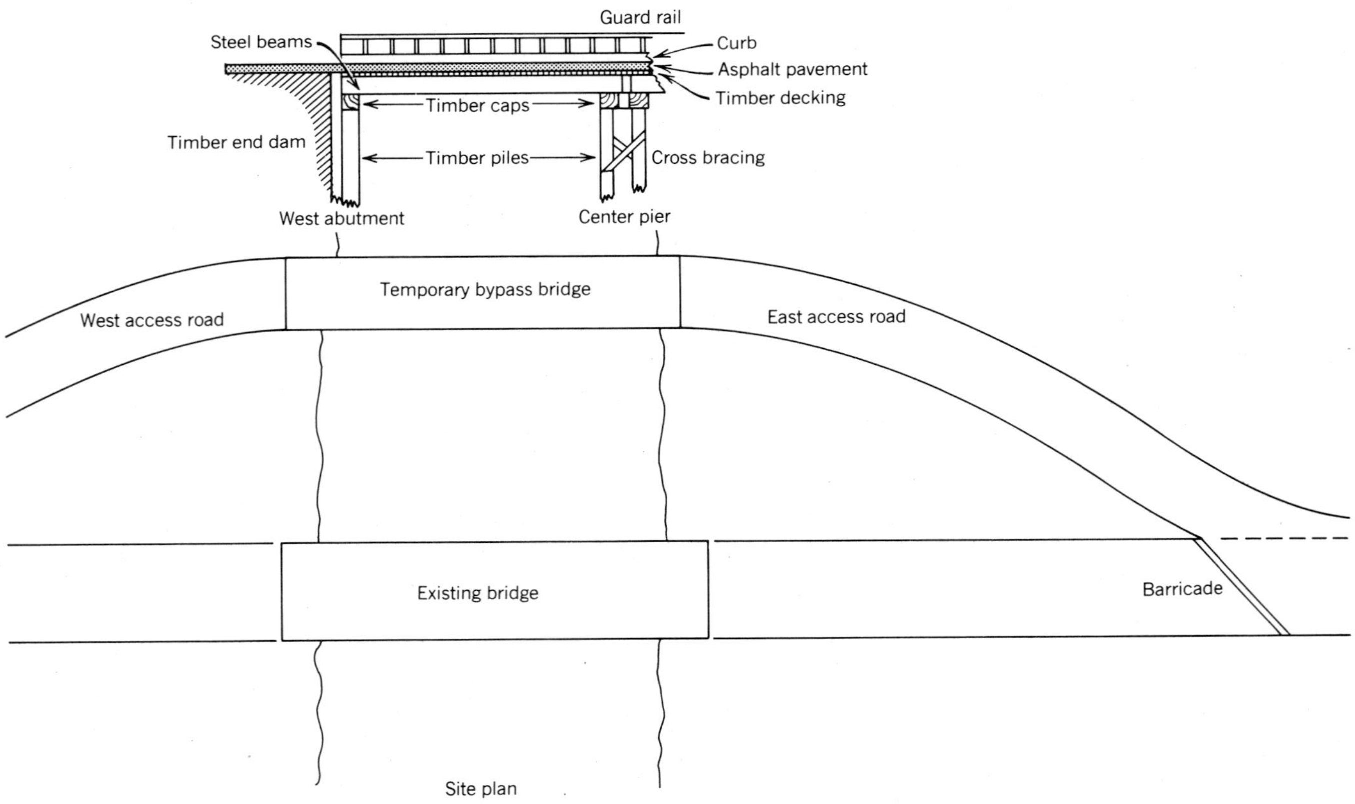

TABLE 3.1

TASK LISTING, EXAMPLE 1

Task No.	Task Description	Estimated Duration, Workdays
1	Survey and layout	1
2	Rough-grade access road on east bank	2
3	Drive timber piles for east abutment	1
4	Construct east abutment	5
5	Drive timber piles for midstream pier	2
6	Complete midstream pier	5
7	Place steel girders east span	2
8	Place timber decking east span	2
9	Drive timber piles west abutment	1
10	Construct west abutment	5
11	Place steel girders west span	2
12	Place timber decking west span	2
13	Rough-grade access road on west bank	2
14	Finish grading access road east bank	1
15	Finish grading access road west bank	1
16	Pave access roads both banks	3
17	Install curbs and gutters on bridge	5
18	Stripe access road	1
19	Erect barricades to site of permanent bridge	1

midstream piles will be driven from the east bank. When the east bank abutment is completed and when the caps have been installed on the midstream pier, the steel beams will be placed for the east span. After the east span decking is installed, the pile driver can be moved onto the east span and the west bank piles can be driven. Equipment other than the pile driver can be driven across the existing bridge to the west bank, therefore, construction of the west bank access road can be started as soon as the equipment is released from the same task on the east bank.

Task Definition

The tasks shown in Table 3.1 have been defined. Task durations were estimated on the basis of an eight-hour workday.

Solution to Example 1

See Figure 3.4 for the bar chart. The scheduled project duration is 40 workdays, or eight weeks. Eight weeks equals 56 calendar days; hence, the planned procedure will result in project completion within the required time. The planned procedure will satisfy the contract requirements.

FIGURE 3.4

SOLUTION TO EXAMPLE 1

Project: Rte 22 By-pass Bridge Owner: NCDOT Contract:Nbr NC-DOT-M-234
Start: To be determined. Contract Project Duration: 60 calendar days.

Task Description	Dur	Start	Finish	Workdays (bar position)
1. Survey Site	1	1	1	X (day 1)
2. Rough Grade East Access Rd	2	2	3	XX (days 2–3)
3. Drive East Bank Piles	1	4	4	X (day 4)
4. Construct East Abutment	5	5	9	XXXXX (days 5–9)
5. Drive Midstream Piles	2	10	11	XX (days 10–11)
6. Construct Mid-stream Pier	5	12	16	XXXXX (days 12–16)
7. Place Girders East Span	2	17	18	XX (days 17–18)
8. Place Deck Timbers East Span	2	19	20	XX (days 19–20)
9. Drive West Bank Piles	1	21	21	X (day 21)
10. Construct West Abutment	5	22	26	XXXXX (days 22–26)
11. Place Girders West Span	2	27	28	XX (days 27–28)
12. Place Deck Timbers W. Span	2	29	30	XX (days 29–30)
13. Rough Grade West Access Rd	2	4	5	XX (days 4–5)
14. Finish Grade East Access Rd	1	31	31	X (day 31)
15. Finish Grade West Access Rd	1	32	32	X (day 32)
16. Pave Access Roads and Bridge	3	33	35	XXX (days 33–35)
17. Install Curbs and Rails on Bridge	5	35	39	XXXXX (days 35–39)
18. Stripe Pavement	1	36	36	X (day 36)
19. Erect Barricades	1	40	40	X (day 40)

Workdays scale: 5 10 15 20 25 30 35 40

TABLE 3.2
TASK DESCRIPTIONS AND DURATIONS, EXAMPLE 2

Task No.	Description	Duration, Weeks
1	Manufacture of new building	6
2	Site preparation and site utilities	2
3	Erect new building	4
4	Relocate manufacturing machinery	1
5	Convert old structure to warehousing	2

Example 2

Prepare a Gantt chart schedule based on calendar day scheduling for the following project. A plant manager plans to build a new pre-engineered building to accommodate a portion of the plant's manufacturing operations. When the new building is completed, manufacturing machinery will be relocated there from an existing building. Then, the area that has been vacated will be converted into warehouse space. The manager desires that the relocation of manufacturing equipment be accomplished during the period June 16 to 23, 1985, because the plant will be shut down at that time and all employees who are not involved in the relocation will be placed on vacation status. The manager desires to accomplish the project in the briefest practical time so as to minimize interference with the plant's normal operations. He considers the task durations listed in Table 3.2 to be realistic.

Manufacture of the new building can commence immediately after an order is placed. Each of the tasks will be performed by a different crew. Prepare a Gantt chart schedule based on the information listed in Table 3.2. Figure 3.5 contains a solution for this problem.

Solution to Example 2

The Gantt chart shown in Figure 3.5 was prepared in light of the various constraints to the initiation of the tasks. The bar for task 4 was plotted first. Then, the bars for the remaining tasks were plotted in accordance with the given constraints. The bar for task 3 was plotted so that building erection would be completed just in time to start relocation of the manufacturing machinery. The bars for tasks 1 and 2 were plotted so that they would be completed just in time to start building erection. The bar for task 5 was plotted so that conversion of the old space will be started as soon as the manufacturing machinery is moved out.

FIGURE 3.5

SOLUTION TO EXAMPLE 2

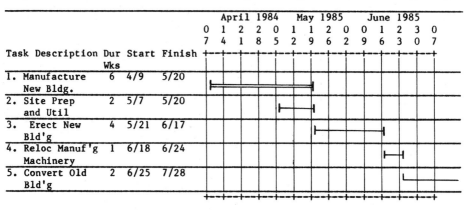

Project: Construction of New Manufacturing Building & Associated Relocations.

				April 1984			May 1985			June 1985			
Task Description	Dur Wks	Start	Finish	0 7	1 4	2 1	2 8	0 5	1 2	1 9	2 6	0 2	0 9	1 6	2 3	3 0	0 7
1. Manufacture New Bldg.	6	4/9	5/20												
2. Site Prep and Util	2	5/7	5/20												
3. Erect New Bld'g	4	5/21	6/17												
4. Reloc Manuf'g Machinery	1	6/18	6/24												
5. Convert Old Bld'g	2	6/25	7/28												

ADVANTAGES AND DISADVANTAGES OF THE BAR CHART METHOD

Advantages

The bar chart schedule is very easy to understand. Almost anyone, regardless of whether or not he or she has any understanding of the principles of scheduling, can look at a bar chart schedule and decipher its meaning. Even experienced schedulers will find a graphic depiction of a project schedule easier to read than a tabular schedule. The bar chart is a very useful format in which to display the results of a schedule prepared by a more contemporary technique.

Disadvantages

The bar chart schedule can be very difficult to prepare, particularly if there are numerous and complex relationships between the tasks that make up the schedule. The construction logic that the scheduler has used in preparing a bar chart cannot be determined by inspection of the chart whereas some of the scheduling techniques that will be covered in subsequent chapters require preparation of logic diagrams. These logic diagrams explicitly depict the logical relationships. By its very nature, a bar chart schedule can be very wide for a project that has a

TABLE 3.3

TASK DESCRIPTIONS AND DURATIONS, EXERCISE 3.1

Task No.	Description	Estimated Duration, Calendar Days
1	Rehabilitate pier 1	90
2	Rehabilitate pier 2	120
3	Rehabilitate storage tank 1	150
4	Rehabilitate storage tank 2	90
5	Rehabilitate rail siding	60
6	Rehabilitate truck loading platform	90

long duration. A tabular schedule for a project with a long duration need be no larger than a tabular schedule for a project with a short duration.

EXERCISES

EXERCISE 3.1
Prepare a bar chart schedule for the following project based on calendar days. Rehabilitate a fuel oil off-loading and distribution complex. The complex contains two oil tanker mooring piers, two 200,000-barrel steel storage tanks, a tank car loading siding, and a tank truck loading platform. The owner desires that the entire project be completed as soon as possible, but he stipulates that the complex must remain operational continuously during the project. Accordingly, work can be in progress on only one of the piers and on one of the tanks simultaneously, and either the rail siding or the truck loading platform must be in operation at all times. The tasks are listed in Table 3.3. Your solution should not indicate a project duration that is greater than 240 calendar days.

EXERCISE 3.2
Draw a bar chart schedule for the project that is described in Example 1 in Chapter 2. Use workday scheduling.

LOGIC DIAGRAMS AND SCHEDULING

4

OBJECTIVES

The Critical Path Method (CPM), the Precedence Method (PM), and the Program Evaluation Review Technique (PERT) are all based on the preparation of logic diagrams. The objectives of this chapter are to introduce the concept of logic diagrams, to define the terms used in logic diagramming, and to explain some of the conventions used in the preparation of logic diagrams. Two types of logic diagrams will be covered: Activity On Arrow diagrams (AOA) and Activity On Node diagrams (AON). The AOA diagram is used in Critical Path Method scheduling (CPM) and in Program Evaluation Review Technique scheduling (PERT). The AON diagram is used in Precedence Method scheduling (PM).

ESSENTIAL TERMS

The reader should understand the meaning of the following terms:

Project

A planned undertaking that involves the performance of work.

Task

Part of the work that makes up a project. The task has been defined, meaning that the work it encompasses has been specified and such attributes as duration have been assigned to it.

Event

The term event, when used in a scheduling context, means a point in time at which some thing, or some things, happen. The first event in a project schedule is that the project starts. The last event in a project schedule is that the project ends. There are numerous intermediate events. One of them might be "the time when the foundations have been poured and the erection of walls and columns can commence." The term event is always used in CPM scheduling; it is less often used in PM scheduling.

Logic Diagrams

A logic diagram (sometimes termed a network) is a graphic depiction of a project. The tasks that make up the project and the logical relationships that exist between those tasks are represented by symbols. There are two basic types of logic diagrams:

> **Activity on Arrow (AOA) Diagrams.** An AOA diagram is made up of arrows, nodes, and words and numbers that are lettered on these arrows and in these nodes. The arrows represent tasks. The nodes are circles that represent events. The CPM and the PERT Method, to be covered in subsequent chapters, are based on AOA logic diagrams. See Figure 4.1a for an example of an AOA logic diagram.

> **Activity on Node (AON) Diagrams.** An AON diagram is also made up of arrows, nodes, and words and numbers. The nodes are depicted with a circle or with a box, and they represent tasks. The arrows represent logical relationships between tasks. The Precedence Method, to be covered in subsequent chapters, is based on AON logic diagrams. See Figure 4.1b for an example of an AON logic diagram.

I-Node and J-Node

The node at the tail end of an arrow is termed the I-node. The node at the head end is termed the J-node. See Figure 4.1c. Note in Figure 4.1a that node 4 is the J-node for arrow A and the I-node for arrow B. In Figure 4.1b, the node representing task B is the I-node for arrow 2, and the node representing task C is the J-node for that same arrow.

Network Analysis

Once the logic diagram (network) has been prepared, it is necessary to make a network analysis. The task data and the logical relationships between the tasks

FIGURE 4.1
THE TWO TYPES OF LOGIC
DIAGRAMS: (a) AOA Logic Diagram;
(b) AON Logic Diagram

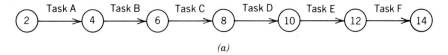

(a)

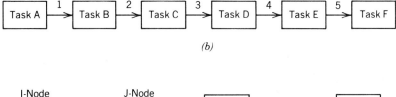

(b)

AOA Diagrams   AON diagrams

(c)

that have been depicted on the diagram are analyzed so as to compute other values needed for the preparation of the schedule. If the Critical Path Method is being used, this analysis may be termed the CPM analysis. If the Precedence Method is being used, the analysis may be termed the PM analysis.

Critical Path

Analysis of either an AOA or an AON logic diagram results in the determination of a critical path through the diagrams. This path can be traced from node to node by passing through the arrows. The longest path, measured in time, that can be traced through the diagram is termed the critical path. Tasks that are located on the critical path are termed critical tasks. If a task that is critical is not completed within its scheduled duration, the project completion will be delayed past its scheduled completion date. If a noncritical task is delayed, there will be no impact on project duration.

LOGICAL RELATIONSHIPS

The following discussion pertains to both AOA and to AON scheduling methods. Each task in a project is logically related to every other task. To specify the logical relationship between two tasks means to specify the order in which the tasks will be performed.

Types of Logical Relationships

There are three possible logical relationships that can exist between a task and another task. These relationships are defined as follows:

Precedent Relationship

Precedent means coming before. If task A is precedent to task B, then at least part of task A must be completed before task B can start. For example, breaking an egg's shell is precedent to frying the egg.

Subsequent Relationship

Subsequent means coming after. If task B is subsequent to task A, then task B cannot start until at least part of task A is completed. Precedence is the opposite of subsequence. If X is precedent to Y, then Y must be subsequent to X. For example, because breaking an egg's shell is precedent to frying the egg, frying the egg is subsequent to breaking the egg's shell.

Concurrent Relationship

If task M is neither precedent nor subsequent to task N, then tasks M and N are concurrent to each other. A concurrent relationship between a pair of tasks does not necessarily mean that the two tasks will be performed simultaneously. It merely means that commencement of work on one of the tasks is not contingent upon completion of some work on the other task. If the two tasks (breaking an egg's shell and frying the egg) that were used as examples above are part of a project to prepare breakfast, and if the breakfast also features toast, then toasting bread will be another task. This third task can be done before, after, or simultaneously with the first two tasks. It is neither precedent nor subsequent to either of them; therefore, it has a concurrent relationship with both of them.

The Basic Logical Relationship

It was stated above that subsequent is the opposite of precedent. The relationship "B is subsequent to A" can be expressed as "A is precedent to B." Hence, it is not necessary to consider subsequence as a separate logical relationship. Furthermore, the concurrent relationship between two tasks merely represents the absence of a precedence relationship between them. Therefore, the basic logical relationship between two tasks can be specified by indicating the precedence, if any, of the two tasks.

Depicting the Logical Relationships

All logical relationships should be shown on the logic diagram. If a logical relationship actually exists between two tasks, and if that relationship is not shown on the diagram, then the network analysis and the resulting schedule will not reflect that relationship. The logical relationships may be depicted explicitly or implicitly. Explicit and implicit depiction of relationships are explained below.

Number of Logical Relationships

A logical relationship exists between every pair of the tasks that make up a project. If a project is made up of N tasks, the number of logical relationships, R, may be found by the equation

$$R = \frac{N!}{2 \times (N - 2)!}$$

Consider the AOA and the AON diagrams shown in Figure 4.1. They represent the same project, which contains six tasks. The total number of pairs of tasks, and the total number of logical relationships between tasks, are determined by the preceding equation.

$$R = \frac{6 \times 5 \times 4 \times 3 \times 2 \times 1}{2 \times (4 \times 3 \times 2 \times 1)} = \frac{720}{48} = 15$$

The pairs of tasks are: A/B, A/C, A/D, A/D, A/F, B/C, B/D, B/E, B/F, C/D, C/E, C/F, D/E, D/F, and E/F. A logical relationship exists between each pair; hence, there are 15 logical relationships.

Explicit Relationships

Fortunately, it is necessary to specify only a small fraction of the logical relationships that exist within a project, those being the explicit relationships. Explicit means distinctly expressed. For example, the relationship (shown in both Figures 4.1*a* and 4.1*b*) that task A is precedent to task B is explicitly depicted on both diagrams. There are five explicit relationships. They are: A is precedent to B, B is precedent to C, C is precedent to D, D is precedent to E, and E is precedent to F.

Implicit Relationships

Implicit means implied. In neither Figure 4.1a nor in Figure 4.1b is task A explicitly depicted as being precedent to task D; however, such a relationship is implied. There are nine implicit relationships in the above network. They include: A is precedent to C, D, E, and F; B is precedent to D, E, and F; C is precedent to E and F; and E is precedent to F. These nine logical relationships have been implicitly expressed.

Activity On Arrow (AOA) Logic Diagrams

The AOA logic diagram will be made up of arrows, representing tasks, and of nodes, representing events, plus words and numbers printed above and below the arrows and within the nodes.

Task Arrows

Figure 4.2 illustrates three different formats for drawing the task arrows of an AOA logic diagram.

The Arc Format. The task arrows are drawn as straight lines and as arcs. Use of this format is not recommended. It is difficult to manually print words on these curved arrows, and it would be very difficult to print the words using a computer printer.

The Sloping Format. The task arrows are drawn as a combination of horizontal, vertical, and sloping straight-line segments. This format is appropriate if the diagram will be drawn manually or by a computer-driven plotting device. It is less appropriate if the diagram will be prepared by using a computer printer. Note how congested the diagram is at nodes [16] and [28] where several arrows originate or terminate.

The Staff Format. The task arrows are drawn as a combination of horizontal and vertical straight-line segments. This format is suitable for diagrams to be drawn manually and for diagrams to be plotted or printed by computer-driven output devices. It is particularly appropriate if numerous arrows will originate or terminate at a particular node. The staff format will often allow reducing the overall dimensions of a logic diagram below the dimensions that would be required using the sloping format. Note that arrows are drawn so that they originate at the right side of a node and terminate at the left side of a node.

FIGURE 4.2
AOA ARROW FORMATS

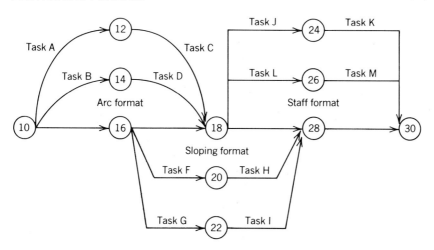

Length of Arrows

Task arrows should contain a horizontal segment that is long enough to allow space for any words or numbers that must be lettered or printed above or below them. Occasionally, a scheduler will prepare an AOA logic diagram in which the task arrows are scaled to the task durations. Even a task having a very brief duration (say, one day) must be represented by an arrow that is long enough (say, 1 inch) to allow for the printing of the task description. Tasks having longer durations (say, 30 days) would be represented by proportionately longer arrows (say, 30 inches). For example, consider the diagram in Figure 4.1a. Assume that task A has a duration of one day and that tasks B, C, D, E, and F have durations of 30 days. If the arrow for task A is drawn 1 inch long, and if the other three arrows are drawn to scale, the overall width of the diagram will be more than 12 feet. Scaling task arrows to task durations is not recommended for general use because the practice often results in excessively wide logic diagrams.

Nodes

The nodes are generally drawn as circles large enough in diameter to allow for the node number to be printed within. Another format, one that is appropriate if the logic diagram is to be printed by a computer printer, is to use a pair of brackets as the node symbol and to print the node number within those brackets. For example, node number 10 might be depicted as ⑩ or [10].

Logical Relationships

The logical relationships between tasks are specified by indicating the I-nodes and the J-nodes for each task arrow. If a node is the J-node for task A and it is also the I-node for task B, then the explicit relationship "A is precedent to B" that exists between the two tasks has been specified. If a node is the J-node for three tasks, and it is also the I-node for five tasks, then 15 ($3 \times 5 = 15$) explicit relationships have been specified.

Activity On Node (AON) Logic Diagrams

The AON diagram will be made up of nodes that represent tasks, of arrows that represent logical relationships between the tasks, and of words and numbers to label these symbols.

Task Nodes

The task nodes will be boxes or circles that are large enough so that the words and numbers required to describe the tasks can be printed within them. Whether boxes or circles are used for nodes is a matter of preference. It is difficult to print a circle with most computer printers. Some printers and all computer-driven plotters can print or plot circles. The use of boxes for nodes seems preferable because more characters can be printed within a box than within a circle of equal width. Figure 4.3 illustrates the depiction of nodes using both the box and the circle format. Note that the left sides of the nodes in this figure have been labeled the start sides and the right sides have been labeled the end sides. It is of significance whether a relationship arrow originates or terminates at the start side or at the end side of a task node.

Relationship Arrows

The arrows on an AON logic diagram, representing logical relationships between tasks, are drawn between the nodes that represent these tasks. One arrow is required for each explicit logical relationship. Some schedulers represent these logical relationships by lines having no arrowheads. The arrowhead positively identifies the precedence of two tasks; hence, the use of arrowheads is recommended. The arrows can be made up of connected straight-line segments (horizontal, vertical, or sloping) and arcs. The author favors the use of the staff format, in which arrows are made up of connected segments of horizontal and vertical lines. The nature of a logical relationship can usually be depicted solely by graphic means; however, some logical relationships used in connection with AON logic diagrams require the entry of words and numbers on the relationship arrows. Arrows for relationships that require entry of data of this kind should contain a horizontal segment of sufficient length.

FIGURE 4.3
BOX-SHAPED VERSUS CIRCLE-
SHAPED NODES: (a) Box Node; (b)
Circle Node.

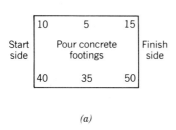 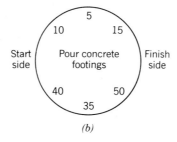

(a)   (b)

Complex Relationships

Several logical relationships are illustrated in the diagram in Figure 4.4. One of
these relationships is termed the simple precedence relationship. The other relationships are termed complex relationships merely to distinguish them from
the simple relationship. The simple precedence relationship is exactly equivalent
to the logical relationship used in the AOA diagram. This relationship implies
that ''A must be completed before B can start.'' Examples of situations in which
use of these various relationships are appropriate will be presented in the chapters
covering the Precedence Method. Consider the diagram shown in Figure 4.4 to
be part of a larger diagram.

FIGURE 4.4
COMPLEX PRECEDENCE
RELATIONSHIPS

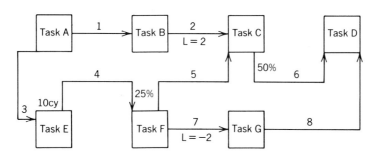

Relationship Arrow 1   Simple Precedence Relationship (End-to-Start Precedence Relationship with No Lag). Task B cannot start until task A is completed.

Relationship Arrow 2   End-to-Start Precedence Relationship with Lag. Task C cannot start until two days after task B is completed.

Relationship Arrow 3   Start-to-Start Precedence Relationship. Task E cannot start until task A starts.

Relationship Arrow 4   Start-to-Start Precedence Relationship with Quantity Lag. Task F cannot start until 10 CY of the work in task E (say, pouring 20 CY of concrete) has been completed.

Relationship Arrow 5   Start-to-Start Precedence Relationship with Percentage Lag. Task C cannot start until 25% of the work in task F has been completed. Note that there is another constraint to starting work on task C; it was specified by relationship arrow 2.

Relationship Arrow 6   End-to-Start Precedence Relationship with Percent Lead. Task D cannot start until all but 50% of the work in task C is completed.

Relationship Arrow 7   End-to-Start Precedence Relationship with Negative Lag. Task G cannot start until two days before task F is completed.

Relationship Arrow 8   End-to-End Precedence Relationship. Task D cannot be completed until task G is completed.

Other Relationships. Other variations of the precedence relationship may be specified using AON diagramming techniques. The chapters on the Precedence Method list some of them.

PRECEDENCE OF NODES AND ARROWS

An earlier section has covered the concept of precedence between tasks. The concept of precedence can also be applied to the symbols that make up a logic diagram. The terms **precedent** and **immediately precedent** will be used in future chapters covering the analysis of logic diagrams.

Precedent

A precedence relationship exists between two arrows if it is possible to draw a continuous line along task arrows that will pass through both of them, always moving the pencil in the direction of the arrows. A precedence relationship exists between two nodes if it is possible to draw a continuous line between them along task arrows, always moving in the direction of the arrows. Similarly, a precedence relationship exists between an arrow and a node if it is possible to draw a continuous line between them along task arrows, always moving in the direction of the arrows.

Immediately Precedent

A node is immediately precedent to another node if the first node is the I-node of an arrow and the second node is that arrow's J-node. An arrow is immediately precedent to its J-node. A node is immediately precedent to the arrow for which it is the I-node.

STRUCTURED LOGIC DIAGRAMS

A structured logic diagram is one that has been drawn in accordance with the rules that are stated below and illustrated in Figure 4.5. The use of structured logic diagrams is recommended for facilitating the numbering of nodes and arrows and for preventing computational errors when the network analysis is being performed.

Orderly Array of Elements

The elements that make up a diagram are nodes and arrows. The symbols that represent nodes should be drawn so that they are located in equally spaced vertical columns. Figures 4.5a and 4.5c illustrate the correct application of this rule, and Figures 4.5b and 4.5d illustrate its incorrect application. Note that in Figure 4.5a, an AOA diagram, and in Figure 4.5c, an AON diagram, the nodes are aligned in vertical columns and the horizontal components of task arrows are aligned. In Figures 4.5b and 4.5d, the nodes are not vertically aligned and the horizontal components are not equally spaced.

Horizontal Components for AOA Arrows

All task arrows for AOA diagrams, including those that represent dummy tasks, should contain a horizontal component. Note in Figure 4.5b that the dummy arrow has no horizontal component. Lacking such a horizontal component, it could be easily overlooked during the network analysis.

FIGURE 4.5
STRUCTURED LOGIC DIAGRAMS: (a)
Structured AOA Diagram; (b)
Unstructured AOA Diagram; (c)
Structured AON Diagram; (d)
Unstructured AON Diagram.

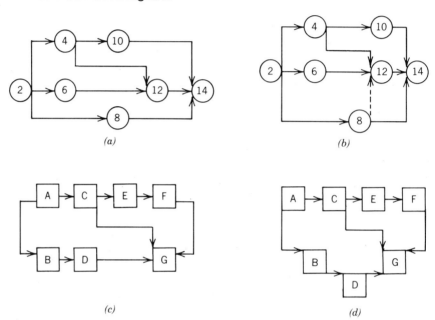

COMPARISON OF THE AOA AND AON TECHNIQUES

Any set of logical relationships that can be depicted by one of the two techniques can be depicted by the other technique. For example, Figure 4.6a is an AON diagram. Figure 4.6b is an AON diagram showing the same logical relationships. Each technique has advantages and disadvantages.

Ease of Learning the Diagramming Techniques

Usually it is easier to learn the AOA diagramming technique than to learn the AON technique, because there is only one simple logical relationship in the AOA technique whereas there are several in the AON technique. On the other

FIGURE 4.6
AN AON LOGIC DIAGRAM AND ITS
AOA LOGICAL EQUIVALENT: (a) AON
Diagram; (b) AOA Equivalent.

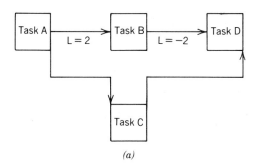

(a)

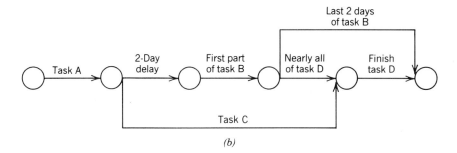

(b)

hand, the AON technique offers a more convenient way to represent complex logical relationships between tasks.

Complexity of Logical Relationships

The AON technique permits the scheduler to specify more readily complex logical relationships between tasks than does the AOA technique. Compare the AON and the AOA diagrams in Figure 4.6. To express the same logic depicted in the AON diagram using AOA notation, it is necessary to define three additional tasks. The actual logical relationships in the real world of construction can be very complex; hence, the AON technique can depict them more realistically.

> **The AOA Logical Relationship.** The single allowable relationship is, "B cannot start until A ends."

FIGURE 4.7
EQUIVALENT LOGIC DIAGRAMS: (a)
AOA Diagram; (b) AON Equivalent;
(c) AON Equivalent with Dummy
Task.

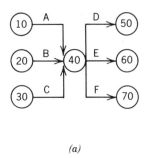

(a)

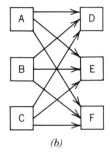

(b)

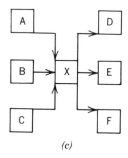

(c)

The AON Logical Relationships. The allowable relationships are, "B cannot start until L days after the end of A," "B cannot start until L days after the start of A," "B cannot end until L days after the end of A," and "B cannot end until L days after the start of A." The word "before" can be used in lieu of the word "after" for all of the above statements of AON logical relationships. As is shown in previous paragraphs, it is possible to modify the statements further so as to use a work quantity as the value for lag.

Ease of Drafting the Diagrams

The example shown in Figure 4.6 illustrates that there will often be fewer nodes and arrows to draw in an AON diagram than in an equivalent AOA diagram.

Some sets of logical relationships can be more readily depicted by using AOA notation than by using AON notation. Figure 4.7 shows parts of a logic diagram using AOA and AON notation. Figure 4.7*a* depicts nine explicit logical relationships using AOA notation. Figure 4.7*b* shows the same nine relationships using AON notation. In the AON technique, one arrow is required for each explicit relationship; hence, nine arrows are drawn. Note that the arrows result in a cluttered diagram. Figure 4.7*c* illustrates the use of a dummy node [X] to reduce this clutter. Dummy task X has zero duration.

THE
CRITICAL PATH
METHOD (CPM)

5

OBJECTIVES

The objectives of this chapter are to introduce the Critical Path Method (CPM), to further develop the principles of logic diagramming that are introduced in Chapter 4, and to illustrate the CPM logical relationships with examples related to construction.

LOGIC DIAGRAMS AND SCHEDULING

The Critical Path Method is based on the establishment of logical relationships between tasks. These logical relationships, which are defined in the discussion that follows, can be depicted by logic diagrams. There are two basic types of logic diagrams, Activity On Arrow (AOA) and Activity On Node (AON) diagrams. See Chapter 4 for discussion and comparison of the two diagramming techniques. The CPM is based on AOA diagrams.

Activity On Arrow (AOA) Diagrams

An AOA diagram is made up of arrows and circles. The arrows represent tasks. The circles (or nodes) represent events. The node at the tail end of an arrow is termed the I-node of this arrow. The node at the head end of an arrow is termed

FIGURE 5.1

PART OF A CPM LOGIC DIAGRAM

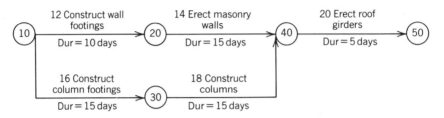

that arrow's J-node. Figure 4.1c (in Chapter 4) illustrates the terms I-node and J-node.

Logical Relationships

The following discussion pertains to the CPM and to AOA logic diagrams. Any pair of the tasks that make up a project are logically related to each other. There are three possible relationships between a pair of tasks. They are defined in the following list and are illustrated in Figure 5.1.

Precedence. Means coming before. If task A is precedent to task B, then task A must be completed before task B can start.

Subsequence. Means coming after. If task B is subsequent to task A, then task B cannot start until task A is completed. Precedence is the opposite of subsequence. If X is precedent to Y, then Y must be subsequent to X.

Concurrency. If task M is neither precedent nor subsequent to task N, then tasks M and N are concurrent to each other.

The logical relationships depicted by the diagram in Figure 5.1 are as follows:

Explicitly Depicted	*Equivalent Statement*
Task 12 is precedent to 14	Task 14 is subsequent to 12
Task 14 is precedent to 20	Task 20 is subsequent to 14
Task 16 is precedent to 18	Task 18 is subsequent to 16
Task 18 is precedent to 20	Task 20 is subsequent to 18

Implicitly Depicted	*Equivalent Statement*
Task 12 is precedent to 20	Task 20 is subsequent to 12
Task 16 is precedent to 20	Task 20 is subsequent to 16

No precedence relationship exists between the following pairs of tasks:

Relationship	*Equivalent Statement*
Task 12 is concurrent with 16	Task 16 is concurrent with 12
Task 12 is concurrent with 18	Task 18 is concurrent with 12
Task 14 is concurrent with 16	Task 16 is concurrent with 14
Task 14 is concurrent with 18	Task 18 is concurrent with 14

It does not follow that because tasks 12 and 14 are concurrent with task 16 that they are concurrent with each other. Neither does it follow that because tasks 16 and 18 are concurrent with 12 they are concurrent with each other.

Note that although tasks 14 and 18 are concurrent with each other, it does not necessarily mean that they will be done simultaneously. Concurrent only means that no precedence relationship exists between a pair of tasks.

INTRODUCTION TO CPM

The Critical Path Method, or CPM, permits the scheduler to compute the critical path through a logic diagram, or network diagram, which represents the project. The critical path passes through tasks that must be completed on schedule if the project is to be completed on schedule. These tasks are called **critical tasks**. The project manager should pay more attention to these critical tasks than to noncritical tasks, because a delay in completing a critical task will delay completion of the project. A delay in completing a noncritical task will not necessarily delay project completion.

CPM Logic Diagram

Assume that part of a project can be represented by the logic diagram shown in Figure 5.1. Assume that this fragment of the total logic diagram contains the critical path.

Attributes of Arrows and Nodes

Note that each task arrow and each node in the diagram shown in Figure 5.1 has been assigned an identifying number and a brief description and that the estimated duration of the task is printed below the arrow that represents the task. Node [10] represents an event, which is a point in time, that point being the time at which it is possible to commence task 12 (construct wall footings) and task 16 (construct column footings). Node [20] is that point in time at which task 12 can be completed and at which task 14 (erect walls) can commence. Node [40] is that point in time at which tasks 14 and 18 can be completed. Node [40] is also the point in time at which both the walls and the columns will be completed and at which it is possible to start task 20 (set girders). Node [50] represents that point in time at which this part of the project can be completed.

Paths Through the Logic Diagram

There are two paths between nodes [10] and [40] in this network. The first path passes through [10] – [20] – [40]. The length of that path is 10 + 15 = 25 days. The second path passes through [10] – [30] – [40]. It has a length of 15 + 15 = 30 days. This second path is the critical path because it is the longest path. Tasks 16 and 18 are critical tasks, because they are on that critical path. The total length of the path [10] – [30] – [40] – [50] is 35 days. If more than 30 days are spent on tasks 16 and 18 combined, this part of the project will require more than 35 days for completion. If one of the noncritical tasks, say, 12, is delayed a few days, the project duration will not be extended, unless the new length of the path [10] – [20] – [40] becomes the longest, or critical, path. Later, we will abbreviate "Dur = X days" to "X," it being understood that a numerical value beneath a task arrow represents the task duration.

Conventions

A convention is a customary practice. The following conventions should be considered. Figure 5.2 contains fragments of logic diagrams which do, and do not, reflect the correct application of these conventions.

Numbering Arrows and Nodes

In numbering the task arrows and the nodes, nonconsecutive numbers were used, making it possible later to add tasks and nodes with appropriate numbers. Some CPM computer programs do not permit entry of task numbers. Such programs simply store task data in the computer memory in the order in which they were entered. Other computer programs have an upper limit on the magnitude of the numbers that can be used for numbering nodes. There is no reason why a task might not be assigned the same number that has been previously used as a node number; but no two tasks, nor any two nodes, should be assigned the same number. An example of the correct application of this convention is shown in Figure 5.2(1). If the scheduler were to decide to add a new task that could

FIGURE 5.2

CORRECT AND INCORRECT
APPLICATION OF CONVENTIONS

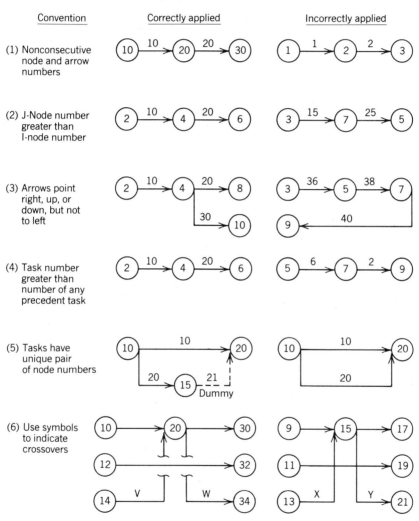

commence after task 10 was completed and that must be completed before task 20 could be started, the scheduler could slip the new task in as task 15. New task 15 would have an I-node of [20] and a J-node of [25]. It would also be necessary to redefine task 20 to indicate that is had an I-node of [25]. If this convention had not been correctly applied, it would have been necessary to renumber all tasks and nodes to the right of the newly inserted task arrow.

FIGURE 5.3
LOGICAL AND ILLOGICAL NODE AND
ARROW NUMBERING

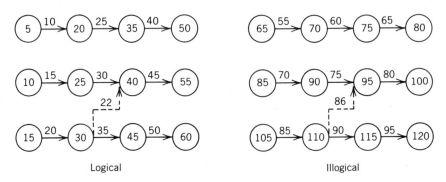

Logical   Illogical

It is good practice first to draw the logic diagram and then to assign numbers to the nodes and to the arrows. Figure 5.3 illustrates a logical and an illogical method for assigning these numbers. The scheduler should work from left to right in assigning numbers, rather than from the top of the diagram to the bottom. Consider that the dummy task arrow was added to both diagrams as an afterthought, after the nodes and arrows were numbered. Note that the arrow for task 22 was added without violation of any of the conventions. The dummy arrow for task 86 violates two of the conventions listed below.

J-Node Number > I-Node Number Convention

It is desirable that nodes be numbered so that the node at the head of an arrow always has a higher number than the node at the tail of that arrow. Figure 5.2(2) illustrates the correct and the incorrect application of this convention. If the convention is adhered to, the scheduler will not be able to inadvertently create a **logic loop**. An example of a logic loop is illustrated in Figure 5.4. Note in Figure 5.4 that for task arrow 8 the J-node number [2] is smaller than the I-node number [4]. This is a violation of the above convention. Also note that task arrow 8 is indicated as being both precedent and subsequent to task arrows 4 and 6, a nonpermissible relationship. This nonpermissible relationship is termed a logic loop. If the convention that J > I had been adhered to, the scheduler would not have been able to create a logic loop. Some computer programs will cycle endlessly if the input data contain a logic loop. Therefore, the input routines for most computer programs will reject input data with a task's I-node larger than its J-node.

FIGURE 5.4
A LOGIC LOOP

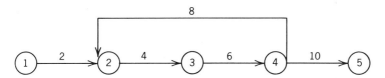

Direction of Arrows

Another convention that will protect against logic loops is to draw arrows so that they point up (↑), down (↓), or to the right (→) but not to the left (←). Figure 5.2(3) illustrates the correct and the incorrect application of this convention. Task arrow 40 points to the left. The scheduler might draw an arrow from node [9] to node [5], thereby creating a logic loop. He would realize that he had created such a loop if he were observing convention (2); otherwise, the logic loop might go undetected at least until an attempt was made to analyze the network. If the analysis was being made by a computer, the computer might cycle continuously. There is an exception to this convention. Often, a diagram will be very wide but not very high. In these instances, the scheduler may use a left-pointing arrow from the right side of the page to the left side so as to continue the diagram at the bottom of the page.

Numbering Tasks

Another convention that is sometimes used is to number tasks so that no task has a higher number than the number of a subsequent task. Adherence to that convention would also have prevented the creation of a logic loop. Some, but not all, CPM scheduling computer programs require that this convention be adhered to. Figure 5.2(4) illustrates the correct and incorrect application of this convention.

Common Node Numbers

Some computer programs will not permit entry of network data in which two task arrows have a common set of node numbers. Adherence to this convention would preclude drawing a diagram in which both task A and task B have I-node numbers of [10] and J-node numbers of [20]. It may be necessary to establish **dummy tasks** to avoid violation of this convention. Dummy tasks will be covered later in this chapter. See Figure 5.2(5) for an illustration of the correct and the incorrect applications of this principle. Note that in the left diagram, dummy task 21 has been drawn. This convention is based upon the logic that is used in some computer programs. An unfortunate consequence of this convention is that introduction of a dummy arrow to preclude two tasks having common node numbers results either in a wider logic diagram or a shortening of the arrow immediately precedent, or immediately subsequent, to the dummy arrow.

Crossovers

In drawing the logic diagram, it may be necessary to have one task arrow cross over another arrow. It is customary to use a crossover symbol in such instances. Use of crossover symbols is illustrated in the left diagram in Figure 5.2(6), where the arrows for tasks V and W are broken. If the arrows for tasks X and Y are not broken, there is a possibility that the reader of the diagram might interpret the diagram as showing that the arrow for task X terminates at node [19] or that the arrow for task Y originates at node [11].

The Basic CPM Logical Relationship

It was stated above that any pair of tasks can be related to each other in three possible ways: a task can be precedent, subsequent, or concurrent with another task. These relationships can be reduced to a single basic relationship which can be stated as follows: task B cannot start until task A ends. This is not equivalent to stating: "Task J *must* start when task I ends." It is equivalent to: "Task I *must* end before task J *can* start." If this basic relationship does not exist between a pair of tasks, then the tasks are concurrent with each other. To illustrate the distinction between the underlined words, consider the statements that follow. Figure 5.5 illustrates the logical relationship.

1. You *cannot* fry an egg until you break its shell.

2. You *can* fry an egg after you break its shell.

3. You *must* break an egg's shell before you fry it.

Note that none of these statements means that you *must* fry an egg immediately after you break its shell.

FIGURE 5.5
LOGICAL RELATIONSHIPS

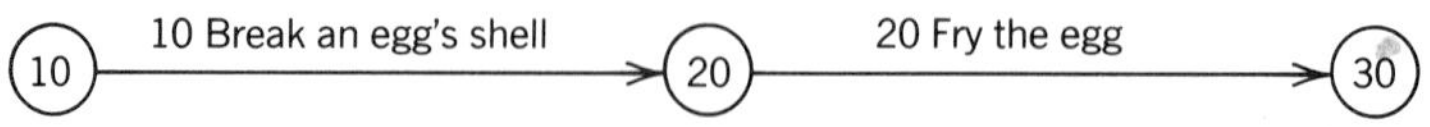

LOGICAL RELATIONSHIPS AS APPLIED TO SCHEDULING

If task M is precedent to task N, then completion of task M is a constraint to the initiation of task N. The scheduler specifies these constraints when he or she drafts the logic diagram. Drafting the logic diagram is an important part of the scheduling process. It requires more knowledge of construction operations than is required for some later phases of the scheduling process. For example, calculation of the critical path is essentially a mechanical operation, one that can be efficiently performed by a computer. To illustrate this point, let us consider a very simple project.

Putting on Your Shoes

Consider this job to be a project that is made up of four tasks: put on left sock, put on right sock, put on and tie laces of left shoe, and put on and tie laces of right shoe. Before we draw the logic diagram, let us determine whether or not there are any absolutely essential logical relationshps between these four tasks. The obvious ones are that putting on the left sock is precedent to putting on the left shoe, and that putting on the right sock is precedent to putting on the right shoe. See Figure 5.6 for a logic diagram that incorporates these two essential logical relationships.

First Try: Unnecessary Constraints

The diagram in Figure 5.6 does include the two essential logical relationships, but it also includes several unnecessary constraints. It does not reflect the possibility of working from right foot to left foot, nor the possibility of putting on both socks before putting on either shoe.

FIGURE 5.6
FIRST TRY; ARBITRARY LOGICAL
CONSTRAINTS

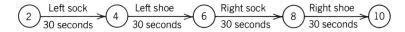

FIGURE 5.7
SECOND TRY; SOME LOGICAL
CONSTRAINTS REMOVED

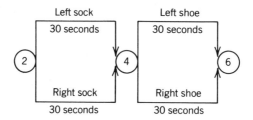

Second Try: Elimination of Unnecessary Constraints

See Figure 5.7. This logic diagram removes some of the unnecessary constraints, but it still indicates that both socks must be donned before either shoe is donned.

Third Try: Removal of All Unnecessary Constraints

See Figure 5.8. This logic diagram removes all unnecessary constraints. However, the diagram implies that you can be putting on two socks, or two shoes, or a sock and a shoe, at one time, a feat beyond the capability of most persons. The logic diagram does not consider the resources available for accomplishment of the tasks. Normal individuals will use all their resources (hands) in performing any of these tasks. Unless additional resources are available (extra-agile hands or a valet), there will be a constraint (a resource constraint) that is not depicted on the diagram.

FIGURE 5.8
THIRD TRY; NO UNNECESSARY
LOGICAL CONSTRAINTS

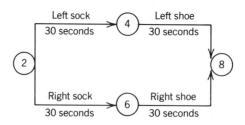

Comparison of the Three Diagrams

Figures 5.6 to 5.8 illustrate that the analysis of even the simplest project requires a use of judgement and that the logic diagramming technique cannot always be relied on to depict the actual conditions that will exist on a project. Figure 5.8 can be considered the best logic diagram because it contains no unnecessary logical constraints. However, the diagram does not reflect that limited resources may prevent simultaneous work on more than one task. Each of the three trial network logic diagrams was based on arbitrary decisions as to how this simple project would be accomplished.

Real Projects

Real projects are more complex. They require assumptions as to how work will be sequenced.

One-Story Building

A one-story steel frame building can be constructed with the floor slab being poured before or after the columns and the roof are erected. A network logic diagram that was prepared on the basis that the floor slab would be poured before the columns and the roof were erected would not reflect the actual construction sequence if the floor slab is poured after the columns and the roof are constructed.

Multiple-Story Building

The construction of a multiple-story commercial office building is often commenced before tenants have been found for all of the floor space. There are technical reasons for accomplishing the interior finish work from the ground floor up, and there are also technical reasons for accomplishing the interior finish work from the top floor down. Regardless of the validity of these technical arguments, it is likely that interior finish work will actually be scheduled on the basis of marketing considerations. If the owner of the building finds a tenant who desires the use of even-numbered floors as soon as possible, this is a very good reason for finishing even-numbered floors before odd-numbered floors. The fact that the information required for an accurate schedule may not be available until well after the project is started does not negate the value of preparing a schedule based on the best information available. It does make it essential that the schedule be promptly revised when better information becomes available.

Fast Tracking

One construction management technique is called **fast tracking**. Under this concept, site development may commence before the construction drawings are completed. It is possible that some material procurement actions, particularly for long lead-time items, may be commenced before design is complete. The reason for taking these early actions is to reduce the overall time for project completion and thereby to reduce the investment cost for the project. The initial logic diagram for a fast-track project will differ considerably from the final logic diagram.

Missile System

It is fairly common, and often justified, in state-of-the-art-type projects to commence construction well before the project design is completed. Consider a major new missile system. The project managers may consider that their new system will be technologically obsolete within 20 years after it was conceived. Based on their experience, they may expect that 5 years will be required to complete the design of the missile, another 3 years to test prototype missiles, 3 years to obtain funding authorization, and 3 years to procure land and to construct the launch sites. If the project managers proceed in a deliberate step-by-step manner, they will produce a system in 14 years that will be technologically obsolete in another 6 years. Under such conditions, it is often justifiable to "bet on the come," thereby expediting project completion by several years. In this example, the project managers have reason to overlap the development stages, perhaps by requesting production funding well before prototype testing is completed. If they are able to decrease the overall time for developing and deploying the system by 2 years, they will have increased the operational life of the system from 6 years to 8 years, or by 33%. Nuclear power plants and other high-technology plants may fall in this category. Given the uncertainty of the tasks that will be performed in the later years, project managers will define these late-year tasks very broadly. As work progresses, and as more information becomes available, they will revise the schedule.

DUMMY TASKS

A dummy task is a task that has zero duration. Dummy task arrows are used for several reasons.

FIGURE 5.9
COMMON I- AND J-NODES

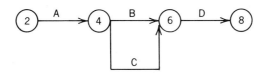

Activity Splitters

The logic diagram shown in Figure 5.9 violates one of the conventions that were described earlier in this chapter. Use of node [4] as the I-node and of node [6] as the J-node for both tasks B and C will cause no problem if the network is analyzed manually. However, many computer programs will reject data if two tasks have a common pair of nodes. See Figure 5.10 for the revised logic diagram with a dummy arrow used as an activity splitter. The arrow for dummy task X is drawn with a dashed line. Dummy tasks have zero duration. Note that the adherence to this convention required lengthening arrow B and making the diagram wider.

Dummy Tasks as Logical Constraints

See Figure 5.11 for the logic diagram of a project as it was originally conceived. Now add the additional logical constraint that task F cannot be started until task A ends. See Figure 5.12 for a revised logic diagram, which includes the dummy task X. This dummy task has a duration of zero. It is drawn with a dashed line. The dummy reflects the logical constraint that task A must be completed before task F can start.

You may experiment by trying to add the logical relationship that F cannot start until A ends without using a dummy task, but you will find that its use is

FIGURE 5.10
DUMMY TASK USED AS ACTIVITY
SPLITTER

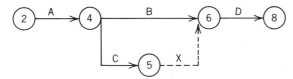

FIGURE 5.11
ORIGINAL LOGIC DIAGRAM

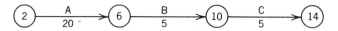

FIGURE 5.12
DUMMY TASK AS A LOGICAL
CONSTRAINT

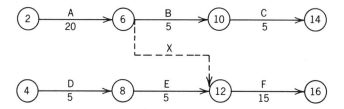

necessary. For example, the diagram in Figure 5.13 is an unsuccessful attempt to show all of the specified constraints without introducing unspecified constraints.

Unnecessary Constraints

The example in Figure 5.13 illustrates one way in which unnecessary constraints are introduced into a network logic diagram. Very frequently, unnecessary constraints are introduced into the diagram simply because the person who is drawing

FIGURE 5.13
UNSUCCESSFUL ATTEMPT TO AVOID
USE OF DUMMY TASK

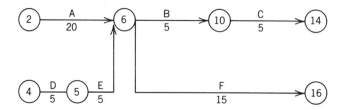

FIGURE 5.14

TASKS 10, 20, AND 22 ARE
NONESSENTIAL CONSTRAINTS

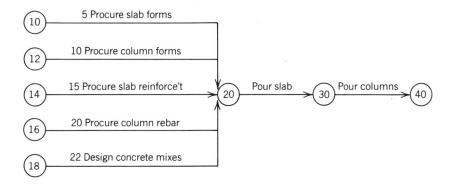

the diagram is either attempting to draw a "tidy" diagram or because he or she has failed to analyze the project properly. Assume that the scheduler desires to show certain procurement actions as constraints to initiation of physical work. A part of the logic diagram is shown in Figure 5.14. The diagram properly indicates that the procurement of slab forms and slab rebar and the design of the concrete mix are precedent to pouring a slab. It improperly indicates that the procurement of column forms and rebar are precedent to pouring the slab.

As another example of unnecessary constraints, consider the partial logic diagram shown in Figure 5.15. Redraw the diagram to show that completion of task E is a constraint to the start of task G and that completion of task D is a constraint to the start of task I. Add no other constraints. Figure 5.16 is an incorrect attempt to add these two constraints, in that it indicates task F as being precedent to task G and task D as being precedent to task H. Figure 5.17 shows

FIGURE 5.15

ORIGINAL DIAGRAM

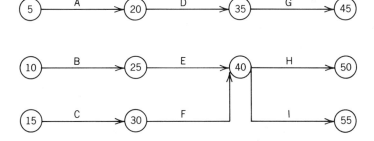

FIGURE 5.16
FIGURE 5.15 WITH INCORRECTLY
DRAWN DUMMY ARROWS

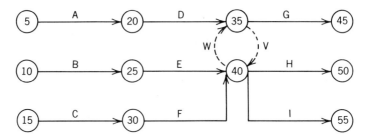

FIGURE 5.17
FIGURE 5.15 WITH CORRECTLY
DRAWN DUMMY ARROWS

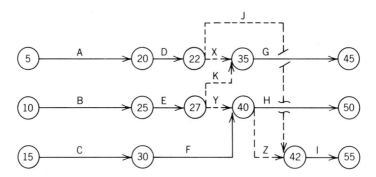

the correctly drawn revised logic diagram. The addition of the two logical constraints required the addition of five dummy tasks. Dummy tasks X, Y, and Z are activity splitters. Dummy tasks J and K are the logical constraints. All five dummy tasks have durations of zero. Note that the dummy arrow J crosses over arrows G and H. Two different crossover symbols are illustrated.

CONTINGENCIES

A contingency is an unusual event that may or may not occur. Some contingencies that will affect the duration of a project are: exceptionally unfavorable weather conditions (rainfall, freezing weather, excessively hot weather, etc.), labor shortages, labor strikes, material shortages, delays by the owner in approving shop drawings, shipping strikes, and the necessity to replace faulty work by the contractor or a subcontractor. Some allowance should be made for these contingencies when preparing the schedule. The scheduler should not assume that the project will be completed under ideal conditions, neither should the schedule be based on the assumption that everything that can possibly go wrong will in fact go wrong.

Some scheduling methods (PERT and Probabilistic Scheduling) allow the scheduler to make three different estimates of the duration for each task: an optimistic estimate, a most likely or average estimate, and a pessimistic estimate. The schedules that are prepared by those methods provide a quantitative estimate of the probability that the project, or any part of the project, will be completed as of any particular date. The Critical Path Method does not allow making three different estimates of task duration; hence, the scheduler must address contingencies in some other manner.

Contingencies Are Exceptional Events

The scheduler should not expect that ideal conditions will prevail throughout the project duration. The scheduler should allow for the normal, and relatively predictable, unfavorable conditions that will exist during the project work.

Rain

If there are normally one or two heavy showers a week during a particular season of the year, schedulers should base their estimates of task durations on that basis. In the southeastern United States, heavy summer showers will occur about once a week. Such a shower will last only part of a day, but an additional day may be required until the ground dries to the point where grading can be performed. Under these conditions, a grading contractor might assume that only five-sevenths of the potential workdays in a week will be available. If the grading contractor estimates that a grading task will require 10 workdays, he should use $10 / (5/7)$ = 14 workdays as the estimated task duration. This normal rainfall is not a contingency. An extended period of rain, perhaps caused by a hurricane, would be a contingency. Although one or two such rains may be expected a year, it is unlikely that one will occur at a time when it will delay a particular task.

Shop Drawing Review

Only a day or so is actually required for an architect–engineer to review a particular shop drawing. However, the architect–engineer may have a thick pile of shop drawings under review when your critical shop drawing arrives. The scheduler should determine from the architect–engineer an estimate of the average review time, and then allow a few days extra for transmission and return of shop drawings when estimating the duration of a task requiring such a review.

Why Worry About Contingencies?

A contingency has been defined as the possible occurrence of a rare event. The determination of the impact of such an event on a project will not necessarily prevent its occurrence. However, it may enable the contractor to plan the work so as to minimize the impact. For example, consider a job done in an area where there is a very short construction season because of severe winter weather. Assume that critical material, say, steel pipe, can only be installed during the construction season and that normal delivery time for the pipe is 90 days. A shipping strike might delay delivery by an additional 90 days. The consequence of such a strike might be the loss of most of the construction season, and the project duration may have to be extended by nearly a year if such a strike occurs. In such a situation, the contractor might decide to arrange to have the pipe delivered early. If the contractor recognizes the impact of such a shipping strike on project duration and project cost while he is still in the contract negotiation stage, he may consider increasing his proposed contract amount to reflect the risk he faces.

Impact of Contingencies on Task and Project Duration

The estimates of task duration that are used in the Critical Path Method are just that—estimates. It is not to be expected that they will exactly correspond with the actual task durations. However, if all the estimates prove to be reasonably accurate, it can be expected that the estimated project duration will be reasonably accurate most of the time. This expectation is based on the assumption that time lost by a contingency's delay of work on one task will be made up by very favorable conditions for another task. The impact that a contingency will have on a project's actual duration depends on whether the tasks that are delayed by this contingency are on the critical path. Some contingencies will have little or no impact on some tasks. For example, rainfall will usually not delay progress on interior finish work, but rainfall will delay outside tasks such as grading or painting. Such delays will include the actual duration of the rainfall plus the additional time for the ground or outside surface to dry.

Allowing for Contingencies

There are three basic approaches to the problem of making an allowance for contingencies. Any one of them, or all of them, can be followed on a specific project.

1. Make no allowance for contingencies when preparing the schedule, but view the estimated project duration as an optimistic estimate. Although it is unlikely that a particular contingency will delay a particular task, it is likely that some contingency will delay some task. It is even likely that several contingencies will delay several tasks, with all of them on the critical path.

2. Increase the estimated durations for tasks that are sensitive to the contingency. If the scheduler estimates that there is a 10% chance that the duration of a particular task will be extended 50% by a contingency, he or she might increase the estimate of that task's duration by 50%. In such a case, there would be a 90% chance that the revised estimate of task duration was too pessimistic. It would be more logical to increase the duration of that task by $0.1 \times 50\% = 5\%$.

3. Define several contingency tasks, such as "weather delay," and assign them an appropriate duration. Include these arrows in the logic diagram and consider them while making the network analysis.

STRENGTHS AND WEAKNESSES OF THE CRITICAL PATH METHOD

The Critical Path Method is well established, with very little variation in the use of conventions. The diagramming technique is easily learned. The principal disadvantage of the method is that the single logical relationship that is allowed is not adequate to express all of the various complex relationships that exist in the real world of project management. For example, it cannot be used to specify that task X will start when task Y starts. If it were desired to specify that task Y could start no earlier than five days after task X is completed, it would be necessary to add a task having a title of "delay" and a duration of five days between the end of task X and the start of task Y. The Precedence Method, covered in Chapter 7, overcomes many of these limitations.

One of the principal benefits to be derived from the preparation of a CPM logic diagram is that its preparation requires detailed analysis of the project. The scheduler or project manager will develop a better understanding of the project as a result of this detailed analysis.

This has been a very brief introduction to the Critical Path Method. The method is described in detail in Chapter 6. The preparation of the logic diagram is an essential first step in applying the method. If any essential logical constraints are omitted from this diagram, or if any nonessential logical constraints are incorporated into the logic diagram, the resulting construction schedule will reflect these errors.

EXERCISES

EXERCISE 5.1

A project includes eight tasks: A, B, C, D, E, F, G, and H. Tasks D and C cannot start until task A ends. Task G cannot start until tasks D and E end. Task B must end before task E starts. Task F cannot start until task C ends. The project is complete when tasks F, G, and H are complete. Draw a CPM logic diagram for the project that includes all of these constraints and *no* others.

EXERCISE 5.2

A project includes six tasks, A through F. Task A is precedent to tasks C and F; task B is precedent to tasks D and E; task C is precedent to task E; and task D is precedent to task F. Draw a CPM diagram reflecting these relationships and *no* others.

EXERCISE 5.3

Draw a CPM logic diagram for the project that was described as Example 1 in Chapter 2.

EXERCISE 5.4

A project to construct a simple concrete block storage building is made up of the tasks listed below. Draw a CPM logic diagram for this project. Observe the previously listed conventions in numbering arrows and nodes. The tasks are not necessarily listed in the order that they will be performed. Do not show logical constraints other than those listed, unless such constraints are clearly essential.

Task	Constraints
A. Survey and layout site	None
B. Clear and grade site	Start after A is completed
C. Construct wall footings	Start after B is completed
D. Pour concrete floor slab	Start after C is completed
E. Erect block walls	Start after C is completed

Task	Constraints
F. Set door and window frames	Perform concurrently with E
G. Set roof joists	Start after E is completed
H. Place roof deck	Start after G is completed
I. Install built-up roof	Start after H is completed
J. Install doors and windows	Start after E, F, and I are completed
K. Paint exterior block	Start after I is completed
L. Install electrical system	Start after I is completed
M. Pave driveway	Start after H is completed
N. Landscape site	Start after M is completed

CALCULATION OF CPM EVENT AND TASK TIMES

6

OBJECTIVE

The preceding chapter describes the procedures for drawing a CPM logic diagram based on Activity On Arrow (AOA) notation. This chapter covers the steps for making the CPM analysis and for completing the CPM schedule. The CPM schedule will consist of a tabulation of time values for the tasks that make up a project. These time values are the estimated start and finish times and the float times for the tasks.

ESSENTIAL TERMS

The terms used in this chapter are described in the discussion that follows. They are grouped in relation to their meanings. It is important that the reader understand these definitions, including the acronyms for the terms involved.

Related to the Network Diagram

The CPM logic diagram is made up of arrows and nodes, with words and numbers printed above and below the arrows and with numbers printed within the nodes. The logic diagram is a graphic depiction of a project, showing the tasks that must be accomplished and the order in which they will be accomplished. Figure 6.1 is an example of a logic diagram.

FIGURE 6.1

CPM LOGIC DIAGRAM

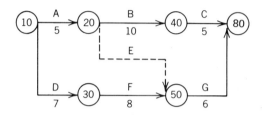

Arrows

The arrows in the diagram of Figure 6.1 represent **tasks**. The task arrows are each assigned a unique task number, which is usually printed on the diagram above the arrow. The tasks are also assigned a short task title or description, which is also printed on the diagram above the arrow. To save space on the diagrams shown in the following sections of this chapter, the task numbers have sometimes been omitted and the task titles have been represented by a capital letter. The duration of each task is printed on the diagram below the arrow that represents the task. Task numbers, task titles, and task durations are termed **task attributes**.

   Real tasks are represented by arrows drawn with solid lines. Real tasks have durations greater than zero. Real tasks usually require the accomplishment of physical work; however, some real tasks merely represent the passage of time. For example, an arrow can be drawn to represent the time that is required for a concrete member to develop the strength that is required so that the forms can be stripped and so that it can support additional construction. Task arrows can be used to represent possible weather delays.

   Dummy tasks are represented by arrows drawn with dashed lines. Task E in Figure 6.1 is a dummy task. Dummy tasks do not require the accomplishment of physical work and have durations of zero. Hence, it is not necessary to print their durations on the diagram. The title of a dummy task may be "dummy," or it may simply be omitted from the diagram. However, dummy tasks must be assigned a task number. The arrows representing dummy tasks are drawn for the reasons indicated in Chapter 5, including the portrayal of logical relationships between tasks.

Nodes and Events

Nodes are graphic symbols (usually a circle enclosing a node number) that represent events. Circles are used to depict nodes in the illustrations of this book. When a node is referrred to in the text, the node number will be enclosed in brackets, for example, [10], [20], and so on. Note that nonconsecutive node numbers have been assigned so as to facilitate the insertion of additional nodes in the diagrams. An event (often called a **milestone**) is a point in time at which something, or several things, can happen, must happen, or have happened. There is always a node at each end of a task arrow. At least one task arrow originates at every node except the terminal node. At least one task arrow terminates at every node except the initial node. The following terms are used in connection with nodes. See Figure 6.1 for the illustration of these terms.

> **I-Node.** The node at the beginning of a task arrow (usually the left end of the arrow) is termed the arrow's I-node. A particular node can be the I-node for several task arrows. Node [20] is the I-node for tasks B and E.

> **J-Node.** The node at the head of the task arrow (usually the right end of the arrow) is termed the arrow's J-node. A paticular node can be the J-node for several task arrows. In Figure 6.1, node [50] is the J-node for tasks E and F.

> **Initial Node.** In every CPM logic diagram, there will be one node (usually at the extreme left of the logic diagram) that represents the event "project start." The initial node may be the I-node for several arrows. It is the J-node for no arrow. Node [10] is the initial node.

> **Terminal Node.** In every CPM logic diagram, there will be one node (usually at the extreme right of the diagram) that represents the event "project completion." The terminal node may be the J-node for several arrows. It is the I-node for no arrow. Node [60] is the terminal node.

Related to the Time of Day

Events are points in time. The possible or required starting times or finishing times for tasks are also points in time. To define a point in time, it is necessary to specify the date and the time of the day. The date can be expressed as a **calendar date**, including the month, the day of the month, and the year. The date can also be expressed as a **work date**, the number of workdays since the project started. The time of day could be expressed as the hour of the day; but in construction scheduling it is customary to use only two times of the day, the **beginning of the day (BOD)** or the **end of the day (EOD)**. Practice varies in respect to use of the two times of the day. Usage depends on the type of schedule being prepared.

Related to the Type of Schedule

The CPM schedule will consist of a tabulation containing task attributes and time values for the tasks that make up a project. The time values are the task times, the estimated times for starting and finishing the tasks, and the task float times. These time values can be expressed in calendar date format, in work date format, or in both formats. Regardless of whether a calendar date format or a work date format is used, these time values consist of two parts, a **date part** and a **time-of-the-day part**.

Work Date Format

The date parts of the time values for starting and for finishing tasks are expressed as elapsed workdays since the project commencement. A complete time value includes a date part, the elapsed workdays since project commencement, and the time of the day. It is customary to use only one time of the day when preparing schedules using the work date format, namely, the end of the day.

Calendar Date Format

The time values for starting and finishing tasks are expressed as calendar dates. A complete time value includes a calendar year, a month of the year, and a day of the month, plus a time of the day. Time values for starting tasks refer to the beginning of the day. Time values for finishing tasks refer to the end of the day.

Calendar Date Format Versus Calendar Date Scheduling

It is more difficult to prepare a schedule based on the calendar date format than on the work date format. However, a calendar date schedule is more convenient to use than is a work date schedule. A schedule may be prepared in work date format, based on the procedures covered in this chapter, and the time values can then be converted to calendar date format. Appendix B contains a table that can be used for this purpose. The resulting schedule will be in calendar date format, but it will not be a true calendar date schedule unless all of the tasks that make up the project have the same work date regime. A work date regime is a set of rules specifying which days are nonworkdays for the various tasks. The different tasks in a project may have different work date regimes. Some tasks (curing concrete) can proceed 7 days a week, whereas other tasks will only be worked on weekdays. The preparation of true calendar date schedules is discussed in Chapter 11.

Equivalence of the End of the Day and the Beginning of the Day

It is assumed that no work is performed between the end of one day and the beginning of the following day. Hence, the end of one day can be considered to be the same point in time as the beginning of the next day.

Work Date Schedules. The end of work date X is equal to the beginning of work date X + 1. The end of the tenth work date is equal to the beginning of the eleventh work date. If work is performed only 5 days a week, and if Friday is the fifteenth work date, then the end of Friday is equivalent to the beginning of the following Monday, the sixteenth work date.

Calendar Date Schedules. The relationship between the end of one date and the beginning of the following date is somewhat more complicated for calendar date schedules. Again assuming that Saturday and Sunday are nonworkdays, either the end of Friday or the end of Sunday could be considered equivalent to the beginning of Monday. These relationships are described in detail in Chapter 11, ''Calendar Date Scheduling.''

Related to Time

Preparation of a CPM schedule involves the determination of time values. The following terms are related to time. Other terms that are also related to time will be defined later in this chapter.

Time Versus Date

As was previously indicated, a complete definition of a time value includes two parts, a date (either a calendar date or a work date) and a time of the day (either the BOD or the EOD). Some schedulers use the words ''time'' and ''date'' interchangeably. In this book the word ''time'' will be used to indicate that the time value includes both a date and a time of the day.

Task Durations (D, or Dur)

Any interval of time (weeks, days, hours, etc.) can be used to specify task durations; however, it is customary to use days in construction scheduling. The following considerations apply to the determination of a task's duration.

Work Time (Workdays). The usual computational procedure for estimating task duration involves the estimation of the total number of hours required to complete the task and the division of this total by the hours of work time in a workday. For example, a task that requires 120 hours will have a duration of 16 workdays of 7.5 hours per day ($^{120}/_{7.5} = 16$). The estimated duration of the task may be adjusted upward to allow for the expectable delays due to bad weather, but no allowance will be made for weekends or holidays. Very often, the computed duration of a task will be other than an integer value. For example, a task that requires 100 hours will have a duration of 12.5 workdays of 8 hours per day. Although it is feasible to prepare a CPM schedule on the basis of noninteger task durations, it is customary to round task durations off to the nearest whole number.

Calendar Time (Calendar Days). The work time that will be required to complete a task is estimated as shown above, but is adjusted upward to reflect nonwork dates such as weekends and holidays.

Workdays Versus Calendar Days. The duration of a task may be expressed in workdays or in calendar days. Although both methods of expressing task duration have advantages and disadvantages, most schedulers will express task duration in workdays. Workdays will be used for task durations in this book.

Event Times

An event is a point in time at which something, or some things, can happen, must happen, or have happened. Every project has a starting event (represented by the initial node), that event being the point in time at which all tasks, other than those that have precedent tasks, can start. Another event might be that point in time at which task X can end and task Y can start. Events are represented by nodes on the CPM logic diagram. Time values for events are termed event times. These values represent points in time; hence, they must include a date and a time of the day. The date part of the event time can be expressed as a calendar date or as a work date. The time-of-the-day part of the value is expressed as the end of the day. Examples are given below to illustrate the time of the day that is being referred to in respect to event times.

> **Early Event Time (EET).** This is the earliest time at which an event can occur, considering the durations of precedent tasks. The initial event in a project (represented by the initial node) will be the project commencement.

Workday Format: EET = 10 means end of the tenth work date.
Calendar Day Format: EET = January 10, 1985, means end of that date.

> **Late Event Time (LET).** This is the latest time at which an event can occur if the project is to be completed on schedule. The terminal event in a project (represented by the terminal node) will be project completion.

Workday Format: LET = 20 means end of the twentieth work date.
Calendar Day Format: LET = January 24, 1985, means end of that date.

Task Times

A task time is the time when a task may start or end. See the preceding discussion concerning the relationship between the beginning of a day and the end of the preceding day. The time of the day part of a task time can be expressed as either the beginning of the day or the end of the day. These times of the day are illustrated in the list that follows:

Early Start Time (ES). This is the earliest time at which a task can be started. The early start time for a task may be specified by a contract provision; it may be dictated by the climate (in arctic regions, earthwork cannot start until the spring thaw); or it may be based on the estimated time at which some precedent task or tasks will be completed. The ES time for pouring a concrete slab is the time at which the forms are installed and the reinforcement has been placed.

Workday Format: ES = 10 means end of the tenth work date.

Calendar Day Format: ES = January 10, 1985, means beginning of that date.

Early Finish Time (EF). This is the earliest time at which a task can be completed if it is started at its ES time and is completed within its estimated duration.

Workday Format: EF = 20 means the end of the twentieth work date.

Calendar Day Format: EF = January 24, 1985, means end of that date.

Late Start Time (LS). The latest time at which a task can be started if it is to be completed by its LF time and if its actual duration is equal to its estimated duration.

Workday Format: LS = 10 means the end of the tenth work date.

Calendar Day Format: LS = January 10, 1985, means the beginning of that date.

Late Finish Time (LF). This is the latest time at which a task can be completed without delaying project completion. For critical tasks, the EF and LF times are identical.

Workday Format: LF = 20 means the end of the twentieth work date.

Calendar Day Format: LF = January 24, 1985, means the end of that date.

Task Float

This is a measure of the difference between a task's early and late start and finish times. The value of a task's float is a measure of how noncritical that task is. The term "slack" is sometimes used. It has the same meaning as float. There are several ways of measuring float.

Total Float (TF). This is the difference between a tasks's LF time and the sum of its ES time and its duration. It is the amount of time that a task's completion may be delayed without delaying project completion. In a later section, it is pointed out that several tasks may share the same total float time.

Free Float (FF). This is the amount of time that a task's completion may be delayed without delaying the start of another task beyond that task's ES time.

Interfering Float (IF). This is the difference between a task's total float and its free float. The completion of a task may be delayed by an amount of time equal to that task's IF without delaying project completion; however, such a delay will delay the start of a subsequent noncritical task.

Julian Date Times

Sometimes a Julian date is used to abbreviate a calendar date. The Julian date is a four-digit number preceded by the letter J. The first digit is the last digit in the four-digit designation of the calendar year, for example, 198*4*. The next three digits represent the sequence of a calendar date within a calendar year, with January 1 being day 1. The Julian date for January 15, 1984, is J4015. The Julian date for December 31, 1985, is J5365. December 31, 1988 (1988 is a leap year), is J8366. The use of Julian dates facilitates finding the number of days between two calendar dates. For example, there are 65 calendar dates between Julian dates J4015 and J4080 inclusive (January 15, 1984 to March 5, 1984). Many office calendars list the last three digits of the Julian date next to the actual calendar date. Appendix B contains a calendar for 1985 showing Julian dates and a listing of a BASIC language computer program that can be used to print calendars for other years. As is the case for calendar date times, the scheduler must be aware of whether reference is being made to the start or the end of a Julian date.

METHODOLOGY

The Critical Path Method is often termed a task-oriented scheduling method, because time values for tasks, rather than for events, are of principal interest to the user. The objective of the CPM is to produce a CPM schedule, a tabulation of task attributes, task times, and task floats. There are four task times: the early start time (ES), the late start time (LS), the early finish time (EF), and the late finish time (LF). These terms, as well as task float, are defined in the discussion on pages 115 to 116. The CPM schedule is produced in three phases, which must be completed in order.

Phases in Preparation of the CPM Schedule

Phase 1   Draw the Logic Diagram

Draw the CPM logic diagram. The logic diagram will depict the logical relationships between the tasks', and the durations of those tasks will be printed on the diagram. This phase is covered in Chapter 5.

Phase 2   Perform the Network Analysis

Event times are computed during the network analysis. Computation of these event times may be considered as an intermediate step in the computation of the task times, which are the time values of principal interest. Events are represented by nodes on the logic diagram. A particular node can represent several different events. For each node, there are two events of interest during this phase. The first of these is the event, "all of the tasks represented by arrows terminating at this node *can* be completed by this time, given the durations of precedent tasks." The event time for this event is the Early Event Time (EET). The second event of interest is, "all of the tasks represented by arrows terminating at this node *must* be completed by this time if the project is to be completed on schedule." The event time for this event is the Late Event Time (LET). The network analysis may be made manually or by a computer. If the analysis is made manually, it is customary to print the results of the computations on the network diagram adjacent to the nodes that represent those events. Some schedulers enclose the values for the EETs in small boxes to the upper left of each node and the values for the LETs in small triangles to the upper right of the nodes. Sets of parentheses are used to enclose the values for EETs and LETs in this book.

The computations involve only the addition and subtraction of integer numbers and are not difficult. To compute the event times, we must make two "passes" through the logic diagram. During each pass, we compute event times and print them on the diagram. The value of an event time is either the sum of, or the difference between, another event time and a task duration. The first pass, called the **forward pass**, is made from left to right to determine the EET for each event. The second pass, called the **backward pass**, is made from right to left to determine the LET for each event. The procedures for performing the network analysis are covered in detail in the next two sections.

Phase 3   Prepare the CPM Schedule

The CPM schedule is a tabulation of task attributes, task times, and task floats. The task times and floats are computed using the event times that were computed in phase 2. During this phase, we must compute for each task: the Early Start Time (ES), the Early Finish Time (EF), the Late Start Time (LS), the Late Finish Time (LF), and the Total Float (TF). We may also compute Free Float (FF) and Interfering Float (IF). The values for each of these task times and float times are computed by using simple equations, which are presented in a subsequent section.

Forward Pass for Early Event Times (EETs)

During the first pass through the logic diagram, the Early Event Times (EETs) are computed. The time of the day for the EETs is the end of the day. These event times must be computed for as many events as there are nodes in the logic diagram. To compute the EET for the event represented by a node, it will be necessary to compute several trial values, one for each task arrow that terminates at the node. The *largest* of these trial values is selected as the EET, and the value is printed on the logic diagram. The initial node is a special case. No arrows terminate at that node; hence, its EET is always zero. Strictly speaking, an event time is an attribute of an event, not of the node that represents the event. The following discussion will often contain references to a node's EET. The reader should construe such references to mean the EET of the event represented by that node.

Node and Arrow Precedence

The concept of precedence has been addressed in previous chapters in respect to the logical relationships between tasks. A similar precedence relationship exists between the nodes and the arrows in a logic diagram. An arrow may be precedent to a node or to another arrow, and a node may be precedent to an arrow or to another node. These precedence relationships can be further categorized as simple precedence or immediate precedence. Consider the CPM logic diagram in Figure 6.2. Table 6.1 lists the precedence relationships that exist between the nodes and the arrows of that diagram.

FIGURE 6.2
CPM DIAGRAM BEFORE
CALCULATING EARLY EVENT TIMES

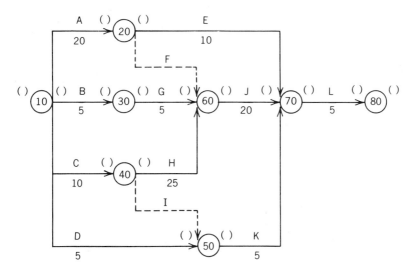

Systematic Determination of EETs

The EETs will be computed by systematically examining the nodes, one at a time, working generally from the left side of the diagram to the right side. Three rules by which the nodes can be systematically examined are listed below. See Figure 6.2 for an illustration of these rules.

Rule 1: Structured Diagrams. A structured CPM logic diagram is one in which the I-node for every task arrow, including those arrows that represent dummy tasks, is physically located to the left of that arrow's J-node. If the CPM diagram is structured, then the EET for any task node can be computed as soon as the EETs have been computed for every node to its left. The diagram in Figure 6.2 is a structured diagram. Assume that the EETs for nodes [10], [20], [30], and [40] have been determined. The EET for either node [50] or node [60] can be calculated next, because the EETs of all nodes to their left have been determined.

Rule 2: Any Diagram. The following rule applies to any CPM logic diagram, regardless of whether it is structured or unstructured, and regardless of whether the convention that the J-node number be greater than the I-node number has been observed. The EET for any node can be computed as soon as the EETs

TABLE 6.1

THE NODE AND ARROW PRECEDENCE RELATIONSHIPS SHOWN IN FIGURE 6.2

Node	Is Precedent to	Is Immediately Precedent to
[10]	[20], [30], [40], [50], [60], [70], [80], A, B, C, D, E, F, G, H, I, J, K, L	[20], [30], [40], [50], A, B, C, D
[20]	[60], [70], [80], E, F, J, L	[60], [70], E, F
[30]	[60], [70], [80], G, J, L	[60], G
[40]	[50], [60], [70], [80], H, I, J, K, L	[50], [60], H, I
[50]	[70], [80], K, L	[70], K
[60]	[70], [80], J, L	[70], J
[70]	[80], L	[80], L
[80]	No node or arrow	No node or arrow
Task	Is Precedent to	Is Immediately Precedent to
A	[20], [60], [70], [80], E, F, J, L	[20], E, F
B	[30], [60], [70], [80], G, J, L	[30], G
C	[40], [50], [60], [70], [80], H, I, J, K, L	[50], [60], H, I
D	[50], [70], [80], K, L	[50], K
E	[70], [80], L	[70], L
F	[60], [70], [80], J, L	[60], J
G	[60], [70], [80], J, L	[70], J
H	[60], [70], [80], J, L	[60], J
I	[50], [70], [80], K, L	[50], K
J	[70], [80], L	[70], L
K	[70], [80], L	[70], L
L	[80]	[80]

have been computed for all nodes that are immediately precedent to it. Again, considering the diagram in Figure 6.2, there are two nodes that are immediately precedent to node [50]. They are nodes [10] and [40]. As soon as the EETs for those two nodes have been determined, the EET for node [50] can be determined. It is not necessary to wait until EETs have been calculated for nodes [20] and [30].

Rule 3: By Node Number. The following rule applies if the convention that the J-node number be larger than the I-node number for every task arrow has been observed. The EET for any task node can be computed as soon as the EETs have been computed for every node having a lower J-node number. The EET for node [30] can be computed as soon as the EETs have been computed for nodes [10] and [20]. This rule is often used in computer programs for CPM scheduling. The next section covers sorting of task listings, a procedure that is often required for computer analysis of the network.

Sorting Task Listings

As indicated in the preceding section, some computer programs require that the tasks be sorted within computer memory before the network analysis is made. There are other reasons for sorting task listings. Some examples follow.

J-Node Sort for CPM Analysis

Rule 3 in the preceding discussion requires that the tasks be considered in their J-node number order, that is, that a task with a J-node number of 10 be considered before a task with a J-node number of 20. Table 6.2 contains two listings of task data for the same project. Note that the left listing shows the tasks in their task number order, while the right listing shows the tasks in their J-node order. If the tasks are listed in J-node order, then rule 3 may be restated as follows: The EET for any tasks's J-node may be computed as soon as all the EETs have been computed for the J-nodes of tasks that are listed before that task.

Other Sorts

The scheduler may want to resort the tasks after the network analysis is completed so that tasks are listed by early start time, by total float, by task number, or by some other criterion or criteria. Tasks may be sorted by several criteria. The right-hand listing in Table 6.2 has actually been sorted twice: first by J-node number, and next by I-node number.

Computing the EETs

Observing one of the rules described above, calculate trial values for the EET for each node in the network. The EET for a node is equal to the largest trial value for that node. There will be one trial value for every arrow that has the

TABLE 6.2

TASK LISTING BEFORE AND AFTER SORTING

	Task Number Sort			J-Node Number, I-Node Number Sort	
Task No.	I-Node No.	J-Node No.	Task No.	I-Node No.	J-Node No.
10	20	70	30	10	20
20	20	60	60	10	30
30	10	20	40	20	40
40	20	40	70	30	40
50	40	60	110	30	50
60	10	30	80	40	50
70	30	40	130	10	60
80	40	50	20	20	60
90	50	60	120	30	60
100	60	70	50	40	60
110	30	50	90	50	60
120	30	60	140	10	70
130	10	60	10	20	70
140	10	70	100	60	70

node as its J-node. Figure 6.3 depicts the I-node and the J-node for task N. Task N has a duration of Dur (N). Equation 6.1 may be used to compute the trial values for a node's EET. Refer to Figure 6.3 while examining Equation 6.1:

$$EET[J] = EET[I] + Dur(N) \qquad (6.1)$$

Equation 6.1 is valid for calculating a trial value for the EET at every node except for the initial node. The EET for the initial node is zero. During the forward pass, you will start at the left side of the diagram and work to the right, calculating the Early Event Time for each node. A trial value for a node's EET must be computed for each arrow terminating at that node.

FIGURE 6.3

EET[J] AND EET[I] OF TASK N

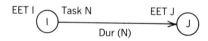

Example 1

Figure 6.2 is a CPM logic diagram. Compute trial values and select the largest as the EET for each node in the diagram. Use one of the systematic approaches described above to establish the order in which you will examine the nodes. If several trial values must be computed for a node, then lightly pencil these values on the diagram. After all trial values have been computed for a node, select the largest value as the EET and print it in the empty set of parentheses that are located just above and just to the left of each node.

Solution to Example 1

Figure 6.4 is a solution to this problem. Rule 3 above was used to establish the order in which the nodes would be evaluated, that is, the nodes were evaluated in ascending node number order. Table 6.3 shows the calculations that were made to determine the trial values for EETs for the various nodes. Those nodes that are located at the J-end (head end) of more than one task arrow require the calculation of more than one trial value for the EET. Both node [60] and node [70] are the J-nodes for three task arrows. Therefore, three trial values were

---

FIGURE 6.4
CPM DIAGRAM WITH EARLY EVENT
TIMES

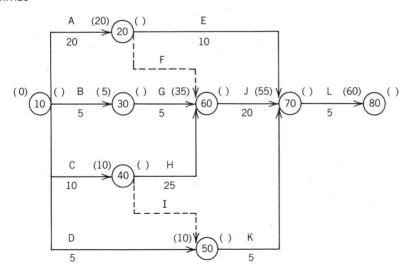

TABLE 6.3

CALCULATIONS FOR THE EARLY EVENT TIMES (EETs)

Node	Selected Value for the EET	Trial Value Calculations
[10]	0	It is the initial node
[20]	20	EET[10] + Dur(A) = 0 + 20 = 20
[30]	5	EET[10] + Dur(B) = 0 + 5 = 5
[40]	10	EET[10] + Dur(C) = 0 + 10 = 10
[50]		EET[10] + Dur(D) = 0 + 5 = 5
[50]	10[a]	EET[40] + Dur(I) = 10 + 0 = 10
[60]		EET[20] + Dur(F) = 20 + 0 = 20
[60]		EET[30] + Dur(G) = 5 + 5 = 10
[60]	35[a]	EET[40] + Dur(H) = 10 + 25 = 35
[70]		EET[20] + Dur(E) = 20 + 10 = 30
[70]	55[a]	EET[60] + Dur(J) = 35 + 20 = 55
[70]		EET[50] + Dur(K) = 10 + 5 = 15
[80]	60	EET[70] + Dur(L) = 55 + 5 = 60

[a]Nodes [50], [60], and [70] are the J-nodes for more than one task. Therefore, it was necessary to compute the EETs for those nodes based on more than one path. The largest computed trial value was selected as the EET.

calculated for the EETs of nodes [60] and [70]. The largest trial value for each node was selected as the EET for that node, and in Figure 6.4 that value is printed within the set of parentheses. These trial values would usually be lightly penciled on the diagram adjacent to the node and would be erased once the largest value had been selected as the EET.

Project Duration

The terminal node should have a computed EET that is larger than the EET for any other node in the network. The estimated project duration is equal to the EET for the terminal node. The estimated project duration for the project depicted at Figure 6.4 is 60 workdays. If the logic diagram has been drawn with multiple terminal nodes (a violation of previously stated conventions), the project duration is equal to the largest EET value for any of them.

Backward Pass for Late Event Times (LETs)

During the forward pass, all the EETs were computed. The largest computed value for any EET was 60 days for terminal node [80]. That value is the project duration. During the backward pass, LETs will be computed. The time of the day for LETs is the end of the day. No node can have an LET that is greater than the project duration. During the forward pass, one or more trial values were computed for the EETs of each node. The largest computed value was selected as the EET. During the backward pass, one or more trial values will be computed for the LETs of each node. The number of trial values that must be calculated for a node is equal to the number of arrows that originate at that node. The *smallest* computed trial value for a node will be selected as its LET.

Node Precedence

The concept of node precedence that was covered in the discussion of the forward pass also applies to the backward pass.

Systematic Evaluation of LETs

Three rules were given for determining the order in which node EETs are calculated. Similar rules apply for determining LETs.

Rule 1: Structured Diagrams.   For structured diagrams, the LET time for a node may be calculated as soon as LETs have been calculated for all nodes to its right. In Figure 6.4, the LET time for node [40] can be calculated as soon as the LETs for nodes [50], [60], [70], and [80] have been calculated.

Rule 2: Any Diagram.   The LET for a node may be calculated as soon as the LETs have been calculated for all nodes to which it is immediately precedent. In Figure 6.4, node [40] is immediately precedent to [60] and [50], and its LET can be calculated as soon as their LETs have been calculated.

Rule 3: Node Number.   If the J > I convention has been observed, the LET for a node can be calculated as soon as the LETs have been calculated for all nodes having a higher J-node number. If the tasks were sorted in a J-node number order, as described in the earlier section covering the forward pass, then the LET for a task's I-node can be computed as soon as the LETs have been computed for the I-nodes of all tasks that are below the task in the listing. In Figure 6.4, the LET for node [40] can be computed as soon as LETs have been computed for nodes [50], [60], [70], and [80].

Computing the LETs

Observing one of the three rules above, and working generally from right to left, compute the LETs for all nodes. Figure 6.5 and Equation 6.2 illustrate the method for computing trial values for the LETs.

$$\text{LET}[I] = \text{LET}[J] - \text{Dur}(N) \qquad (6.2)$$

FIGURE 6.5
LET[J] AND LET[I] OF TASK N

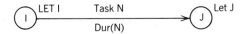

Equation 6.2 is valid for every node except the terminal node. The LET for the terminal node is equal to the project duration. If there are multiple terminal nodes, then each of them will have an LET equal to project duration.

Example 2

Compute all LETs for the diagram shown in Figure 6.4. Start at the right side of the diagram and work to the left, calculating trial values for the LET for each node. There will be as many trial values for a node as there are immediately subsequent arrows. Pencil the trial values for LETs on the diagram above and to the right of the nodes.

Solution to Example 2
Figure 6.6 contains the LETs for all tasks. The selected value for the LET of each node was the smallest of the trial values that was computed for that node,

FIGURE 6.6
CPM DIAGRAM WITH LATE EVENT TIMES

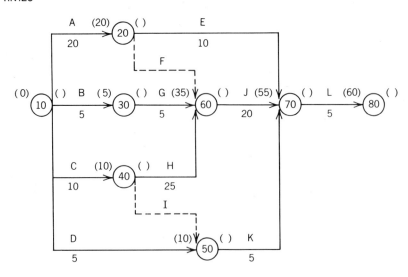

TABLE 6.4
CALCULATIONS FOR THE LATE EVENT TIMES (LETs)

Node	Selected Value for the LET	Trial Value Calculations
[80]	60	It is the terminal node and its LET = project duration
[70]	55	LET[80] − Dur(L) = 60 − 5 = 55
[60]	35	LET[70] − Dur(J) = 55 − 20 = 35
[50]	50	LET[70] − Dur(K) = 55 − 5 = 50
[40]	10[a]	LET[60] − Dur(H) = 35 − 25 = 10[a]
[40]		LET[50] − Dur(I) = 50 − 0 = 50
[30]	30	LET[60] − Dur(G) = 35 − 5 = 30
[20]		LET[70] − Dur(E) = 55 − 10 = 45
[20]	35[a]	LET[60] − Dur(F) = 35 − 0 = 35[a]
[10]		LET[20] − Dur(A) = 35 − 20 = 15
[10]		LET[30] − Dur(B) = 30 − 5 = 25
[10]	0[a]	LET[40] − Dur(C) = 10 − 10 = 0[a]
[10]		LET[50] − Dur(D) = 50 − 5 = 45

[a]Several of the nodes are I-nodes for more than one task arrow; for example, node [10] is the I-node for task arrows A, B, C, and D. A trial value for the LET of node [10] had to be computed for each task arrow. The smallest trial value was selected as the LET for the node. The LET for the initial node must be equal to zero. If it is not equal to zero, then you have made a computational error.

and that value is printed in the parentheses above and to the right of the nodes. Table 6.4 indicates that the calculations that were made to obtain the trial values. Rule 3 was observed, that is, LETs were calculated for the nodes in inverse node number order.

Calculate Task Times

Four task times (ES, EF, LS, and LF) must be calculated for each task. Refer to page 115 for their full definitions. These task times are computed on the basis of the event times that were computed in the two preceding sections. Use Figure 6.7 and Equations 6.3 to 6.6 to compute the task times:

$$ES(N) = EET[I] \qquad (6.3)$$

$$LF(N) = LET[J] \qquad (6.4)$$

$$EF(N) = EET[I] + Dur(N) \quad \text{or} \quad EF(N) = ES(N) + Dur(N) \quad (6.5)$$

$$LS(N) = LET[J] - Dur(N) \quad \text{or} \quad LS(N) = LF(N) - Dur(N) \quad (6.6)$$

FIGURE 6.7
EET AND LET FOR I-NODE AND
J-NODE OF TASK N

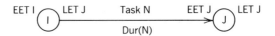

Example 3

The logic diagram for this example is the same as the one that was used in the preceding examples. Figure 6.6 contains that diagram. All EETs and LETs are indicated. It is possible to calculate the task times and to print them directly on the logic diagram. Often it is preferable to print the task times on the CPM schedule rather than on the logic diagram. There are four tasks times for each task; hence, it would be necessary to write four values on the diagram for each arrow. The logic diagram is already crowded with data. The addition of more data would necessitate drawing the logic diagram to a larger scale. Table 6.5 is a partly completed project schedule. The EET for the I-node and the LET for the J-node of each task are listed in this table to facilitate the calculation of task

TABLE 6.5
CPM SCHEDULE WITH EVENT TIMES[a]

Task	I-Node	J-Node	Dur	EET(I)	LET[J]	ES	EF	LS	LF	TF	FF	IF
A	[10]	[20]	20	0	35							
B	[10]	[30]	5	0	30							
C	[10]	[40]	10	0	10							
D	[10]	[50]	5	0	50							
E	[20]	[70]	10	20	55							
F	[20]	[60]	0	20	35							
G	[30]	[60]	5	5	35							
H	[40]	[60]	25	10	35							
I	[40]	[50]	0	10	50							
J	[60]	[70]	20	35	55							
K	[50]	[70]	5	10	55							
L	[70]	[80]	5	55	60							

[a]Event and task times are as of EOD.

times. Normally, these EETs and LETs would not be printed in the CPM schedule. All data in that table were taken from the logic diagram. No further reference to the logic diagram is required to complete the schedule. Using Equations 6.3 to 6.6 or the alternates to Equations 6.5 and 6.6, complete the columns in Table 6.5 that are headed ES, EF, LS, and LF. It is suggested that you start at the top of the table and compute the values in the order ES, LF, EF, and LS.

Solution to Example 3
The task times are listed in Table 6.6. Note that task times are printed for the dummy tasks, as well as for actual tasks. Review the definitions of task times on page 115.

Meaning of Task Times
The four computed task times for task E have the following meanings: (1)Task E can start no earlier than the end of the twentieth workday. (2) Task E can be finished no earlier than the end of the thirtieth workday. (3) Task E must be started no later than the end of the forty-fifth workday, if the project is to be completed by the end of the sixtieth workday. (4) Task E must be completed by the end of the fifty-fifth workday, if the project is to be completed by the end of the sixtieth workday. Four statements like these can be made about each of the other real tasks. The statements can also be made concerning dummy tasks.

TABLE 6.6
CPM SCHEDULE WITH TASK TIMES[a]

Task	I-Node	J-Node	Dur	EET(I)	LET[J]	ES	EF	LS	LF	TF	FF	IF
A	[10]	[20]	20	0	35	0	20	15	35			
B	[10]	[30]	5	0	30	0	5	25	30			
C	[10]	[40]	10	0	10	0	10	0	10			
D	[10]	[50]	5	0	50	0	5	45	50			
E	[20]	[70]	10	20	55	20	30	45	55			
F	[20]	[60]	0	20	35	20	20	35	35			
G	[30]	[60]	5	5	35	5	10	30	35			
H	[40]	[60]	25	10	35	10	35	10	35			
I	[40]	[50]	0	10	50	10	10	50	50			
J	[60]	[70]	20	35	55	35	55	35	55			
K	[50]	[70]	5	10	55	10	15	50	55			
L	[70]	[80]	5	55	60	55	60	55	60			

[a]Event and task times are as of EOD.

Significance of Task Times

Although the four statements above that concern task E are stated in a declarative manner, they are only the results of an analytical process that was based on assumptions the scheduler has made concerning task durations and the sequence in which tasks will be performed. It is unlikely that actual task durations will be exactly as estimated. Actual crew sizes may be larger or smaller than assumed by the scheduler when he or she estimated task durations. Delays caused by weather will be longer or shorter than anticipated. The field personnel may have performed the tasks in a different sequence than visualized by the scheduler. Some of the constraints depicted on the diagram may not have been essential.

Recall that the start and the finish times for all tasks are expressed as the end of the day. Dummy task F has an early start time as of the end of the twentieth day and an early finish time as of the end of the twentieth day, a correspondence that is appropriate considering its zero duration. If the start times of tasks had been expressed as the beginning of the day, and if the finish times were expressed as the end of the day, then dummy task F would have an early start time as of the beginning of the twenty-first day and an early finish time of the end of the twentieth day. This apparent paradox is explainable in that the end of a day and the beginning of the following day are considered identical.

Calculate Float Times

Total Float (TF)

This value is also termed **slack time**. It is a measure of how noncritical a task may be. Table 6.6 lists ES, EF, LS, and LF times for the tasks. Task A *can* be started on its ES date of zero (end of day 0 = start of day 1), but it need not be started until its LS date of 15 (end of day 15). Similarly, task A can be finished at its EF date of 20, but it need not be completed until its LF date of 35. Total float is the difference between an LS and an ES date or the difference between an LF and an EF date. Three equations that will yield a task's total float are (the three equations yield identical results):

$$TF(N) = LET[J] - EET[I] - Dur(N) \qquad (6.7a)$$

$$TF(N) = LF(N) - EF(N) \qquad (6.7b)$$

$$TF(N) = LS(N) - ES(N) \qquad (6.7c)$$

Example 4

Using one of the equations above, complete the column headed TF in Table 6.6.

TABLE 6.7

CPM SCHEDULE WITH TASK TIMES AND TOTAL FLOAT VALUES[a]

Task	I-Node	J-Node	Dur	EET(I)	LET[J]	ES	EF	LS	LF	TF	FF	IF
A	[10]	[20]	20	0	35	0	20	15	35	15		
B	[10]	[30]	5	0	30	0	5	25	30	25		
C	[10]	[40]	10	0	10	0	10	0	10	0		
D	[10]	[50]	5	0	50	0	5	45	50	45		
E	[20]	[70]	10	20	55	20	30	45	55	25		
F	[20]	[60]	0	20	35	20	20	35	35	15		
G	[30]	[60]	5	5	35	5	10	30	35	25		
H	[40]	[60]	25	10	35	10	35	10	35	0		
I	[40]	[50]	0	10	50	10	10	50	50	40		
J	[60]	[70]	20	35	55	35	55	35	55	0		
K	[50]	[70]	5	10	55	10	15	50	55	40		
L	[70]	[80]	5	55	60	55	60	55	60	0		

[a]Event and task times are as of EOD.

Solution to Example 4

Table 6.7 contains the values for total float as well as the task times.

Critical Tasks

Note that tasks C, H, J, and L have zero total float. Therefore, these four tasks are termed critical tasks. If the actual durations of tasks C, H, J, or L exceed their estimated durations, then the project duration will be longer than 60 days.

Noncritical Tasks

The actual durations of the other tasks may exceed their estimated durations to some extent without delaying project completion past the end of the sixtieth workday. These other tasks are noncritical. They have various degrees of non-criticality. Tasks A and F have total floats of 15 workdays, whereas task D has a total float of 45 workdays. Tasks A and F are closer to being critical than is task D. A subsequent section contains a discussion of total float as a shared commodity.

Test for Criticality

The use of one of Equations 6.7a to 6.7c positively identifies the critical tasks, those having total float of zero being critical. Often, the scheduler will outline the critical path on the logic diagram without calculating total float. Figure 6.8

FIGURE 6.8

TEST FOR TASK'S CRITICALITY

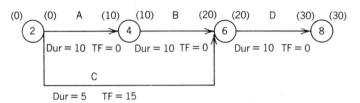

contains a fragment of a logic diagram. Many students have been observed concluding that all four tasks shown are critical. Do not make the mistake of believing that a task is critical simply because both its I-node and its J-node are on the critical path. A node is on the critical path if its EET equals its LET. For task C, EET(I) = LET(I) and EET(J) = LET(J); therefore, both nodes of task C are on the critical path. For a task to be critical, both of its nodes must be on the critical path, but Equation 6.7a must yield a total float value of zero. Note that task C in Figure 6.8 is not critical. Even though EET[2] = LET[2] and EET[6] = LET[6], TF(C) = 20 − 0 − 5 = 15. A critical task has TF of zero.

The Critical Path

Figure 6.9 is the CPM diagram for Example 4, with all of the arrows that have zero total float drawn with darkened lines. The path, or paths, through the network that can be followed along these darkened arrows is the critical path; hence, the name of this method, the Critical Path Method.

Float Patterns

The arrows for the noncritical tasks in Figure 6.9 have been labeled with their total float values. Several patterns are revealed by a study of Figure 6.9.

Pattern 1.
The critical path is continuous from the initial node to the terminal node. Sometimes, the path will fork at a node into two or more critical paths, but each of these critical paths will be continuous, and they will all converge at some subsequent node.

Pattern 2
If only one task arrow terminates at a node and only one task arrow originates at that node, then the two tasks will have the same total float. See node [30]. Both tasks B and G have the same total float.

FIGURE 6.9

CPM DIAGRAM WITH CRITICAL PATH
OUTLINED AND TOTAL FLOAT

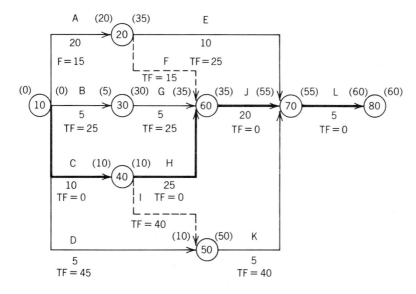

General Pattern

Patterns 1 and 2 are special cases of a general pattern that may be stated as follows: The lowest total float value for any arrow terminating at a node will be equal to the lowest total float value for any arrow originating at that node. Table 6.8 illustrates this general float pattern. Consider node [50]. Two arrows terminate there. The one that has the lowest total float has TF = 40. The one arrow originating there has TF = 40. Consider node [40]. One arrow terminates there, having TF = 0. Two arrows originating there; the one with the lowest total float has TF = 0.

Total Float Is a Shared Commodity

A task's total float can be shared with other tasks. Both task B and task G have TF = 25. The maximum delay that can occur in the two tasks combined without delaying the project is 25 days. A chain of noncritical tasks is a path that can be traced between any two or more nodes passing only through noncritical arrows. Such a chain must originate on a node on the critical path and must terminate on a node on the critical path, but it can pass through no other nodes on the critical path. All the tasks on such a chain share total float. If one of these tasks uses some of its total float, then there will be less total float available for other tasks on that chain. Five chains of noncritical tasks are depicted in the diagram

TABLE 6.8
ILLUSTRATION OF GENERAL TOTAL FLOAT PATTERN[a]

| | Arrows Terminating at Node | | | Arrows Originating at Node | |
Task	I J	Node	Task	I J	
A	[10] − [20] TF = 15*	[20]	E	[20] − [70] TF = 25	
			F	[20] − [60] TF = 15*	
B	[10] − [30] TF = 25*	[30]	G	[30] − [60] TF = 25*	
C	[10] − [40] TF = 0*	[40]	H	[40] − [60] TF = 0*	
			I	[40] − [50] TF = 40	
D	[10] − [50] TF = 45	[50]	K	[50] − [70] TF = 40*	
I	[40] − [50] TF = 40*				
F	[20] − [60] TF = 15	[60]	J	[60] − [70] TF = 0*	
G	[30] − [60] TF = 25				
H	[40] − [60] TF = 0*				
E	[20] − [70] TF = 25	[70]	L	[70] − [80] TF = 0*	
J	[60] − [70] TF = 0*				
K	[50] − [70] TF = 40				

[a]The lowest value of TF for an arrow terminating at a node has been labeled with an asterisk. Similarly, the lowest value of TF for an arrow originating at a node has been labeled with an asterisk. The labeled values are equal.

in Figure 6.8. They are [10]–[20]–[60], [10]–[20]–[70], [10]–[30]–[60], [10]–[50]–[70], and [40]–[50]–[70]. The tasks located on any of those five chains share at least some of their total float with all of the other tasks located on the same chain.

Free Float and Interfering Float

These values are also a measure of a task's noncriticality, or slack time.

Free Float (FF)

This is the slack time available to a task which, if used, will not delay the start of a subsequent task beyond its early start time. A task's free float can be calculated with Equation 6.8, shown below and illustrated in Figure 6.7. Only those tasks that are located at the end (right side) of a chain of noncritical tasks have free float.

$$FF(N) = EET[J] - EET[I] - Dur(N) \tag{6.8}$$

Interfering Float (IF)

A task's interfering float is the difference between the tasks's total float and its free float. If a task's IF float is used, the start of some subsequent task will be interfered with (delayed beyond its ES time). Interfering float can be calculated by using Equation 6.9, shown here and illustrated in Figure 6.7.

$$IF(N) = LET[J] - EET[J] \qquad (6.9)$$

Example 5

Using the two equations above, calculate the values for free float and for interfering float for the logic diagram that was used in the preceding examples and print the computed values in Table 6.7.

Solution to Example 5

Table 6.9 contains the computed values for all float and task times. Figure 6.10 is the logic diagram with free float values printed on the arrows for all tasks that

TABLE 6.9

CPM SCHEDULE WITH ALL TASK TIMES AND FLOATS[a]

Task	I-Node	J-Node	Dur	EET(I)	LET[J]	ES	EF	LS	LF	TF	FF	IF
A	[10]	[20]	20	0	35	0	20	15	35	15	0	15
B	[10]	[30]	5	0	30	0	5	25	30	25	0	25
C	[10]	[40]	10	0	10	0	10	0	10	0	0	0
D	[10]	[50]	5	0	50	0	5	45	50	45	5	40
E	[20]	[70]	10	20	55	20	30	45	55	25	25	0
F	[20]	[60]	0	20	35	20	20	35	35	15	15	0
G	[30]	[60]	5	5	35	5	10	30	35	25	25	0
H	[40]	[60]	25	10	35	10	35	10	35	0	0	0
I	[40]	[50]	0	10	50	10	10	50	50	40	0	40
J	[60]	[70]	20	35	55	35	55	35	55	0	0	0
K	[50]	[70]	5	10	55	10	15	50	55	40	40	0
L	[70]	[80]	5	55	60	55	60	55	60	0	0	0

[a]Event and task times are as of EOD.

FIGURE 6.10

CPM DIAGRAM WITH FREE FLOAT

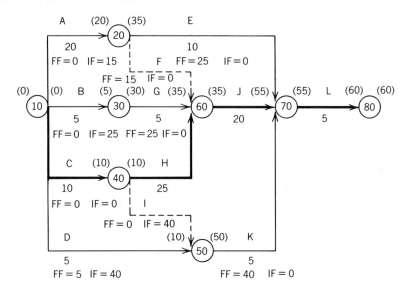

have free float. The path through nodes [10] – [30] – [60] is termed a **chain of arrows**. Usually, only the last arrow in a chain has free float. In a few instances, when two chains of noncritical tasks intersect, a task may have free float even though it is not the last task in the chain. The free float values for the task of the example are labeled on the diagram in Figure 6.10. Note that task D has free float. In this instance, task G has free float, while task B does not. Task G can be delayed by 25 days without delaying the start of any other task, assuming that task G can start on its early start date. The last arrow in a chain of arrows is analogous to the last runner in a relay race. Great acclaim, or shame, greets the last runner, depending on whether he won or lost the race. Lesser acclaim, or shame, is the lot of the preceding runners. Great pressure is sometimes placed on a foreman who is responsible for the last task in a chain of tasks to get the project back on schedule.

Schedulers are divided in opinion as to whether total float or free float is the most significant measure of a task's noncriticality, with a majority considering total float as more significant than free float. A case could be made that free float is equally significant, because delay in the completion of a noncritical task may result in delay of the start of a subsequent task. A subcontractor who has contracted to start this subsequent task on a particular date might claim damages if he is unable to start on that date. The conclusion is that the significance of one type of float, as compared to another type, depends on the circumstances and on how the data will be used.

CPM SCHEDULING ON MICROCOMPUTERS

There are two general types of computer programs. Compiled, or machine language programs, run very fast. Interpreter programs run much slower, but the user can modify the programs to suit his or her own purposes. Appendix B contains BASIC computer language programs for scheduling. They can be run as interpreter programs, or they can be compiled and run as machine language programs. Numerous CPM computer programs that can be run on microcomputers are commercially available. The following are factors that should be taken into consideration when choosing a microcomputer and scheduling software.

Scheduling Programs Versus Integrated Construction Management Programs

Much of the data that must be entered into the computer for scheduling purposes is common to data that are needed for financial management and cost estimating purposes. An integrated program contains various modules, one for scheduling, another for cost estimating, and so forth. Data entered into one module can be passed to another module. It will be very difficult to patch together separate scheduling programs and estimating programs. If it is your intent to automate cost estimation, financial management, and the like, as well as scheduling, then you should consider purchasing integrated software and a computer system that is capable of running that software. However, you should also recognize that an integrated system may perform several functions—each of them in a mediocre manner. A thorough demonstration of the computer system and its software is necessary.

Computer Memory Requirements

Computer memory consists of rapid access memory (RAM) and of nonvolatile memory (floppy disks or hard disks). The standard microcomputer intended for business use will contain at least 64K (about 64,000 bytes) of RAM. Consider a byte of RAM as the capacity to store one digit or one letter. Some of the 64K of RAM is not available for storage of data describing the construction project because it is required to store the computer interpreter language (BASIC) and the program that will produce the schedule. A typical 64K microcomputer may have about 30K of RAM available for storing data describing a project.

The data storage requirements per task depend on the desired completeness of the task description and on the type and capabilities of the scheduling program. At least about 50 bytes of data storage will be required for a minimum task description; hence, the 64K microcomputer could potentially handle up to 30,000/50 = 600 tasks. A minimum task description would allow input of only integer values for task and node numbers and might restrict their magnitude to some arbitrary value (say, 600). This would limit the length of task descriptions to about 24 characters, and it would not permit the input of costs codes, task costs, and other such data. The program would allow only workday scheduling, and it might not include desirable features such as data resequencing, data editing, and project expediting. Therefore, the actual size of the project that a micro-computer might handle, with fewer restrictions and more capabilities, would be considerably less than 600. Note that many scheduling programs are written so that they are unable to exploit RAMs in excess of 64K. In addition to an adequate RAM, the computer system should have adequate nonvolatile memory in the form of floppy disks, hard disks, or both.

Computer Speed

Computer analysis of any but the most trivial scheduling problems will require substantial time, from minutes to hours. The newest microcomputers are termed 16-bit machines (versus the 8-bit machines of a few years ago). The 16-bit machines will run programs at about twice the speed of 8-bit machines. Even more important, 16-bit machines can utilize the larger RAM capacities that are becoming available (256K and up).

Should You Buy a Package

Assuming that you do not already have a computer, you may decide to purchase a package of software and hardware after the package has been demonstrated to you on the type of scheduling problems that you intend to solve. If you already own a computer, then you may decide simply to buy a software program that will run on your computer.

LIMITATIONS OF THE CRITICAL PATH METHOD

Simple Nature of CPM Logical Relationship

The simple nature of the CPM logical relationship makes it difficult to specify such real relationships as "task B can start when task A is half finished" or "task D must start as soon as task C is finished."

Reliability of Task Times

The task times are computed on the basis of an analysis of the network logic diagram and on estimates of task duration. The logic diagram represents the scheduler's concept of the sequence in which tasks will be accomplished. In most instances, the estimated task durations will not prove to be exactly correct, nor will the tasks be performed in the exact sequence visualized by the scheduler. Hence, it is not to be expected that the actual task times will correspond exactly with the scheduled task times. However, if the estimated task durations are reasonably accurate and if the logic diagram corresponds reasonably with the construction sequence that will actually be followed, the task times should be sufficiently accurate for project management purposes.

ADVANTAGES OF THE CRITICAL PATH METHOD

The CPM is well established. Many contractors and owners use it. The CPM schedule can be used for project management purposes. Using the data contained in the schedule, the scheduler can prepare a Gantt chart schedule. The schedule, the Gantt chart, and the logic diagram can serve as the basis for other construction management functions to be covered in subsequent chapters.

EXERCISES

EXERCISE 6.1
Based on the CPM diagram shown in Figure 6.11, calculate all event and task times and all task floats. Enter the computed values in the blank CPM schedule form shown in Table 6.10.

FIGURE 6.11
LOGIC DIAGRAM FOR EXERCISE 6.1

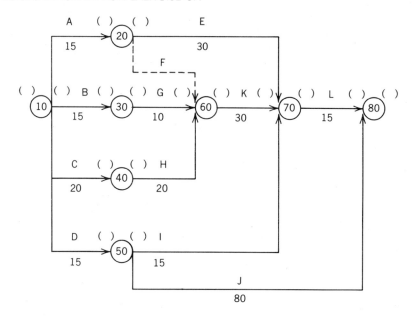

TABLE 6.10
BLANK CPM FORM FOR EXERCISE 6.1[a]

Task	I-Node	J-Node	Dur	EET(I)	LET(J)	ES	EF	LS	LF	TF	FF	IF
A												
B												
C												
D												
E												
F												
G												
H												
I												
J												
K												
L												

[a]Event and task times are as of EOD.

EXERCISE 6.2
Draw and analyze a CPM logic diagram for the project described in Example 1 in Chapter 3 and illustrated in Figure 3.3. Use the same task durations that were given for that example and the same constraints to the initiation of tasks that were used in the problem. Compute all task times and all task floats. Outline the critical path on the diagram. Use workday scheduling methods.

EXERCISE 6.3
Draw a CPM logic diagram for the project described as Example 1 in Chapter 2. Use the task durations that were given in the solution to that problem. In drawing the diagram, use the logical constraints on the basis of your understanding of construction procedures. Analyze the network and outline the critical path. Prepare a CPM schedule and draw a Gantt chart for the project. Program CPM in Appendix B may be used for preparing the schedule and the Gantt chart.

EXERCISE 6.4
Draw the logic diagram for the project that was described in Table 6.2.

THE
PRECEDENCE
METHOD
(PM)

7

OBJECTIVES

The objectives of this chapter are to introduce the Precedence Method (PM), to further develop the principles of logic diagramming that are covered in Chapter 4 and that apply to the PM, and to illustrate PM logical relationships related to construction. The examples of logic diagramming shown in this chapter cover only the diagramming of relationships between a pair of tasks. Chapter 8 covers the diagramming of an entire project involving many tasks and many logical relationships. Chapter 8 also presents procedures for making the network analysis and for preparing schedules.

INTRODUCTION TO THE PRECEDENCE METHOD (PM)

The Precedence Method (PM), like the Critical Path Method (CPM), is widely used in the construction industry. Its principal advantage is that it allows the user to specify more complex relationships between construction tasks than does the CPM. The reader may wish to review Chapter 4, which introduces and compares CPM and PM logic diagrams.

Comparison of CPM and PM Logic Diagrams

Any project that can be diagrammed using the CPM can be diagrammed using the PM, and vice versa. Figure 7.1 contains both a CPM and a PM logic diagram for the same project. The project involves construction of a small structure having

FIGURE 7.1
EQUIVALENT CPM AND PM LOGIC
DIAGRAMS: (a) CPM Diagram;
(b) PM Diagram.

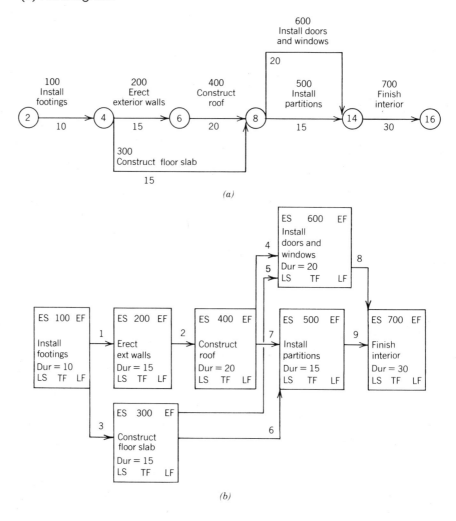

(a)

(b)

load-bearing exterior walls and nonload-bearing interior partitions. The two diagrams depict exactly the same constraints and construction logic. In this instance, the two diagrams are of about equal size and complexity. Note that the PM diagram contains more information than does the CPM diagram.

In the CPM diagram in Figure 7.1a, arrows represent tasks and nodes represent events. The nodes are depicted as small circles containing the event number. The logical relationship between tasks is specified when the task arrows are assigned I-node and J-node numbers. The CPM diagram was drawn in violation of one of the CPM conventions. Note that tasks 500 and 600 have common I-nodes and J-nodes. It would have been necessary to draw a dummy ''activity splitter'' arrow splitting either task 500 or task 600 to observe the convention. The result would have been a wider diagram.

The PM diagram shown in Figure 7.1b illustrates the symbols used in the PM. Note that tasks are represented by nodes (boxes). Within these boxes are printed a task number, a task description, and a task duration. Also printed within the boxes are computed task time values, including Early Start Time (ES), Early Finish Time (EF), Late Start Time (LS), Late Finish Time (LF), and Total Float (TF). For this example, the acronyms for these task times are printed within the task nodes rather than their numerical values. The values listed thus far in this section have the same meaning that they had when they were used with the Critical Path Method. The procedures for calculating task time values differ from those used with the CPM. They will be covered in Chapter 8. The diagram in Figure 7.1b also contains arrows, which represent the logical relationships between pairs of tasks. Each arrow representing a relationship has been assigned a unique number that is printed above the arrow. Note that arrow 5 crosses over arrow 7.

Although the CPM and the PM logic diagrams shown in Figure 7.1 both depict the same project, and the same logical relationships between the activities that make up the project, it would not be correct to conclude that the PM is simply a different way of doing what can be done by CPM. In this example, only one kind of logical relationship is depicted between the various tasks that make up the project; task B cannot be started until task A is completed. The PM allows the use of four kinds of logical relationships between tasks, with each type of relationship having three forms. These logical relationships are described in this chapter.

Logical Relationships

For the Precedence Method, as is true for the Critical Path Method, logical relationships may exist between the two tasks that make up a pair of tasks. In the case of the PM, the logical relationship actually exists between a part (start or end) of one task and a part (start or end) of a second task. As is the case for the CPM, logical relationships may be depicted **explicitly** or **implicitly**. (Review the meaning of these terms as described on page 118.) The CPM depicts explicit relationships by assignment of node numbers to the various tasks. In Figure 7.1a, two tasks have a J-node of [8] and two tasks have an I-node of [8]; $2 \times 2 = 4$ explicit logical relationships have been depicted at node [8]. There are four nodes that serve as the J-node for a task and an I-node for another task. The total number of explicit relationships shown are $1 \times 2 + 1 \times 1 + 2 \times 2 + 2 \times 1 = 9$. In the PM, explicit logical relationships between a pair of tasks are depicted by relationship arrows. One relationship arrow depicts one explicit logical relationship; hence, there are nine arrows.

The relationship between a pair of tasks can include a **lag**, with a negative lag value being a **lead**. The value of a relationship lag is printed below the relationship arrow. Zero values are usually omitted from the diagram. The two diagrams in Figure 7.2 illustrate two ways of drawing arrows between nodes when there is a lag or lead involved. For this example, the objective is to depict the relationship that task 1040 can commence 2 days before task 1020 is completed. In the first example, the relationship is indicated by an arrow drawn from the end (right side) of one task node to the start (left side) of a second task node.

FIGURE 7.2
FORMATS FOR LINKING NODES WITH ARROWS: (a) Preferred Format for Linking Task Nodes with Arrows. (b) Alternative Format for Linking Task Nodes with Arrows.

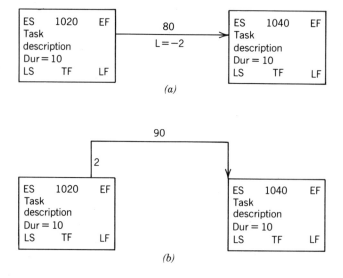

Arrow 80 has been labeled with a lag value of -2. A negative lag is a **lead**; hence, the start of task 1040 can lead the end of task 1020 by 2 days. In the second example, arrow 90 is drawn from near the end (2 days before the end) of node 1020 to the start of node 1040. In this book, arrows will be drawn as in Figure 7.2*a*, that is, with arrows originating and terminating at either the start side or the end side of a task node.

Critical Path Method Logical Relationship

There is one type of logical relationship that can be depicted in the CPM logic diagram. This relationship illustrated in Figure 7.1*a*, can be stated in two forms, with the two forms having exactly the same meaning:

> **Conditional Form.** Task 200, erect exterior walls, can start no earlier than the time when task 100, install footings, has been completed.

> **Imperative Form.** Task 100, install footings, must be completed before task 200, erect exterior walls, can start.

Precedence Method Logical Relationships

There are four types of logical relationships that can be depicted in the PM logic diagram, with each type having three variants. Figure 7.3 illustrates the four types of PM logical relationship. The abbreviations ES, SS, EE, and SE are used to describe these types of relationship in the discussion that follows. If the first letter in any of these abbreviations is S, then the arrow originates at the start side (left side) of a task node. If the first letter is E, then the arrow originates at the end side (right side) of a task node. The second letter in the abbreviations indicates whether the arrow terminates at the start side (S) or the end side (E) of a task node. The four relationships depicted in Figure 7.3 are each represented by an arrow. It is not necessary to label these arrows by type, as has been done in this figure, because it is evident whether the arrow originates at the start or the end of a node, and it is evident whether it terminates at the start or end of a second node. The four arrows are labeled with a **lag value.** Lag values can be positive, zero, or negative. The lag value is printed on the diagram just below the relationship arrow. Zero lag values are usually omitted from the diagram.

It should be recognized that *PM logical relationships are between parts of tasks.* Examine the diagram in Figure 7.4. The diagram contains two task nodes and two relationship arrows. Arrow 1 represents a start-to-start (SS) relationship. Its meaning is that task 85, install rigid insulation between brick and block walls, can start no earlier than two days after the start of task 70, erect brick and block masonry wall. Arrow 2 represents an end-to-end (EE) relationship. Its meaning is that task 70, erect brick and block masonry wall, can end no earlier than three days after the end of task 85, install rigid insulation between brick and block.

FIGURE 7.3

THE FOUR PM LOGICAL
RELATIONSHIPS: (a) End to Start
(ES); (b) Start to End (SE); (c) Start
to Start (SS); (d) End to End (EE).

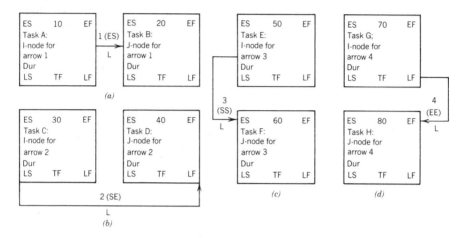

In this instance, the start of task 70 is precedent to the start of task 85, whereas the end of task 85 is precedent to the end of task 70. It would not be correct to state that task 70 is precedent to task 85 or that task 85 is precedent to task 70. The precedence relationship exists between a part of one task and a part of another task.

The CPM includes the convention that a tasks arrow's J-node number should be larger than its I-node number, that convention being a guard against the inclusion of logic loops. *The J > I convention is not applicable to the PM*. Note in Figure 7.4 that the task node for task 70 is the I-node for relationship arrow 1, with task node [85] being the arrow's J-node. For arrow 2, node [85] is the I-node and node [70] is the J-node.

PM logical relationships facilitate depicting partial concurrency. Again referring to Figure 7.4, we see that there are actually several construction activities involved. They include laying (and reinforcing) concrete block, installing brick ties between alternate courses of block, installing rigid insulation on the exterior of the block, and laying face brick. All of this work could have been included within a single task—construct and insulate block wall. However, the work has been divided into the two tasks, one to be performed by a masonry crew and the other to be performed by an insulation crew. The most efficient way to do the work would be to have the masons erect a section of block wall, have the insulaters cover that section, and have the masons install the face brick over the insulation. The masons would be the first to start work and the last to finish

FIGURE 7.4
I-NODE/J-NODE DESIGNATION

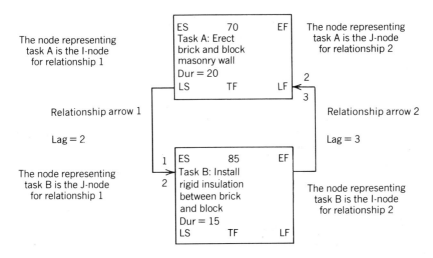

The node representing
task A is the I-node
for relationship 1

ES   70   EF
Task A: Erect
brick and block
masonry wall
Dur = 20
LS   TF   LF

The node representing
task A is the J-node
for relationship 2

2
3

Relationship arrow 1

Relationship arrow 2

Lag = 2

Lag = 3

The node representing
task B is the J-node
for relationship 1

1
2

ES   85   EF
Task B: Install
rigid insulation
between brick
and block
Dur = 15
LS   TF   LF

The node representing
task B is the I-node
for relationship 2

work. The insulaters would work along with the masons for most of the time. The two tasks are partially concurrent. It would have been necessary to define two tasks as "delays" if this logical relationship had been specified with the CPM.

EXAMPLES OF PM LOGICAL RELATIONSHIPS

Logical relationships exist between a part of one task and a part of a second task. They are represented by arrows, which should always be drawn with arrowheads. Lag values, other than zero values, are printed on the logic diagram below the arrows. Each arrow should be assigned a unique number, that is, no other arrow should have the same number. An arrow may be assigned a number that has been used to identify a task node. Task nodes should be assigned unique numbers. The logical relationships are illustrated in Figures 7.5 to 7.11. Each illustration is accompanied by two statements of the logical relationship: one in conditional form, and the other in imperative form. The two forms have exactly the same meaning. The two forms are presented so as to facilitate the explanation of the more complex relationships discussed later in this chapter. Each pair of statements is accompanied by an additional statement that clarifies the limits of the depicted relationship.

End-to-Start (ES) Relationships

This is the most frequently used of the four PM logical relationships. See Figure 7.5, in which three applications of this relationship are illustrated.

End to Start with Zero Lag

This relationship is the same as the CPM logical relationship. See arrow 40 in Figure 7.5.

> **Conditional Form.** The installation of reinforcing bars for a suspended slab can start no earlier than the time that construction of the forms for the slabs is completed.

> **Imperative Form.** The construction of the forms for a suspended slab must be completed before the installation of slab reinforcing bars can start.

FIGURE 7.5

END-TO-START (ES) LOGICAL
RELATIONSHIPS WITH ZERO,
POSITIVE, AND NEGATIVE LAGS

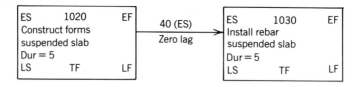

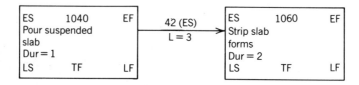

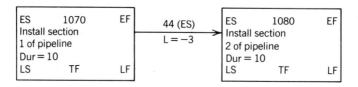

Neither statement means that the installation of reinforcing bars *must* commence immediately after the form construction is completed.

End to Start with Positive Lag

Stripping (removing) the forms for a suspended slab cannot commence for some time (say, three days) after the slab concrete is placed in the forms. This delay allows time for the concrete to gain sufficient strength so that it can support its own weight. See arrow 42 in Figure 7.5.

> **Conditional Form.** Form stripping can start no earlier than three days after the concrete pour is completed.

> **Imperative Form.** The concrete pour must be completed at least three days before form stripping can start.

Neither statement means that form stripping *must* start 3 days after the pour is completed.

End to Start with Negative Lag (Lead)

Assume that two sections of pipeline are to be constructed and that both sections require the use of a trenching machine for the first 7 days of their 10-day durations. Further assume that only one trenching machine is available. The machine will be available for use on the second section 7 days after the first section is started, or 3 days before it is completed. Hence, starting the second section leads the completion of the first section by 3 days. See arrow 44 in Figure 7.5.

> **Conditional Form.** The installation of the second section of pipeline can start no earlier than 3 days before the time that the first section of pipeline can be completed.

> **Imperative Form.** The installation of the first section of pipeline must be completed no later than 3 days after the time that installation of the second section can start.

Neither statement means that the installation of the second section *must* start 3 days before the first section is completed.

Start-to-Start (SS) Relationships

This type of relationship is often expressed so as to specify full or partial concurrency of tasks. Figure 7.6 illustrates this type of relationship. The diagram will usually be more compact if the diagram is drawn so that the related pair of tasks are one above the other. It is desirable that the arrow that links such a

FIGURE 7.6
START-TO-START (SS) LOGICAL
RELATIONSHIPS WITH ZERO,
POSITIVE, AND NEGATIVE LAGS

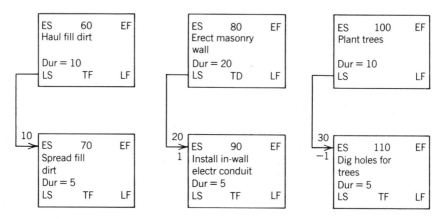

stacked pair of tasks have a horizontal segment over which the arrow number, and beneath which the arrow lag value, can be printed. It is further desirable that the arrow number and the lag value be printed near the arrow's head end.

Start to Start with Zero Lag

It is necessary that fill dirt be spread as it is hauled and dumped at a fill site. Tasks 60 and 70 have been separately defined because the hauling will be done by a subcontractor, whereas spreading will be done by the general contractor. However, the two tasks should be done nearly concurrently. Arrow 10 indicates that spreading cannot start until hauling starts.

> **Conditional Form.** Spreading fill dirt can start no earlier than the start of hauling the dirt.
>
> **Imperative Form.** Hauling fill dirt must start no later than the time that spreading can start.

Neither statement means that spreading *must* start as soon as hauling starts, which is the desired relationship. A later section describes how to specify that spreading will start no sooner than, and no later than, the start of hauling.

Start to Start with Positive Lag

Assume that electrical conduit is to be installed in a masonry wall as the wall is erected. The installation of the conduit cannot start until about a day after wall erection starts and should be done concurrently with wall erection thereafter. Arrow 20 partially specifies the desired relationship.

Conditional Form. The installation of electrical conduit can start no earlier than one day after wall erection starts.

Imperative Form. Wall erection must start no later than one day before the time that installation of conduit can start.

Neither statement means that conduit installation *must* start one day after wall erection starts.

Start to Start with Negative Lag

It is not desirable to dig the holes for a large number of trees and then to leave the holes open for an extended period of time before the trees are planted. Open holes are a safety hazard. In this instance, the project owner has specified that trees will be planted within one day after their holes are dug. Obviously, a tree cannot be planted until its hole is dug. The relationship that is depicted by arrow 30 only satisfies one of the desired constraints, that hole digging can start no earlier than one day before the tree planting starts. It leaves open the possibility that hole digging can start after tree planting starts.

Conditional Form. The hole digging can start no earlier than one day before tree planting starts.

Imperative Form. Tree planting must start no later than one day after hole digging starts.

Neither statement means that hole digging *must* start before tree planting starts.

End-to-End (EE) Relationships

These relationships are illustrated in Figure 7.7. Note that the tasks are the same as those used to illustrate start-to-start relationships. End-to-end relationships are often used in conjunction with start-to-start relationships to indicate partial concurrency between tasks.

End to End with Zero Lag

The spreading of the fill dirt cannot be completed until all the fill dirt has been hauled. See arrow 12.

Conditional Form. The completion of spreading can be no earlier than the completion of hauling.

Imperative Form. Hauling must be completed before spreading can be completed.

Neither statement would preclude the completion of spreading well after the completion of hauling.

FIGURE 7.7
END-TO-END (EE) LOGICAL
RELATIONSHIPS WITH ZERO,
POSITIVE, AND NEGATIVE LAGS

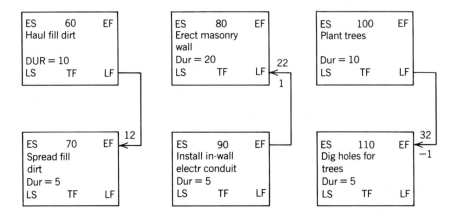

End to End with Positive Lag

It is necessary that the electricians work almost concurrently with masons—the masons starting one day earlier and finishing one day later than the electricians. Arrow 22 specifies that the masons will still have one day's work after the electricians are finished.

> **Conditional Form.** The masons can finish the wall no earlier than one day after the electricians complete installation of conduit.

> **Imperative Form.** The electricians must complete installation of conduit no later than one day before the time that masons can complete construction of the wall.

Neither statement would preclude the completion of the conduit installation well before the completion of the wall.

End to End with Negative Lag

A start-to-start relationship arrow was previously drawn to preclude the start of hole digging earlier than one day before tree planting starts. The EE arrow 32 is drawn to indicate that hole digging can be finished no earlier than one day before tree planting is finished.

> **Conditional Form.** Hole digging can be completed no earlier than one day before the time that tree planting is completed.

Imperative Form. Tree planting must be completed no later than one day after the time that hole digging can be completed.

Neither statement means that hole digging *must* be completed before tree planting is completed.

Combined Use of SS and EE Relationships

The preceding sections described the use of SS and EE arrows to depict relationships between the three pairs of tasks shown in Figures 7.6 and 7.7. In no case did the arrows that were drawn completely depict the desired logical relationships. Additional arrows must be drawn to specify the precise logical relationships. Recall that one arrow specifies one logical relationship between a pair of tasks.

Haul and Spread Fill Dirt

This task involves hauling and spreading of fill dirt. It is essential that spreading commence almost immediately after hauling starts, and that spreading be done continuously throughout the period during which the hauling takes place. Note that the estimated duration of the hauling task is 10 days whereas the estimated duration of the spreading task is only 5 days. The estimates of task duration were based on quantity of soil to be handled and upon the capacities of the hauling and spreading equipment. Ideally, the equipment to be used for the two tasks would have equal production rates, and the two tasks would have equal durations. Assume that such a balancing of resources was not possible in this instance. Additional arrows must be drawn to depict the desired logical relationship. See Figure 7.8.

Meaning of Diagram Based Only on Arrows 10
and 12
The spreading cannot start until hauling starts and the spreading cannot be finished until the hauling is finished. However, spreading could start well after hauling starts and spreading could be finished well after hauling is finished.

Draw Additional Arrows to Specify Logic Precisely

Conditional Form for Arrow 10. Spreading can start no earlier than the time that hauling starts.

Imperative Form for Arrow 11. Spreading must start no later than the time hauling starts.

FIGURE 7.8

COMBINED USE OF SS AND EE
RELATIONSHIPS

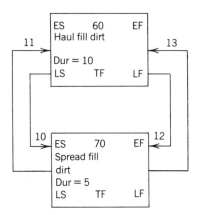

Combined Meaning. Spreading will start when hauling starts.

Conditional Form for Arrow 12. Spreading can end no earlier than the time that hauling ends.

Imperative Form for Arrow 13. Spreading must end no later than the time that hauling ends.

Combined Meaning. Spreading will end when hauling ends.

Significance of the Four Arrows

The procedures for making the network analysis and calculating task times will be described in Chapter 8. These procedures will lead to the calculation of identical task times for tasks 60 and 70. That is to say, the following identities will exist: ES(60) = ES(70), EF(60) = EF(70), LS(60) = LS(70), and LF(60) = LF(70). However, task 70, spread fill dirt, will have a larger computed total float than will task 60, haul fill dirt. The diagram indicates that the two tasks can and must start and end simultaneously.

Doubled-Headed Arrows

An arrowhead could be drawn at both ends of arrow 10 and at both ends of arrow 12, thereby making it unnecessary to draw arrows 11 and 13.

Erect Masonry and Install Conduit

The diagrams in Figures 7.6 and 7.7 fail to depict precisely the desired construction logic. Figure 7.9 illustrates the use of multiple arrows to specify the desired relationships.

Meaning Based Only on Arrows 20 and 22

Conduit installation cannot start until one day after wall construction starts, but it could start considerably later. Wall construction cannot be finished until one day after conduit installation is finished, but it could be finished much later.

Draw Additional Arrows

Arrows 21 and 23 have been added to define more precisely the relationship. For the time being, refer only to the left diagram in Figure 7.9.

> **Conditional Form for Arrow 20.** Conduit installation can start no earlier than one day after the wall erection starts.

> **Imperative Form for Arrow 21.** Conduit installation must start no later than one day after the wall erection starts.

> **Combined Meaning.** Conduit installation will start one day after the wall erection starts.

> **Imperative Form for Arrow 22.** Conduit installation must be completed no later than one day before the completion of the wall erection.

> **Conditional Form for Arrow 23.** Conduit installation can be completed no earlier than one day before the start of the wall erection.

> **Combined Meaning.** Conduit installation will be completed one day before the end of the wall erection.

FIGURE 7.9

DOUBLE-HEADED START-TO-START
AND END-TO-END ARROWS: (a)
Multiple Arrows; (b) Double-Headed
Arrows.

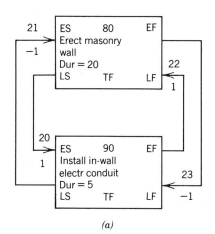 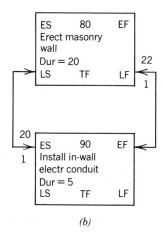

(a)   (b)

Significance of Multiple Arrows

The conduit installation will start one day after the wall erection starts and will be finished one day before the wall erection is finished. The computed task times for the two tasks will be identical; task 90, install in-wall electrical conduit, will have a larger total float than will the other task.

Use of Double-Headed Arrows

Refer to the right diagram in Figure 7.9. Note that double-headed SS and ES arrows have been used and that arrows 21 and 23 have been deleted. The right diagram has the same meaning as the left diagram. Particularly note the placement of the relationship numbers and the lag values. They should be positioned together to preclude misunderstanding. For arrow 20, the lag value is positioned near node 90; the double-headed arrow means that task 90 will start one day after the start of task 80.

Lag Values Must Be Equal When Multiple Arrows Are Used

Refer to the left diagram in Figure 7.9. Arrows 20 and 21 have equal lag values (the values have opposite signs). This must be true when there are two SS or two EE arrows connecting a pair of nodes. If a double-headed arrow is used to represent two SS arrows, or two EE arrows, the arrow number may be placed at either end of the doubled-headed arrow, but care should be taken that the lag value has the correct sign and is printed by the arrow number.

Tree-Planting Tasks

Figure 7.10 illustrates the use of multiple arrows and doubled-headed arrows to tie together the start of the hole-digging and tree-planting tasks that were previously used to illustrate SS and EE relationships. The objective is to have the diagram show that tree planting will start and end one day after hole digging starts and ends.

Draw Additional Arrows to Specify Logic Precisely

Refer to the left diagram in Figure 7.10. Arrows 31 and 33 have been added to those drawn in preceding illustrations.

> **Conditional Form for Arrow 30.** The hole digging can start no earlier than one day before the time that tree planting can start.
>
> **Imperative Form for Arrow 31.** The hole digging must start no later than one day before the time that tree planting can start.
>
> **Combined Meaning.** Hole digging will start one day before tree planting starts.
>
> **Conditional Form for Arrow 32.** Hole digging can be completed no earlier than one day before the time that tree planting can be completed.

FIGURE 7.10
DOUBLE-HEADED START-TO-START
AND END-TO-END ARROWS: (a)
Multiple Arrows; (b) Double-Headed
Arrows.

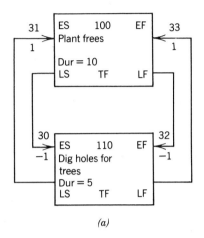

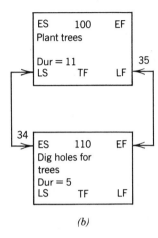

(a)   (b)

Imperative Form for Arrow 33. Hole digging must be completed no later than one day before the time that tree planting can be completed.

Combined Meaning. Hole digging will be completed one day before tree planting is completed.

The significance of the four arrows is that the tree planting will start and end one day after the hole digging starts and ends. The original statement of the problem was that a tree must be planted within one day after its hole was dug. Multiple SS and EE arrows have been used to ensure that this requirement was met. The same objective could have been met by extending the duration of the tree-planting task to 11 days and by using doubled-headed SS and EE arrows with no lags to link the two nodes. The right diagram in Figure 7.10 illustrates this solution.

Combined Use of ES and SE Relationships

The use of the start-to-end arrow has not yet been illustrated because the relationship is very seldom depicted alone. It is almost always used in conjunction with an ES arrow to tie the end of one task together with the start of another task. See Figure 7.11 for some diagrams that illustrate the combined use of ES

FIGURE 7.11

COMBINED USE OF ES AND SE
RELATIONSHIPS

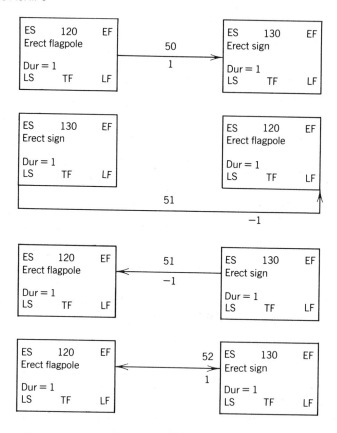

and SE arrows. Assume that a crane will be used to erect a flagpole and then to erect a sign. It is desired that the sign erection begin exactly one day after the end of the flagpole erection task.

The top diagram in Figure 7.11 shows arrow 50, an end-to-start relationship with a lag of one day. The next diagram shows arrow 51, an SE relationship with a lead of one day. The third diagram is the logical equivalent of the second diagram; it also shows arrow 51 with a lead of one day. Note that the arrow points to the left, a violation of normal diagramming conventions. The first and the third diagrams have the meanings stated below.

Conditional Form for Arrow 50. Sign erection can start no earlier than one day after the completion of flagpole erection.

Imperative Form for Arrow 51. Sign erection must start no later than one day after the completion of flagpole erection.

Combined Meaning of Arrows 50 and 51. Sign erection will start one day after the completion of flagpole erection.

The double-headed ES/SE arrow, arrow 52, is the equivalent of arrows 50 and 51. Note that the arrow number and the relationship lag are positioned near task 50, erect the sign. If they had been positioned at the left side of arrow 52, the meaning would be that flagpole erection would end one day after the sign erection started. If the arrow number and a lag value of -1 had been positioned near the left end of the double-headed arrow, the correct relationship would have been depicted.

EXERCISES

EXERCISE 7.1
Draw task nodes and relationship arrows to depict the following situation. One task involves the placement of a lightweight concrete topping on a large roof. The second task involves the placement of a built-up roof over the topping. Both tasks have estimated durations of five days. The built-up roof should not be placed over a section of the roof until the topping has cured for three days, but it should be placed as soon as possible thereafter.

(a) Use SS and EE arrows to depict the relationship.

(b) Use ES and EE arrows to depict the relationship.

EXERCISE 7.2
Draw task nodes and relationship arrows to depict the following situation. One task involves hanging gypsum board on the walls and ceiling of a large building. The task has a duration of 20 days. A second task, having a duration of 10 days, involves painting that gypsum board. Painting cannot start until 3 days after a piece of gypsum board is hung.

(a) Use ES and EE arrows to depict the relationship.

(b) Use SS and EE arrows to depict the relationship.

EXERCISE 7.3
Diagram several pairs of related tasks for the kinds of construction work that you are familiar with. Use the permissible logical relationships described in this chapter.

CALCULATION OF PRECEDENCE METHOD TASK TIMES AND FLOATS

8

OBJECTIVES

The preceding chapter covers the procedures for diagramming the logical relationships between a pair of tasks based on the Activity On Node (AON) notation that is used in the Precedence Method (PM). It also describes the four basic PM logical relationships (ES, SS, EE, and SE) and the meaning of the positive, zero, and negative lags that are associated with the relationships; then it presents examples of the use of the various relationships with lag values. The objectives of this chapter are to describe the diagramming of the entire project, the calculation of task times and float, and the advantages and disadvantages of the Precedence Method.

TASKS AND RELATIONSHIPS

The following terms will be used in this chapter. It is essential that the reader understand these definitions. Other terms will be defined later in the chapter.

Tasks

Tasks are represented on the logic diagram by nodes. Nodes are drawn as boxes, within which are printed task attributes such as task number, task description, task duration, the four task times, task float, and others that the scheduler may desire.

Task Times

Task times are computed values that are applicable to the tasks that make up a project. There are four task times. Procedures for calculating them will be covered in a subsequent section.

Early Start (ES) Time
This is the earliest time at which a task can be started, given the duration of precedent tasks and other constraints depicted in the logic diagram.

Early Finish (EF) Time
This is the earliest time at which a task can be finished if it is started at its ES time and if it is completed within its estimated duration.

Late Start (LS) Time
This is the latest time at which a task can be started without delaying project completion, assuming that it will be completed within its estimated duration.

Late Finish (LF) Time
This is the latest time at which a task can be completed without delaying project completion.

Task Float

Task float is a measure of how critical a task, or a part of a task, is. There are three kinds of task float. Equations for computing these task float values will be presented following their definitions. The solutions for the equations require values for the task times that were just defined. Procedures for calculating the task time values are covered in subsequent sections.

Task Total Float (TF)
A task that has zero total float is a critical task. It must be started at its ES time, completed within its estimated duration, and completed by its LF date; otherwise, the project completion will be delayed. The total float for task N may be computed by Equation 8.1:

$$TF(N) = LF(N) - ES(N) - Dur(N) \qquad (8.1)$$

Task Starting Float (SF)
The starting of a task may be critical even though the task itself is not critical. If the starting of a task is precedent to the starting of another task, and if that second task is critical (TF = 0), then starting the first task may be critical. The starting of a task is critical if its ES time equals its LS time. Any task that has

zero TF will also have zero SF. The starting float for task N may be calculated by Equation 8.2:

$$SF(N) = LS(N) - ES(N) \qquad (8.2)$$

Task Finish Float (FF)

Note that the acronym FF does not mean free float as it did in the Critical Path Method. The completion of a task may be critical even when the task itself is not critical. If the completion of a task is precedent to the completion of another task that is critical (TF = 0), then the completion of the first task may be critical. The completion of a task is critical if the task's EF time equals its LF time. Any task that has zero TF will also have zero FF. The finish float for task N may be calculated by Equation 8.3:

$$FF(N) = LF(N) - EF(N) \qquad (8.3)$$

Logical Relationships and Relationship Float (RF)

The logical relationships between tasks are depicted on the logic diagram as arrows. An arrow shows a relationship between two tasks; more specifically, it shows a relationship between a part of one task and a part of a second task. The relationship may contain a lag value (These relationships are discussed in Chapter 7.) Relationships also have float values. An arrow may or may not be on the critical path. It will be on the critical path if it has a zero value for RF. Critical relationship arrows connect the critical parts of task nodes. The total float for relationship R may be computed by Equations 8.4 to 8.7. The values for the task times at the relationship arrow's I-node (task node at arrow's tail end) and J-node (task node at the arrow's head end) must be known to calculate relationship float.

$$\text{ES Arrows: } RF(R) = LS(J) - EF(I) - Lag(R) \qquad (8.4)$$

$$\text{SS Arrows: } RF(R) = LS(J) - ES(I) - Lag(R) \qquad (8.5)$$

$$\text{EE Arrows: } RF(R) = LF(J) - EF(I) - Lag(R) \qquad (8.6)$$

$$\text{SE Arrows: } RF(R) = LF(J) - ES(I) - Lag(R) \qquad (8.7)$$

DIAGRAMMING THE PROJECT

Chapter 7 covers diagramming the relationships between a pair of tasks. This section discusses diagramming the entire project. The project logic diagram will contain one node for each task. Arrows will be used to depict logical relationships between those tasks.

Characteristics of Logic Diagrams

A satisfactory logic diagram will have the characteristics described hereafter. The diagram must be comprehensive, correctly depicting all essential logical relationships between the tasks that make up the project. It should contain no unnecessary logic arrows, and it should be legible.

The scheduler who prepares the logic diagram needs a thorough knowledge of the construction procedures that will be followed. If he lacks knowledge on some aspect of the project, he should seek advice from those persons who have that knowledge. Field personnel, such as project superintendents, often have a deeper understanding of the construction process than anyone else. The scheduler should consider consulting them while preparing the schedule rather than preparing the schedule on the basis of assumed construction procedures that may not be followed. If the project superintendent has been appointed by the time the schedule is to be prepared, the scheduler should consider having several coordination meetings with the superintendent to clarify the actual construction sequences that will be followed.

Comprehensive

Any work activity that affects the time at which other work activities can start must be defined as a task and included in the logic diagram. Chapter 2, ''Task Definition,'' listed a number of kinds of work activity that are often overlooked when logic diagrams are prepared. These include preconstruction tasks such as obtaining permits and bonds; engineering tasks such as preparing and reviewing shop drawings; and procurement tasks such as fabricating components and purchase and delivery of long lead-time materials.

Logical Relationships Correctly Shown

The logic arrows represent constraints to the starting or the finishing of tasks. Completion of a built-up roof and installation of exterior doors and windows are termed **closing in** the building. Closing in the building is usually considered a constraint to starting the installation of interior finish materials that may be damaged by rain. If a certain task, say, installing gypsum wallboard on interior walls, cannot be done until the building is closed in, then a logic arrow, or logic arrows, must reflect that constraint. The constraint may be explicitly depicted or it may be implicitly expressed, but it must be shown on the diagram.

Figure 8.1 illustrates the explicit and implicit expression of logical relationships. Note that in Figure 8.1*a* an arrow explicitly shows that the completion of the built-up roof is precedent to the start of wallboard installation. Figure 8.1*b* explicitly shows that the completion of the built-up roof is precedent to starting the interior frame partitions, and its explicitly shows that starting the interior frame partitions is precedent to starting installation of the wallboard. Hence, an implicit relationship has been depicted, namely, that completion of the built-up roof is precedent to starting installation of the wallboard. Even though Figure 8.1*b* shows the desired constraint, the scheduler could draw another arrow in the diagram shown at Figure 8.1*b* from the completion of the

FIGURE 8.1
EXPLICIT VERSUS IMPLICIT
RELATIONSHIPS: (*a*) Explicit
Relationship Between Tasks 10 and
30; (*b*) Implicit Relationship Between
Tasks 10 and 30.

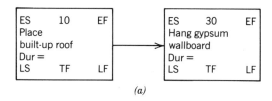

(*a*)

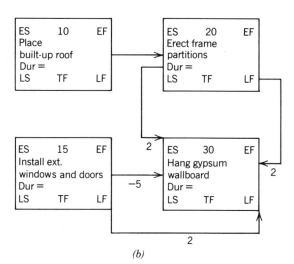

(*b*)

roof to the start of wallboard installation, thereby explicitly depicting the relationship. The scheduler generally would not do so, because PM diagrams can become very cluttered if relationships are duplicated. Figure 8.1*b* also contains an additional task node, the installation of exterior doors and windows, and arrows explicitly expressing the relationship of this additional task to the wallboard installation task. Closing in the building was not defined as a task; rather it is a project condition that encompasses several defined tasks. This project condition is a constraint to the initiation of work on another group of tasks that involve installation of materials that could be damaged by rain.

The installation of materials cannot start until at least some of the materials have been procured, and it cannot be completed until all the materials have been procured. The painting of wall surfaces cannot be completed until all these wall surfaces have been installed. The resilient flooring for a slab cannot be installed until the slab has been installed. These are obvious construction relationships when so stated. The relationships must be depicted on the logic diagram.

Concurrency

One of the principal virtues of the Precedence Method is that it permits the scheduler to easily show partial concurrence between a pair of tasks. Figure 8.1*b* indicates that the installation of gypsum wallboard over interior frame walls could start shortly after the erection of these walls starts. It is not necessary to complete the erection of all the partitions before starting to cover some of them with wallboard. Figure 8.1*b* also shows that it would be possible to finish covering the frame walls with gypsum wallboard shortly after the last wall had been erected. It also shows that hanging the wallboard could start before all the exterior doors and windows have been installed, but it could not be completed until after all these doors and windows had been installed. If it is feasible to perform tasks semiconcurrently, then the logic diagram should reflect that possibility.

No Unnecessary Constraints

As will become evident as you continue reading this chapter, PM logic diagrams can become very complex. Some schedulers may ''tie in'' a task node to another node simply to make the diagram more readable. The introduction of logic arrows that do not represent essential construction constraints will result in unrealistic schedules.

No Logic Loops

Figure 8.2 depicts a logic loop. In this example, the diagram specifies that task B cannot start until task A is completed and task A cannot be started until task B is completed. Although the illogical nature of this diagram is apparent, it is

FIGURE 8.2
A LOGIC LOOP

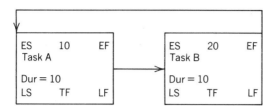

easy to insert logic loops into complex PM diagrams. A subsequent section will cover some PM conventions that help guard against logic loops, but the basic way of avoiding logic loops is to avoid depicting any relationship on the diagram that is not essential.

Figure 8.3 shows a PM logic diagram that contains several logic loops. A logic loop exists where it is possible to trace a path from a point on the diagram through the diagram back to the starting point. The path of a logic loop can pass through arrows in the direction of the arrows, through nodes from left to right,

FIGURE 8.3
THREE LOGIC LOOPS: A, B, AND C

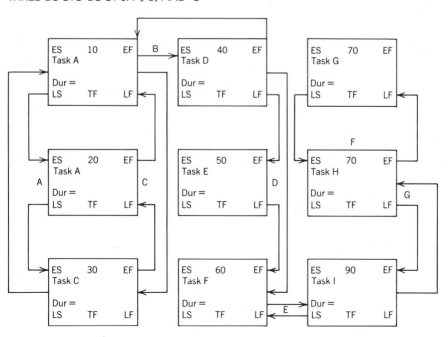

and vertically along either side of nodes. There are three logic loops in this diagram. They are made up of the three arrows and the three nodes that surround the letters A, B, and C. The arrows and nodes surrounding the letters D and F superficially resemble a logic loop, but no such loops exists. Note that you cannot trace a continuous path, moving in the directions specified above that will surround the letter D or the letter F. A double-headed arrow is actually a form of a logic loop, but it is a permissible logic loop. Note that the two arrows surrounding the letter E and the two arrows surrounding the letter G are equivalent to double-headed arrows, and they do form logic loops. A subsequent section will explain why double-headed arrows are a permissible form of logic loop.

No Improperly Dangling Task Nodes

A task node that has no arrow terminating at its left side is a **start-dangling** node. A node that has no arrow originating at its right side is a **finish-dangling** node. There must be at least one start-dangling and at least one finish-dangling node in each logic diagram. There may be more than one of each type. There may also be groups of nodes that are not connected to the balance of the diagram. There is nothing intrinsically wrong with having numerous start-dangling or finish-dangling nodes in a diagram, as long as their dangling nature makes sense from a practical construction point of view. See Figure 8.4 for an illustration of dangling nodes. The nodes for tasks 10, 20, 30, 50, and 70 are start-dangling. The diagram shows no tasks as being precedent to the start of these five tasks. Task 10 calls for the procurement of foundation rebar (assume that the task also includes the preparation and review of shop drawings). Task 20 calls for surveying the site. Task 50 calls for the procurement of steel columns (again, assume the task includes the preparation and review of shop drawings). All three of these tasks can start on the first day of the project; therefore, all three of them are properly indicated as being start-dangling. The node for task 50 was placed near node [80], to which it is immediately precedent, instead of at the extreme left of the logic diagram, thereby avoiding having a long arrow. The node for task 70, pour floor slab, is improperly shown as start-dangling. Several other construction operations are precedent to pouring this slab.

Three nodes, [40], [60], and [900], are shown as finish-dangling. Node [900] is the final task in the project. Hence, it is properly shown as finish-dangling. Task [40], construct foundations, is incorrectly shown as finish-dangling; completion of the foundations is precedent to many other tasks.

Task nodes [30] and [60] are shown as being unconnected to the rest of the network. Assuming that grading the roadbed can be started on the first day of the project and that the completion of the paving is not precedent to any other project work, the dangling nature of these two task nodes is proper. Actually, it is likely that some work, such as surveying and erosion control, should be shown as precedent to the grading.

Some schedulers will object to having more than one start-dangling node, and

FIGURE 8.4
DANGLING TASKS

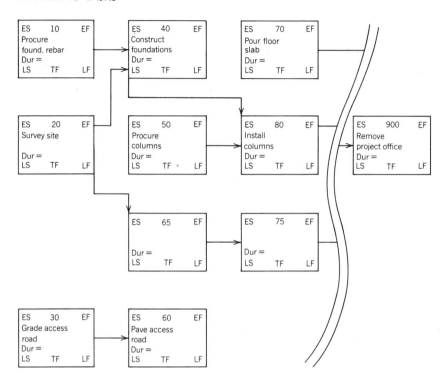

more than one finish-dangling node, on a logic diagram. If that is the case, they can draw a dummy (having zero duration) task node at the extreme left of the diagram. Then, they should draw end-to-start arrows with zero lag from that dummy node to all real task nodes that are start-dangling. Similarly, they should draw another dummy task node at the extreme right of the diagram and draw end-to-start arrows from all real finish-dangling nodes to that dummy node. They should not connect all the start-dangling nodes together with start-to-start arrows, nor should they connect all the finish-dangling nodes with end-to-end arrows. Start-to-start arrows and end-to-end arrows should be reserved for use when there is an actual construction reason for their use; they should not be used to tidy up a diagram.

Consequences of Improperly Dangling Task Nodes

The PM network analysis that will be covered in subsequent sections results in the calculation of task times. If a node is start-dangling, its computed early start time will be zero. If the node is finish-dangling, its computed late finish time will be equal to the projection duration. In the example above, the consequence of showing task node 40 as finish-dangling is that the computed late finish time for the task construct foundations will be equal to the project duration. It is not sufficient to tie this finish-dangling task node into a dummy terminal node; it must be tied into some task node that makes construction sense.

Legibility

It is essential that the logic diagram be completely legible and understandable. It is nearly impossible to determine the logical relationships between tasks if the diagram itself is sloppy or hard to understand. Students may try to save time and effort by drawing a slovenly diagram, intending to redraw it once they have determined the logical relationships. Such an attempt to save time is counter-productive.

Drawing the Logic Diagram

Dimensions of Nodes (Boxes) and Spacing Between Nodes

A task node should be about 1.5 inch × 1.5 inch. That is large enough to print a 24-character task description and seven numerical values (ES, EF, LS, LF, TF, duration, and task number). The nodes should be spaced about 1.5 inch apart, both vertically and horizontally. Such spacing will be sufficient to allow drawing arrows that pass between the nodes. These dimensions apply to the finished logic diagram.

The First Draft

You should start off with a wide sheet of paper because logic diagrams tend to be wide, usually wider than they are high. The reverse side of used fanfold computer paper is very satisfactory for preparing a draft logic diagram. Get a section that is about 5 feet long and turn it on its side. The 1.5 inch × 1.5 inch dimensions recommended for nodes is satisfactory for a first draft, but the nodes should be spaced about twice as far apart as they will be spaced in the finished diagram, since almost invariably you will discover that you have omitted a task node from the draft diagram. This overlooked node usually belongs right in the middle of the diagram. If the columns of nodes are spaced about 3 inches apart, there will be space to insert the overlooked node. If the columns are spaced about 1.5 inch apart, which is satisfactory for the final diagram, there will not be enough space to insert additional nodes.

Skip ahead and examine Figure 8.7, a finished logic diagram. Now assume that you have discovered the need for an additional node, and that the node should be placed between nodes 70 and 110. There is not enough space for the insertion of a node in that location. The rows of nodes should also be spaced about 3 inches apart for the first draft. Again referring to Figure 8.7, imagine your frustration if you decided you needed another node box between nodes 60 and 70. Just as used computer paper can be used for a very wide sheet, it can be used for a very tall sheet. Simply tape together several long pieces of computer paper. You may decide that you should start with a piece of paper that is 10 feet long and 2 feet high and that you should space the rows and columns of nodes about 5 inches apart. Then, your afterthoughts can be incorporated into the draft diagram with a minimum of erasing.

One student devised a very practical method for drawing draft logic diagrams. He used 2 inch square self-adhesive pieces of paper for the task nodes. He was able to shift these nodes about on a larger piece of paper at will until they were correctly positioned.

Structured Diagrams

All logic diagrams in this chapter are structured diagrams, meaning that the task nodes are drawn in equally spaced rows and columns. The logic arrows are drawn as vertical and horizontal segments, with every arrow having a horizontal segment. The relationship arrow number is printed above that horizontal segment, and the arrow lag, if any, is printed below the horizontal segment. Examine Figure 8.5. Note that arrows 10 and 20 share a vertical line segment, the shared portion being termed a **staff**. The use of staffs enables the scheduler to draw a more compact and less cluttered logic diagram. A staff may be connected to the head end of one arrow and to the tail end of several arrows, or it may be connected to the tail end of one arrow and to the head end of several arrows. If two or more arrows are connected to a staff at their head ends, and if two or more arrows are connected to the same staff at their tail ends, the meaning will not be clear.

Note that arrow numbers for arrows 10, 20, 30, and 40 are printed on the diagram so that there is no doubt which logical relationship they identify. Compare the positioning of these arrow numbers to the positioning of the numbers for arrows 90 and 110. Arrow numbers should be printed on a horizontal segment of the arrow that is not shared by any other arrow. Compare the arrows numbered 50 and 60 to the arrows numbered 70 and 80. Because arrows 70 and 80 share a horizontal line segment, it is possible to misinterpret the diagram. The above rules are not sacrosanct; any absolutely clear technique may be used for drawing the arrows and for positioning the arrow numbers.

Avoid Crossovers

Many times it will be impossible to draw a logic diagram without having one logic arrow cross over another arrow. Figure 8.6a illustrates a crossover. Note

FIGURE 8.5
DRAWING ARROWS AND PLACEMENT OF ARROW NUMBERS

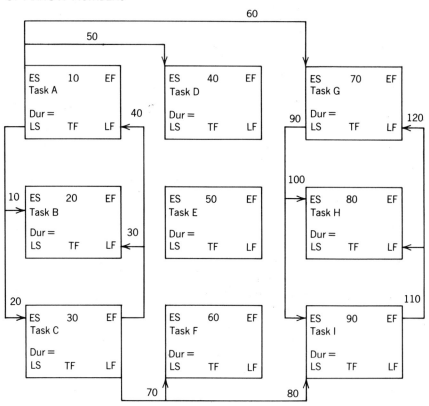

that line break symbols have been used to indicate that the arrow originating at node [10] and terminating at node [40] crosses over another arrow. The number of crossovers in a diagram may be reduced by the use of dummy task nodes. Figure 8.6b illustrates exactly the same logical relationships as does figure 8.6a, but no crossover has been required. In this instance, both nodes [10] and [20] were precedent to both nodes [30] and [40], requiring four arrows. If five nodes were all precedent to all five additional nodes, 25 arrows would have been required, with enough crossovers to result in an illegible diagram.

Conventions

Conventions are rules that are meant to make a diagram easier to read and to reduce the chances that a logic error will creep into the diagram.

FIGURE 8.6
USE OF DUMMY TASKS TO
ELIMINATE CROSSOVERS:
(a) Crossovers; (b) Crossovers
Eliminated by Dummy Node.

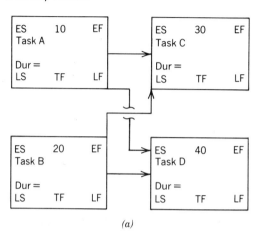

(a)

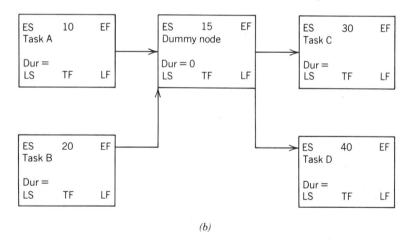

(b)

Arrow Direction

One convention is to draw logic arrows so that they point to the right, up, or down but never to the left. Note that many arrows in the illustrations for this chapter have a short horizontal segment that points to the left but that no arrows have an overall direction to the left. The reason for having a short left-pointing horizontal segment for an arrow is to provide space upon which the arrow number can be printed. An exception to this convention is the case in which a logic diagram is very wide but not very high. In such instances, it may be desirable to print the second half of the diagram below the first half on the same sheet of paper, and one or more left-pointing arrows will be needed to connect the end of the first half to the beginning of the second half.

Node Numbering

Node numbers merely serve for purposes of identification. Any consistent system may be used for assigning them. However, a particular number should be used as the node number for only one node. It is preferable to construct the logic diagram completely and then to number the nodes from left to right and from the top down. This system has been used for numbering the nodes in all of the diagrams in this chapter.

A convention that was used in the Critical Path Method was to always have the node number at the head of an arrow larger than the node number at the tail of the arrow. That system is not feasible in the Precedence Method. Examine arrows 20 and 40 in Figure 8.5. Node 10 is at the tail of arrow 20 and node 30 is at its head. However, node 10 is at the head of arrow 40, with node 30 at the tail.

Arrow Numbering

The same system should be used for numbering arrows as was used for numbering nodes, that is, you should start at the upper left and work from left to right and from top to bottom. Arrow numbers should be unique, that is, no two arrows should have the same arrow number. Some computer programs require the assignment of arrow numbers so that they are indicative of the precedence of the arrows. Other programs, including the one for which a BASIC language program listing is printed in Appendix B, permit the assignment of arrow numbers in any arbitrary manner. The following section describes a procedure by which arrow numbers can be assigned so that they are indicative of precedence.

Numbering Arrows in Accordance with Their Precedence

The procedure described hereafter has been used to number the arrows in the examples given in this chapter. Examine Figure 8.7, a fairly complex logic diagram. During the network analysis phase, to be covered in a subsequent section, it is necessary to consider the impact of relationships on task times. For example, it is necessary to compute the early start time for node [100]. That time cannot be computed until the early finish time has been computed for node [60]. The ES time for node [100] will be equal to the EF time for node [60] plus the lag, if any, for arrow 110. It is evident that you cannot start the network analysis by computing task times for node [100]. It is not so evident that you

FIGURE 8.7
NUMBERING NODES AND ARROWS

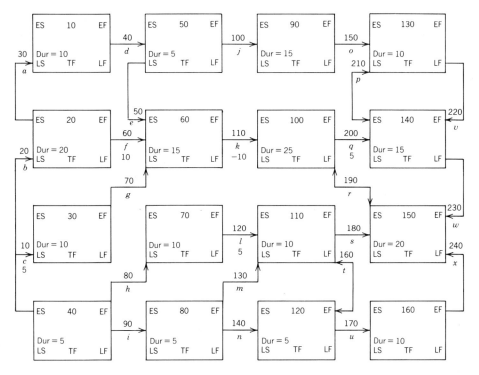

cannot start with node [10]. In fact, the initial node in this diagram is node [40]; it is the only left-dangling node in the diagram. Figure 8.7 also contains three double-headed arrows, a permissible type of logic loop. The exact order in which the various nodes and arrows should be considered can be very confusing.

The following rules govern the systematic assignment of arrow numbers so that the numbers can be used during the network analysis phase to determine the order in which nodes and arrows should be considered. Each arrow in Figure 8.7 has been assigned an identifying lowercase letter. The discussion of this procedure will use this letter to identify an arrow until a number will have been assigned.

Rules for Assignment of Numbers to Arrows Having a Single Head

The diagram in Figure 8.7 contains three double-headed arrows: 160, 190, and 210. All other arrows have single heads.

Rule 1. An arrow originating at the left side of a node may be assigned a number after all arrows terminating at the left side of that node have been assigned a number.

Rule 2. An arrow originating at the right side of a node may be assigned a number after all arrows terminating at either side of the node have been assigned a number.

Application of Rules 1 and 2

To start the numbering process, examine the nodes of the diagram in Figure 8.7. Only node [40] meets the conditions of either rule 1 or rule 2. Because there are no unnumbered arrows terminating at the left side of the node [40], rule 1 allows the numbering of arrows b and c. It does not matter which of them is numbered first. The arrows were numbered in increments of 10 so that appropriate numbers can be assigned to any arrows that are added as afterthoughts. At this point, arrow a can be numbered by rule 1; and arrows f, g, h, and i can be numbered by rule 2. The numbering procedure was continued until arrow o was given the number 150.

Table 8.1 shows the order in which numbers were assigned to the arrows and the rationale for assignment of these numbers. If, after applying rules 1 and 2, some arrows cannot be assigned a number, it is an indication that a logic loop exists in the diagram. If the logic loop results from the use of double-headed arrows, it may still be possible to continue assigning numbers according to the rules given in a subsequent section.

Rules for Assignment of Numbers to Arrows Having Double Heads

After numbers have been assigned to the arrows lettered a to o, it was no longer possible to continue assignment of arrow numbers based on rules 1 and 2. This

TABLE 8.1

RATIONALE FOR ASSIGNMENT OF NUMBERS TO SINGLE-HEADED ARROWS

Arrow No.	Assigned to Arrow	Rule No.	Arrow No.	Assigned to Arrow	Rule No.
10	c	1	20	b	1
30	a	1	40	d	2
50	e	1	60	f	2
70	g	2	80	h	2
90	i	2	100	j	2
110	k	2	120	l	2
130	m	2	140	n	2
150	o	2			

is an indication that there is a logic loop in the diagram. In this instance, there are three logic loops, all of them resulting from the use of double-headed arrows lettered *p*, *r*, and *t*. A logic loop caused by double-headed arrows is a permissible logic loop; however, additional rules are required to number those arrows, and special procedures must be applied during the network analysis phase.

The following rules permit the assignment of numbers to double-headed arrows. These rules will be used in conjunction with rules 1 and 2 to complete the numbering of the arrows. The rules given below are adequate for diagrams in which there is no more than one double-headed arrow connecting to a side of a task node. Although the rules could be extended to encompass more complex diagrams, their application is not considered practical for manual network analyses.

Rule 3. If a double-headed arrow connects the starting sides (left sides) of two nodes and if no arrow that has not been assigned a number terminates at the left side of either node (excepting the double-headed arrow), then the double-headed arrow may be assigned the next arrow number. After applying this rule, try to apply rules 1 and 2 to number additional arrows. Arrow *p* cannot be numbered by this rule until arrow *q* is numbered.

Rule 4. If a double-headed arrow connects the end sides (right sides) of two nodes and if no arrow that has not been assigned a number terminates at either side of either node (excepting the double-headed arrow), then the double-headed arrow may be assigned the next number. After applying this rule, attempt to apply rules 1 and 2. Arrow *t* meets the conditions for this rule and is numbered 160. Then, arrows *u* and *s* can be numbered 170 and 180 respectively, by rule 2.

Rule 5. If a double-headed arrow connects the right side of one node and the left side of a second node and if no arrow not having been assigned a number terminates at either side of the first node (excepting the double-headed arrow), and if no arrow not having been assigned a number terminates at the left side of the second node (excepting the double-headed arrow), then the double-headed arrow may be assigned the next number. After applying this rule, try to apply rules 1 and 2. Arrow *r* meets this rule and is numbered 190. Next, arrow *q* can be numbered 190 by rule 2.

Rules 3 to 5 are used in conjunction with rules 1 and 2 to complete the numbering of the arrows. Table 8.2 indicates the order and the rationale for numbering the remaining arrows. There can be more than one correct solution to the arrow-numbering procedure; hence, it may be possible to number the arrows differently than is indicated in Table 8.2. Figure 8.7 shows the diagram with numbered logic arrows.

If it is impossible to assign numbers to all arrows by using the above rules,

TABLE 8.2
RATIONALE FOR ASSIGNMENT OF NUMBERS TO REMAINING ARROWS[a]

Arrow No.	Assigned to Arrow	Rule No.	Arrow No.	Assigned to Arrow	Rule No.
160	t	4	170	u	2
180	s	2	190	r	5
200	q	2	210	p	3
220	v	2	230	x	2
240	w	2			

[a]Arrow x could have been numbered immediately after numbering arrow u. Arrow w could have been numbered immediately after numbering arrow v.

then the logic diagram is too complicated to be solved by the given rules, or it may contain a logic loop. In either case, the diagram must be either simplified or the logic loop must be eliminated before the analysis may proceed. These rules allow logical numbering of arrows as long as no more than one double-headed arrow terminates at one side of any node. The PM scheduling program listed in Appendix B will cope with a situation in which there are double-headed arrows (not more than one double-headed arrow connecting to a side of a node), but the time for network analysis may be quite long.

METHODOLOGY

In the Critical Path Method, it is necessary to compute event times as a preliminary step to the computation of task times. Such a preliminary step is not required for the Precedence Method.

Phases of Schedule Preparation

The PM schedule is prepared in three phases. They must be performed in the indicated order.

Phase 1. Draw the Logic Diagram

Plot the nodes in a **structured** manner. Structured means that the nodes will be aligned in vertical columns and that if two tasks are logically related in an end-to-start manner, the node at the J-end of the relationship arrow is physically located to the right of the node at the I-end of the arrow. Relationship arrows can point to the right, upward, or downward, but they should not point to the left. Although a portion of relationship arrow 30 in Figure 8.7 points to the left, the overall direction of that arrow is upward. The logic diagram will contain a great amount of information. To preclude a cluttered and illegible diagram, it is important to draw the diagram at an adequate scale. Having drawn the nodes and the relationship arrows, it is necessary to number the nodes and the arrows. It is desirable that a logical system be used to number the arrows. Such a system is described in a previous section.

Phase 2. Perform the Network Analysis

The network analysis comprises three operations: the **forward pass**, the determination of **project duration**, and the **backward pass**. The Early Start times (ESs) and the Early Finish times (EFs) are computed during the forward pass. The largest EF time calculated for any task is taken as the project duration. The Late Start times (LSs) and the Late Finish times (LFs) are computed during the backward pass. Subsequent sections cover these operations.

Phase 3. Prepare the Schedule in Tabular Form

The table should show **task times** and **task floats**. A Gantt chart may be prepared to supplement the tabular schedule.

The Forward Pass

The forward pass is made to determine the Early Start times (ESs) and the Early Finish times (EFs). There may be several trial values computed for each of these times, with these trial values lightly penciled on the diagram. The largest trial value is selected as the task time (ES or EF, as appropriate) and is printed within the node, with the other trial values erased.

Rules for Computing Trial Values for ES and EF Times

The following rules govern the computation of these trial values.

Rule 1.   The smallest possible value for an ES or an EF time is zero. If there is no reason to assign a larger value for one of these times, then assign a value of zero for the time.

Rule 2.   The smallest possible value for a time at the head of a relationship arrow is the early time at the tail of that arrow plus the arrow's lag. For ES and EE arrows, the early time is the EF time. For SS and SE arrows, the early time is the ES time. Note that if an arrow has a negative value for lag, its value must be added algebraically, which is equivalent to the subtraction of its absolute value.

Rule 3. The smallest possible value for a task's EF time is the task's ES time plus its duration.

Rule 4. Consider the relationship arrows in the order of their numbers, with the numbers having been assigned in accordance with the procedure described in the previous section.

Rule 5. Immediately after all arrows terminating at the left side of a node have been considered, apply rule 3 above to determine whether the EF time has been affected.

Figure 8.8 is a PM logic diagram before network analysis. Figure 8.9 contains the same diagram with values entered for the ES and EF times for each task node. Figure 8.8 contains ES, SS, and EE arrows with zero, positive, and

FIGURE 8.8

THE PM DIAGRAM BEFORE NETWORK
ANALYSIS

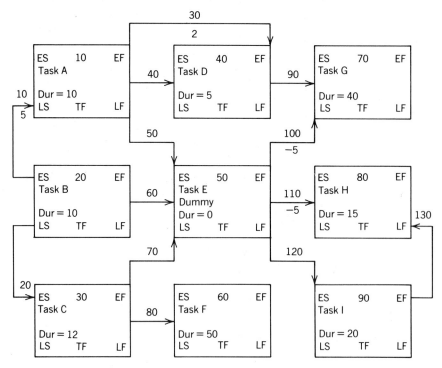

FIGURE 8.9
THE FORWARD PASS

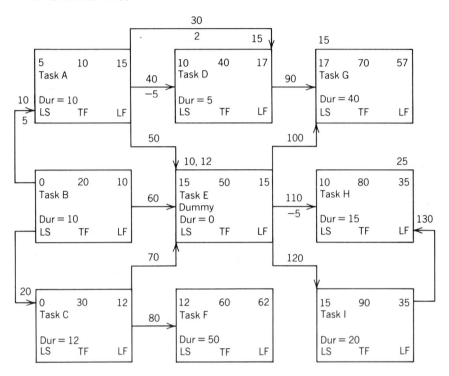

negative lags. It does not contain any SE arrows, nor any double-headed arrows. Note that a dummy task node, 50, has been plotted so as to reduce the number of crossovers. Also note that there are two finish-dangling nodes, 60 and 70. In this instance, the EF time for node 60 is greater than for any other node, even though node 60 is not at the extreme right of the diagram. Task 50 will be the last task to be completed, at the end of the sixty-second workday; hence, the project duration is 62 workdays. Table 8.3 indicates the order and the rationale for calculating the ES and EF task times for this project. The largest computed trial value for each task time has been marked with an asterisk in this table.

Project Duration

The largest value for an Early Finish (EF) time that was computed during the forward pass is the project duration. In the example above, the project duration is 62 days, based on the EF time for task 60. All tasks must be completed by

TABLE 8.3

TRIAL VALUES FOR EARLY START AND EARLY FINISH TIMES[a]

Node No.	Rule Used	Selected Values for		Trial Value Calculations
		ES	EF	
20	1	0		No precedent tasks, therefore ES(20) = 0*
	3		10	EF(20) = ES(20) + Dur(20) = 0 + 10 = 10*
10	2	5		ES(10) = ES(20) + Lag 10 = 0 + 5 = 5*
	3		15	EF(10) = ES(10) + Dur(10) = 5 + 10 = 15*
30	2	0		ES(30) = ES(20) + Lag 20 = 0 + 0 = 0*
	3		12	EF(30) = ES(30) + Dur(30) = 0 + 12 = 12*
40	2		17	EF(40) = EF(10) + Lag 30 = 15 + 2 = 17*
	2	10		ES(40) = EF(10) + Lag 40 = 15 − 5 = 10*
	3			EF(40) = ES(40) + Dur(40) = 10 + 5 = 15
50	2	15		ES(50) = EF(10) + Lag 50 = 15 + 0 = 15*
	2			ES(50) = EF(20) + Lag 60 = 10 + 0 = 10
	2			ES(50) = EF(30) + Lag 70 = 12 + 0 = 12
	3		15	EF(50) = ES(50) + Dur(50) = 15 + 0 = 15*
60	2	12		ES(60) = EF(30) + Lag 80 = 12 + 0 = 12*
	3		62	EF(60) = ES(60) + Dur(60) = 12 + 50 = 62*
70	2	17		ES(70) = EF(40) + Lag 90 = 17 + 0 = 17*
	2			ES(70) = EF(50) + Lag 100 = 15 + 0 = 15
	3		57	EF(70) = ES(70) + Dur(70) = 17 + 40 = 57*
80	2	10		ES(80) = EF(50) + Lag 110 = 15 − 5 = 10*
	3			EF(80) = ES(80) + Dur(80) = 10 + 15 = 25
90	2	15		ES(90) = EF(50) + Lag 120 = 15 + 0 = 15*
	3		35	EF(90) = ES(90) + Dur(90) = 15 + 20 = 35
80	2		35	EF(80) = EF(90) + Lag 130 = 35 + 0 = 35*

[a]The largest trial value calculated for a task time (either an ES or an EF) is marked with an asterisk. That same value was selected as the task time.

the end of the sixty-second workday if the project is to be completed by that time.

In this example, the node having the largest EF time was not located at the extreme right of the diagram. This resulted because task 60 had a long duration and was finish-dangling. Even if there is only one finish-dangling node, which is located at the extreme right of the diagram, it is possible that the largest value for an EF time may be at some other node. The largest value for an EF time, regardless of where the node having that value is located, is the project duration.

The Backward Pass

The backward pass will be completed working generally from right to left. During the backward pass, the Late Start (LS) and the Late Finish (LF) times will be computed. There may be several trial values computed for each of these times, with the smallest trial value selected as the task time.

Rules for Computing LSs and LFs

The following rules govern the computation of LSs and LFs.

Rule 1.   The largest possible value for any LS or LF time is the project duration, as computed in the previous paragraph.

FIGURE 8.10
THE BACKWARD PASS

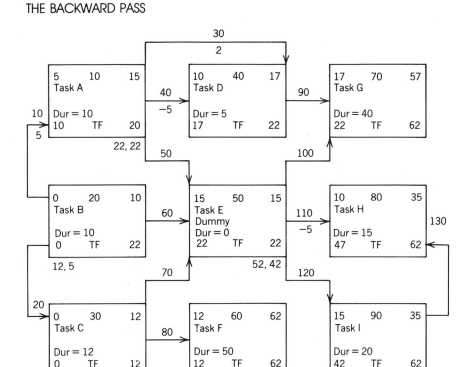

Rule 2. The largest possible value for a time at the tail of an arrow is the late time at the head of the arrow less the arrow's lag. If the arrow is a SS or an ES arrow, the late time is the LS time. If the arrow is an EE or an SE arrow, the late time is the LF time. If the lag value is negative, then it must be subtracted algebraically, which is equivalent to adding its absolute value.

Rule 3. The largest possible value for a task's LS time is its LF time minus its duration.

TABLE 8.4
TRIAL VALUES FOR LATE START AND LATE FINISH TIMES[a]

Node No.	Rule Used	Selected Values for LS	LF	Trial Value Calculations
80	1		62	Finish-dangling node; LF = Project duration*
	3	47		LS(80) = LF(80) − Dur(80) = 62 − 15 = 47*
70	1		62	Finish-dangling node; LF = Proj. duration*
	3	22		LS(70) = LF(70) − Dur(70) = 62 − 40 = 22*
60	1		62	Finish-dangling node; LF = Proj. duration*
	3	12		LS(60) = LF(60) − Dur(60) = 62 − 50 = 12*
90	2		62	LF(90) = LF(80) − Lag 130 = 62 − 0 = 62*
	3	15		LS(90) = LF(90) − Dur(90) = 62 − 20 = 42*
50	2			LF(50) = LS(90) − Lag 120 = 42 − 0 = 42
	2			LF(50) = LS(80) − Lag 110 = 47 + 5 = 52
	2		22	LF(50) = LS(70) − Lag 100 = 22 − 0 = 22*
	3	22		LS(50) = LF(50) − Dur(50) = 22 − 0 = 22*
40	2		22	LF(40) = LS(70) − Lag 90 = 22 − 0 = 22*
	3	17		LS(40) = LF(40) − Dur(40) = 22 − 5 = 17*
30	2		12	LF(30) = LS(60) − Lag 80 = 12 − 0 = 12*
	2			LF(30) = LS(50) − Lag 70 = 22 − 0 = 22
	3	0		LS(30) = LF(30) − Dur(30) = 12 − 12 = 0*
20	2		22	LF(20) = LS(50) − Lag 60 = 22 − 0 = 22*
10	2			LF(10) = LS(50) − Lag 50 = 22 − 0 = 22
	2			LF(10) = LS(40) − Lag 40 = 17 + 5 = 22
	2		20	LF(10) = LF(40) − Lag 30 = 22 − 2 = 20*
	3	10		LS(10) = LF(10) − Dur(10) = 30 − 10 = 10*
20	2	0		LS(20) = LS(30) − Lag 20 = 0 − 0 = 0*
	2			LS(20) = LS(10) − Lag 10 = 10 − 5 = 5

[a]The smallest computed trial value for an event time (either LS or LF time) was selected as the event time. These smallest values are marked with an asterisk.

Rule 4.   Consider the relationship arrows in the inverse order of their arrow numbers.

Rule 5.   Immediately after an LF time has been computed, apply rule 3 above to determine whether the LS time has been affected.

Figure 8.10 (page 185) shows the tasks LS and LF times. Table 8.4 indicates the trial values that were computed for these times and the rationale for their computation. Note that the relationship arrows have been considered in inverse order of their numbers. Also note that no later start time is less than zero. In some instances, a trial value may be negative. If so, use zero as the trial value.

THE CRITICAL PATH AND FLOAT VALUES

Float Values

Equations 8.1 to 8.3, given earlier in this chapter, allow the calculation of the task float values for Total Float (TF), Start Float (SF), and Finish Float (FF). Equations 8.4 to 8.7 allow the calculation of Relationship Float (RF).

The Critical Path

The critical path is continuous from the beginning of the project to the end of the project. The path may fork into two or more paths. It is drawn through arrows and through parts of nodes in accordance with the following rules. Both tasks (nodes) and relationships (arrows) can be on the critical path.

Rule 1.   If a task's ES time equals its LS time (SF = 0), the start of the task is critical.

Rule 2.   If a task's EF time equals its LF time (FF = 0), the end of the task is critical.

Rule 3.   If both the start and the end of a task are critical, then the task may be critical. However, having its start and its finish both critical is not an adequate criterion for the task itself being critical. (See Figure 8.11, where it is demonstrated that task 30 is not critical, although both its start and finish are critical.)

Rule 4.   A task is critical if its Total Float (TF) is equal to zero. Total float is equal to LF − Dur − ES.

FIGURE 8.11
NONCRITICAL TASK WITH CRITICAL
START AND FINISH

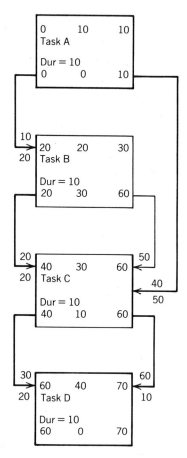

Rule 5.   An arrow is critical if its Relationship Float (RF) is zero. The RF will always be zero for double-headed arrows, regardless of whether the arrows do, or do not, connect to the critical path. Double-headed arrows that do not form a link in the chain of tasks making up a critical path may be critical, but they are not on the critical path.

For the application of the rules, see Figure 8.12, which indicates the critical path for the problem just solved. Total float values are printed on the diagram,

FIGURE 8.12

TOTAL FLOAT AND THE CRITICAL
PATH

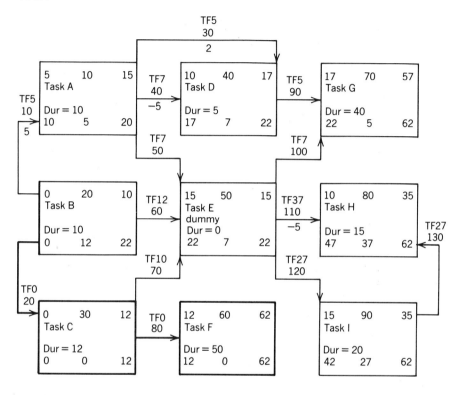

both for tasks and for relationship arrows. The float values for relationship float
are labeled TF because relationship float is a kind of total float.

A Computer Solution

Figure 8.13 is a computer solution for the project depicted by the diagram in
Figure 8.12. A listing for the computer program is shown in Appendix B. Figure
8.14 is a Gantt chart for the same project, also produced by the program in
Appendix B. Note that the Gantt chart only covers workdays 1 through 70 because
the paper is only wide enough for 80 columns. The bar chart in Figure 8.13 can

FIGURE 8.13
COMPUTER SOLUTION TO NETWORK
SHOWN IN FIGURE 8.7

SCHEDULE FOR PROJECT IN FIGURE 8.7 — EARLY START BAR CHART

PAGE NUMBER : 1

TASK#	DUR	DESCRIPTION	ES	EF	LS	LF	TF
20	20	TASK B	0	20	0	20	0
10	10	TASK A	0	10	20	30	20
40	5	TASK D	0	5	30	35	30
30	10	TASK C	5	15	20	30	15
70	10	TASK G	5	15	35	45	30
80	5	TASK H	5	10	45	50	40
50	5	TASK E	10	15	45	50	35
120	5	TASK L	10	15	55	60	45
90	15	TASK I	15	30	50	65	35
110	10	TASK K	20	30	50	60	30

60 15 TASK F

160 10 TASK P

100 25 TASK J

150 20 TASK O

140 15 TASK N

130 10 TASK M

LOGICAL RELATIONSHIPS

SEQ	ARROW#	LAG	TYPE	INODE	JNODE	TF
1	10	5	SS	40	30	15
3	30	0	SS	20	10	20
5	50	0	SS	50	60	20
7	70	0	ES	30	60	15
9	90	0	ES	40	80	40
11	110	-10	ES	60	100	0
13	130	0	ES	80	110	40
15	150	0	ES	90	130	35
17	161	0	EE	120	110	30
19	180	0	ES	110	150	30
21	190	0	ES	100	150	0
23	200	5	ES	100	140	0
25	211	0	SS	140	130	0
27	230	0	EE	140	150	0

SEQ	ARROW#	LAG	TYPE	INODE	JNODE	TF
2	20	0	SS	40	20	0
4	40	0	ES	10	50	20
6	60	10	ES	20	60	0
8	80	0	ES	40	70	30
10	100	0	ES	50	90	35
12	120	5	ES	70	110	30
14	140	0	ES	80	120	45
16	160	0	EE	110	120	30
18	170	0	ES	120	160	40
20	240	0	EE	160	150	40
22	191	0	SE	150	100	0
24	210	0	SS	130	140	0
26	220	0	EE	130	140	5
28	0	0		0	0	0

FIGURE 8.14
COMPUTER-GENERATED GANTT
CHART TO ACCOMPANY FIGURE 8.13

PAGE NUMBER: 1   SHEET NBR: 1

```
000000000000000000000000000000000000000000000000000000000000000000000
000000000011111111112222222222333333333344444444445555555555566666666667
123456789012345678901234567890123456789012345678901234567890123456789012345678901234567890
     +       +       +       +       +       +       +       +       +       +       +       +       +       +
CCCCCCCCCCCCCCCCCCCCC
     +       +       +       +       +       +       +       +       +       +       +       +       +       +
EEEEEEEEEEFFFFFFFFFFFFFFFFFFFFFF
     +       +       +       +       +       +       +       +       +       +       +       +       +       +
EEEEEFFFFFFFFFFFFFFFFFFFFFFFFFFFFFFFFFF
     +       +       +       +       +       +       +       +       +       +       +       +       +       +
  EEEEEEEEEEEFFFFFFFFFFFFFFFFFF
     +       +       +       +       +       +       +       +       +       +       +       +       +       +
  EEEEEEEEEEEFFFFFFFFFFFFFFFFFFFFFFFFFFFFFFFFFF
     +       +       +       +       +       +       +       +       +       +       +       +       +       +
EEEEEFFFFFFFFFFFFFFFFFFFFFFFFFFFFFFFFFFFFFFFFFFFFFFF
     +       +       +       +       +       +       +       +       +       +       +       +       +       +
     EEEEEFFFFFFFFFFFFFFFFFFFFFFFFFFFFFFFFFFFFFFFFF
     +       +       +       +       +       +       +       +       +       +       +       +       +       +
     EEEEEEEEEEEEEEEEEEEEEFFFFFFFFFFFFFFFFFFFFFFFFFFFFFFFFFFFF
     +       +       +       +       +       +       +       +       +       +       +       +       +       +
       EEEEEEEEEEEEEEEEEEFFFFFFFFFFFFFFFFFFFFFFFFFFFFFFFFFFFFFFFFF
     +       +       +       +       +       +       +       +       +       +       +       +       +       +
         EEEEEEEEEEEFFFFFFFFFFFFFFFFFFFFFFFFFFFFF
     +       +       +       +       +       +       +       +       +       +       +       +       +       +
                  CCCCCCCCCCCCCCC
     +       +       +       +       +       +       +       +       +       +       +       +       +       +
         EEEEEEEEEEFFFFFFFFFFFFFFFFFFFFFFFFFFFFFFFFFFFFFFFF
     +       +       +       +       +       +       +       +       +       +       +       +       +       +
                  CCCCCCCCCCCCCCCCCCCCCCCCCCC
     +       +       +       +       +       +       +       +       +       +       +       +       +       +
                                          CCCCCCCCCC
     +       +       +       +       +       +       +       +       +       +       +       +       +       +
                                          CCCCC
     +       +       +       +       +       +       +       +       +       +       +       +       +       +
                                          EEEEE
     +       +       +       +       +       +       +       +       +       +       +       +       +       +
```

be taped to the schedule in Figure 8.12. Additional sheets can be produced to contain the bar chart for the remaining duration of the project. These can be taped side by side to cover the entire project duration.

ADVANTAGES AND DISADVANTAGES OF THE PRECEDENCE METHOD

Advantages

The Precedence Method (PM) allows the scheduler to depict complex relationships between the tasks that make up a project. These relationships are particularly useful in depicting semiconcurrency between tasks. These relationships have both sequential and concurrent characteristics. Such relationships are usually more appropriate for construction scheduling than are the purely sequential relationships that are permissible between a pair of tasks in the Critical Path Method (CPM).

The PM has fewer restrictive conventions than does the CPM. It also permits the drafting of more compact logic diagrams than does the CPM.

Disadvantages

The PM is not as well established as is the CPM. Hence, there is more variation in the use of conventions than is encountered in the CPM.

The complex nature of the logical relationships permitted by the PM makes the PM network analysis more complicated than the CPM network analysis. These allowable complex logical relationships should not be depicted simply because they are available. Not only do complex relationships make manual analysis more difficult, they also slow down a solution by computer programs. The scheduler should restrict the use of double-headed arrows to the situations where this use is essential.

There are fewer commercially available computer programs based on the PM than on the CPM, and there are fewer construction practitioners who are familiar with the PM than with the CPM. However, the PM is gaining an increasing acceptance within the construction industry.

EXERCISES

EXERCISE 8.1
Make a network analysis of the complex PM diagram shown in Figure 8.7.
Figure 8.15 contains a solution for this exercise.

FIGURE 8.15

A COMPLEX PM DIAGRAM

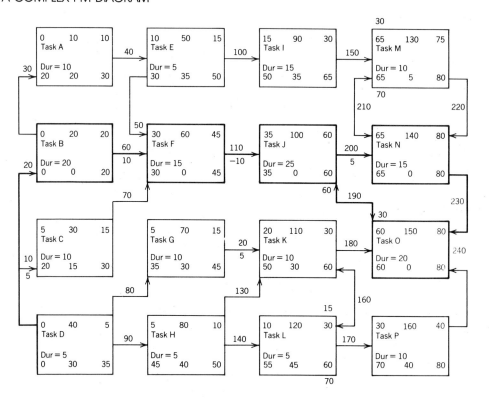

EXERCISE 8.2
Make a network analysis of the portion of a project that is depicted in Figure 8.16.

FIGURE 8.16
EXERCISE 1: PM LOGIC DIAGRAM
FOR PART OF A PROJECT

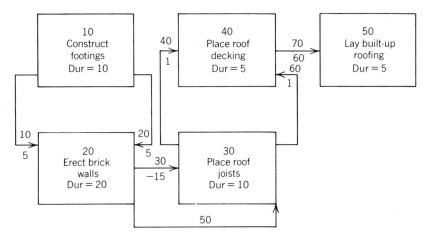

EXERCISE 8.3   A Project with Sequential/Concurrent Characteristics
Many construction projects appear to be sequential in nature. For example, road construction involves route surveying, clearing, grading, the placement of base course, paving, and final tasks such as striping the traffic lanes and installing traffic signs. Although these tasks are somewhat sequential in nature (clearing cannot start until after some surveying has been done), the tasks also have concurrent characteristics (clearing can be started before all route surveying is completed). The PM is well suited for depicting these sequential/concurrent relationships between tasks. Figure 8.17 depicts such a project. It also illustrates the compact nature of a PM diagram compared with a CPM diagram. All duration and lag values are expressed in calendar weeks. Determine the project duration.

FIGURE 8.17
EXERCISE 2: A SEQUENTIAL/
CONCURRENT PROJECT

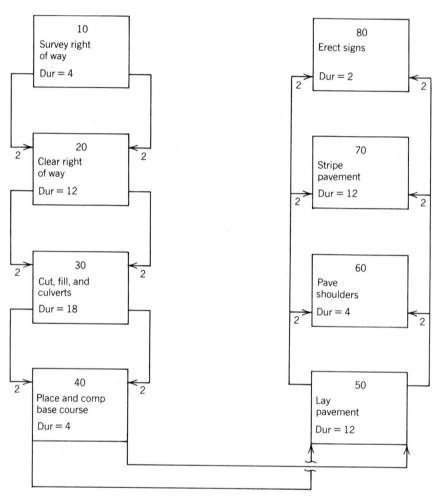

EXERCISE 8.4
Draw a logic diagram for the project that was described in Example 1 in Chapter 2. Use the same task durations that were used for Exercise 6.3; however, exploit the PM capability of depicting semiconcurrent relationships between tasks. Prepare a project schedule and a Gantt chart. Determine whether the capabilities of the PM have enabled you to schedule this project in a shorter time than was practical with the CPM.

PROGRAM EVALUATION REVIEW TECHNIQUE (PERT)

9

OBJECTIVE

The objective of this chapter is to provide an understanding of the fundamentals of the Program Evaluation Review Technique (PERT) and of the strengths and weaknesses of that technique. PERT was developed about 1958 by the US Navy and its contractors as a technique for managing the development and production of the Polaris missile system. The technique was given credit for saving about two years in the development of this weapons system, and it has enjoyed widespread usage since then. It is not widely used in the construction industry. This chapter briefly describes PERT because it is an established technique with some features that are applicable to construction management. Other techniques also contain these features in a more useful form. There have been many embellishments to the original PERT method since 1958.

It is assumed that the reader is completely familiar with the Critical Path Method (CPM) as described in Chapters 5 and 6. Many of the computational techniques and the logic diagramming techniques that are used in PERT are nearly identical to the techniques used in CPM. This chapter emphasizes the differences between PERT and CPM techniques.

INTRODUCTION TO PERT

The PERT Method shares many similarities with the Critical Path Method (CPM) and, to a lesser degree, with the Precedence Method (PM). PERT, like the

Critical Path and the Precedence Methods, is based on the analysis of logic diagrams (networks). As is true for CPM, PERT uses an Activity On Arrow (AOA) diagramming technique, meaning that arrows are used to represent tasks and nodes are used to represent events. PERT, unlike CPM and PM, was developed as an event-oriented technique, meaning that the principal objective is to compute event times. The CPM and PM are task-oriented, meaning that the principal objective is to compute task times. Nevertheless, although PERT was developed as an event-oriented method, it can be used to compute task times. The discussion of PERT in this chapter will focus on the computation of task times.

The PERT Method enables the user to estimate not only the most probable project duration but also to estimate the probability that the project, or any portion of the project, will be completed within any particular time period. Even though PERT does allow estimation of these probabilities, PERT itself is a deterministic method as defined below.

The CPM, the PM, and the PERT are all **deterministic** methods, meaning that all computed values (event times, project durations, etc.) are completely determined by the data used to compute them. Given the same logic diagram and the same task durations, there can be only one correct solution for the project duration using PERT. One scheduler could compute project duration several times, or different schedulers could compute project duration. Barring computation errors, the computed project durations would not differ. Even though PERT allows the scheduler to compute the probability that the project duration will exceed some specified value, the methods used are deterministic, and the computed probability will not vary regardless of how often the computations are repeated. A **probabilistic** method introduces chance into the computation procedures. It may seem paradoxical, but the introduction of chance may actually improve the accuracy of computed values such as project duration. This improvement results because a deterministic method usually requires the use of assumptions that will simplify the computation process. A probabilistic method permits the scheduler to dispense with some of these assumptions and, by repeating the computations several times and then averaging the results, to compute an answer that is more accurate than one that can be obtained by a deterministic method. Chapter 10 describes a probabilistic method that can be used with CPM and PM.

PERT TASK AND EVENT VALUES

The PERT Method was developed as an event-oriented method. Technically, the times that must be estimated are the times that will transpire between events.

Events are points in time that are separated by some form of activity or even inactivity. The following discussion is based on the concept that events are separated in time by tasks and that the estimated duration of these tasks represents the estimate of time between the events.

Estimates of Task Duration

With the PERT Method, three different estimates of duration are made for each task, whereas a single estimate of task duration is made with CPM and PM. The persons who developed PERT considered that the uncertainties associated with a research and development program made it infeasible to use a single estimate for the time between events. In the following sections, several symbols will be introduced. Lowercase symbols pertain to task-related values, whereas uppercase symbols pertain to event values.

Three estimates are made of the duration of each task. They are as follows:

Optimistic Estimate (t_o)**.** This is the estimated time required to complete the task if everything goes well. You may visualize the optimistic estimate as the duration that would be bettered not more than one time in 100 repetitions of the task.

Pessimistic Estimate (t_p)**.** This is the estimated time required to complete a task if nearly everything goes wrong. You may visualize the pessimistic estimate as the duration that would be bettered 99 times in 100 repetitions of the task. You should not include in your pessimistic estimate rare events such as a biblical flood, but only events that might reasonably be expected during the project duration.

Most Likely Estimate (t_m)**.** This is the length of time that will be required to accomplish the task more often than any other time if the task is repeated many times. This definition actually is an estimate of the **modal** duration. An alternative definition used by some authors is that t_m is the time required to complete the task 50% of the times that it is repeated. This second definition is an estimate of the **median** duration.

The distinction between a modal estimate and median estimate is based on the science of statistics. The distinction is not important for the purposes of construction scheduling. The most likely duration is not necessarily the average of the optimistic and the pessimistic estimates. Most schedulers can visualize more bad breaks than good breaks when they are making this estimate. Despite such pessimistic forebodings, the scheduler will usually recognize that a run of really bad breaks is not very probable; hence, the *most likely* estimate is usually closer to the optimistic estimate than it is to the pessimistic estimate.

Because all subsequent computations in the PERT Method are based on the three estimates of task duration that have just been defined, you may properly conclude that it is essential that these estimates be accurate. In fact, it is as difficult to make an accurate estimate for these three durations as it is to make an accurate single estimate of duration in the CPM and the PM. Some schedulers may "play it safe" and submit unrealistically high pessimistic estimates of task duration. Other schedulers may submit unrealistically low optimistic durations. Any estimate of task duration is of a subjective nature, based on the scheduler's assumptions as to the resources that will be available for commitment to the task and of possible contingencies that may impede the completion of the task.

Still, the idea of requiring the scheduler to submit three estimates of task duration has merit. In general, the average of three guesses as to the value of an unknown will be more accurate than a single guess. The author has tested this thesis numerous times in the classroom by requiring students to make individual estimates of a task's duration before the task had been analyzed. Although the guesses by individual students will differ widely from the duration as it is finally computed, the average of their guesses will usually be fairly close to the computed value. The author has also required individual students to make optimistic and pessimistic guesses as to a task's duration. In most instances, these students have been able to bracket the computed duration.

Effective Task Duration (t_e)

Having made the three estimates of task duration, it is then necessary to compute the effective duration for each task. The effective task duration may be thought of as an estimate of the mean (average) duration. This value, as computed by Equation 9.1, will be used in the PERT network analysis:

$$t_e = \frac{t_o + 4t_m + t_p}{6} \qquad (9.1)$$

Task Standard Deviation (d)

It is also necessary to compute for each task its standard deviation using Equation 9.2. These task standard deviations will be used to compute task variance, described below.

$$d = \frac{t_p - t_o}{6} \qquad (9.2)$$

Task Variance (*v*)

The square of a task's deviation is known as the task's variance. The values for task variance, as computed by Equation 9.3, will be used to compute event variance:

$$v = d^2 \tag{9.3}$$

Event Variance (*V*)

The variance for an event is equal to the sum of the task variances for critical tasks that are precedent to that event. The event variance is used to compute the event deviation:

$$V = \Sigma v_{cp} \tag{9.4}$$

where v_{cp} is the task variance of the critical tasks precedent to the event.

Event Deviation (*D*)

The event deviation is equal to the square root of the event variance. It is used to compute the probability that an actual event time will be larger or smaller than some specified value:

$$D = \sqrt{V} \tag{9.5}$$

NORMAL DISTRIBUTION

Normal Distribution Concept

Many natural phenomena (the PERT Method assumes that task durations are among such phenomena) have values that are normally distributed, meaning that the values associated with such phenomena vary in a normal and predictable manner and in accordance with the "normal distribution equation." For example, assume that the average time for a mason to complete the task of laying 1000 face bricks, using first-class worksmanship, is 20 hours. An expert mason working under optimum conditions may be able to complete the task in only 10 hours, whereas a less expert mason working under unfavorable conditions may require

30 hours to complete the task. It is conceivable that some super-expert masons working under very favorable conditions might be able to lay 1000 bricks in less than 10 hours, and it is also conceivable that some really poor masons working under very unfavorable conditions may require more than 30 hours to do the job. However, it is very unlikely that the actual time required will be outside the range of 10 to 30 hours.

If one were to test a large number of masons under various conditions, the actual recorded times to lay 1000 bricks would tend to cluster around the average time of 20 hours, with only a few times being near the extreme high and low limits of 30 and 10 hours, respectively. There are a number of ways in which these recorded times might be distributed around the central value of 20 hours, the normal distribution being only one of those ways. A curve, often called a **bell-shaped curve**, can be used to represent the normal distribution. Numerous statistical tables and statistical formulas are available that will enable the user to determine the values associated with this type of distribution; hence, it is very convenient to assume that task durations will vary in accordance with the normal distribution equation.

One can visualize a number of circumstances in which the values for task durations would not be normally distributed. For example, a labor union might prohibit a mason from laying more than 500 bricks a day, and a contractor might discharge any mason who lays less than 500 bricks a day. In such an instance, nearly all masons would lay exactly 500 bricks a day. As a less extreme example, a contractor might be required to comply with equal opportunity laws by hiring as masons a substantial number of women and minorities, even though these new employees had little or no working experience as masons. Until the new employees gained experience, the durations for the new employees would be expected to cluster around one average, while the durations for the experienced employees would cluster around a different and higher average. This type of distribution is termed a **bimodal distribution**.

Frequency Distribution Analysis

Assume that a task was repeated a large number of times, say, 50 times, and that its duration was recorded each time. The actual durations varied from less than 6 days to more than 10 days. Table 9.1 contains the data that might have been recorded. Note that the data in Table 9.1 are organized so that the number of occurrences has been recorded for equal intervals of time, in this case of one day's length. If the range of project durations had been larger, it might have been convenient to use a larger interval, say, 2 or 3 days.

The data in Table 9.1 have been used to construct the **frequency distribution histogram** in Figure 9.1. The number of occurrences in each interval is expressed

TABLE 9.1

NUMBER OF OCCURENCES IN 100 INSTANCES

Task Duration, Days	Number of Occurrences	Percent Occurrences
5–5.99	1	2
6–6.99	7	14
7–7.99	17	34
8–8.99	17	34
9–9.99	7	14
10–10.99	1	2
Total	50	100

as the percent of total occurrences. The total area enclosed by the histogram is 100%.

In Figure 9.2 a **normal distribution curve (bell-shaped curve)** has been superimposed on the frequency distribution histogram of Figure 9.1. Statisticians would say that the normal curve encloses a unit area if the values of the ordinates are expressed as decimal fractions and if the abscissas are expressed as standard deviations. For the purposes of this discussion, we will specify that the area enclosed by the normal curve has a value of 100%, the same area that was enclosed by the frequency distribution histogram. The width of the normal curve is infinite; however, 99.5% of its area will be enclosed within the range of −3 and +3 standard deviations. A standard deviation is one-sixth of the base of that part of a bell-shaped curve that encloses 99.5% of the area beneath the curve.

Figure 9.3 is the normal distribution curve with the frequency distribution

FIGURE 9.1

FREQUENCY DISTRIBUTION
HISTOGRAM

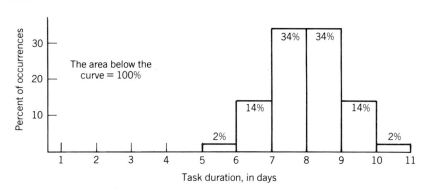

Task duration, in days

FIGURE 9.2

NORMAL CURVE SUPERIMPOSED ON
FREQUENCY DISTRIBUTION
HISTOGRAM

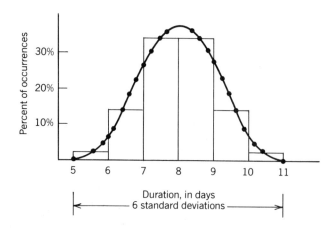

histogram deleted. Note that the *total area under the curve* is assumed to be 100%, very close to the actual area of 99.5%. If the total area of the curve is divided into six subareas by equally spaced vertical lines, then the area of each subarea will be as shown in Figure 9.3. Figure 9.4 also shows the normal curve; however, the task duration values have been printed beneath the values for standard deviations. The probability of completing the task in a specified time or less is equal to the area below the curve and to the left of a vertical line

FIGURE 9.3

AREAS ENCLOSED BY NORMAL
CURVE AND STANDARD DEVIATIONS

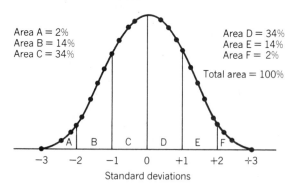

FIGURE 9.4
TASK DURATIONS COMPARED TO
STANDARD DEVIATIONS FROM MEAN

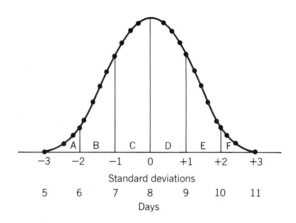

passing through that time. The probability of it taking more than a specified time to complete a task is the area below the curve and to the right of the vertical line. The area enclosed by the curve and the horizontal baseline is 100%. About 68% of the area is between −1 and +1 standard deviations, about 95% is between −2 and +2 standard deviations, and about 100% is between −3 and +3 standard deviations.

Table 9.2 indicates the area enclosed by the curve, the baseline, a vertical line drawn through zero standard deviation, and a vertical line drawn through the specified standard devitation. Note that the areas are rounded off to whole percentages, sufficiently precise for construction scheduling purposes. Also note

TABLE 9.2
AREA BETWEEN NORMAL CURVE, X-AXIS, AND Y-AXIS

Standard Deviation	Area, %	Standard Deviation	Area, %	Standard Deviation	Area, %
0.0	0	1.0	34	2.0	48
0.1	4	1.1	36	2.1	48
0.2	8	1.2	38	2.2	49
0.3	12	1.3	40	2.3	49
0.4	16	1.4	42	2.4	49
0.5	19	1.5	43	2.5	49
0.6	23	1.6	45	2.6	50
0.7	26	1.7	46	—	—
0.8	29	1.8	46		
0.9	32	1.9	47	3.0	50

that the area enclosed by vertical lines drawn through any standard deviation between 2.6 and 3.0 is equal to 50%.

The following examples illustrate how Table 9.2 is used to compute probabilities. The areas under the curve are expressed as probability percentages.

The area under the normal curve and to the left of a vertical line drawn through zero standard deviation is 50%. Likewise, the area under the curve and to the right of that same vertical line is also 50%. From Table 9.2, we can determine the area enclosed by the normal curve, a vertical line drawn through zero standard deviation, and a second vertical line drawn through any other standard deviation. For example, the enclosed area is 34% if the second vertical line is drawn through one standard deviation. Table 9.2 is used regardless of whether the second vertical line is drawn through $+1$ standard deviation or -1 standard deviation.

Knowing that the area enclosed by the curve and vertical lines drawn through zero and one standard deviation is 34%, we can determine the area to the left of the second vertical line. If that second vertical line is drawn through -1 standard deviation, then the area to its left is $50\% - 34\% = 16\%$. Figure 9.5 illustrates this calculation. However, if the second vertical line is drawn through $+1$ standard deviation, then the area to its left is $50\% + 34\% = 84\%$.

The area to the left of a vertical line drawn through -0.5 standard deviation is $50\% - 19\% = 31\%$. The area to the left of a vertical line drawn through $+1.7$ standard deviations is $50\% + 46\% = 96\%$.

The above examples are meant to illustrate the use of the data in Table 9.2. Table 9.2 will actually be used to calculate the probability of events occurring at specified times.

FIGURE 9.5
PROBABILITY AS FUNCTION OF AREA
ENCLOSED

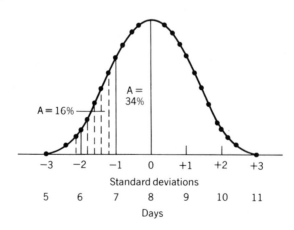

THE PERT NETWORK AND COMPUTATION OF EVENT TIMES

Example 1   Calculate Event Times and Event Probabilities

This problem focuses on computing event times and the probability of attaining events at specified times. A subsequent example focuses on task times. The procedures used in this example are also used for the next example.

Diagramming the Project and Computing Task and Event Values

Construct the Logic Diagram. Draw the PERT network diagram, using the same diagramming techniques and conventions that were used for drawing CPM diagrams. List the optimistic, most likely, and pessimistic estimates for task durations. Figure 9.6 contains the logic diagram with estimated task durations for this problem.

Compute Effective Task Durations and Task Standard Deviations. Using Equations 9.1 and 9.2, calculate the effective task durations and standard deviations. The values for t_e and d are shown in Figure 9.7. The values for t_o, t_m, and t_p will not be used in subsequent calculations, so they have been deleted from the diagram in Figure 9.7.

The Forward Pass for *Te*. The symbol *Te* is equivalent to **EET** used in the Critical Path Method. T_e is used for the PERT early event time to be consistent with terminology used in other books covering PERT. Make a forward pass through the network, just as you did for CPM, and calculate the early event

---

FIGURE 9.6
PERT DIAGRAM WITH THREE
ESTIMATED DURATIONS PER TASK

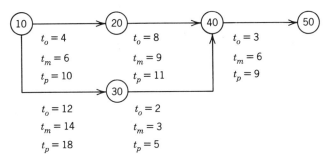

FIGURE 9.7
PERT DIAGRAM WITH TASKS'
EFECTIVE DURATIONS AND
STANDARD DEVIATIONS

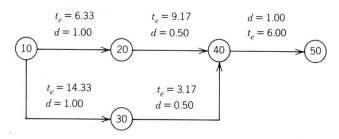

times (T_e's), using the values of t_e for task durations. The T_e's are enclosed in parentheses in Figure 9.8. In making the forward pass, more than one trial value may be computed for the early event time of an event. Along the path [20]–[40], the trial value for T_e [40] is $6.33 + 9.17 = 15.5$. Along the path [30]–[40], the trial value is $14.33 + 3.17 = 17.5$. Select the largest trial value as T_e [40], or 17.5 days.

Project Duration. The largest value that has been computed for any T_e is the most likely project duration, in this case, 23.5 days. There is a 50% probability that the project can be computed in this time or less.

Backward Pass for T_l. The symbol T_l has the same meaning as **LET** in CPM. Make a backward pass through the network and calculate the late event times (T_l's). During the backward pass, several trial values may be computed for the Late Event Time. Along the path [30]–[10], the trial value for T_l [10] = 14.33 − 14.33, or zero. Along the path [20]–[10], the trial value is $8.33 − 6.33$, or

FIGURE 9.8
PERT DIAGRAM WITH EARLY EVENT
TIMES

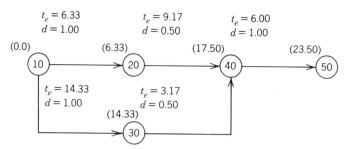

FIGURE 9.9
PERT DIAGRAM WITH LATE EVENT
TIMES

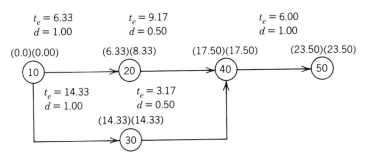

2.00. Choose the smaller value. If the late event time of the initial node is not equal to zero, you have made an error. Figure 9.9 shows the Late Event Times.

The Critical Path, Event Slack Time, and Task Float. Any node for which $T_e = T_l$ is on the critical path and has zero slack time. Event slack time **(Ts)** is equal to T_l less T_e. Event slack time for event E may be computed by Equation 9.6. The only event having slack time in Figure 9.10 is the event represented by node [20]. Its slack time is $8.33 - 6.33$ or 2.00 days. Task total float **(TF)** is equal to T_l at the head (J-node end) of the task arrow less T_e at the tail (I-node end) of the arrow less the task's effective duration t_e. Total float for task N may be computed by Equation 9.7. A task having a zero total float is on the critical path. The total floats for the noncritical tasks are labeled in Figure 9.10, and the critical path has been emphasized. Event slack time is analogous to task total float. It is an indication of how critical it is to attain an event at some specified time. The estimated median project duration is 23.50 days, that is,

FIGURE 9.10
PERT DIAGRAM WITH CRITICAL PATH
OUTLINED

$t_e = 6.33$ $t_e = 9.17$ $t_e = 6.00$
$d = 1.00$ $d = 0.50$ $d = 1.00$

(0.0)(0.00)   (6.33)(8.33)   (17.50)(17.50)   (23.50)(23.50)

(10) $TF = 2.0$ → (20) $TF = 2$ → (40) $TF = 0$ → (50)

$t_e = 14.33$ $t_e = 3.17$
$d = 1.00$ $d = 0.50$

(14.33)(14.33)

$TF = 0$ → (30) $TF = 0$

there is a 50% probability that the project will be completed in 23.50 days or less.

$$T_s(E) = T_l(E) - T_e(E) \tag{9.6}$$

$$TF(N) = T_l(J) - T_e(I) - t_e(N) \tag{9.7}$$

Probability Analysis for Example 1

Compute the probability that some event along the critical path will be attained at some specified scheduled time (T_x). For example, find the probability that event [40] will be attained in 16.0 days, as opposed to its early event time (T_e) of 17.5 days.

Find the Event Variance (V). The event variance $V(40)$ is equal to the sum of the task variances (v) of all precedent tasks along the critical path. Recall that task variance is equal to the square of the task's standard deviation. The event variance $V(40)$ in this case is $\Sigma\ 1^2 + 0.5^2 = 1.25$.

Find the Event Standard Deviation (D). The square root of the event variance is the event's standard deviation. The event standard deviation $D(40)$ is $\sqrt{1.25}$, or 1.1 days.

Find the Difference Between the Specified Time (Tx) and the Early Event Time (Z). The symbol Z represents the time difference between a specified time (T_x) and an early event time (T_e) with time expressed in event standard deviations. The value of Z for event E may be computed by Equation 9.8. In this example, the value of Z is $(16.0 - 17.5)/1.1$, or -1.4 standard deviations.

$$Z(E) = \frac{(T_x - T_e)}{D} \tag{9.8}$$

Find the Area and the Probability. Using the table of standard deviations presented in a previous section, find the area equivalent to $Z = -1.4$. In this case, that area is 42%. The probability of attaining event [40] in 16 or less days is $50\% - 42\% = 8\%$.

IMPACT OF NONCRITICAL PATHS ON PROJECT DURATION

Example 2

The preceding example illustrates the procedure for computing event times and the probability that an event would be attained at a specified time. The calcu-

TABLE 9.3
TABULATION OF TASK DATA FOR EXAMPLE 2

Task	I-Node	J-Node	t_o	t_m	t_p	t_e	d
Construct wall footings	2	4	10	15	20	15.00	1.67
Construct column footings	2	6	25	30	40	30.83	2.50
Dummy task	4	8	0	0	0	0.00	0.00
Erect walls	4	10	20	30	40	30.00	3.33
Dummy task	6	8	0	0	0	0.00	0.00
Erect columns	6	10	10	15	25	15.83	2.50
Pour roof slab	10	12	20	25	35	25.83	2.50
Pour floor slab	8	12	10	15	20	15.00	1.67

lations are based only on data for tasks on the critical path. This example illustrates the effect of noncritical tasks on project duration and event times.

The PERT Logic Diagram for Example 2
A phase of a construction project contains six real tasks. Optimistic, median, and pessimistic estimates of task duration have been made for each task. The tasks are described in Table 9.3, which also shows the computed values for each task's effective duration and task deviation. Figure 9.11 is the CPM logic diagram for the task. The forward pass and the backward pass have been made so as to compute event times. The values for the early event times and the late event times (T_e and T_l) appear in the parentheses above the nodes.

Project Duration and Critical Path. The computed median project duration is 72.5 days, meaning that there is a 50% probability that the actual duration will

FIGURE 9.11
PERT DIAGRAM FOR EXAMPLE 2

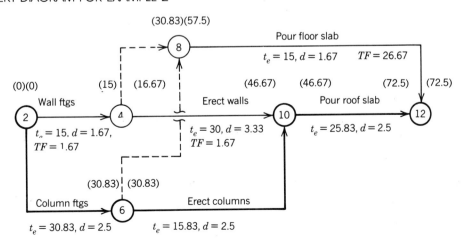

be 72.5 days or less. The critical path has been outlined. The critical path passes through nodes [2], [6], [10], and [12].

Computing Probabilities for Other Project Durations. Compute the probability that the project can be completed in 70 days or less.

Find the Event Variance for the Terminal Event. Sum the task variances along the critical path to obtain the event variance for the terminal event (project completion). This event variance is $2.5^2 + 2.5^2 + 2.5^2 = 18.75$.

Find the Event Standard Deviation. The event standard deviation for the terminal node is $\sqrt{18.75} = 4.33$ days.

Find the Value of Z. Determine how many event standard deviations the specified event time for event [12], 70 days, would differ from the most likely event time, 72.5 days. Z has the value: $(70 - 72.5) / 4.33$, or 0.6 standard deviation.

Find the Probability of Occurrence. Determine the probability that the event time of node [12] will be 0.6 standard deviation less than its most likely time. From Table 9.2, the corresponding area between vertical lines through $Z = 0.00$ and $Z = 0.64$ is about 23%. The probability that the project will be completed in 70 days is $50\% - 23\% = 27\%$.

Effect of Noncritical Tasks on Expected Project Duration. Note that the most likely project duration of 72.5 days for this project was based entirely on the effective durations of the tasks along the critical path. The two tasks along the path [2]–[4]–[10] are not critical; they both have slack times equal to $46.67 - 30 - 15$ or 1.67 days. Even though these two tasks are not critical, there is some chance that their actual durations may exceed the effective durations of the critical tasks along the path [2]–[6]–[10]. Compute the probability that the event time of node [10] will be greater when based on these noncritical tasks than it was based on the critical tasks. T_e for node [12] based on these noncritical tasks is $15 + 30 = 45$ days. For these two noncritical tasks to become critical, their combined actual durations would have to become 46.67 days, or 1.67 days more than the sum of their most likely durations. The sum of their variances is $1.67^2 + 3.33^2$, or 13.87. Hence, the event deviation based on the noncritical tasks would be the square root of that value, or 3.72 days. The value for Z is $1.67/3.72$, or 0.5 standard deviation. From Table 9.2, there is a $50\% + 19\%$, or 69%, chance that their combined durations would be 46.67 days or less. There is a $100\% - 69\%$, or 31%, chance that their combined durations will be more than 46.67 days. The actual probability that the event time for node [10] will be equal or less than 46.67 days is $0.50 \times 0.69 = 0.35$, or 35% rather than 50%. The effect of ignoring noncritical, but nearly critical, tasks is to compute an overly optimistic estimate of event times. Because the task along the path [8]–[12] is not even close to being critical, ignoring its effect will have little impact on the computed most likely project duration.

PERT TASK TIMES BY
COMPUTER SCHEDULING

Example 3

This example illustrates the calculation of task times by the PERT Method. It features a development project for a condominium complex. Although there is some uncertainty concerning how much time will be required to design and build the structures, there is a great deal more uncertainty concerning the time that will be required to sell the condominium units. The complex will be constructed in three phases. Construction of the second and third phases will not commence until 75% of the condominium units in the preceding phase have been sold. The diagram in Figure 9.12 represents the project. It shows optimistic, most likely, and pessimistic estimates of task duration. The problem has been solved using

FIGURE 9.12

PERT DIAGRAM FOR CONDOMINIUM
PROJECT

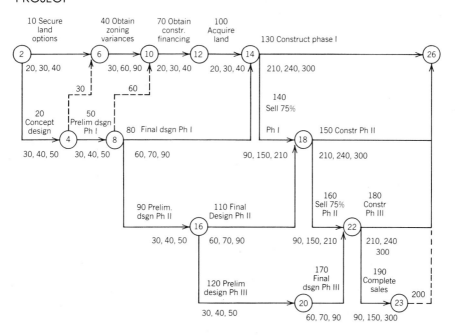

FIGURE 9.13
COMPUTER SOLUTION FOR
CONDOMINIUM PROJECT SCHEDULE

Schedule for Condominium Project.

TSK#	I-#	J-#	DURATIONS					ES	EF	LS	LF	TF	FF
			OPT.	MED.	PESS.	EFF.	DEV.						
10	2	6	20.0	30.0	40.0	30.0	3.3	0.0	30.0	10.0	40.0	10.0	10.0
			Secure Land Options										
20	2	4	30.0	40.0	50.0	40.0	3.3	0.0	40.0	0.0	40.0	0.0	0.0
			Concept Design										
30	4	6	0.0	0.0	0.0	0.0	0.0						
			Dummy										
40	6	10	30.0	60.0	90.0	60.0	10.0	40.0	100.0	40.0	100.0	0.0	0.0
			Obtain Zoning Variances										
50	4	8	30.0	40.0	50.0	40.0	3.3	40.0	80.0	48.3	88.3	8.3	0.0
			Prelim Design Ph I										
60	8	10	0.0	0.0	0.0	0.0	0.0						
			Dummy										
70	10	12	20.0	30.0	40.0	30.0	3.3	100.0	130.0	100.0	130.0	0.0	0.0
			Obtain Construction Loan										

	i	j	Description	a	m	b	t_e							
80	8	14	Final Design Ph I	60.0	70.0	90.0	71.7	5.0	80.0	151.7	88.3	160.0	8.3	8.3
90	8	16	Prelim Design Ph II	30.0	40.0	50.0	40.0	3.3	80.0	120.0	198.3	238.3	118.3	0.0
100	12	14	Acquire Land	20.0	30.0	40.0	30.0	3.3	130.0	160.0	130.0	160.0	0.0	0.0
110	16	18	Final Design Ph II	60.0	70.0	90.0	71.7	5.0	120.0	191.7	238.3	310.0	118.3	118.3
120	16	20	Prelim Design Ph III	30.0	40.0	50.0	40.0	3.3	120.0	160.0	348.3	388.3	228.3	0.0
130	14	26	Construct Ph I	210.0	240.0	300.0	245.0	15.0	160.0	405.0	460.0	705.0	300.0	300.0
140	14	18	Sell 75% Ph I	90.0	150.0	210.0	150.0	20.0	160.0	310.0	160.0	310.0	0.0	0.0
150	18	26	Construct Ph II	210.0	240.0	300.0	245.0	15.0	310.0	555.0	460.0	705.0	150.0	150.0
160	18	22	Sell 75% Ph II	90.0	150.0	210.0	150.0	20.0	310.0	460.0	310.0	460.0	0.0	0.0
170	20	22	Final Design Ph III	60.0	70.0	90.0	71.7	5.0	160.0	231.7	388.3	460.0	228.3	228.3
180	22	26	Construct Ph III	210.0	240.0	300.0	245.0	15.0	460.0	705.0	460.0	705.0	0.0	0.0
190	22	23	Complete Sales	90.0	150.0	300.0	165.0	35.0	460.0	625.0	540.0	705.0	80.0	0.0
200	23	26	Dummy	0.0	0.0	0.0	0.0	0.0	0.0	0.0	0.0	0.0	0.0	0.0

a PERT computer program, a BASIC listing of which may be found in Appendix B. All estimated task durations are in calendar days.

The PERT Project Schedule. Figure 9.13 is a computer-generated schedule for the above project. Note that the optimistic, median, and pessimistic estimates of task duration have been used to compute effect (mean) task durations and task deviations, which are included in the printout. Task times are also computed and printed on the schedule. There is a 50% probability that the project will be completed within 705 calendar days.

Probability Analysis by Computer. Figure 9.14 is a probability analysis generated by the PERT computer program. The program enables users to determine the event times that have a 0%, 5%, 10%, 15%, and so forth, probability of occurrence for any specified node. For this project, there is a 0% probability that the project can be completed in 603 workdays or less. There is a 100% probability that the project can be completed in 807 days or less. Both of these probabilities were computed on the basis of the variances of the precedent tasks.

FIGURE 9.14
COMPUTER SOLUTION FOR
DETERMINATION OF EVENT
PROBABILITIES

```
PROBABILITY OF EVENT OCCURENCE BY SPECIFIED TIMES ALONG SPECIFIED PATHS
NODE NUMBER:      26
TASK#     20 TASK VARIANCE=  11.1 CUMULATIVE VARIANCE=   11.1
TASK#     40 TASK VARIANCE=100.0 CUMULATIVE VARIANCE=  111.1
TASK#     70 TASK VARIANCE=  11.1 CUMULATIVE VARIANCE=  122.2
TASK#    100 TASK VARIANCE=  11.1 CUMULATIVE VARIANCE=  133.3
TASK#    140 TASK VARIANCE=400.0 CUMULATIVE VARIANCE=  533.3
TASK#    160 TASK VARIANCE=400.0 CUMULATIVE VARIANCE=  933.3
TASK#    180 TASK VARIANCE=225.0 CUMULATIVE VARIANCE=1158.3
   WORK DAYS ROUNDED OFF TO NEAREST WHOLE NUMBER
   603 649 661 670 676 682 687 696 705 714 723 728 734 740 749 761 807
    0%   5% 10% 15% 20% 25% 30% 40% 50% 60% 70% 75% 80% 85% 90% 95%100%
PROBABILITY OF EVENT OCCURENCE BY SPECIFIED DAY




PROBABILITY OF EVENT OCCURENCE BY SPECIFIED TIMES ALONG SPECIFIED PATHS
NODE NUMBER:      14
TASK#     20 TASK VARIANCE=  11.1 CUMULATIVE VARIANCE=   11.1
TASK#     30 TASK VARIANCE=   0.0 CUMULATIVE VARIANCE=   11.1
TASK#     40 TASK VARIANCE=100.0 CUMULATIVE VARIANCE=  111.1
TASK#     70 TASK VARIANCE=  11.1 CUMULATIVE VARIANCE=  122.2
TASK#    100 TASK VARIANCE=  11.1 CUMULATIVE VARIANCE=  133.3
   WORK DAYS ROUNDED OFF TO NEAREST WHOLE NUMBER
   125 141 145 148 150 152 154 157 160 163 166 168 170 172 175 179 195
    0%   5% 10% 15% 20% 25% 30% 40% 50% 60% 70% 75% 80% 85% 90% 95%100%
PROBABILITY OF EVENT OCCURENCE BY SPECIFIED DAY
```

Of course, these probabilities are determined (this is a deterministic method) on the basis of the three estimates of task duration for each task. In fact, the project may never be completed if sales do not meet the developer's expectations.

Critical Tasks Considered. The probability analysis for project duration was based on considering all the critical tasks on the critical path leading to the terminal node. Actually, this program allows the user to consider variances along any path he or she desires.

Task Times. The user could also determine probabilities of other matters of interest. For example, when purchasing the options to buy land, the developer would specify the expiration date of an option. In that case he would determine the date at which there was a 100% probability that land acquisition could be completed. A probability analysis indicates that there is a 100% probability that all land will be acquired by the end of the 195th day, so land options should not expire before the end of the 195th day. Note that the probability analysis was based on the most critical tasks precedent to the event in question, the completion of land acquisition.

ADVANTAGES AND DISADVANTAGES OF THE PERT METHOD

Advantages of the PERT Method

The method does permit calculation of the probability of completing the project at specified times, a feature not present in the Critical Path and Precedence Methods. PERT has been used and developed for many years. A substantial amount of computer software is available for solving problems based on the PERT Method.

Disadvantages

The PERT Method, like the CPM and PM, yields results that are entirely dependent on the accuracy of the estimates of task duration. A theoretical deficiency of the PERT Method is that computed values of early event times, and of probabilities for attainment of events at specified times, are based solely on the durations of tasks that are on the critical path. If the network contains several concurrent critical or nearly critical paths, then the PERT Method will yield results for these event times that will be too optimistic. The mathematical computations required for the PERT Method are not complex, but they are so tedious as to make the use of the method impractical for manual solution of any but the smallest project networks.

PROBABILISTIC SCHEDULING (MONTE CARLO METHOD)

10

OBJECTIVES

The objectives of this chapter are to discuss probabilistic scheduling in general; to describe a particular probabilistic scheduling method—the Monte Carlo Method; to describe the circumstances in which a probabilistic method should be considered for construction scheduling purposes; and to compare the Monte Carlo Method with the PERT Method.

It is assumed that the reader is familiar with the CPM, the PM, and the PERT scheduling method which are described in Chapters 5 to 9. PERT is used to analyze projects that have been diagrammed using Activity On Arrow (AOA) notation. A computer program, **AOAPERT**, will be introduced in this chapter that is useful for analyzing projects diagrammed using AOA notation by probabilistic methods. It will also analyze projects using the PERT techniques covered in Chapter 9. A second program, **AONPERT**, is introduced that will analyze projects diagrammed using Activity On Node (AON) techniques. This second program uses the deterministic PERT approach and a probabilistic approach for projects diagrammed by the AON technique used for the Precedence Method (PM). For the purposes of this chapter, the term PERT is used to refer to both the AOA and the AON versions of the method. The acronyms AOAPERT and AONPERT are used to specify the two versions of the method when such a distinction is necessary. The Monte Carlo Method has some similarities to these PERT Methods, although the PERT Methods are not themselves probabilistic methods. In some instances, the Monte Carlo Method will result in more reliable schedules than will the PERT Methods.

OVERVIEW OF THE MONTE CARLO METHOD

The Monte Carlo Method may be used for analyzing logic diagrams that have been drawn using either the AOA or the AON notation.

Reasons for Using the Monte Carlo Technique

The scheduler will usually choose the CPM or PM when there is little uncertainty concerning task durations. If there is uncertainty about task durations, the scheduler may use PERT to estimate the probability of completing projects at specified times. If certain other conditions exist, namely, multiple critical or nearly critical paths through the project's logic diagram, the scheduler may decide to use the probabilistic methods discussed in this chapter.

Uncertainty

The Monte Carlo technique should be used only if there is uncertainty concerning task durations and, in the case of AON diagrams, relationship lags. Use of the technique is so time consuming that all but the most trivial schedules must be analyzed by a computer, and considerable time is required even for a computer solution. Later sections of this chapter illustrate the amount of effort required to make a Monte Carlo analysis. If the schedulers are confident that their estimated task durations will be very close to the actual times that will be required to accomplish the tasks, then they should use the Critical Path Method or the Precedence Method. In nearly all instances, there will be some uncertainty concerning task durations and relationship lags. Uncertainty is covered in more detail later in this chapter.

When there is uncertainty about task durations and about relationship lags, there will necessarily be uncertainty about the computed values for event times and task times. The deterministic PERT Methods (AOAPERT and AONPERT) can be used to compute the probability that any of these computed times will have specified values. For example, the PERT Methods might enable the scheduler to estimate that there is a 90% probability that a task can be completed in 180 days or less. If there were no uncertainty about task durations, then either the CPM or the PM would enable the scheduler to state that the project will be completed in some specified time.

Multiple Critical Paths

In both the PERT Methods (AOAPERT and AONPERT), a critical path through the network can be computed, with this path passing through various nodes and arrows on the logic diagram. The path can fork into several parallel critical paths. Furthermore, there can be other paths through the diagram that are nearly critical, that is, the nodes and the arrows on those paths have very low total floats. The existence of multiple critical, or nearly critical, paths through the network is an indication that the probabilistic Monte Carlo Method should be used rather than the deterministic PERT Methods. The latter require very little more computational effort than the CPM and the PM, and they can yield solutions to scheduling problems that are nearly as accurate as those that can be produced by the Monte Carlo Method. However, both the deterministic AOAPERT and AONPERT Methods will result in overly optimistic estimates of project duration and of task and event times if the logic diagram contains multiple critical or nearly critical paths.

A Brief Description of the Monte Carlo Method

The method requires that the network diagram be analyzed numerous times. Each such analysis is termed a **run**. The results of each run are stored in computer memory or are recorded in the case of manual analyses. The results can include event times (for AOA diagrams) or task times (for AOA and AON diagrams); however, microcomputer memory capacity may preclude storing all the results if the analysis is to be repeated many times. The stored data are then analyzed to determine average and median event and task times and to determine the frequency distribution of such times.

For example, a network diagram might be analyzed 100 times to determine project duration. The average computed project duration might be 180 days. The smallest project duration found during these 100 runs might have been 150 days and the largest duration might have been 220 days. The scheduler could then conclude that there is nearly a 100% probability that the actual project duration will be somewhere in the range of 150 to 220 days. If only 10 of the computed project durations are greater than 195 days, then the scheduler could conclude that there is a 90% probability that the actual project duration will not exceed 195 days. The scheduler will have more confidence in the Monte Carlo solution if he or she has made many runs (say, 1000) than if he or she has made only a few runs (say, 10). However, the computational effort required for a Monte Carlo analysis is proportional to the number of runs, so the scheduler will generally make only 25 to 100 runs. The results produced will vary in successive runs because effective task durations and effective relationship lags (for AON diagrams) will be recomputed for each run with some random variation in these values.

The effective values for task durations and for relationship lags will be based on the scheduler's estimates of optimistic, central, and pessimistic values for durations and lags. However, the effective value is also based on chance, usually on a random number. It may seem that the use of chance as an element of the analysis is illogical; however, the use of chance is an essential element of the Monte Carlo Method. The use of chance is a guarantee that the scheduler will not unconsciously introduce bias into the computations.

ESSENTIAL TERMS

The following terms are used in this chapter. The reader should study them now and refer to them again when they are discussed later in the text.

Deterministic Procedure

In this procedure, the results are completely dependent on the input data. If the same procedure is repeated numerous times, the results will always be the same. The CPM, the PM, and the PERT Method are all deterministic. Given the same input data (logical relationships between tasks and task durations), the results (event times, task times, and probability of event occurrence at particular times) will always be the same.

Probabilistic Procedure

In this procedure, chance is introduced into the computation of the results. Chance is introduced into the Monte Carlo analysis by using random numbers to compute some of the time values that will be used in analyzing the project network diagram.

Random Numbers

Random numbers are numbers that can be obtained from a table of random numbers or numbers generated by a computer program. The numbers that are listed in such a table will range between a lower limit and an upper limit, say, zero to 100. Although each number within this range is represented an equal number of times, there is no pattern to the location of the numbers within the table. Numbers are extracted from these tables by entering them at any point and by using the numbers as they are printed. The user should not skip over any of the printed numbers. Appendix C contains a list of random numbers.

Estimated and Computed Time Values

The definitions that follow apply to projects that have been diagrammed by using either AOA or AON notation. Although some of the definitions are phrased so that they pertain to task durations, they can also be applied to relationship lags.

Optimistic Estimate of Task Duration (t_o)

These estimates apply with both AOA and AON procedures. They are the durations the scheduler believes would not be bettered more than one time in 100 repetitions of a task. See page 201 for a further discussion of this term.

Pessimistic Estimate of Task Duration (t_p)

These estimates apply with both AOA and AON procedures. They are the durations the scheduler believes could be bettered 99 times in 100 repetitions of the task. See page 201 for a further discussion of this term.

Central Value Estimate of Task Duration (t_c)

These estimates apply with both AOA and AON procedures. The value of the estimates will be somewhere between the optimistic and the pessimistic estimates of task duration. The central value estimate is not necessarily the average of the optimistic and the pessimistic estimates, although it will usually be approximately equal to that average. The meaning the scheduler places on this term will determine its value. The section on page 201 covers this term in more detail.

Effective Task Duration (t_e)

This is a computed duration for each task that will be used during the Monte Carlo analysis. Random numbers are used in computing this value. It will usually have a value that is close to the central value estimate, but it may range anywhere from the optimistic to the pessimistic duration. The Monte Carlo Method involves making the network analysis numerous times, with each analysis termed a run. The effective duration of a task will change from run to run. The term **effective duration** is also used in the deterministic PERT Methods. Effective durations for use in the PERT Methods are computed deterministically, that is, without the introduction of chance.

Estimated Relationship Lags (L)

This term is applicable only for projects diagrammed using AON notation. The Precedence Method requires the assignment of a lag value for each relationship arrow. When making a Monte Carlo analysis of an AON diagram, three estimates must be made of the lag value, an **optimistic estimate (L_o)**, a **central estimate (L_c)**, and a **pessimistic estimate (L_p)**. These values may be zero, positive, or negative. From these values, and using random numbers, **effective values of lag (L_e)** may be computed. The effective values will change from run to run.

Frequency Distribution of Time Values

The scheduler must make three estimates of the duration for each task and, for the AON method, the relationship lags. The scheduler must also assume a frequency distribution for these values. The actual task durations will be between the pessimistic and the optimistic values and will tend to cluster around the estimated central value estimates. The scheduler can make many different assumptions as to how the time values will be distributed.

Three commonly used assumptions are described below and are illustrated in Figures 10.1 to 10.3. Although the assumptions are described in the context of task durations, exactly the same assumptions can be made concerning relationship lags for AON diagrams. During the Monte Carlo analysis, an effective value for task duration will be computed for each task for each run, with that effective value being computed on the basis of the three estimated durations, of the assumed distribution, and of a random number between zero and 100. In each of the three figures, an effective duration has been computed on the basis that the random number was 16, meaning that there is a 16% probability that the actual duration will be equal or less than the computed effective duration.

Normal Distribution

This assumption was used for the PERT Method. The scheduler makes estimates for the optimistic, the central, and the pessimistic durations. The central estimate could be of the mean, of the median, or of the modal value. A mean value is an average value. It is not necessarily the average of the optimistic and the pessimistic values. Rather, it is the average of the durations that would occur if the task were to be repeated a large number of times. The median value is that time which would be exceeded 50% of the time if the task were repeated a large number of times. The modal value is that time which would be required more frequently than any other time.

The scheduler has no way of knowing the exact value of the mean, median, or modal task duration. Hence, all three values are simply estimates. Having made the three estimates, the scheduler assumes that actual task durations will be in the range from an optimistic to a pessimistic estimate and that a frequency distribution graph would resemble the normal distribution curve (bell-shaped curve) described in Chapter 9 in connection with the PERT Method. The PERT Method was based on the input of an average value as the central value. An ''effective'' duration was computed based on these input values using the equations presented in Chapter 9. It was then assumed that the actual distribution of task durations could be represented by a symmetrical normal distribution curve. The data used for the example illustrated in Figure 10.1 are not symmetrical about the central value of 15 days. Hence, the assumption that they can be represented by a symmetrical curve would introduce some error into the calculations. Figure 10.1 illustrates normal distribution of task durations between an optimistic value of 10 and a pessimistic value of 25, with the central value of 15 considered a mean value. Note that the depicted curve is not symmetrical but is skewed to the right. A normal distribution curve has infinite width; however, most of its area (99.5%) will be between the optimistic and the pessimistic durations. The effective duration is approximately 13 days, based on selection of the random number 16.

FIGURE 10.1
SKEWED NORMAL DISTRIBUTION
CURVE

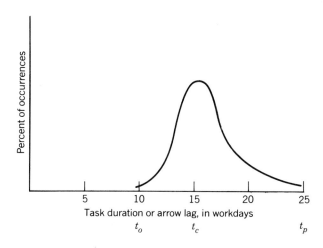

This assumption concerning frequency distribution has a major disadvantage when applied to Monte Carlo scheduling. The mathematical equations that define either a symmetrical or a skewed normal distribution curve are complex. Although a computer can compute a single effective duration based on normal distribution very rapidly, the Monte Carlo Method requires that numerous runs (network analyses) be made. Hence, an effective duration must be computed for each task for each run. For example, a network that contains 100 tasks may be analyzed 100 times. Hence, the assumption of normal distribution would require solving the normal distribution equation 10,000 times, an excessively time-consuming effort even for a computer.

Triangular Distribution with Modal Value as Central Value

Figure 10.2 illustrates this kind of distribution. The estimated optimistic and pessimistic values are as previously described. An estimated modal value is used for the central value, the modal value being the time that would most frequently be required if the task were repeated many times. The area beneath the triangle is 100%, meaning that if the task was repeated numerous times, all actual durations will be in the range from optimistic to pessimistic. Note that the triangle is skewed to the right. The area to the right of the central (modal) value is twice as large as the area to the left of the central value; this means that 67% of the times the task was repeated, the actual duration would be greater than the modal

FIGURE 10.2
TRIANGULAR DISTRIBUTION WITH
MODAL VALUE AS CENTRAL VALUE

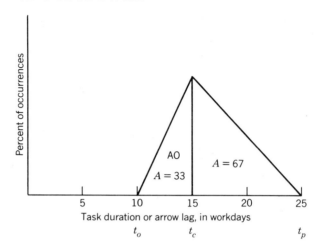

duration of 15 days. This assumed distribution will be used in the discussion of Monte Carlo scheduling in this chapter.

Equations 10.1 to 10.3 may be used to compute the effective durations and the effective relationship lags for this type of frequency distribution. The symbols t_o, t_c, t_p, and t_e have been previously defined. The symbol R is for a random number having a value between 0 and 100. The symbol AO represents the area to the left of the central value:

$$AO = 100 \times \frac{t_c - t_o}{t_p - t_o} \tag{10.1}$$

If R is equal to or less than AO, then use Equation 10.2. If R is greater than AO, then use Equation 10.3.

$$t_e = t_o + (t_c - t_o) \sqrt{\frac{R}{AO}} \tag{10.2}$$

$$t_e = t_p - (t_p - t_c) \sqrt{\frac{100 - R}{100 - AO}} \tag{10.3}$$

$$\text{Example: } AO = 100 \times \frac{15 - 10}{25 - 10} = 33.3$$

$$\text{Assume } R = 16$$

Since R is 16, which is less than AO, use Equation 10.2:

$$t_e = 10 + (15 - 10) \sqrt{\frac{16}{33.3}} = 13.46 \text{ days}$$

CAUTION: It is mathematically impossible to divide any number by zero.

If $t_o = t_p$, then the denominator in Equation 10.1 will be equal to zero. In this case, t_e is equal to t_o.

If $AO = 0$, then the denominator in Equation 10.2 will be equal to zero. In this case, use Equation 10.3, regardless of the value of R. If $AO = 100$, then the denominator in Equation 10.3 will be equal to zero. In this case, use Equation 10.2, regardless of the value of R.

If $R = 0$, then $t_e = t_o$. If $R = 100$, then $t_e = t_p$.

Triangular Distribution with Median Value as
Central Value

Figure 10.3 illustrates this kind of distribution. The estimated optimistic and pessimistic durations are as previously described. Note that the distribution diagram consists of two triangles, with 50% of the area being enclosed by each of them. Equations 10.2 and 10.3 may also be used for computing the effective times for this type of distribution. However, the value of AO is always equal to 50.

FIGURE 10.3
TRIANGULAR DISTRIBUTION WITH
MEDIAN VALUE AS CENTRAL VALUE

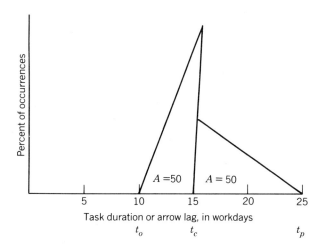

For example, when R is 16, which is less than 50, use Equation 10.2:

$$t_e = 10 + (15 - 10) \sqrt{\frac{16}{50}} = 12.83 \text{ days}$$

Comparison of Assumed Distributions

As previously indicated, the normal distribution assumption has been rejected for use in the Monte Carlo Method because the solution of a normal distribution equation for many times to obtain effective durations would be too time consuming. The two triangular distributions permit computation of effective durations in a reasonable amount of time. The assumption of normal distribution will result in a tighter clustering of effective durations about the central value than will the assumption of either of the two triangular distributions. The Monte Carlo programs are based on a triangular distribution with a modal value as the central value.

MORE ON ESTIMATING TASK DURATIONS AND RELATIONSHIP LAGS

Task Durations

The optimistic estimate of task duration should not be based on the assumption that job conditions will be perfect and that craftsmen and equipment will operate at absolute peak performance levels. Although all of these conditions could theoretically exist throughout the time a task is in progress, it is very unlikely that they will exist. It is quite likely that a task that has an extended duration will be delayed, at least briefly, by a spell of unfavorable weather; and it is also likely that production by craftsmen will be reduced, even if only slightly, by factors beyond the control of management. There may be minor reductions in the production rate of equipment, again resulting from unpredictable factors. It is very likely that at least one of these negative factors may exist for a short period of time. Hence, the optimistic estimate should represent the scheduler's estimate of the duration that could not be bettered by more than one time in 100 repetitions of the task.

Similarly, the pessimistic estimate should not be based on the assumption that everything that can go wrong will go wrong, and will stay wrong, for the entire period the task is in progress. If pessimism is carried to the ultimate and ridiculous extreme, then the pessimistic estimate of task duration might be "forever."

Rather, the pessimistic estimate should represent the scheduler's judgement as to the time that could be bettered 99 times in 100 repetitions of the task.

Admittedly, these two estimates will be of a subjective nature, and two competent schedulers could make different estimates as to their value.

Relationship Lags

As was indicated in Chapters 7 and 8 on Precedence Method scheduling, there may be zero, positive, or negative lags between the start (or end) of one task and the start (or end) of another task. Use of lag values allows the scheduler to depict partial concurrence between tasks. The use of lag values is permissible for AON diagrams being solved by the Monte Carlo Method, just as it was for the Precedence Method. Equations 10.1 to 10.4 may be used to compute effective values for lags by substituting L_o, L_c, L_p, and L_e for the symbols t_o, t_c, t_p, and t_e, respectively. The variance for a task lag is equal to $(L_p - L_o)/6$.

COMPUTER PROGRAMS AOAPERT AND AONPERT

Two computer programs, titled AOAPERT and AONPERT, are listed in Appendix B. Both programs have the capability of producing both deterministic PERT solutions and probabilistic Monte Carlo solutions. Program AOAPERT is to be used if the project is diagrammed using AOA notation, whereas AONPERT is to be used when AON notation has been used to diagram the project. Each program has two routines. The first of these, the PERT routine, produces a **deterministic** solution. The second routine, the Monte Carlo routine, produces a **probabilistic** solution.

PERT Routines

Both program AOAPERT and AONPERT require the input of optimistic, central-value, and pessimistic estimates of task durations. Program AONPERT also requires the input of optimistic, central-value, and pessimistic estimates of relationship lag values. Both programs compute effective task durations, and AONPERT also computes effective relationship lag values. Both programs compute task variances, and AONPERT also computes lag variances. Both programs then make a network analysis using the effective values of task duration and, for AON diagrams, effective lag values. Both programs then perform a probability analysis for a user-specified event time. The specified event time must be an early event time for the AOAPERT program or an early finish time for the AONPERT program.

The user must specify the node number of the event for which a probability analysis is desired and the path through the network over which variances are to be summed. This may be a critical path or any other path the user desires. The program then prints the probability analysis. Examples of program output are given in later sections of this chapter.

The AOAPERT program computes the effective task durations in accordance with the equation presented in Chapter 9 for the PERT Method. The AONPERT program computes the effective values for task durations and relationship lags on the basis of an assumed triangular distribution, with the central value being a modal value. Equations 10.4 and 10.5 may be used to compute these values:

$$t_e = t_o + \frac{2}{3} \times \left(\frac{t_c - t_o}{t_p - t_o} \right) + \frac{1}{3} \times \left(\frac{t_p - t_c}{t_p - t_o} \right) \tag{10.4}$$

$$L_e = L_o + \frac{2}{3} \times \left(\frac{L_c - L_o}{L_p - L_o} \right) + \frac{1}{3} \times \left(\frac{L_p - L_c}{L_p - L_o} \right) \tag{10.5}$$

Monte Carlo Routines

For both AOAPERT and AONPERT, the same values that were used as input for the PERT routine will be used for the Monte Carlo routine. The user must specify the event for which a Monte Carlo analysis is to be made. The user must also specify the number of Monte Carlo runs to be made. It is suggested that 100 runs be made for this routine. For both AOA and AON diagrams, the assumed frequency distribution of task durations (and for AON diagrams, lag values) are triangular, with the central value being a modal value. These effective durations are recomputed each run using a random number and in accordance with Equations 10.1 to 10.3.

AOA Diagrams

The user specifies a node number for the Monte Carlo probability analysis. The program then analyzes the network for as many runs as the user has specified. On each run, the early event time for the specified event node is recorded in computer memory. These recorded early event times are then sorted in ascending order (smallest event time at the top of the list). The program then produces a printout showing the event times that have a 0%, 5%, 10%, and so on, probability of occurrence. The user may specify the output of the early event times that were calculated on each run.

AON Diagrams

The user specifies the task node number for which a Monte Carlo probability analysis is desired and the number of runs to be made. The program computes the early finish times for that task which have a probability of occurrence of 0%, 5%, 10%, and so on. The user may call for output of all the early finish times computed on the various runs.

Similarities and Differences Between the Monte Carlo Routines

On each of the runs (repetitions of the network analysis), effective values must be computed for task durations and, in the case of an AON diagram, of relationship lags. These values are computed using Equations 10.1 to 10.3. The two programs result in the production of a probability analysis by probabilistic means. In the case of AOAPERT, the probability analysis will be for the early event time of a specified event, whereas for AONPERT, the analysis will be for the early finish time of a specified task.

The selection of an early event time for analysis by AOAPERT was based on the desire to make the program as similar as possible to the well-established PERT Method. The selection of the early finish time of a task for analysis by AONPERT was based on the belief that that value would be most useful to the scheduler. Both programs may be revised to generate a probability analysis for other time values. Because the Monte Carlo routines are very time and computer-memory consuming, it is not feasible to make a probability analysis for all time values during a single set of runs.

MANUAL AND COMPUTER SOLUTIONS USING PERT AND MONTE CARLO METHODS

Manual Solutions

It is not feasible to manually solve any but the most trivial scheduling methods by the Monte Carlo Method. The following example merely indicates the procedures by which the method is accomplished using a computer.

Example 1

This example involves both a PERT and a Monte Carlo analysis of a simple project. The objective of the example is to determine the probability that the project can be completed within 50 days. Figure 10.4 contains a simple AOA

FIGURE 10.4

SIMPLE CPM DIAGRAM WITH
MULTIPLE ESTIMATES OF TASK
DURATIONS

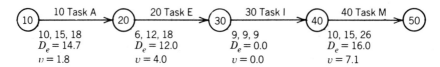

logic diagram with four task arrows. The estimated optimistic, central, and pessimistic durations of the tasks are printed beneath the task arrows. The effective duration values of each task, as well as their variances, that will be used in the PERT analysis are also printed below the arrows. These effective values were computed using the equations given in Chapter 9 for the PERT Method. The three estimates of task duration will be used in the Monte Carlo solution, but effective values for durations will be computed as described in preceding sections of this chapter.

Manual Solution by PERT Method

The steps of the manual PERT solution follow.

Step 1. Find the most likely project duration. It is equal to the early event time of terminal node [50] and it is the sum of the effective durations of the tasks along the path [10]–[20]–[30]–[40]–[50]. The most likely project duration is: 14.7 + 12.0 + 9.0 + 16.0, or 51.7 days.

Step 2. Find the project duration standard deviation. This is equal to the square root of the sum of the task variances along the critical path. It is equal to: 1.8 + 4.0 + 0.0 + 7.1, or 3.6 days.

Step 3. Find the number of standard deviations difference between 50 days and 51.7 days. It is (50 − 51.7)/3.6, or −0.5 standard deviation. This value was represented by the symbol Z in Chapter 9.

Step 4. Find the area associated with a Z value of 0.5. From Table 9.2, this area is 19%.

Step 5. Find the probability that the project can be completed in 50 days. The area to the left of the computed Z value on the normal distribution curve is 50% − 19%, or 31%. There is a 31% chance that the project can be completed in 50 days.

TABLE 10.1

RANDOM TASK DURATIONS AND RESULTING EARLY EVENT TIMES

Run	Effective Durations for Task No.				Early Event Times for Node No.				
No.	10	20	30	40	[10]	[20]	[30]	[40]	[50]
1	11.1	9.4	9.0	23.0	0.0	11.1	20.5	29.5	52.5
2	16.1	14.4	9.0	24.2	0.0	16.1	30.5	39.5	63.7
3	11.2	8.3	9.0	13.9	0.0	11.2	19.5	28.5	42.4
.	.	.	.	.	.	.	.	.	.
.	.	.	.	.	.	.	.	.	.
.	.	.	.	.	.	.	.	.	.
100	9.3	12.2	9.0	14.7	0.0	9.3	21.5	30.5	45.2

Manual Solution by Monte Carlo Method

Table 10.1 contains some of the effective task durations that would have been computed using Equations 10.1 to 10.3. The solution of Equation 10.1 was required for each task duration for each run, with a different random number being used for each solution. Although the network analysis was made 100 times (100 runs), only the computed effective durations for four of these runs are shown in Table 10.1. On each of the 100 runs, the effective durations shown in Table 10.1 were computed. Then, a network analysis was made to determine the early event times for nodes [10] to [50]. These early event times are shown in Table 10.1. After each run was completed, the computed early event time for node [50] was recorded. After 100 runs, these recorded times were sorted in ascending order (with the shortest time at the top). Then, the list was examined to find the first time value that was equal to 50 days. That time value was the thirty-fifth item on a list containing 100 items. Hence, the probability of completing the project in 50 days or less is 35%.

Comparison of Manual Analysis by the Two Methods

A manual solution by the PERT Method, as outlined for this simple project in the preceding discussion, required only a few minutes. The manual solution by the Monte Carlo Method required several hours. It involved solving Equation 10.1 400 times (one time per task per run) and solving either Equation 10.2 or 10.3 an equal number of times. The time required would have been reduced if fewer runs had been made; however, it should be apparent that manual solution by the Monte Carlo Method is not feasible. The computed probability of the early event time for node [50] being equal or less than 50 days was 35% by the Monte Carlo Method versus 31% by the PERT Method. This discrepancy is discussed in a later section.

Computer Solutions

Example 2

This example features exactly the same project used in Example 1. The project is depicted by the logic diagram in Figure 10.4. Program AOAPERT was used for the solution. Examine Figure 10.5, which contains both the PERT and the Monte Carlo solutions. The task data input to the computer was used for both solutions. These data consisted of the task descriptions and task arrow I-nodes and J-nodes plus optimistic, central-value, and pessimistic estimates of task duration. On completion of the data input, the program produced a PERT schedule. Note that Figure 10.5 shows the input data plus calculated values for effective task durations; task standard deviations; task times (ES, LS, EF, and LF); and task total floats (TFs). At this point, the user could call for a PERT probability analysis, a Monte Carlo probability analysis, or both.

Deterministic PERT Solution

The network was analyzed by the deterministic PERT method to determine the event times and the total float values of the tasks. In this instance, it is evident that all task arrows and all event nodes are on the critical path. The location of the critical path or paths would not be so evident in a more complex logic diagram. The user then called for a probability analysis for the early event time for the event represented by node [50], namely, project completion. He could have called for a probability analysis for the early event time of some other node. Note that the printout shows the smallest and the largest possible early event times for this node, 35 and 71 days, respectively. There is essentially no probability that this event time will be as small as 35 days or larger than 71 days. However, if every task were completed in its optimistic duration, then the project duration would be 35 days; and if every task required its pessimistic duration, the project duration would be 71 days.

The user was then called on to specify the arrow numbers of the tasks that are precedent to the node in question, in this case, node [50]. In a more complex diagram, the user might have desired to make a probability analysis for a non-critical node. In this case, all the critical arrows precedent to node [50] were specified. The program then computed and listed the variances for each of the specified arrows. It also listed the cumulative variance of the specified arrows. It computed and listed the event standard deviation, which is the square root of the cumulative variance.

Next, the program computed and printed the early event times for node [50] that had 0%, 5%, 10%, and so on, probability of occurrence. These probabilities were computed by using data stored in computer memory which are equivalent to that in Table 9.2. Note that the probability of the early event time of node [50] being equal or less than 50 days is 30%, nearly the same as the 31% probability that was computed manually above. This small discrepancy resulted from using rounded-off values in the manual analysis. Probability analyses for any other nodes could have been called for and printed.

Probabilistic Monte Carlo Solution

The Monte Carlo computer solution uses the three estimates of task description that were input for the PERT solution. However, the effective values for task durations were recomputed for each run as described in the previous section on manual analysis. Task variances are not used in the Monte Carlo solution. The output shows all of the computed early event times for node [50] and the minimum, mean, and maximum early event times that were computed for node [50] in the 100 runs. Output of these values is optional. Preceding these values is the probability analysis for the node in question, node [50]. This analysis is in the same format as the PERT analysis.

Note that the listed probability for the early event time for node [50] being 50 days or less is 40% versus 31% for the PERT analysis. Part of this discrepancy results from the fact that early event times are rounded off to the nearest whole day. Examination of the list of 100 computed early event times indicates that the probability is actually 36% (50.15 days is the thirty-seventh item in a list of 100 items). The remaining discrepancy results from the probabilistic nature of the Monte Carlo procedure, from the assumed shape of the frequency distribution curve for durations, and from the skewness of task duration distributions.

Variability in Monte Carlo Results.   If the Monte Carlo analysis were to be made again using the same input data, the results would differ from those in the first run. This is to be expected because Monte Carlo results are based on chance. The variation in the results from successive Monte Carlo analyses will be minimized, but not eliminated, if each analysis involves a large number of runs.

Skewness in Task Durations.   The PERT Method is implicitly based on symmetrical distributions of task durations, whereas the Monte Carlo Method takes skewness into account. Note that the frequency distribution for task 40 is skewed to the right. Most estimates of task duration will be skewed to the right, that is, schedulers tend to be more pessimistic than they are optimistic.

Assumed Shape of Task Duration Frequency Distribution Curves.   The PERT Method is based on an assumed normal distribution curve, whereas the Monte Carlo Method is based on an assumed triangular distribution curve. The area of a normal curve is more concentrated near its central value than is that of a triangular curve.

Comparison of Monte Carlo and PERT Results

In this instance, the Monte Carlo solution yielded a more optimistic estimate of the probability of completing this project in 50 days than did the PERT solution.

FIGURE 10.5
COMPUTER-GENERATED PERT AND
MONTE CARLO ANALYSIS OF
SIMPLE CPM DIAGRAM

SIMPLE AOA LOGIC DIAGRAM

*********** PERT SCHEDULE **************

TSK#	I-#	J-#	DURATIONS OPT.	MED.	PESS.	EFF.	DEV.	ES	EF	LS	LF	TF	FF
10	10	20	10.0	15.0	18.0	14.7	1.3	0.0	14.7	0.0	14.7	0.0	0.0
			TASK A
20	20	30	6.0	12.0	18.0	12.0	2.0	14.7	26.7	14.7	26.7	0.0	0.0
			TASK E
30	30	40	9.0	9.0	9.0	9.0	0.0	26.7	35.7	26.7	35.7	0.0	0.0
			TASK I
40	40	50	10.0	15.0	26.0	16.0	2.7	35.7	51.7	35.7	51.7	0.0	0.0
			TASK M

NODE NUMBER: 50 SMALLEST AND LARGEST POSSIBLE EET'S FOR NODE ARE: 35 71

*** PROBABILITY ANALYSIS BY PERT METHOD ***

TASK# 10 TASK VARIANCE=	1.8 CUMULATIVE VARIANCE= 1.8
TASK# 20 TASK VARIANCE=	4.0 CUMULATIVE VARIANCE= 5.8
TASK# 30 TASK VARIANCE=	0.0 CUMULATIVE VARIANCE= 5.8
TASK# 40 TASK VARIANCE=	7.1 CUMULATIVE VARIANCE= 12.9

EVENT DEVIATION = 3.6
COMPUTED EET'S ROUNDED OFF TO NEAREST WHOLE NUMBER
PERT PROBABILITY

0%	5%	10%	15%	20%	25%	30%	40%	50%	60%	70%	75%	80%	85%	90%	95%	100%
41	46	47	48	49	49	50	51	52	53	54	54	55	55	56	58	62

OF EET BEING EQUAL OR LESS THAN ABOVE TIMES

**** PROBABILITY ANALYSIS BY MONTE CARLO METHOD ****

PROBABILITY BASED ON 100 MONTE CARLO SIMULATIONS.

0%	5%	10%	15%	20%	25%	30%	40%	50%	60%	70%	75%	80%	85%	90%	95%	100%
42	45	47	47	48	49	49	50	51	52	54	56	56	57	58	60	64

OF EET FOR NODE BEING EQUAL OR LESS THAN ABOVE TIMES.

COMPUTED EARLY EVENT TIMES

42.41	42.98	42.99	44.17	45.23	46.04	46.33	46.90	46.90	46.93
46.96	47.00	47.25	47.30	47.32	47.50	47.62	47.94	47.94	48.04
48.17	48.25	48.53	48.56	48.56	48.73	48.74	48.83	48.88	49.09
49.54	49.70	49.81	49.86	49.93	50.15	50.15	50.16	50.30	50.41
50.41	50.42	50.47	50.48	50.48	50.51	50.51	50.52	50.61	50.64
50.76	50.77	51.09	51.16	51.51	51.88	51.94	52.06	52.21	52.28
52.28	52.34	52.40	52.48	52.51	53.00	53.09	53.4·	53.60	54.31
54.47	54.94	55.49	55.65	55.69	55.75	55.86	55.88	56.05	56.08
56.08	56.15	56.17	56.63	57.42	57.50	57.54	57.87	57.95	57.97
58.12	59.04	59.05	59.28	59.82	60.33	61.41	62.73	63.47	63.66

SMALLEST, MEAN AND MAXIMUM VALUES ARE: 42.41 51.96 63.66

The discrepancy is small. Either solution is satisfactory, considering the subjective nature of the estimates of task duration that were their bases.

Time Requirements for PERT and Monte Carlo Solutions

The PERT solution to this problem required only a few seconds after the data input to the computer. Printout time required about a minute, mostly to print the PERT schedule. If another probability analysis were desired for a different node, that analysis could have been made and printed out in a few seconds. The Monte Carlo solution for this simple problem required nearly 5 minutes of computer time. If an analysis were required for a different node, that new analysis would also require about 5 minutes. It is feasible to make a Monte Carlo probability analysis for only one time value per set of Monte Carlo runs because of limitations in computer memory.

Example 3

This example features a more complex logic diagram than was used in Examples 1 and 2. Figure 10.6 contains an AOA logic diagram with 16 task arrows. This diagram will be used to illustrate the effect of multiple critical or nearly critical paths. The top chain of tasks in this figure contains the same task arrows and estimated durations that were used for Figure 10.4. Except for the three arrows originating at node [10], all task arrows in the three remaining chains have the same estimated durations as those in the same column in the top chain. Two sets of task durations have been assigned to the three arrows originating at node [10]. One set contains task durations that will make the chains nearly critical, whereas the other set will make the chains quite noncritical. The analysis will be made to determine the statistical probability of completing the project at various times; hence, the time value selected for analysis is the EET for node [50].

One Critical Path and Three Nearly Critical Paths

Task durations have been used for arrows 12, 14, and 16 so that the chains for which they are the initial arrow will be nearly critical. Figure 10.7 contains a PERT schedule based on these durations. Note that all arrows on the chain made up of arrows 10, 20, 30, and 40 have zero total float. All other arrows in the diagram have a total float value of 1.

The PERT statistical analysis is based only on the critical path that contains arrows 10, 20, 30, and 40. The Monte Carlo analysis is based on 100 runs. Compare the median (50% probability) value for the EET of node [50] as it was

FIGURE 10.6
CPM DIAGRAM WITH ONE CRITICAL
AND THREE NEARLY CRITICAL PATHS

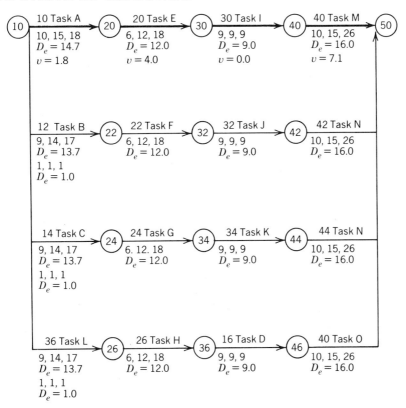

computed by the PERT and by the Monte Carlo methods. The Monte Carlo Method results in a value of 57 days versus 52 days by the PERT Method. This is as would be expected, because the Monte Carlo Method considers all paths to node [50], one of which is critical and three of which are nearly critical. The PERT Method ignores all tasks except those along a single critical path. Compare the PERT probability analysis in Figure 10.7 to that in Figure 10.5. The probability values are identical, even though the diagram on which Figure 10.5 is based contained only four arrows.

Only One Critical Path
Figure 10.8 contains the PERT schedule for the same logic diagram; however, the durations used for arrows 12, 14, and 16 have been reduced so as to make

FIGURE 10.7
COMPUTER ANALYSIS OF DIAGRAM IN FIGURE 10.6

AOA LOGIC DIAGRAM WITH ONE CRITICAL PATH AND THREE NEARLY CRITICAL PATHS

*********** PERT SCHEDULE ************

| TSK# | I-# | J-# | DURATIONS | | | | DEV. | ES | EF | LS | LF | TF | FF |
			OPT.	MED.	PESS.	EFF.							
10	10	20	10.0	15.0	18.0	14.7	1.3	0.0	14.7	0.0	14.7	0.0	0.0
			TASK A										
12	10	22	9.0	14.0	17.0	13.7	1.3	0.0	13.7	1.0	14.7	1.0	0.0
			TASK B										
14	10	24	9.0	14.0	17.0	13.7	1.3	0.0	13.7	1.0	14.7	1.0	0.0
			TASK C										
16	10	26	9.0	14.0	17.0	13.7	1.3	0.0	13.7	1.0	14.7	1.0	0.0
			TASK D										
20	20	30	6.0	12.0	18.0	12.0	2.0	14.7	26.7	14.7	26.7	0.0	0.0
			TASK E										
22	22	32	6.0	12.0	18.0	12.0	2.0	13.7	25.7	14.7	26.7	1.0	0.0
			TASK F										
24	24	34	6.0	12.0	18.0	12.0	2.0	13.7	25.7	14.7	26.7	1.0	0.0
			TASK G										
26	26	36	6.0	12.0	18.0	12.0	2.0	13.7	25.7	14.7	26.7	1.0	0.0
			TASK H										
30	30	40	9.0	9.0	9.0	9.0	0.0	26.7	35.7	26.7	35.7	0.0	0.0
			TASK I										
32	32	42	9.0	9.0	9.0	9.0	0.0	25.7	34.7	26.7	35.7	1.0	0.0
			TASK J										

34	34	44	9.0	9.0	9.0	9.0	0.0	25.7	34.7	26.7	35.7	1.0	0.0	TASK K
36	36	46	9.0	9.0	9.0	9.0	0.0	25.7	34.7	26.7	35.7	1.0	0.0	TASK L
40	40	50	10.0	15.0	26.0	16.0	2.7	35.7	51.7	35.7	51.7	0.0	0.0	TASK M
42	42	50	10.0	15.0	26.0	16.0	2.7	34.7	50.7	35.7	51.7	1.0	1.0	TASK N
44	44	50	10.0	15.0	26.0	16.0	2.7	34.7	50.7	35.7	51.7	1.0	1.0	TASK O
46	46	50	10.0	15.0	26.0	16.0	2.7	34.7	50.7	35.7	51.7	1.0	1.0	TASK P

NODE NUMBER: 50 SMALLEST AND LARGEST POSSIBLE EET'S FOR NODE ARE: 35 71

*** PROBABILITY ANALYSIS BY PERT METHOD ***

```
TASK#  10  TASK VARIANCE=   1.8   CUMULATIVE VARIANCE=   1.8
TASK#  20  TASK VARIANCE=   4.0   CUMULATIVE VARIANCE=   5.8
TASK#  30  TASK VARIANCE=   0.0   CUMULATIVE VARIANCE=   5.8
TASK#  40  TASK VARIANCE=   7.1   CUMULATIVE VARIANCE=  12.9
EVENT DEVIATION =   3.6
```

COMPUTED EET'S ROUNDED OFF TO NEAREST WHOLE NUMBER

PERT PROBABILITY

```
 0%  5% 10% 15% 20% 25% 30% 40% 50% 60% 70% 75% 80% 85% 90% 95% 100%
 41  46  47  48  49  50  51  52  53  54  55  56  58  62
```

OF EET BEING EQUAL OR LESS THAN ABOVE TIMES

**** PROBABILITY ANALYSIS BY MONTE CARLO METHOD ****

PROBABILITY BASED ON 100 MONTE CARLO SIMULATIONS.

```
 0%  5% 10% 15% 20% 25% 30% 40% 50% 60% 70% 75% 80% 85% 90% 95% 100%
 49  51  52  53  54  55  57  58  59  60  61  62  67
```

OF EET FOR NODE BEING EQUAL OR LESS THAN ABOVE TIMES.
SMALLEST, MEAN AND MAXIMUM VALUES ARE: 49.19   56.70   66.64

FIGURE 10.8
COMPUTER ANALYSIS WITH NO
NEARLY CRITICAL PATHS

AOA LOGIC DIAGRAM WITH ONE CRITICAL PATH AND NO NEARLY CRITICAL PATHS

*********** PERT SCHEDULE ************

TSK#	I-#	J-#	DURATIONS OPT.	MED.	PESS.	EFF.	DEV.	ES	EF	LS	LF	TF	FF
10	10	20	10.0	15.0	18.0	14.7	1.3	0.0	14.7	0.0	14.7	0.0	0.0
			TASK A										
12	10	22	1.0	1.0	1.0	1.0	0.0	0.0	1.0	13.7	14.7	13.7	0.0
			TASK B										
14	10	24	1.0	1.0	1.0	1.0	0.0	0.0	1.0	13.7	14.7	13.7	0.0
			TASK C										
16	10	26	1.0	1.0	1.0	1.0	0.0	0.0	1.0	13.7	14.7	13.7	0.0
			TASK D										
20	20	30	6.0	12.0	18.0	12.0	2.0	14.7	26.7	14.7	26.7	0.0	0.0
			TASK E										
22	22	32	6.0	12.0	18.0	12.0	2.0	1.0	13.0	14.7	26.7	13.7	0.0
			TASK F										
24	24	34	6.0	12.0	18.0	12.0	2.0	1.0	13.0	14.7	26.7	13.7	0.0
			TASK G										
26	26	36	6.0	12.0	18.0	12.0	2.0	1.0	13.0	14.7	26.7	13.7	0.0
			TASK H										
30	30	40	9.0	9.0	9.0	9.0	0.0	26.7	35.7	26.7	35.7	0.0	0.0
			TASK I										
32	32	42	9.0	9.0	9.0	9.0	0.0	13.0	22.0	26.7	35.7	13.7	0.0
			TASK J										

34	34	44		9.0	9.0	9.0	9.0	0.0	13.0	22.0	26.7	35.7	13.7	0.0
36	36	46	TASK K	9.0	9.0	9.0	9.0	0.0	13.0	22.0	26.7	35.7	13.7	0.0
40	40	50	TASK L	10.0	15.0	26.0	16.0	2.7	35.7	51.7	35.7	51.7	0.0	0.0
42	42	50	TASK M	10.0	15.0	26.0	16.0	2.7	22.0	38.0	35.7	51.7	13.7	13.7
44	44	50	TASK N	10.0	15.0	26.0	16.0	2.7	22.0	38.0	35.7	51.7	13.7	13.7
46	46	50	TASK O	10.0	15.0	26.0	16.0	2.7	22.0	38.0	35.7	51.7	13.7	13.7
			TASK P											

NODE NUMBER: 50 SMALLEST AND LARGEST POSSIBLE EET'S FOR NODE ARE: 35 71

*** PROBABILITY ANALYSIS BY PERT METHOD ***

TASK# 10 TASK VARIANCE=   1.8 CUMULATIVE VARIANCE=   1.8
TASK# 20 TASK VARIANCE=   4.0 CUMULATIVE VARIANCE=   5.8
TASK# 30 TASK VARIANCE=   0.0 CUMULATIVE VARIANCE=   5.8
TASK# 40 TASK VARIANCE=   7.1 CUMULATIVE VARIANCE= 12.9
EVENT DEVIATION = 3.6

COMPUTED EET'S ROUNDED OFF TO NEAREST WHOLE NUMBER

PERT PROBABILITY

0%	5%	10%	15%	20%	25%	30%	40%	50%	60%	70%	75%	80%	85%	90%	95%	100%
41	46	47	48	49	50	51	52	53	54	55	55	56		58		62

OF EET BEING EQUAL OR LESS THAN ABOVE TIMES

**** PROBABILITY ANALYSIS BY MONTE CARLO METHOD ****

PROBABILITY BASED ON 100 MONTE CARLO SIMULATIONS.

0%	5%	10%	15%	20%	25%	30%	40%	50%	60%	70%	75%	80%	85%	90%	95%	100%
41	45	47	48	49	50	51	53	53	53	55	55	56	57	58	60	63

OF EET FOR NODE BEING EQUAL OR LESS THAN ABOVE TIMES.
SMALLEST, MEAN AND MAXIMUM VALUES ARE: 41.01   52.48   63.37

them, as well as the subsequent arrows in their chains, quite noncritical. Note that all tasks, except those in the top chain, now have total float values of 13.7. The PERT probability analysis is identical to that of the preceding PERT analyses.

Note that the Monte Carlo probability analysis yields values very close to those resulting from the PERT analysis. This is as would be expected. A total float value of 13.7 is more than three times the PERT-computed event deviation for node [50]. Although there is some possibility that the actual durations of tasks along one of the noncritical chains may have an impact on project duration, it is unlikely that such may be the case.

Monte Carlo Solution Time

Each of the Monte Carlo solutions shown in Figures 10.7 and 10.8 required approximately 10 minutes to solve on a microcomputer. The time could have been reduced by 50% by making only 25 runs rather than 100. However, the scheduler would have less confidence in a probability analysis based on only 25 runs. The author has solved the problem illustrated in Figure 10.7 using 25, 100, and 500 runs. Even successive analyses based on the same number of runs have resulted in differences in computed median and mean project durations of one or two days.

Example 4

This example illustrates the AONPERT deterministic scheduling method and the application of the probabilistic Monte Carlo Method to schedules diagrammed using AON notation. The schedule is for a condominium development project, a type of project in which financing and marketing considerations may involve more uncertainty than do construction operations. The project involves construction of amenities (a clubhouse, swimming pool, tennis courts, etc.) and of condominium units. The condominium units will be constructed in two phases, with more units in phase I than in phase II. They will be constructed using factory-manufactured modular units. Manufacture of the units will not be commenced until 50% of the units in the phase of which they are a part have been sold. Marketing of phase II units will not commence until 50% of the phase I units have been sold. Other constraints to the tasks that make up this project are depicted on the AON logic diagram in Figure 10.9. Note that some of the relationship arrows in the logic diagram have lag values, with several having negative lag values (leads). For example, starting the erection of the phase I units may lead (begin before) the completion of all foundations for those units.

FIGURE 10.9
ACTIVITY ON NODE DIAGRAM FOR CONDOMINIUM PROJECT

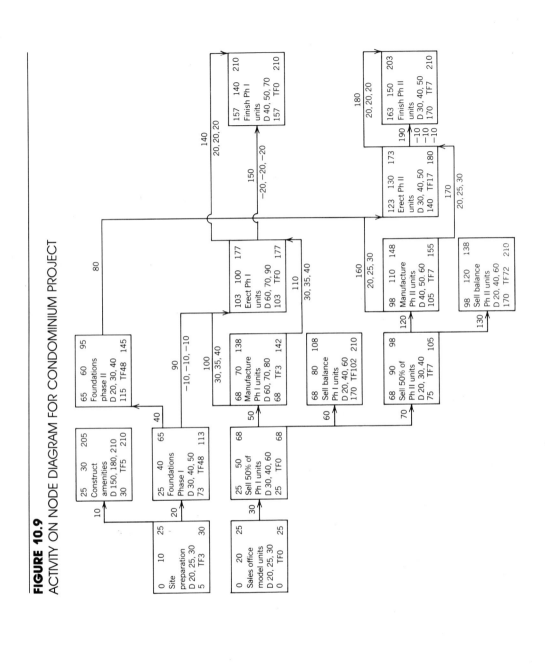

FIGURE 10.10
AON-PERT SCHEDULE FOR
CONDOMINIUM PROJECT

TWO-PHASED CONDOMINIUM PROJECT
PERT SCHEDULE

SEQ	TASK#	DURATIONS OPT MOD PESS EFF	Description	ES	EF	LS	LF	TF	SF	FF
1	10	20 25 30 25.0	Site Preparation	0.0	25.0	5.0	30.0	5.0	5	5
2	20	20 25 30 25.0	Sales Offc & Model Units	0.0	25.0	0.0	25.0	0.0	0	0
3	30	150 180 210 180.0	Construct Amenities	25.0	205.0	30.0	210.0	5.0	5	5
4	40	30 40 50 40.0	Foundations Phase I	25.0	65.0	73.3	113.3	48.3	48	48
5	50	30 40 60 43.3	Sell 50% of Ph I Units	25.0	68.3	25.0	68.3	0.0	0	0
6	60	20 30 40 30.0	Foundations Phase II	65.0	95.0	115.0	145.0	50.0	50	50
7	70	60 70 80 70.0	Manufacture Ph I Units	68.3	138.3	68.3	141.7	3.3	0	3
8	80	20 40 60 40.0	Sell Balance Ph I Units	68.3	108.3	170.0	210.0	101.7	102	102
9	90	20 30 40 30.0	Sell 50% of Ph II Units	68.3	98.3	75.0	105.0	6.7	7	7
10	100	60 70 90 73.3	Erect Ph I Units	103.3	176.7	103.3	176.7	0.0	0	0
11	110	40 50 60 50.0	Manufacture Ph II Units	98.3	148.3	105.0	155.0	6.7	7	7

SEQ	RLT#								
12	120	20	40	60	40.0	Sell Balance Ph II Units	98.3	138.3	170.0	210.0	71.7	72	72
13	130	30	40	50	40.0	Erect Ph II Units	123.3	173.3	140.0	180.0	16.7	17	7
14	140	40	50	70	53.3	Finish Ph I Units	156.7	210.0	156.7	210.0	0.0	0	0
15	150	30	40	50	40.0	Finish Ph II Units	163.3	203.3	170.0	210.0	6.7	7	7

SEQ	RLT#	LAGS				TYPE	INODE	JNODE	TOTAL FLOAT
		OPT	MOD	PESS	EFF				
1	10	0	0	0	0.0	ES	10	30	5.0
2	20	0	0	0	0.0	ES	10	40	48.3
3	30	0	0	0	0.0	ES	20	50	0.0
4	40	0	0	0	0.0	ES	40	60	50.0
5	50	0	0	0	0.0	ES	50	70	0.0
6	60	0	0	0	0.0	ES	50	80	101.7
7	70	0	0	0	0.0	ES	50	90	6.7
8	80	-5	-5	-5	-5.0	ES	60	130	50.0
9	90	-10	-10	-10	-10.0	ES	40	100	48.3
10	100	30	35	40	35.0	SS	70	100	0.0
11	110	30	35	40	35.0	EE	70	100	3.3
12	120	0	0	0	0.0	ES	90	110	6.7
13	130	0	0	0	0.0	ES	90	120	71.7
14	140	20	20	20	20.0	EE	100	140	13.3
15	150	-20	-20	-20	-20.0	ES	100	140	0.0
16	160	20	25	30	25.0	SS	110	130	16.7
17	170	20	25	30	25.0	EE	110	130	6.7
18	180	20	20	20	20.0	EE	130	150	16.7
19	190	-10	-10	-10	-10.0	ES	130	150	6.7

FIGURE 10.11
PROBABILITY ANALYSIS FOR
CONDOMINIUM PROJECT

```
SMALLEST POSSIBLE EF TIME FOR TASK #  140 IS  160.00
LARGEST  POSSIBLE EF TIME FOR TASK #  140 IS  270.00
PROBABILITY OF EF TIME BEING EQUAL OR LESS THAN LISTED VALUES

PROBABILITY ANALYSIS BY PERT METHOD
TASK  NBR  20 VARIANCE=    2.8 CUMULATIVE VARIANCE    2.8
TASK  NBR  50 VARIANCE=   25.0 CUMULATIVE VARIANCE   27.8
TASK  NBR 100 VARIANCE=   25.0 CUMULATIVE VARIANCE   52.8
TASK  NBR 140 VARIANCE=   25.0 CUMULATIVE VARIANCE   77.8
ARROW NBR  30 VARIANCE=    0.0 CUMULATIVE VARIANCE   77.8
ARROW NBR  50 VARIANCE=    0.0 CUMULATIVE VARIANCE   77.8
ARROW NBR 100 VARIANCE=    2.8 CUMULATIVE VARIANCE   80.6
ARROW NBR 150 VARIANCE=    0.0 CUMULATIVE VARIANCE   80.6
  0%   5%  10%  15%  20%  30%  40%  50%  60%  70%  80%  85%  90%  95% 100%
 183  195  198  201  202  205  208  210  212  215  218  219  222  225  237
```

PROBABILITY ANALYSIS BY MONTE CARLO METHOD
BASED ON 100 MONTE CARLO SIMULATIONS, AVERAGE EF TIME = 209.53

0%	5%	10%	15%	20%	30%	40%	50%	60%	70%	80%	85%	90%	95%	100%
184	192	196	199	201	204	207	209	212	215	218	220	224	228	229

SMALLEST POSSIBLE EF TIME FOR TASK # 150 IS 150.00
LARGEST POSSIBLE EF TIME FOR TASK # 150 IS 260.00
PROBABILITY OF EF TIME BEING EQUAL OR LESS THAN LISTED VALUES

PROBABILITY ANALYSIS BY PERT METHOD
TASK NBR   20 VARIANCE= 2.8 CUMULATIVE VARIANCE 2.8
TASK NBR   50 VARIANCE= 25.0 CUMULATIVE VARIANCE 27.8
TASK NBR   90 VARIANCE= 11.1 CUMULATIVE VARIANCE 38.9
TASK NBR 110 VARIANCE= 11.1 CUMULATIVE VARIANCE 50.0
TASK NBR 150 VARIANCE= 11.1 CUMULATIVE VARIANCE 61.1
ARROW NBR 30 VARIANCE= 0.0 CUMULATIVE VARIANCE 61.1
ARROW NBR 70 VARIANCE= 0.0 CUMULATIVE VARIANCE 61.1
ARROW NBR 120 VARIANCE= 0.0 CUMULATIVE VARIANCE 61.1
ARROW NBR 170 VARIANCE= 2.8 CUMULATIVE VARIANCE 63.9
ARROW NBR 190 VARIANCE= 0.0 CUMULATIVE VARIANCE 63.9

0%	5%	10%	15%	20%	30%	40%	50%	60%	70%	80%	85%	90%	95%	100%
192	203	206	208	209	212	214	216	218	220	223	224	226	229	240

AONPERT Deterministic Schedule

Program AONPERT, a BASIC listing which is printed in Appendix B, was used to prepare the schedule shown in Figure 10.10. Equations 10.4 and 10.5 were used to compute the effective durations and the effective lags, plus the duration variances and the lag variances for the preparation of this schedule. There is one critical path, which passes through nodes [20], [50], [100], and [140] and through arrows 30, 50, 100, and 150. There are several nearly critical paths. One that has a total float of 5 days passes through nodes [10] and [30] and through arrow 10. Another nearly critical path, having a total float of 3.3 days, passes through node [70] (manufacture phase I units) and arrow 70. Still another, having total float of 6.7 days, passes through nodes [20], [50], and [90], [110], and [150] and through arrows 30, 70, 120, 170, and 190. This latter noncritical path shares two nodes and one arrow with the critical path.

Based on an examination of this deterministic schedule, the scheduler decides to make a probability analysis for the critical path and for the noncritical path that terminates at node [150]. Surprisingly, the schedule indicates that the phase I units will be completed later than the phase II units. The scheduler might decide to reappraise some of the estimated task durations and relationship lags for this reason.

Probability Analyses

Figure 10.11 contains the probability analyses for the EETs of nodes [140] and [150]. A PERT probability analysis was made for each node. One Monte Carlo analysis was made for node [140], and two Monte Carlo analyses were made for node [150]. The second Monte Carlo analysis made for node [150] was based on only 25 runs. The PERT and the Monte Carlo frequency distributions were quite close when 100 Monte Carlo runs were made but less so when only 25 runs were made. Even though the total float values for some of the noncritical paths are quite low, most of the tasks and arrows on those paths are not precedent to the terminal event on the critical path.

Earlier in this chapter, it was stated that the existence of multiple critical and nearly critical paths was a clear indication that the Monte Carlo technique should be considered. This criterion should be revised to state that the existence of multiple critical or nearly critical paths precedent to a critical or nearly critical node is an indication that the Monte Carlo Method should be considered. About 15 minutes was required for making 100 Monte Carlo runs for this project.

SUMMARY

The use of the Monte Carlo Method should be considered only when the following conditions exist:

1. There is considerble uncertainty concerning task durations and relationship lags.

2. There are multiple critical or nearly critical paths that are precedent to a critical or nearly critical task.

The Monte Carlo Method requires much more computational effort than do deterministic methods. The effort required is proportional to the number of tasks involved and to the number of Monte Carlo runs that are made. The solution of all but the most trivial problems requires the use of a computer. The total time to solve a scheduling problem by a computer includes data entry time, computation time, and printout time. If the scheduler has a microcomputer that he or she can dedicate to a Monte Carlo solution for several hours while he or she performs other work, then the demands for computation effort will not preclude the use of the Monte Carlo Method.

The author has used the two programs presented in this chapter to make 1000 runs for projects having 100 tasks. The solution time was not recorded; however, the printout was ready the next morning. If the programs were compiled into machine language, execution time would be reduced significantly. If the programs were revised so that they would make frequency distribution analyses of several time values, the computation effort would be increased by about 10% for each additional time value.

The computer memory requirements (RAM) for execution of these programs amount to about 800 bytes per task, assuming that 100 Monte Carlo runs will be made. This requirement is over and above the RAM requirements for running a deterministic scheduling program. If the programs were revised to make frequency distribution analyses for several time values, then additional RAM requirements would increase proportionally to the number of values being analyzed.

CALENDAR DAY SCHEDULING

11

OBJECTIVES

Task times (ES, EF, LS, and LF) and event times (EET and LET) are made up of two parts: a date part and a time-of-the-day part. Thus far in this book, event times and task times have been expressed with workday dates making up the date part of these times and the end of the day being the time of the day. For instance, a project is scheduled to be completed at the end of the mth work date or an event is scheduled to occur at the end of the nth work date. This chapter covers the principles of calendar date scheduling, the advantages and disadvantages of calendar date and work date scheduling, and some of the terms used in connection with calendar date scheduling.

WORK DATE SCHEDULING VERSUS CALENDAR DATE SCHEDULING

There are advantages and disadvantages incident to the use of work dates and of calendar dates.

Work Dates

The use of work dates for the date part of event times and task times is convenient for the scheduler for several reasons. Task durations are usually estimated in workdays, such durations being equal to the amount of work to be done divided by the work that can be done in a workday. Schedules are often prepared before the actual project starting date is known; hence, it may not be practical to prepare the schedule based on calendar dates. Although the use of work dates is convenient for preparing the schedule, the scheduler and other persons who use the schedule for management purposes will find that they must often convert the task times into calendar date format. For example, a purchase order for materials must include a required delivery date. A required delivery date that was expressed as a work date would be meaningless to a vendor.

Calendar Dates

Schedules with the date part of task times expressed as calendar dates are convenient for use in project management; however, it is somewhat more difficult to prepare a schedule based on calendar dates than to prepare a schedule that is based on work dates. Calendar date scheduling is particularly useful when the schedule must be periodically updated. There are three different methods by which a calendar date schedule may be prepared. Later sections of this chapter illustrate two of these methods and describe the third.

ESSENTIAL TERMS

Time of the Day

In the examples shown in previous chapters, the time-of-the-day part of event times and task times has been the end of the day. Use of this single time of the day has simplified some of the calculations. It is desirable to use two times of the day for calendar date schedules.

> **Task Starting Times (ES and LS).** These times will be expressed so that the beginning of the day is the time of the day. An ES time of January 14, 1985, means the beginning of that date.
>
> **Task Finish Times (EF and LF) and Event Times (EET and LET).** These times will be expressed so that the end of the day is the time of the day. An EF time of January 18, 1985, means the end of that date.

Task Durations

Task durations may be expressed in workdays or in calendar days. Because the actual calendar day duration of a task depends not only on the total amount of work to be done and the amount of work that can be done in a workday but also on the number of holidays and other nonworkdays that will occur while the task is in progress, it is difficult to estimate the calendar day duration of most tasks.

The calendar day duration of some tasks may be independent of holidays. For example, the time required for cast-in-place concrete to develop sufficient strength to permit stripping the forms is a function of mix design and weather conditions. The duration of such a task may be expressed in calendar days. Other kinds of tasks for which it is easier to estimate a calendar day duration than a workday duration include the following:

> **Contractual Requirements.** This kind includes tasks in which another party (a vendor or a subcontractor) may be contractually obligated to deliver material or to perform a service within a specified calendar day period.

> **Climatic Conditions.** This kind includes delays defined as tasks. These delays may be expected to occur because of climatic conditions. In northern climates, it may be impractical to perform earthwork when the ground is frozen.

> **Occupancy.** These are tasks that represent delays that will occur because of the occupancy of a facility. For example, renovation work on school classrooms can be performed only during the periods when school is not in session.

Workday Regimes

A workday regime is a set of rules specifying which calendar dates will be work dates. Several different regimes may have to be defined to cover all the tasks that make up a project. Typical regimes are listed below. These regimes are listed as examples; many other regimes could be defined. It is convenient to have calendars that will facilitate converting calendar dates to work dates for the various defined regimes. The scheduler can prepare such charts by numbering the days on an office calendar, skipping over the days that are nonworkdays.

> **Example Regime 1.** Every calendar day is a workday. This regime is appropriate for use with tasks (curing of concrete or delivery of goods and services within a contractually specified number of calendar days) whose durations are not dependent on holidays and other nonworkdays. A Julian date calendar represents this regime. Figure 11.1 is a Julian calendar for 1985. Note that the days of the year are numbered consecutively from January 1 to December 31. A Julian date calendar can be produced for any year using Program JULIAN, the BASIC listing of which is included in Appendix B. Many office calendars have the Julian dates printed along with the calendar dates. The scheduler can quickly convert a normal calendar to a Julian date calendar by numbering the dates consecutively.

> **Example Regime 2.** Every calendar day is a workday except for those calendar dates that are legal holidays (January 1, July 4, December 25, etc.).

FIGURE 11.1
JULIAN DATE CALENDAR

DAY OF WEEK AND JULIAN DATE FOR CALENDAR YEAR   1985

DOM	JAN	FEB	MAR	APR	MAY	JUN	JUL	AUG	SEP	OCT	NOV	DEC
1	T001	F032	F060	M091	W121	S152	M182	T213	S244	T274	F305	S335
2	W002	S033	S061	T092	T122	S153	T183	F214	M245	W275	S306	M336
3	T003	S034	S062	W093	F123	M154	W184	S215	T246	T276	S307	T337
4	F004	M035	M063	T094	S124	T155	T185	S216	W247	F277	M308	W338
5	S005	T036	T064	F095	S125	W156	F186	M217	T248	S278	T309	T339
6	S006	W037	W065	S096	M126	T157	S187	T218	F249	S279	W310	F340
7	M007	T038	T066	S097	T127	F158	S188	W219	S250	M280	T311	S341
8	T008	F039	F067	M098	W128	S159	M189	T220	S251	T281	F312	S342
9	W009	S040	S068	T099	T129	S160	T190	F221	M252	W282	S313	M343
10	T010	S041	S069	W100	F130	M161	W191	S222	T253	T283	S314	T344
11	F011	M042	M070	T101	S131	T162	T192	S223	W254	F284	M315	W345
12	S012	T043	T071	F102	S132	W163	F193	M224	T255	S285	T316	T346
13	S013	W044	W072	S103	M133	T164	S194	T225	F256	S286	W317	F347
14	M014	T045	T073	S104	T134	F165	S195	W226	S257	M287	T318	S348
15	T015	F046	F074	M105	W135	S166	M196	T227	S258	T288	F319	S349
16	W016	S047	S075	T106	T136	S167	T197	F228	M259	W289	S320	M350
17	T017	S048	S076	W107	F137	M168	W198	S229	T260	T290	S321	T351
18	F018	M049	M077	T108	S138	T169	T199	S230	W261	F291	M322	W352
19	S019	T050	T078	F109	S139	W170	F200	M231	T262	S292	T323	T353
20	S020	W051	W079	S110	M140	T171	S201	T232	F263	S293	W324	F354
21	M021	T052	T080	S111	T141	F172	S202	W233	S264	M294	T325	S355
22	T022	F053	F081	M112	W142	S173	M203	T234	S265	T295	F326	S356
23	W023	S054	S082	T113	T143	S174	T204	F235	M266	W296	S327	M357
24	T024	S055	S083	W114	F144	M175	W205	S236	T267	T297	S328	T358
25	F025	M056	M084	T115	S145	T176	T206	S237	W268	F298	M329	W359
26	S026	T057	T085	F116	S146	W177	F207	M238	T269	S299	T330	T360
27	S027	W058	W086	S117	M147	T178	S208	T239	F270	S300	W331	F361
28	M028	T059	T087	S118	T148	F179	S209	W240	S271	M301	T332	S362
29	T029		F088	M119	W149	S180	M210	T241	S272	T302	F333	S363
30	W030		S089	T120	T150	S181	T211	F242	M273	W303	S334	M364
31	T031		S090		F151		W212	S243		T304		T365

Example Regime 3. Every calendar day is a workday except for those calendar dates that are legal holidays or Sundays. This regime is appropriate for use with tasks the scheduler believes to be so critical that overtime pay for Saturday work is justified.

Example Regime 4. Every calendar day is a workday except for legal holidays, Sundays, and Saturdays. This regime is appropriate for use with

FIGURE 11.2
REGIME 4 WORK DATE/CALENDAR
DATE CONVERSION CALENDAR

REGIME #4 - SATURDAYS, SUNDAYS AND LEGAL HOLIDAYS ARE NON-WORK DAYS.

NON-WORK DAYS ARE:
SUN SAT
```
 850101  850105  850106  850112  850113  850119  850120  850126  850127  850202
 850203  850209  850210  850216  850217  850223  850224  850302  850303  850309
 850310  850316  850317  850323  850324  850330  850331  850406  850407  850413
 850414  850420  850421  850427  850428  850504  850505  850511  850512  850518
 850519  850525  850526  850601  850602  850608  850609  850615  850616  850622
 850623  850629  850630
```

WORKDAYS ARE

```
  1-WED-850102    2-THU-850103    3-FRI-850104    4-MON-850107    5-TUE-850108
  6-WED-850109    7-THU-850110    8-FRI-850111    9-MON-850114   10-TUE-850115
 11-WED-850116   12-THU-850117   13-FRI-850118   14-MON-850121   15-TUE-850122
 16-WED-850123   17-THU-850124   18-FRI-850125   19-MON-850128   20-TUE-850129
 21-WED-850130   22-THU-850131   23-FRI-850201   24-MON-850204   25-TUE-850205
 26-WED-850206   27-THU-850207   28-FRI-850208   29-MON-850211   30-TUE-850212
 31-WED-850213   32-THU-850214   33-FRI-850215   34-MON-850218   35-TUE-850219
 36-WED-850220   37-THU-850221   38-FRI-850222   39-MON-850225   40-TUE-850226
 41-WED-850227   42-THU-850228   43-FRI-850301   44-MON-850304   45-TUE-850305
 46-WED-850306   47-THU-850307   48-FRI-850308   49-MON-850311   50-TUE-850312
 51-WED-850313   52-THU-850314   53-FRI-850315   54-MON-850318   55-TUE-850319
 56-WED-850320   57-THU-850321   58-FRI-850322   59-MON-850325   60-TUE-850326
 61-WED-850327   62-THU-850328   63-FRI-850329   64-MON-850401   65-TUE-850402
 66-WED-850403   67-THU-850404   68-FRI-850405   69-MON-850408   70-TUE-850409
 71-WED-850410   72-THU-850411   73-FRI-850412   74-MON-850415   75-TUE-850416
 76-WED-850417   77-THU-850418   78-FRI-850419   79-MON-850422   80-TUE-850423
 81-WED-850424   82-THU-850425   83-FRI-850426   84-MON-850429   85-TUE-850430
 86-WED-850501   87-THU-850502   88-FRI-850503   89-MON-850506   90-TUE-850507
 91-WED-850508   92-THU-850509   93-FRI-850510   94-MON-850513   95-TUE-850514
 96-WED-850515   97-THU-850516   98-FRI-850517   99-MON-850520  100-TUE-850521
101-WED-850522  102-THU-850523  103-FRI-850524  104-MON-850527  105-TUE-850528
106-WED-850529  107-THU-850530  108-FRI-850531  109-MON-850603  110-TUE-850604
111-WED-850605  112-THU-850606  113-FRI-850607  114-MON-850610  115-TUE-850611
116-WED-850612  117-THU-850613  118-FRI-850614  119-MON-850617  120-TUE-850618
121-WED-850619  122-THU-850620  123-FRI-850621  124-MON-850624  125-TUE-850625
126-WED-850626  127-THU-850627  128-FRI-850628
```

tasks the scheduler believes not to be so critical as to justify any premium pay. Figure 11.2 is a workday/calendar day conversion chart for this regime. This chart was produced by Program REGIME, a BASIC listing of which is included in Appendix B. Program REGIME can also be used to prepare a conversion chart for any desired regime.

Example Regime 5. Every calendar day is a workday except for legal holidays, Sundays, Saturdays, and dates between November 15 and February 15. This regime is appropriate for use with an earth-moving task the scheduler believes impractical to perform during the extremely cold part of the year.

METHODS FOR PREPARING CALENDAR DAY SCHEDULES

Described in this section are three methods for preparing calendar day schedules. The methods are listed in order of increasing difficulty. Two of the methods will be illustrated using the project whose CPM diagram is in Figure 11.3. This project involves the construction of a combined gasoline service station and convenience store. The store will be in a prefabricated metal building. Additional features of the completed project include buried gasoline tanks, gasoline pumps, underground site utilities (electrical, water, and drains), and paving. All of the task durations are expressed in workdays except for task 10, which has a duration expressed in calendar days. The project is scheduled to start at the beginning of Monday, January 14, 1985.

It is convenient to represent calendar dates numerically. There are several conventions for doing this, including the MMDDYY and the YYMMDD format. January 14, 1985 would be represented as 011485 or 850114 depending on the convention used. The YYMMDD format facilitates the comparison of two dates to determine which is later and may be preferable for this reason.

Method 1 Hybrid Schedule

This schedule is termed a hybrid schedule because it is initially prepared as a workday schedule, with all task times calculated in work date format. Subsequently, by using a workdate/calendar date conversion chart such as the one shown in Figure 11.2, one can convert these task times to calendar date format. It is necessary that all task durations be expressed in workdays. If most of the tasks have been defined as Regime 4 tasks, then any non-Regime 4 tasks must have their durations recomputed as though they were Regime 4 tasks. For example, task 10 has a duration of 30 calendar days. Recompute its duration as 30 CD × (5 WD/7 CD) = 21.4 workdays. This value has been rounded off to the integer value of 22 workdays. If most of the tasks were Regime 3 tasks (6 workdays per week), then the factors 6/7 and 6/5 would be used to recompute

FIGURE 11.3
LOGIC DIAGRAM FOR SERVICE
STATION/CONVENIENCE STORE
PROJECT

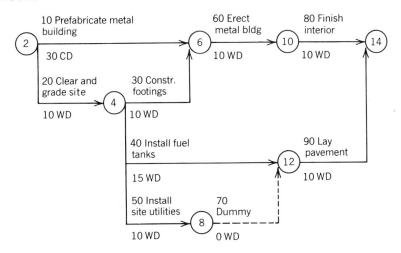

the durations of Regime 1 and Regime 4 tasks, respectively. This procedure is not exact because it does not take into account occasional legal holidays that occur on weekdays. The objective is to convert all durations to workdays.

Figure 11.4 is the CPM diagram with all task durations converted to workdays. All event times have been computed in work date format and have been printed on the diagram. These EET and LET times are work dates as of the end of the day. Note that the EET for the initial node is 8, rather than zero. The project start date of January 14, 1985, is the ninth workday for Regime 4. Because event times are expressed as of the end of the day, the project will start at the end of the eighth work date. If the project start date is unknown, or if the scheduler objects to using a nonzero value for the EET of the initial node, then he or she may use zero for that EET. It will then be necessary to add a value (in this case 8) to all computed work date task times before converting them to calendar dates. Having set the EET of the initial node as 8, the CPM analysis has been made exactly as has been previously illustrated. Note that the LET of the initial node is equal to its EET. Table 11.1 is the CPM schedule with all task times shown both in work date and in calendar date format. Figure 11.2 was used to make this conversion.

Table 11.1 is the CPM schedule for this project with task times shown both in work date and in calendar date formats. In computing calendar date task times

---

FIGURE 11.4
DIAGRAM WITH CALENDAR
DURATIONS CHANGED TO
WORK DAY DURATIONS

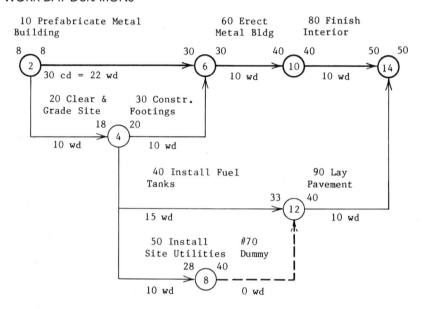

for Table 11.1, values were taken from the conversion chart in Figure 11.2. The calendar date values were computed as follows:

Early Finish Time
The EF time for each task is the calendar date that corresponds to the task's EF time expressed in workdays. For example, the EF time for task 10 was work date 30. From Figure 11.2, work date 30 corresponds to calendar date 850212. The task's EF time is the end of February 12, 1985.

Late Finish Time
The LF time for each task is the calendar date that corresponds to the task's LF time expressed as a work date. For example, the LF time of task 20 was work date 20. From Figure 11.2, work date 20 corresponds to calendar date 850129. The task's LF time is the end of January 29, 1985.

Early Start Time
The ES time for each arrow is the calendar date that corresponds to the task's work date ES time plus 1. For example, the ES time for task 90 was work date

TABLE 11.1

CPM HYBRID SCHEDULE—TIMES IN CALENDAR DATE AND WORK DATE FORMAT[a]

Tsk No.	I-N No.	J-N No.	Dur, WD	Description	ES	EF	LS	LF	TF
10	2	6	22	Prefabricate metal building	850114 (8)	850212 (30)	850114 (8)	850212 (30)	0
20	2	4	10	Clear and grade site	850114 (8)	850125 (18)	850116 (10)	850129 (20)	2
30	4	6	10	Construct footings	850128 (18)	850228 (28)	850130 (20)	850212 (30)	2
40	4	12	15	Install fuel tanks	850128 (18)	850215 (33)	850206 (25)	850226 (40)	7
50	4	8	10	Install site utilities	850128 (18)	850228 (28)	850213 (30)	850226 (40)	12
60	6	10	10	Erect metal building	850213 (30)	850226 (40)	850213 (30)	850226 (40)	0
70	8	12	0	Dummy arrow	850211 (28)	850208 (28)	850227 (40)	850226 (40)	12
80	10	14	10	Finish interior	850227 (40)	850312 (50)	850227 (40)	850312 (50)	0
90	12	14	10	Lay pavement	850218 (33)	850301 (43)	850227 (40)	850312 (50)	7

[a]All work date times are as of the end of the day. Calendar date start times are as of the beginning of the day. Calendar date finish times are as of the end of the day.

33. Because the workdate ES time is expressed as of the end of day 33, the calendar date ES time will be the calendar date that corresponds to work date 34. The task's ES time is the beginning of calendar date 850218.

Late Start Time

The LS time for each arrow is the calendar date that corresponds to the task's work date LS time plus 1. For example, task 40 has a work date LS time of 25. The task's LS time is the beginning of calendar date 850206.

Total Float

The total float for a task could be expressed in workdays or in calendar days. The author prefers to express TF in workdays. Workday TF is computed using work date event times and task durations as described in Chapter 6.

Method 2   Bar Chart Method of Preparing Calendar Date Schedule

Figure 11.5 illustrates a second method for preparing a calendar date schedule. The bar chart has a heading that contains each calendar date of the project duration in the YYMMDD format. Stationery stores and drafting supply stores sell forms that can be readily modified for this purpose. The heading also lists the day of the week for each calendar date. The body of the chart is ruled off in columns, with Sundays and Saturdays marked with periods. The body is also ruled off in lines, with one line for each task of the project.

Task 10 is a Regime 1-type task, that is, it can be worked every day. It has a duration of 30 calendar days. Note that 30 X marks have been plotted for task 10, and note that the X marks are plotted regardless of the day of the week. Task 20 can also start on January 14, 1985, and it has a duration of 10 workdays. Note that 10 X marks have been plotted for task 10, but Saturdays and Sundays have been skipped over because task 20 is a Regime 4-type task. Task 20 has an EF date of January 25, 1985. By an inspection of the logic diagram in Figure 11.4, it is determined that task 30 can commence when task 20 is completed. Although task 20 can be completed on Friday, January 25, 1985, task 30 cannot be started until Monday, January 28, 1985. Again by an inspection of the logic diagram, it is determined that task 90 can commence when both tasks 40 and 50 have been completed. The respective completion dates of these two tasks are February 15, 1985, and February 8, 1985. Hence, task 90 can commence on the first weekday after February 15, 1985, or on February 18, 1985. The project completion date is March 12, 1985, the same date that was computed using the hybrid method.

The bar chart method of preparing a calendar date schedule is very easy to learn. It permits the scheduler to take into account several different workday regimes that apply to the various tasks. The ES and the EF times of the tasks can be read directly from the bar chart.

The Critical Path

A determination of the critical path requires that the scheduler understand the float patterns that are described in Chapter 6.

Common J-Nodes

If two or more arrows have common J-nodes on the logic diagram but are plotted on the bar graph to end at different times, then only the task that has the latest completion time can be critical. For example, both tasks 80 and 90 have a J-node of [14]. Because task 80 is plotted to end after task 90 ends, task 90 cannot

FIGURE 11.5
CALENDAR DATED BAR CHART

```
                        Calendar Dates
          Y 888888888888888888888888888888888888888888888888888888888888
          Y 555555555555555555555555555555555555555555555555555555555555
          M 000000000000000000000000000000000000000000000000000000000000
          M 111111111111111111222222222222222222222222222233333333333333333
          D 111111222222222223300000000001111111111222222222000000000011111111
          D 456789012345678901123456789012345678901234567812345678901234567
        DOW MTWTFSSMTWTFSSMTWTFSSMTWTFSSMTWTFSSMTWTFSSMTWTFSSMTWTFSSMTWTFSS
```

Tsk Nbr	Dur											
10	30 cd	XXXXXXXXXXXXXXXXXXXXXXXXXXXXXX										
20	10 wd	XXXXX	XXXXX									
30	10 wd			XXXXX	XXXXX							
40	15 wd			XXXXX	XXXXX	XXXXX						
50	10 wd			XXXXX	XXXXX							
60	10 wd						XXX	XXXXX	XX			
70	0 wd											
80	10 wd									XXX	XXXXX	XX
90	10 wd								XXXXX	XXXXX		

be critical. Similarly, tasks 10 and 30 have a common J-node, with 10 plotted to end after 30 ends. Hence, task 30 cannot be critical.

Continuous Critical Path
The critical path is continuous from the initial node to the terminal node. If task 90 is not critical, then neither task 40 nor task 50 can be critical, and task 60 must be critical. Because tasks 30, 40, and 50 have been determined to be noncritical, task 20 must be noncritical. Because task 60 has been determined to be critical and task 30 to be noncritical, task 10 must be critical.

Total Float
Although it is possible to compute the total float of the noncritical tasks, such a determination would require a fairly difficult logical analysis. If the scheduler considers that the determination of actual total values is important, then he will find method 1 above or method 3 below more appropriate than the bar chart method. Alternatively, he may express total float in calendar days.

Method 3   An Exact Method, CPM Analysis Based on Calendar Dates

The third method for calendar date scheduling involves computing event times in calendar dates. The calendar date for the EET of the initial node would be one calendar day before the actual calendar date of project commencement. A forward pass and a backward pass would be made. In computing the trial values for EETs, it would be necessary to convert the EET at the I-node of the arrow to a work date, using a conversion chart. The trial value at the J-node of the arrow would be equal to the EET at its I-node plus its duration. Again using the conversion chart, the trial value for the EET at the J-node would have to be converted back to a calendar date. A similar procedure would be used during the backward pass to compute trial values for LETs.

In computing task times and total floats, more references would have to be made to the conversion charts. The procedure sounds complicated, and it is complicated. In fact, it is unsuitable for manual solutions. Computer programs can be used to compute calendar date schedules by using this method. Such programs can include routines that will compute the conversion tables and store them in RAM. If this procedure is used, a great deal of computer memory must be dedicated to the storage of these conversion table data. Alternatively, the computer programs can contain routines that will check every calendar date to determine whether it is a work date or a non-work date for the routine involved. Such routines greatly increase the required computation time.

Notwithstanding the disadvantage of the method just described, it is the only method that will result in true calendar date schedules for projects that include tasks defined as belonging to various regimes and that will correctly compute total float in workdays.

SUMMARY

Three methods are presented in this chapter for preparing a schedule in calendar date format. All three methods require considerably more effort than would be required using the work date format, and the third method is too tedious to be used for manual solutions. However, the first two methods will produce results that are sufficiently accurate for construction scheduling purposes. Many computer programs enable the scheduler to produce calendar date schedules. Some of these programs are based on the first (or hybrid) method, and others are based on the third (exact) method.

UPDATING
THE
SCHEDULE

12

OBJECTIVES

This chapter describes the reasons for updating a construction schedule and two methods for updating schedules. Although Activity On Arrow (AOA) diagrammed schedules are used for examples, the principles that are covered also pertain to Activity On Node (AON) diagrammed schedules. PERT and Monte Carlo schedules can also be updated by using the principles presented. The following discussion is based on the premise that the project logic diagram will be unchanged. The problems encountered in simultaneously revising the diagram and updating the schedule are considered in a subsequent section titled ''Revision of the Logic Diagram.''

REASONS FOR UPDATING
CONSTRUCTION SCHEDULES

A schedule is a time-phased plan for accomplishing the tasks that make up a project. It is based on specified logical relationships between the tasks and on estimated task durations. It is very unlikely that the actual task durations will be exactly as estimated. It is also unlikely that the actual construction sequence will be exactly as depicted in the logic diagram. Furthermore, there may be additions or deletions to the scope of a construction project that will affect the times that tasks can be started and completed. Reliance on the original project schedule throughout the duration of a project after additional information has become available is very much like using a road map that you have purchased in an antique bookshop.

There are really only two reasons for not updating a construction project schedule. First, it is possible, but not likely, that every task may have an actual duration that is equal to its estimated duration, and that the tasks are performed in the exact sequence visualized when the project was originally scheduled. Second, a few contractors prepare a schedule because the contract documents require them to do so, even though they have no plans to use the schedule as a management tool. When the author sees a schedule hanging in a project field office, with no evidence that it has been revised, he always wonders which of these two reasons explains its virginal, although somewhat sun-faded and fly-speckled, condition.

Updating the Schedule to Reflect Current Project Status

The contractor and the owner have a vital interest in knowing the overall project completion status. If the project is behind schedule, both parties should be concerned as to what can be done to get the project back on schedule. In contract construction, the owner will make periodic progress payments to the contractor. It is customary for contractors to submit invoices (requests for partial payment) at fixed intervals, say, once a month. In these invoices, the contractor will claim that he has completed some specified percentage of the total project work. His claimed earnings are equal to the claimed percentage times the contract amount. The owner will review the contractor's claims and, if he finds them reasonable, will make a partial payment to the contractor, often retaining some percentage of the claimed earnings until the project is completed. The retained percentage may be dependent on whether or not the project was on schedule at the time the invoice was submitted. It is very much to the contractor's financial advantage that the owner find his claims reasonable. Prompt payment of the contractor's requests for partial payment will reduce the contractor's need to borrow working capital. Other parties who have an interest in knowing a project's overall completion status might include bonding companies and banks.

Updating the Schedule to Restore Its Original Usefulness as a Management Tool

The construction project schedule can be a useful management tool. It can be used by project managers to coordinate the activities of subcontractors and by procurement specialists to coordinate the delivery of materials, and for many similar purposes. To the extent that the schedule is out of date, its value for these management purposes will be degraded.

Updating the Schedule So That It May Be Used for Evaluation of Procedures, Performances, and Causes for Delay

If a contract falls behind schedule, all concerned will inevitably wonder why it has fallen behind schedule. Perhaps the schedule itself was unrealistic. Perhaps unusual weather was the problem. Maybe owner-instituted changes in project scope are responsible. Answering these questions can be very important. The late completion of a contract may result in the assessment of liquidated damages against a contractor; it will certainly result in the incurrence of project overhead costs for an extended period. If the cause can be attributed to the owner, or to a specific vendor or subcontractor, the contractor may be able to justify an increase in the contract amount, or relief from liquidated damages. Or the contractor may be able to obtain some compensation from those responsible for the delays.

If the fault lies within the contractor's own company (possibly with himself), he may be able to take corrective action, such as additional training for those involved. If the project is being completed ahead of schedule, then an "atta-boy/atta-girl," possibly accompanied by a more tangible reward, may be in order. It is sometimes difficult to determine the actual impact on overall project status that has resulted from completing a particular task in more or less than its estimated duration.

METHOD 1 UPDATING THE SCHEDULE USING THE BAR CHART

This updating method will be used for Example 1. The application of the method results only in determining the project's current status. The example deals with a schedule for the construction of a pre-engineered warehouse building. The project has been scheduled using a Gantt chart as the only scheduling tool. Figure 12.1 is the original bar chart schedule for this project. A total of 13 tasks are shown on the chart. It is not evident just which considerations led the scheduler to draw the chart as depicted. The project has a scheduled duration of 15 weeks. The schedule is to be updated using information that is available as of the end of the eighth week. Note that time-scaled bars represent the periods of time during which the scheduler expects the various tasks to be in progress.

The bar chart lists two specific items of information for each task. First, the estimated duration of each task is listed on the chart. Second, the percentage of the total project work the task involves is listed. For example, the construction of footings represents 2% of the total project work. There are several ways of computing the percentage of the total project work represented by a specific task. These ways will be covered in the discussion that follows. Note that at the bottom of Figure 12.1 there is a line titled "Scheduled Cumulative %." The numbers printed on this line represent the cumulative percentage of the total project work that will be completed at the end of each week during the project's scheduled 15-week duration. Also note that the chart contains an S-shaped curve. This curve graphically represents the scheduled cumulative percentage of project completion as of the end of each week during the scheduled project duration. The procedures for computing the cumulative percentage completion will be covered in the next section. The S-shaped progress curve is characteristic of construction projects. It indicates that progress is slow when the project first starts, picks up speed later, and then is slow again in the final phases of the project.

Task Status as of End of the Eighth Week

Figure 12.2 depicts the status of the project as of the end of the eighth week. Five tasks have been completed, and their actual start and finish dates are shown by the time-scaled bars on the Gantt chart. The bars that represent actual task status are drawn beneath the bars that represent scheduled task status. Often, the bars that represent actual task status will be drawn using a colored pencil. Three other tasks have been started but are not yet completed. The status of each task is listed in the "Curr Stat" column. The bars originate at the time the tasks were actually started, and they terminate at the time the tasks were actually finished or at the end of the eighth week, whichever is earlier.

Note the penciled number in each one-week-long section of the task bars. These numbers represent the percentage of the total project work that was completed in that task during that week. For those tasks that are 100% complete at the end of the eighth week, the sum of the penciled numbers equals the percentage of total project work represented by the task. The line at the bottom of the page titled "Actual Completion %" is completed one column at a time, starting from the left, with the value being equal to the value for the previous week plus the sum of the penciled numbers above and in the same column. In this example, the actual cumulative project completion at the end of the eigth week is 40%. The line titled "Scheduled Completion %" was completed in the same manner but by using the task bars that represent scheduled task starts and finishes. Two S-curves have been plotted, representing scheduled and actual percentage completion of the project. These two curves will be found on Figure 12.3. The bottom line on this figure, titled "Deviation," indicates the difference between scheduled and actual project completion as of the end of each week.

FIGURE 12.1
BAR CHART FOR WAREHOUSE PROJECT

PROJECT: ACME Warehouse Project   Updated As Of:

Weeks

Task	Dur Wks	Pct Tot	Curr Stat
Site Preparation	2	2	
Construct Footings	2	2	
Pour Floor Slab	2	6	
Erect Columns and Girders	3	6	
Set Roof Joists	3	9	
Install Metal Roof	3	9	
Install Metal Wall Panels	3	15	
Install Doors and Windows	3	12	
Install HVAC System	4	8	
Install Electrical System	4	8	
Install Sprinkler System	3	9	
Install Moveable Partitions	3	6	
Pave Drives and Hardstands	2	6	
Landscape Site	2	2	

Week columns: 1 2 3 4 5 6 7 8 9 10 11 12 13 14 15 16

Project Status: 100%, 90%, 80%, 70%, 60%, 50%, 40%, 30%, 20%, 10%, 0%

	1	3	7	12	17	25	40	54	67	74	83	93	98	99	100
Scheduled Cumulative %															
Actual Cumulative %															
Deviation %															

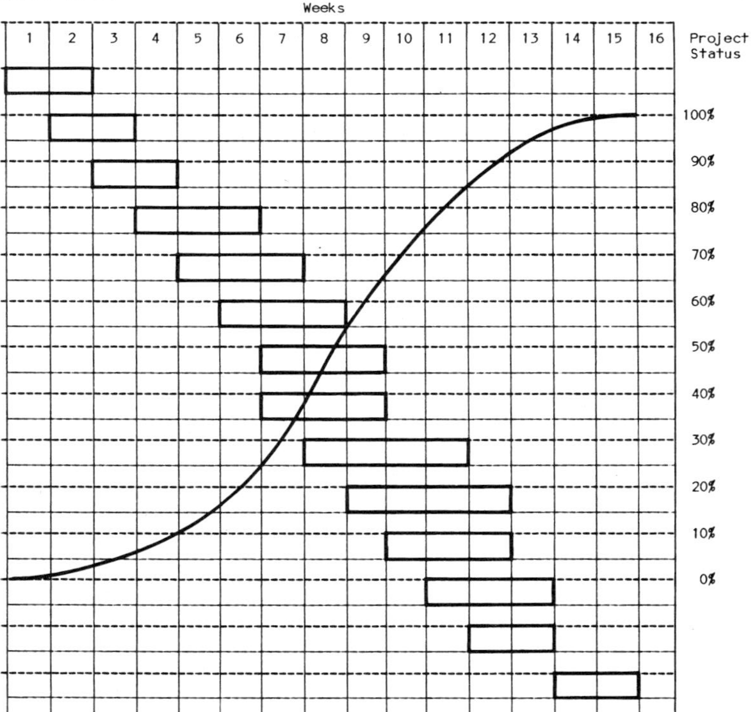

FIGURE 12.2
PERCENT COMPLETION CALCULATION

PROJECT: ACME Warehouse Project   Updated As Of: End of 8 th Week

Weeks

Task	Dur Wks	Pct Tot	Curr Stat	1	2	3	4	5	6	7	8	9	10	11	12	13	14	15	16	Project Status
Site Preparation	2	2	100		2															100%
Construct Footings	2	2	100		1	1														90%
Pour Floor Slab	2	6	100			1	1													80%
Erect Columns and Girders	3	6	100				3	3												70%
Set Roof Joists	3	9	100					2	2	2										50%
Install Metal Roof	3	9	67					3	3	3										50%
Install Metal Wall Panels	3	15	33						3	3	5									40%
Install Doors and Windows	3	12	33								4									30%
Install HVAC System	4	8	0																	20%
Install Electrical System	4	8	0																	10%
Install Sprinkler System	3	9	0																	0%
Install Moveable Partitions	3	6	0																	
Pave Drives and Hardstands	2	6	0																	
Landscape Site	2	2	0																	
Scheduled Cumulative %				1	3	7	12	17	25	40	54	67	74	83	93	98	99	100		
Actual Cumulative %				0	1	3	7	12	17	25	40									
Deviation %				-1	-2	-4	-5	-5	-8	-15	-14									

FIGURE 12.3
UPDATED BAR CHART FOR WAREHOUSE PROJECT

PROJECT: ACME Warehouse Project   Updated As Of: End of 8 th Week

Task	Dur Wks	Pct Tot	Curr Stat	1	2	3	4	5	6	7	8	9	10	11	12	13	14	15	16	Project Status
Site Preparation	2	2	100																	
Construct Footings	2	2	100																	
Pour Floor Slab	2	6	100																	
Erect Columns and Girders	3	6	100																	
Set Roof Joists	3	9	100																	
Install Metal Roof	3	9	67																	
Install Metal Wall Panels	3	15	33																	
Install Doors and Windows	3	12	33																	
Install HVAC System	4	8	0																	
Install Electrical System	4	8	0																	
Install Sprinkler System	3	9	0																	
Install Moveable Partitions	3	6	0																	
Pave Drives and Hardstands	2	6	0																	
Landscape Site	2	2	0																	
Scheduled Cumulative %				1	3	7	12	17	25	40	54	67	74	83	93	98	99	100		
Actual Cumulative %				0	1	3	7	12	17	25	40									
Deviation %				-1	-2	-4	-5	-5	-8	-15	-14									

Project Status scale: 100%, 90%, 80%, 70%, 60%, 50%, 40%, 30%, 20%, 10%, 0%

Utility of the Updated Bar Chart

The updated bar chart schedule very clearly indicates whether a project is ahead of, on, or behind schedule. It should serve well for computing and for proving the contractor's claimed current earnings for invoice purposes. However, the schedule does not answer several important questions. First, what impact will past delays have on the actual completion date? Second, why has the project fallen behind schedule?

A casual examination of the bar chart reveals that the first task to be started, namely, site preparation, started a week after its scheduled starting date and all other tasks that have been started have started a week after their scheduled times. You might surmise that project completion will be one week later than originally scheduled. In fact, you do not know the rationale of the scheduler when he plotted the bars. The scheduled starting date for the installation of the sprinkler system may have been based on the scheduled starting or completion date of one of the tasks listed above. On the other hand, the starting date may have been based on the ability of the supplier to fabricate the system components. If this is the case, the installation of the sprinkler system may be able to start at the beginning of the tenth week as originally scheduled. The task to install roof joists started a week behind schedule. Was all of that one-week delay attributable to the one-week delay in starting the erection of columns and girders? Was the scheduled finish date for completion of the joist installation caused entirely by the one-week delay in the finish of the column and girder erection, or were there other causes?

METHOD 2 UPDATING THE SCHEDULE BY NETWORK ANALYSIS

This method of updating the schedule will clearly indicate why the project is ahead of schedule or behind schedule. If the late initiation of work on a task or the slow performance of work on the task is responsible for project delay, those causes will be pinpointed. It will produce projections of the times that unstarted tasks can be started and unfinished tasks can be completed. It will also indicate whether there have been any changes in the project's critical path.

Essential Terms

The reader should understand the meaning of the following terms:

Times of the Day

Beginning Of Day (BOD)

The BOD is the time of day that is used in connection with the starting of a project or a task when the date is in calendar date format.

End Of Day (EOD)

The EOD is the time of day that is used in connection with the completion of a project or task when the date is in calendar date format. The EOD is the time of day for the start and finish of tasks and projects when the date is in work date format.

End Of Work Date (EWD)

This term is actually redundant when the schedule is in work date format because it has the same meaning as EOD. However, the acronym will be used in this section to emphasize that times are as of the end of a work date.

Update Time

This is the time, expressed in workdays, at the end of which data have been submitted for updating the schedule. It is not the date on which the updating report was prepared.

Projected Values

A projected value may be a task duration or a task start or finish time. Projected values may be based on equations that are presented in the following text, or they may be computed during the CPM network analysis. They may also be based on the scheduler's informed judgment. For example, progress on a partly completed task may have been so slow that computations indicate the task's actual duration will be much larger than its estimated duration. If the scheduler is aware that the task will be completed on a double-shift basis, he or she may elect to substitute his or her judgment-based value for the calculated value of the task duration. In any case, the projected values will be used to produce the revised schedule.

Durations

Five terms are used in connection with a task's duration. In all cases, durations are expressed in workdays (WD).

Estimated Duration

This is the originally estimated task duration.

Actual Duration

This term applies only to tasks that have been finished. It is the actual task duration and is equal to the task's actual finish time less its actual start time.

Projected Duration

This term applies only to tasks that have not been completed. It is the expected elapsed time between a task's starting time and its finish time. It may be computed on the basis of a task's starting time and its percent completion as of the update time. Alternatively, it may be a value that the scheduler considers more appropriate than the computed value.

Effective Duration

This is the difference between a task's actual or projected completion time and the time that it could have been, or could be, started based on the status of precedent tasks.

Duration Deviation

This is the difference between a task's effective duration and its etimated duration. The duration deviation is positive when the task has taken longer to complete than was originally scheduled. It is negative if the task has been completed in less than its scheduled time. The duration deviation is the principal indicator of why a task is off schedule.

Task Status

This is the percent completion of a task as of the update time. Ideally, the percent completion should represent the ratio between the value of the work done on a task and the task's total value. It should not merely represent the ratio between the time the task has been in progress and the task's estimated duration.

Scheduled Status

This is the percent completion of a task as of the update time based on the original schedule.

Actual Status

This is the percent completion reported by field personnel based on their observation of actual progress.

Task Start and Finish Times

Scheduled Start and Finish Times

These are the Early Start Times (ESs) and the Early Finish Times (EFs) that are computed based on the originally estimated task durations.

Actual Start and Finish Times

These terms apply to tasks that have actually been started and, if appropriate, finished as of the update time. The times are as of the end of the day.

Projected Start and Finish Times

These terms are revised early start times and early finish times for unfinished tasks. They are based on the actual and projected start and finish times of precedent tasks. They may be computed values or they may be values the scheduler considers more appropriate than the computed values.

Total Float

Total float is measured in workdays. There are two terms used for total float.

Scheduled Total Float (TF)

This value is computed on the basis of the original network diagram and original estimated task durations.

Revised Total Float (TF-R)

This value is computed based on actual and projected task durations. It is an indicator of the current criticality of completed and unfinished tasks.

Preparatory Steps: Status as of End of Workday Zero (EWD 0)

Step 1. Draw Logic Diagram

Figure 12.4 contains the project's CPM logic diagram. The estimated durations and the total floats (TFs) for all tasks are printed beneath the task arrows. The early event times (EETs) and the late event times (LETs) are printed above and below the event nodes, respectively. Values for durations, total floats, EETs, and LETs are enclosed in parentheses to indicate that they are based on the originally estimated task durations. This diagram will be the basis of another logic diagram to be prepared each time the project schedule is updated. None of the values printed on this diagram will change during subsequent updates. Make a copy for use in the first update. Outline the critical path on the original copy of the logic diagram.

Step 2. Prepare Update Form

This form will be used in conjunction with the logic diagram to update the schedule. The values entered during this preparatory step will not change during

FIGURE 12.4

ORIGINAL CPM DIAGRAM

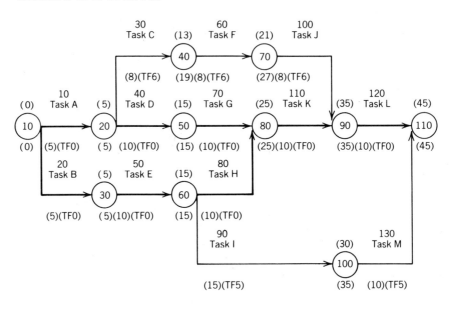

subsequent updates. Make a copy for use in the first update. Complete the following columns on the form shown in Table 12.1.

1. Column a, Task Numbers.

2. Column b, Estimated Task Durations.

3. Column i, Estimated Early Start Times. These values are equal to the EET at the I-node of each task arrow on the logic diagram shown in Figure 12.4.

4. Column l, Estimated Early Finish Times. These values are equal to the column i values EET(I), plus the column b values, Estimated Task Duration.

5. Column o, Scheduled Total Float. These values are equal to the LETs at the task arrows' J-nodes less the column i values less the column b values.

TABLE 12.1

UPDATE FORM AS OF END OF WORKDAY 0

Time of Update: End of Workday 0

Task No. (a)	Duration, Workdays					Status, %		Start, End of Workday			Finish, End of Workday			Total Float, Workdays	
	Est (b)	Act (c)	Proj (d)	Eff (e)	Dev (f)	Schd (g)	Act (h)	Schd (i)	Act (j)	Proj (k)	Schd (l)	Act (m)	Proj (n)	Schd (o)	Rvsd (p)
10	5							0			5			0	
20	5							0			5			0	
30	8							5			13			6	
40	10							5			15			0	
50	10							5			15			0	
60	8							13			21			6	
70	10							15			25			0	
80	10							15			25			0	
90	15							15			30			5	
100	8							21			29			6	
110	10							25			35			0	
120	10							35			45			0	
130	10							30			40			5	

TABLE 12.2

SUPERINTENDENT'S PROJECT STATUS REPORT

Report for Project: Acme Warehouse   As of: 1/25/85 (EWD 10)
Project Start Date: January 14, 1985 (EWD 0)

Task No.	Actual Start Time BOD, EWD M/D/Y		Actual Finish Time EOD, EWD M/D/Y		Task Status, %	Projected Start Time BOD, EWD M/D/Y		Projected Finish Time EOD, EWD M/D/Y		Projected Duration, Workdays
10	1/15/85	1	1/22/85	7	100					
20	1/16/85	2	1/22/85	7	100					
30	1/23/85	7			50					
40	1/24/85	8			20					
50	1/23/85	7			40					
60										
70										
80										
90										
100										
110										
120										
130										

First Update as of End of Workday 10 (EWD 10)

Assume that the project superintendent has submitted the project status report shown in Table 12.2. The superintendent has reported several dates in the month/day/year format. He has reported start dates as of the beginning of the day and finish dates as of the end of the day. The scheduler has converted these times to workday format with all times as of the end of the day. He used Table 11.2 to make these conversions. Use copies of the update form and the CPM diagram that you prepared as a preparatory step to update the schedule as of the end of workday 10. Refer to Table 12.3 and to Figure 12.5 as you study the following sections.

TABLE 12.3

UPDATE FORM AS OF END OF WORKDAY 10

Time of Update: End of Workday 10

Task No. (a)	Duration, Workdays					Status, %		Start, End of Workday			Finish, End of Workday			Total Float, Workdays	
	Est (b)	Act (c)	Proj (d)	Eff (e)	Dev (f)	Schd (g)	Act (h)	Schd (i)	Act (j)	Proj (k)	Schd (l)	Act (m)	Proj (n)	Schd (o)	Rvsd (p)
10	5	6		7		100	100	0	1		5	7		0	0
20	5	5		7		100	100	0	2		5	7		0	3
30	8		6	6		63	50	5	7		13		13	6	9
40	10		10	11		50	20	5	8		15		18	0	0
50	10		8	8		50	40	5	7		15		15	0	3
60	8			8				13		13	21		21	6	9
70	10			10				15		18	25		28	0	0
80	10			10				15		15	25		25	0	3
90	15			15				15		15	30		30	5	8
100	8			8				21		21	29		29	6	9
110	10			10				25		28	35		38	0	0
120	10			10				35		38	45		48	0	0
130	10			10				30		30	40		40	5	8

FIGURE 12.5

CPM DIAGRAM WITH UPDATE DATA
AS OF EOD 10

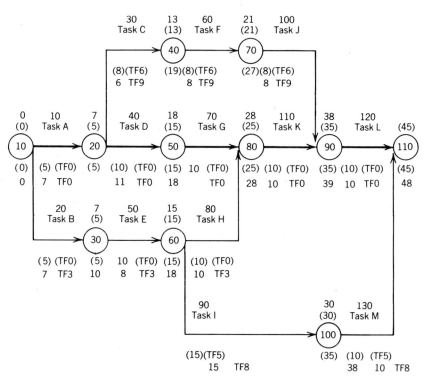

The symbols to be used in this section have the following meanings.

Ut represents the update time. All times, including *Ut*, are as of the end of a workday.

Vx represents a computed or actual value that is to be entered, or has been entered, in column x of the update form (Table 12.1). For example, *Vc* is the actual duration of a task, and the value is to be entered in column c of the update form.

EET-R and *LET-R* are revised values for early event times and late event times based on computations made during the updating process.

Step 1. Enter Update Time

Enter the number 10 in the space at the top of the update form. This is the update time, meaning that all data in the form represents the status of tasks as of the end of workday 10.

Step 2. Enter All Actual Start Times

These data are taken from Table 12.2. Enter these end-of-workday values in column j of the update form. Column j values are entered for tasks 10, 20, 30, 40, and 50 because the field superintendent has reported these tasks as actually started.

Step 3. Enter All Actual Finish Times

These data are taken from Table 12.2. Enter these end-of-workday values in column m of the update form. Also pencil these values above the J-nodes of completed tasks on the logic diagram as a trial value for the node's *EET-R*. Column m values are entered for tasks 10 and 20, which the superintendent has reported as completed.

Step 4. Enter All Actual Durations

Any task that has been reported as actually finished should also have been reported as actually started. The difference between the actual finish time and the actual start time is the actual duration. Enter the actual duration value in column c. Values have been entered for tasks 10 and 20.

Step 5. Make Copies of Update Form and Logic Diagram

All data entered thus far are the actual dates that will not change for subsequent updates. Make a copy of the update form and of the logic diagram for use in subsequent updates.

Step 6. Enter All Actual Task Status Data

The superintendent has reported the actual status of tasks 10, 20, 30, 40, and 50. Enter these completion percentages in column h of the update form.

Step 7. Complete Column g (Scheduled Status) of Update Form

The values in this column represent the scheduled percent completion for the tasks as of the update time. The values for tasks that have column i values (scheduled start times) equal to or greater than the update time are equal to zero. For other tasks (e.g., tasks 10, 20, 30, 40, and 50), the values to be entered in column g can be computed by Equation 12.1. For noninteger numbers, round off to the nearest integer number:

$$Vg = \frac{100(Ut - Vi)}{Vb}, \text{ but not over } 100\% \qquad (12.1)$$

Step 8. Enter Projected Durations for Started but Unfinished Tasks

These are computed values to be entered in column d of the update form. Use Equation 12.2 to determine the values. For noninteger numbers, round off to the nearest integer value:

$$Vd = \frac{100(Ut - Vj)}{Vh} \qquad (12.2)$$

If the scheduler has firm information that the duration of a task will be other than as computed by Equation 12.2, he or she should enter that value in column d.

Step 9. Enter All Projected Start Times Based on Judgment

If the scheduler has firm knowledge that an unstarted task will start at a known future time, he or she should enter that time in column k. Use this option sparingly; normally, the values in column k will be computed values. No values have been entered on this basis for this update.

Step 10. Enter Projected Finish Times

There are two situations in which a projected finish time should be entered. For either of these situations, enter the projected finish time in column n and pencil the value as a trial value for the *EET-R* above the task's J-node on the logic diagram.

1. For started but unfinished tasks, use Equation 12.3. This equation was used for tasks 30, 40, and 50. If the scheduler has firm knowledge that

the task will be finished at some different time, he or she may enter that time in column n.

$$Vn = Vj + Vd \qquad (12.3)$$

2. For any unstarted task for which a projected start time has been entered but no projected duration has been entered, enter a projected finish time. That time will be computed on the basis of Equation 12.4 or it will be based on the scheduler's judgment. This option was not used for this update.

$$Vn = Vk + Vb \qquad 12.4)$$

Step 11. Enter Projected Durations Based on Projected Start and Finish Times

The projected duration is equal to the difference between projected finish time and projected start time. No values were computed on this basis for this update.

Step 12. Enter Effective Duration Values

Thus far, one of two duration values have been entered for some of the tasks. They are the actual and the projected durations. A third duration value must now be determined, the **effective duration**. The effective duration is not necessarily equal to the actual duration. The effective duration includes both the actual duration and any delays in starting a task after the time that it could be started. It is necessary to refer to the logic diagram in Figure 12.5 to determine this value. The effective duration is to be computed on one of the bases below and then entered in column e of the update schedule and printed below the task arrow on the logic diagram.

1. For actually finished tasks, Ve is the difference between the tasks actual finish time and the previously entered trial value for the *EET-R* of the task arrow's I-node. The value Ve was thus computed for tasks 10 and 20.

2. For tasks that have a projected finish time, Ve is the difference between that time and the *EET-R* of the task arrow's I-node. The value was thus computed for tasks 30, 40, and 50.

3. For unstarted tasks that have been assigned a projected duration based on the schedulers judgment but have not been assigned projected start and finish times, the effective duration is equal to that projected duration.

4. For all other tasks (those having neither actual nor projected finish times, nor projected durations), the effective duration is equal to the estimated duration.

Step 13. Enter Effective Durations on Logic Diagram

Print all effective durations (from column e of update form) beneath the task arrows on the logic diagram. Do not enclose them in parentheses.

Step 14. Make a CPM Network Analysis

Make the CPM analysis using the effective task durations. If a trial value for the *EET-R* of a node has already been printed on the diagram (steps 3 and 10) and a second trial value for the *EET-R* is computed during the network analysis, then use the larger value for the *EET-R*. Make both a forward pass to compute *EET-R* values and a backward pass to compute *LET-R* values. Print these EET-R and LET-R values on the logic diagram. Do not enclose them in parentheses.

Step 15. Complete the Update Form

Complete column k (projected start time) for any task not having a value printed in this column. The value is equal to the *EET-R* at the task arrow's I-node. Complete column n (projected finish time) for any task not having a value printed in this column. The value is equal to the task's column k value (projected start time) plus its column e value (effective duration). Complete column p (revised total float). A task's total float is equal to the *LET-R* at its J-node less its *EET-R* at its I-node less its effective duration. Complete column f (duration deviation). The column f value is equal to the column e value (effective duration) less the column b value (estimated duration).

Analyze Project Status

The values entered in the update schedule permit an analysis of overall project status. Refer to Table 12.2. and Figure 12.5. Values printed above and below the event nodes and below the task arrows are not enclosed in parentheses. They represent values that are effective as of this update time.

Impact of Task Performance on Project Status

Column f (duration deviation) is a measure of the effective duration of a task compared to its estimated duration. Effective duration includes not only a task's actual duration, but also the delays in starting a task after it could have been started. The revised project duration is three days longer than the originally estimated project duration. Tasks 10 and 40 were originally critical and are still critical. Between them, the two tasks have effective durations that are three days longer than their estimated durations. Hence, the project delay resulted from slow performance on task 10 and from a delay in starting either task as soon as it could have been started. Task 20 was started two days later than the time it could have been started but was completed within its estimated duration. Because task 20 was on the original critical path, its slow start would have affected project duration. However, rapid completion of task 50 may make up for this delay.

Current Critical Path
Table 12.3 indicated the current total floats of all tasks. The manager should concentrate on those tasks having zero total float to get the project back on schedule. He or she should consider transferring resources from noncritical tasks to critical tasks.

Second Update as of End of Workday 20 (EWD 20)

The project manager and the superintendent have taken some steps to get the project back on schedule. The superintendent's project status report as of January 28, 1985 (1/28/85 or EWD 20), is shown as Table 12.4. Prepare a revised schedule update form and logic diagrams based on the copies of previously prepared forms and diagrams.

Post Data from Superintendent's Report

The data from the superintendent's project status report are posted on Figure 12.6 and on Table 12.5 using the 15-step procedure illustrated previously. The superintendent has made a projection for the starting time of unstarted task 90. He has also made a projection for the finish times of started but unfinished tasks 60 and 70.

During the posting of data, the *EET-R* for node [80] was assigned a trial value of 23 in accordance with step 10. During the CPM analysis, a larger trial value for that *EET-R* was computed and was selected as the *EET-R*.

Revised Project Status

The CPM analysis now indicates that the project will be completed in its original 45-day duration. The schedule as of EWD 10 indicated the project would be 3 days late. The main reason for the improvement in project status is that task 70 now has an effective duration of 6 days versus its estimated duration of 10 days. The critical path has shifted so that tasks 10, 40, and 70 are no longer critical;

TABLE 12.4

SUPERINTENDENT'S PROJECT STATUS REPORT

Report for Project: Acme Warehouse   As of: 2/8/85 (EWD 20)

Project Start Date: January 14, 1985 (EWD 0)

Task No.	Actual Start Time BOD, M/D/Y	EWD	Actual Finish Time EOD, M/D/Y	EWD	Task Status, %	Projected Start Time BOD, M/D/Y	EWD	Projected Finish Time EOD, M/D/Y	EWD	Projected Duration, Workdays
10	1/15/85	1	1/22/85	7	100					
20	1/16/85	2	1/22/85	7	100					
30	1/23/85	7	1/30/85	13	100					
40	1/24/85	8	2/ 5/85	17	100					
50	1/23/85	7	2/ 1/85	15	100					
60	1/31/85	13			90			2/12/85	22	
70	2/ 6/85	17			50			2/13/85	23	
80	2/ 4/85	15			50					
90						2/11/85	20			
100										
110										
120										
130										

FIGURE 12.6
CPM DIAGRAM WITH UPDATE DATA
AS OF EOD 20

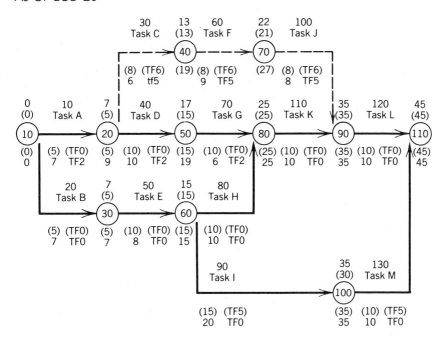

TABLE 12.5
UPDATE FORM AS OF END OF WORKDAY 20

Task No. (a)	Duration, Workdays					Status, %		Start, End of Workday			Finish, End of Workday			Total Float, Workdays	
	Est (b)	Act (c)	Proj (d)	Eff (e)	Dev (f)	Schd (g)	Act (h)	Schd (i)	Act (j)	Proj (k)	Schd (l)	Act (m)	Proj (n)	Schd (o)	Rvsd (p)
10	5	6		7	2	100	100	0	1		5	7		0	2
20	5	5		7	2	100	100	0	2		5	7		0	0
30	8	6		6	-2	100	100	5	7		13	13		6	5
40	10	9		10	0	100	100	5	8		15	17		0	2
50	10	8		8	-2	100	100	5	7		15	15		0	0
60	8		9	9	1	88	90	13	13		21		22	6	5
70	10		6	6	-4	50	50	15	17		25		23	0	2
80	10			10	0	50	50	15	15		25		25	0	0
90	15		15	20	5	33	0	15			30		35	5	0
100	8			8	0	0	0	21			29		30	6	5
110	10			10	0	0	0	25			35		35	0	0
120	10			10	0	0	0	35			45		45	0	0
130	10			10	0	0	0	30			40		45	5	0

however, tasks 90 and 130 have become critical. It appears that the expediting actions on task 70 were slightly overdone, that task now having 2 days of total float.

SUMMARY

Method 1 is fairly easy to learn and to use. It yields useful information on current project status, but it obscures the reasons that a project is off schedule. Method 2 yields complete information on the reasons that a project is off schedule, but it is difficult to learn and to use. Other methods for updating a schedule exist. Many of these methods are incorporated into scheduling computer programs. Ideally, they will result in the output of data similar to that produced by method 2.

EXPEDITING THE PROJECT

13

OBJECTIVE

This chapter describes a method for expediting a construction project at the least cost.

ESSENTIAL TERMS

Expediting

To expedite a project is to take measures that will result in the project's being completed earlier than if these measures had not been taken. The two basic ways of expediting a project are to resequence the tasks that make up the project and to accelerate (crash) some or all of these tasks. If one assumes that the original project schedule was prepared so as to complete the project at minimum cost, then it follows that any revision of that schedule will result in increased costs. In fact, it is often possible to expedite a project without increasing, and possibly decreasing, total costs.

Unnecessary Constraints

A scheduler may specify completion of one task as a constraint to the initiation of a second task, even though such a logical relationship is not essential. Often, the simplest and most economical method for expediting a project is to delete

FIGURE 13.1
WALLBOARD INSTALLATION AS
CONSTRAINT TO WALLBOARD
PAINTING

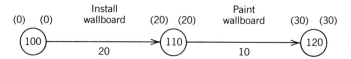

nonessential constraints. For example, assume that the scheduler has specified that all interior wallboard must be installed before any of that wallboard may be painted. This constraint will certainly eliminate any coordination problems between the wallboard installers and the painters. However, its specification may unnecessarily delay project completion. Figure 13.1 indicates the impact on project duration of this unnecessary constraint.

For the example shown in Figure 13.1, completion of the two tasks will require 30 days if the indicated constraint is observed. In Figure 13.2, the unnecessary constraint has been removed, but the duration of the wallboard painting task has been increased to 22 days to reflect the fact that the painting of the wallboard cannot be completed until some time after all of it is installed. The revised duration for the two tasks is 22 days. The Precedence Method (PM) diagram in Figure 13.3 allows this relationship to be depicted more clearly.

In general, constraints should be avoided, unless they are essential. A precedent/subsequent relationship between any pair of tasks involves a constraint. As much as is practical, tasks should be indicated as being concurrent with each other. Use of the PM, as opposed to the CPM, will allow use of precedent/subsequent relationships without unduly prolonging project duration, particularly if the start-to-start and the end-to-end logical relations are used unstead of end-to-start relationships.

FIGURE 13.2
WALLBOARD PAINTING CONCURRENT
WITH WALLBOARD INSTALLATION

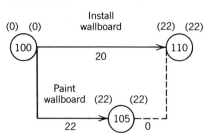

FIGURE 13.3
PRECEDENCE DIAGRAM SHOWING
TASK CONCURRENCY

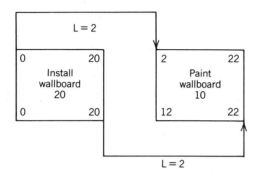

Total Project Direct Costs

Total project direct costs include task costs and project overhead costs, with the latter category being closely related to project duration. If some of the tasks are crashed, there may be an increase in task costs but a greater reduction in project overhead costs.

Penalties and Bonuses

If the project is being performed under a contract, the contract provisions may include penalty and bonus clauses. Liquidated damages are charges that are assessed against a contractor who completes a project later than the date specified in the contract. The purpose of these charges is to reimburse the contractee for losses that he or she may suffer as a result of late performance by the contractor. The amount of these charges is usually specified in the contract in dollars per day of late completion. Although liquidated damages are not considered penalties in a legal sense, they have the nature of a penalty for practical purposes. A bonus is a premium added to the contract price for each day the project is completed earlier than the specified date. It will be to the project manager's financial advantage to incur additional task costs in expediting a project as long as these additional costs are less than the bonuses to be earned or the penalties to be avoided.

Seasonal Considerations

By expediting the early phases of a project (at increased costs for some of the tasks in the early phases), it may become feasible to perform tasks within later phases of the project during a season when that work can be performed more efficiently and at decreased cost. In areas where severe cold weather occurs, it may be necessary to take special (costly) protective measures in order to pour concrete, lay bricks, and so on, during below-freezing weather. In such circumstances, it might be economically feasible to perform site grading, foundation construction, and the like, on a multiple-shift basis during the summer and fall so that concrete and masonry work can be completed before the onset of freezing weather.

Freeing Resources

A project manager may wish to expedite one project so as to make certain that the resources committed to that project, such as manpower and equipment, become available for use on another project.

Effect of Expediting on Cash Flow

It is not always advantageous to expedite a project, even if it can be expedited at negligible cost. Cash flow is covered in Chapter 15. The cash flow problem may be aggravated if a project is expedited.

CRASHING TASKS AND CRASHING THE PROJECT

Both tasks and projects may be completed in less than their normal duration. To completely crash a task is to complete that task in the minimum possible time, by means of working for extended hours and on multiple shifts and by committing to it all of the manpower and equipment that can be used to reduce the task's duration. A completely crashed project is one in which every measure that would contribute to reduction in project duration has been taken.

Note that a project may be completely crashed without completely crashing every task within the project. Figure 13.4 illustrates a project that contains a number of tasks. All of the tasks are "crashable," meaning that they can be completed in less than their normal duration, but at more than their normal cost. Shown on the diagram are normal and crash durations and the normal and crash costs for each task. Also shown on the diagram are the event times if all tasks are completed in their normal durations. Below these values are printed the event times if all tasks are completed in their crash durations. Total floats are indicated for both of these alternatives. Normal project duration is 55 days and normal project cost it $38,800. If all tasks are completely crashed, then project duration

FIGURE 13.4
CPM ANALYSIS USING NORMAL
AND CRASH TASK DATA

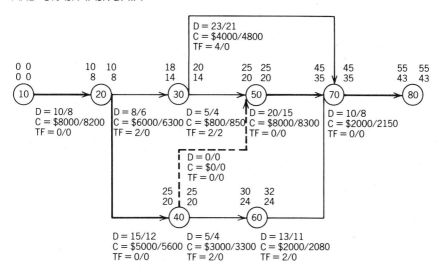

is reduced to 43 days and project cost is increased to 41,580. Note that if all tasks are completely crashed, task [30]–[50] will have 2 days' total float. This indicates that crashing that task was unnecessary, in that it had no effect on project duration. Hence, the project could have been crashed to 43 days at a cost of $41,530 without crashing task [30]–[50].

It is rarely feasible to completely crash either a task or a project. Rather, the objective usually will be to expedite the project to some desired duration by taking those measures that will attain this goal at the least cost. A later section of this chapter outlines a procedure by which a project may be expedited to any desired duration at the least cost.

Crashing Tasks

A task may be crashed by doing the following:

1. Working the tasks on multiple shifts. Personnel on nighttime shifts must be paid a premium wage and are usually less productive than persons working during daylight hours.

2. Working extended hours or extended days. Personnel working more than normal hours per day or more than normal hours per week must be paid a premium wage for the overtime hours. Although their pro-

duction per day or per week will be greater than if they had worked normal hours, their production per hour will decrease and their production per dollar of wage cost will decrease even more rapidly.

3. Bringing larger equipment or additional equipment onto the jobsite. The cost of having an item of equipment on the jobsite is a function of its hourly cost and a delivery/return cost. If an item of equipment will be used only a day or so, the delivery/return costs may represent a large part of the total cost.

4. Putting more men on the job. There is a practical limit to how many men can simultaneously be working on a task without getting in each other's way. Furthermore, the productivity of a worker is usually low when the worker is first committed to a task, improving as his or her knowledge of the task increases. If a task is manned too heavily, it will be completed before the craftsmen have had the opportunity to develop that increased productivity.

5. By using more costly, but more quickly installed, materials.

Only critical tasks need to be crashed. Examine the CPM diagram in Figure 13.5. The durations listed below the task arrows are normal durations (the durations that will be required if the most economical construction procedures are followed). Each of the three tasks can be crashed a maximum of 3 days at the additional cost per day of crashing indicated on the diagram.

Step 1.
There is no reason to crash tasks B and C until they become critical. Therefore, crash task A by one day at an added cost of $100. Figure 13.6 indicates the project schedule with task A crashed by one day.

FIGURE 13.5
PROJECT BEFORE EXPEDITING

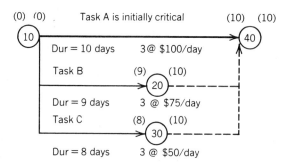

FIGURE 13.6
PROJECT AFTER CRASHING TASK A:
CUMULATIVE EXPEDITING COST =
$100

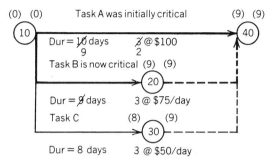

Step 2.
Crash task A by one additional day and crash task B by one day. The total added cost will now be $275 = (2 × $100) + (1 × $75). See Figure 13.7 for the schedule following these expediting actions.

Step 3.
Crash each task by one day. The total added cost is now $500 = (3 × $100) + (2 × $75) + (1 × $50). The project cannot be further expedited because task A has been crashed by 3 days, and it was earlier stipulated that the individual tasks could be crashed by a maximum of 3 days. Even though tasks B and C can be further crashed, such action would not further expedite project completion. See Figure 13.8 for the diagram after the project has been completely crashed.

FIGURE 13.7
AFTER CRASHING TASKS A AND B:
CUMULATIVE COST = $275

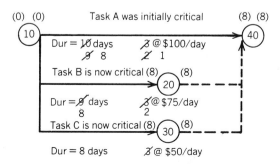

FIGURE 13.8
AFTER CRASHING TASKS A, B, AND
C: CUMULATIVE COST = $500

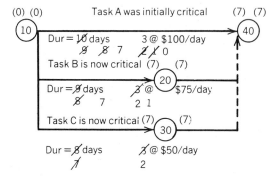

Further Development of Technique

The example depicted in Figures 13.5 and 13.8 is only an introduction to the expediting technique. A subsequent section develops this technique in detail.

ESTIMATES OF TASK COSTS AND TASK DURATIONS

Estimated task costs are related to estimated task durations. There are numerous assumptions an estimator can make concerning the resources that will be used to complete a task; hence, there can be numerous estimates of task duration, each such estimate of task duration having a corresponding estimate of task cost. As a practical matter, an estimator will not consider every conceivable way in which a task can be accomplished. Rather, he will limit his consideration to those techniques with which he is familiar and to those that require resources he believes to be available. The estimator will also make assumptions on such matters as the expected weather conditions that will affect task duration. Hence, it is not to be expected that the estimated "normal," or least-cost, task duration will invariably prove to be either the lowest possible such estimate or that it will prove to be accurate. Still, most estimators will be able to prepare several alternative estimates of task duration and related task cost for many tasks.

Usually, the cost of completing a task will be increased as the task duration is decreased. It is frequently assumed that the relationship between task cost and task duration is **linear**. For example, assume that the estimator considers two ways in which a task can be accomplished. One way will cost $10,000 and require 5 days, whereas the other way will cost only $5000 but will require 10

FIGURE 13.9

TASK DURATION VERSUS TASK
COST

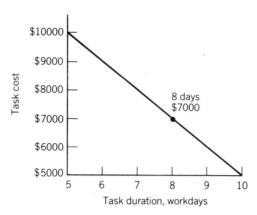

days. It may eventually prove desirable to accomplish the task in some duration
that is between 5 and 10 days.

Figure 13.9 graphically illustrates an assumed linear relationship between task
duration and task cost. Based on the assumption of linearity, it should cost $7000
to accomplish the task in 8 days. The assumed relationship is actually an inverse
relationship. The estimated cost could have been calculated algebraically by
using Equation 13.1:

$$Ci = Cl + \frac{(Cs - Cl)(Dl - Di)}{Dl - Ds} \qquad (13.1)$$

where

Cl = Cost for long duration in $
Cs = Cost for short duration in $
Ci = Cost for intermediate duration in $
Dl = Long duration in days
Ds = Short duration in days
Di = Intermediate duration in days

Example:

$$\text{Cost (8 days)} = \$5000 + \frac{(\$10,000 - \$5000)(10 - 8)}{10 - 5} = \$7000$$

Is the assumption of linearity valid? Assume that a task involves the excavation
of 5000 cubic yards (CY) of earth for a building foundation. The estimator has
determined that the most economical method for excavating the earth would be
to use a backhoe that will already be on the jobsite. The backhoe has an average

TABLE 13.1

TASK COSTS AS A FUNCTION OF WORKDAY LENGTH

Workday Hours	Daily ROP at 62.5 CYH, CY	Task Dur., Days	Straight-Time Work			Overtime Work			Grand Total[a]
			Hours	Hourly Rate	Total	Hours	Hourly Rate	Total	
8	500	10.0	80	$12.50	$1000				$5000
9	562	8.8	71	$12.50	$ 889	9	$18.75	$169	$5058
10	625	8.0	64	$12.50	$ 800	16	$18.75	$300	$5100
11	687	7.3	58	$12.50	$ 727	22	$18.75	$413	$5140
12	750	6.7	53	$12.50	$ 667	27	$18.75	$506	$5173

[a]Total for column includes wage costs and $4000 equipment cost.

rate of production of 62.5 CY per hour (CYH), or 500 CY per 8-hour day (CYD). The normal task duration would be 5000 CY/500CYD = 10 days. The backhoe's operating cost is $50.00 per hour, and the operator's wage costs are $12.50 per hour. Hence, the hourly cost will be $62.50 and the cost per 8-hour day will be $500.00. The total normal task cost will be 10 days × $500 per day = $5000. This task will be on the project's critical path, so the estimator considers expediting it to reduce project duration. The estimator considers two options for expediting the task.

Option 1. Operate the backhoe for more than 8 hours a day. The backhoe's hourly operating cost will remain $50, but the operator's wage costs will be increased by 50% for all hours worked in excess of 8 hours per day (HPD). Table 13.1 contains the computations for the task's cost for various

FIGURE 13.10

TOTAL TASK COST AND DURATION
AS FUNCTION OF WORKDAY LENGTH

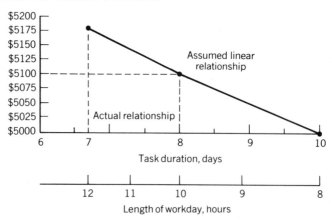

TABLE 13.2
TASK COST AS A FUNCTION OF INCREASED EQUIPMENT COMMITMENT

Task Duration, Days	Equipment	Days Operated	Operating Cost	Delivery Cost	Total Cost
10	First backhoe	10	$5000	$0	$5000
8	First backhoe	8	$4000	$0	
	Second backhoe	2	$1000	$1000	$6000
6	First backhoe	6	$3000	$0	
	Second backhoe	4	$2000	$1000	$6000
5	First backhoe	5	$2500	$0	
	Second backhoe	5	$2500	$1000	$6000

task durations. For this example, it is assumed that the backhoe rate of production will remain at 62.5 CYH, even though the extended workday should result in decreased operator efficiency. Figure 13.10 graphically illustrates the relationship between task cost and task duration. The relationship is nearly linear, and an assumption of linearity is appropriate.

Option 2. Bring a second backhoe onto the jobsite. The second backhoe will be similar to the first one in every respect except that a delivery/return cost of $1000 will be incurred, regardless of how many days the second backhoe is used on the job. Both backhoes will be operated 8 hours a day; hence, the hourly operational cost (including operator's wages) will be $62.50 per hour, or $500 per day. Table 13.2 illustrates that the cost of expediting the task will be the same, regardless of how many days the task is expedited. In this instance, as illustrated in Figure 13.11, the relationship between task duration and task cost is not linear.

FIGURE 13.11
TOTAL TASK COST AS FUNCTION
OF TASK DURATION

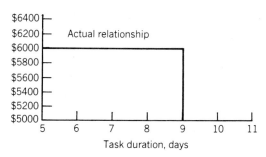

Task duration, days

EXPEDITING PROJECTS AT LEAST COST BY CPM

The least-cost method of expediting a project schedule based on the CPM by any desired time is described below. The method includes procedures for revising the total float of noncritical tasks as critical tasks are crashed.

Step 1. Draw the CPM Diagram

Show the number of days that each task can be crashed, the cost per day to crash each crashable task, and the total float of each task.

Step 2. Draw Sections

The sections must pass vertically through the diagram. A section can pass through any task except those that are critical but noncrashable. As the expediting process is continued, additional tasks will become critical, and the remaining crashability of some tasks will be reduced as a result of the expediting process.

Step 3. Find the Least-Cost Section

The least-cost section is the one in which the sum of the crash costs for the **critical** tasks that it passes through is the lowest.

Step 4. Crash All the Critical Tasks on the Least-Cost Section

The number of days these tasks can be crashed will be the least of:

   1. The remaining crashability of any critical task through which the section passes.

   2. The total float of any noncritical task through which the section passes.

Step 5. Reduce the Crashability of Crashed Tasks

Post the diagram with the remaining crashability of all crashed critical tasks.

Step 6. Reduce the Total Float of Noncritical Tasks Cut by Section

Reduce the total float of any noncritical task through which the section passes if that noncritical task is concurrent with all crashed critical tasks.

Step 7. Reduce the Total Float of Other Noncritical Tasks

Reduce the total float of any other noncritical task in the network so that the lowest total float of any arrow originating at a node is equal to the lowest total float of any arrow terminating at the node.

Step 8. Repeat Process as Often as Possible

Repeat steps 2 through 7 until the project duration has been reduced to the desired value or until it can be reduced no further.

Example 1   CPM Diagram Before Expediting

Figure 13.12 shows the CPM diagram before expediting. Beneath each arrow is printed the normal task duration and the crash task duration and the normal task cost and the crash task cost. A CPM analysis has been made, and all event times are printed above the nodes. The initial project duration is 55 days.

Possible Sections
Figure 13.13 shows the CPM diagram with only the total float and the crash properties indicated for the tasks. Also shown are six possible sections that can be drawn vertically through the diagram. Note that no section passes through critical dummy task [30]–[50]. A section cannot pass through any critical task

---

FIGURE 13.12
CPM DIAGRAM BEFORE EXPEDITING:
DURATION = 55 DAYS

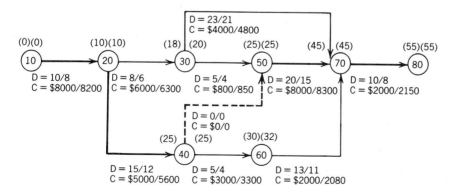

FIGURE 13.13

TOTAL FLOAT AND CRASH
PROPERTIES OF TASKS

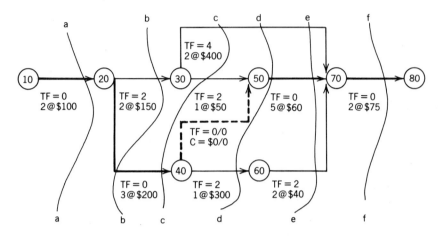

unless that task has remaining crashability, and dummy tasks, having zero duration, cannot be crashed.

First Cut
See Figure 13.14 and Table 13.3. Of the six possible sections, section d–d has
the least cost. Crash task [50]–[70] by 2 days. Although this task has 5 days of

FIGURE 13.14

FIRST CUT: DURATION = 53 DAYS

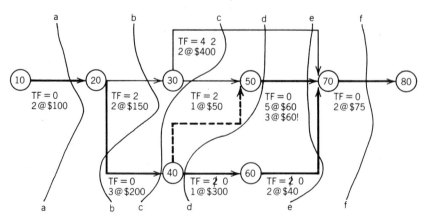

TABLE 13.3

TABULATION OF SECTION CRASH COSTS BEFORE FIRST CUT

Section	Cuts Critical Tasks	Crash Cost, $ per Day For Task	For Section	Crash Section, Days	Crash Cost for Action, $
a–a	[10]–[20]	100	100		
b–b	[20]–[40]	200	200		
c–c	[20]–[40]	200	200		
d–d	[50]–[70]	60	60	2	120
e–e	[50]–[70]	60	60		
f–f	[70]–[80]	75	75		

crashability, tasks [40]–[60] and [60]–[70] will become critical after task [50]–[70] has been crashed 2 days. Post the diagram showing that the crashability of [50]–[60] has been reduced from 5 days to 3 days. Tasks [30]–[70], [40]–[60], and [60]–[70] are all concurrent with crashed critical task [50]–[70], so reduce their total floats by 2 days. Tasks [40]–[60] and [60]–[70] have become critical. In this instance, two sections had equal crash costs. In such instances, either section may be selected. The project duration after the first cut is 53 days, and the cumulative expediting cost is $120.

Second Cut

See Figure 13.15 and Table 13.4. As a result of the first cut, tasks [40]–[60] and [60]–[70] have become critical. The cost of a cut through section d–d has increased from $60 to $360, and the cost of a cut through section e–e has increased from $60 to $100. Section f–f is now the least costly section at $100 a day. Crash task [70]–[80] by 2 days, the amount of that task's crashability. Post the diagram to show that task [70]–[80] has no remaining crashability. Because there are no tasks that are concurrent with this crashed critical task, there are no changes in the total float of other tasks. The project duration after the second cut is 51 days, and the cumulative expediting cost is $270.

Third Cut

See Figure 13.16 and Table 13.5. Both sections a–a and e–e have section costs of $100 per day. It does not matter which of them is selected. Crash task [10]–[20] by 2 days. Post the diagram to indicate that the task has no remaining

FIGURE 13.15
SECOND CUT: DURATION = 51
DAYS

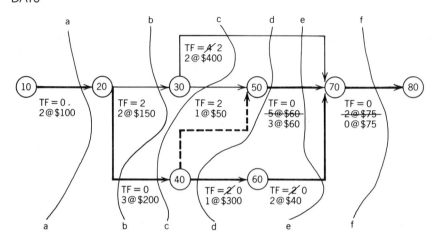

TABLE 13.4
TABULATION OF SECTION CRASH COSTS BEFORE SECOND CUT

Section	Cuts Critical Tasks	Crash Cost, $ per Day For Task	For Section	Crash Section, Days	Crash Cost for Action, $
a–a	[10]–[20]	100	100		
b–b	[20]–[40]	200	200		
c–c	[20]–[40]	200	200		
d–d	[40]–[60] [50]–[70]	300 60	360		
e–e	[50]–[70] [60]–[70]	60 40	100		
f–f	[70]–[80]	75	75	2	150

FIGURE 13.16
THIRD CUT: DURATION = 49 DAYS

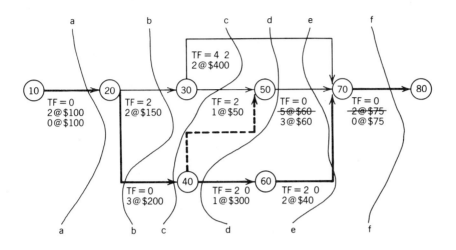

TABLE 13.5
TABULATION OF SECTION CRASH COSTS BEFORE THIRD CUT

Section	Cuts Critical Tasks	Crash Cost, $ per Day		Crash Section, Days	Crash Cost for Action, $
		For Task	For Section		
a–a	[10]–[20]	100	100	2	200
b–b	[20]–[40]	200	200		
c–c	[20]–[40]	200	200		
d–d	[40]–[60]	300	360		
	[50]–[70]	60			
e–e	[50]–[70]	60	100		
	[60]–[70]	40			
f–f	Can no longer be cut				

ms 450

crashability. Crashing this task does not affect the total float of any other task. The current project duration is 49 days, and the cumulative expediting cost is $470.

Fourth Cut

See Figure 13.17 and Table 13.6. During the previous cut, it was determined that a cut through section e–e costs $100. Crash tasks [50]–[70] and [60]–[70] by 2 days. Reduce the crashability of those two tasks by 2 days. Task [30]–[70] is concurrent with both the two crashed tasks, so reduce its total float from 2 days to zero days. Examine node [30]. The lowest total float of an arrow originating at the node is now zero days, so the lowest total float of a node terminating at the node must be zero days. Change the total float of task [20]–[30] to zero days. The current project duration is 47 days, and the cumulative expediting cost is $670.

Fifth Cut

See Figure 13.18 and Table 13.7. The current project duration is 45 days, and the cumulative expediting cost is $1370.

Sixth Cut

See Figure 13.19 and Table 13.8. The current duration is 44 days, and the cumulative expediting cost is $1870.

Seventh Cut

See Figure 13.20 and Table 13.9. No additional expediting is possible after the tasks on this section are crashed. Current duration is 43 days, and cumulative expediting cost is $2730.

Nonlinear Nature of Project Expediting Curve

Table 13.10 is a tabulation of the expediting actions that were made to reduce project duration from 55 days to 43 days. Note that in the column titled "Expediting Cost per Day," the entries are in ascending order. If they had not been in ascending order, it would have been an indication that the tasks were crashed in a sequence that would not result in the least-cost solution to the expediting problem. Figure 13.21 depicts the nonlinear nature of the relationship between project duration and project cost (or project expediting cost). In the early stages of the expediting process, it was possible to expedite the project by crashing only one task, with that task having a low crash cost. In the final stages of the process, it was necessary to crash several tasks to expedite the project, with those tasks having high crash costs.

FIGURE 13.17
FOURTH CUT: DURATION = 47 DAYS

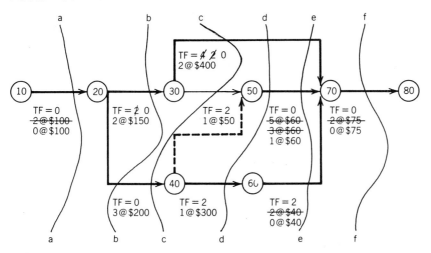

TABLE 13.6
TABULATION OF SECTION CRASH COSTS BEFORE FOURTH CUT

Section	Cuts Critical Tasks	Crash Cost, $ per Day For Task	Crash Cost, $ per Day For Section	Crash Section, Days	Crash Cost for Action, $
a–a	Section can no longer be cut				
b–b	[20]–[40]	200	200		
c–c	[20]–[40]	200	200		
d–d	[40]–[60] [50]–[70]	300 60	360		
e–e	[50]–[70] [60]–[70]	60 40	100	2	200
f–f	Section can no longer be cut				

FIGURE 13.18
FIFTH CUT: DURATION = 45 DAYS

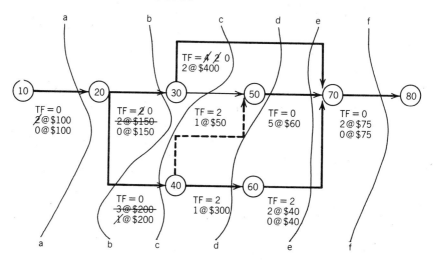

TABLE 13.7
TABULATION OF SECTION CRASH COSTS BEFORE FIFTH CUT

Section	Cuts Critical Tasks	Crash Cost, $ per Day For Task	Crash Cost, $ per Day For Section	Crash Section, Days	Crash Cost for Action, $
a–a	Section can no longer be cut				
b–b	[20]–[30]	150		2	700
	[20]–[40]	200			
c–c	[20]–[40]	200	600		
	[30]–[70]	400			
d–d	[30]–[70]	400			
	[40]–[60]	300			
	[50]–[70]	60	760		
e–e	Section can no longer be cut				
f–f	Section can no longer be cut				

FIGURE 13.19
SIXTH CUT: DURATION = 44 DAYS

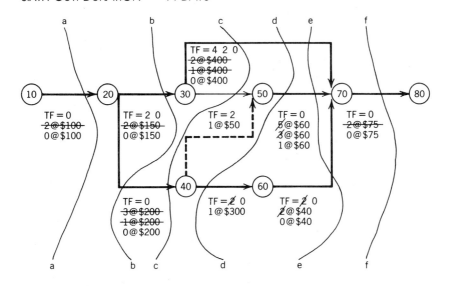

TABLE 13.8
TABULATION OF SECTION CRASH COSTS BEFORE SIXTH CUT

Section	Cuts Critical Tasks	Crash Cost, $ per Day For Task	Crash Cost, $ per Day For Section	Crash Section, Days	Crash Cost for Action, $
a–a	Can no longer be cut				
b–b	Can no longer be cut				
c–c	[20]–[40]	200			
	[30]–[70]	400	600	1	600
d–d	[30]–[70]	400			
	[40]–[60]	300			
	[50]–[70]	60	760		
e–e	Can no longer be cut				
f–f	Can no longer be cut				

FIGURE 13.20
SEVENTH CUT: DURATION = 43
DAYS

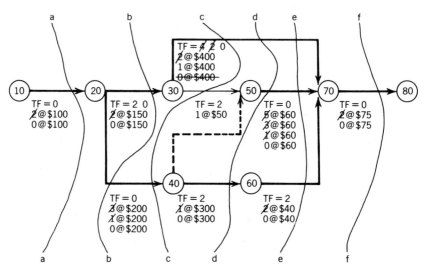

TABLE 13.9
TABULATION OF SECTION CRASH COSTS BEFORE SEVENTH CUT

Section	Cuts Critical Tasks	Crash Cost, $ per Day For Task	For Section	Crash Section, Days	Crash Cost for Action, $
a–a	Can no longer be cut				
b–b	Can no longer be cut				
c–c	Can no longer be cut				
	[30]–[70]	400			
	[40]–[60]	300			
d–d	[50]–[70]	60		1	760
e–e	Can no longer be cut				
f–f	Can no longer be cut				

TABLE 13.10

TABULATION OF EXPEDITING COSTS

Cut No.	Crash Tasks	Crash Cost, $ per Day	Expediting Cost per Day, $	Expedite Project, Days	Revised Duration, Days	Cumulative Cost, $
0	Before expediting		NA	NA	55	0
1	[50]–[70]	60	60	2	53	120
2	[70]–[80]	75	75	2	51	270
3	[10]–[20]	100	100	2	49	470
4	[50]–[70]	60				
	[60]–[70]	40	100	2	47	670
5	[20]–[30]	150				
	[20]–[40]	200	350	2	45	1370
6	[20]–[40]	200				
	[30]–[70]	400	600	1	44	1970
7	[30]–[70]	400				
	[40]–[60]	300				
	[50]–[70]	60	760	1	43	2730

FIGURE 13.21
PROJECT DURATION VERSUS
PROJECT LENGTH

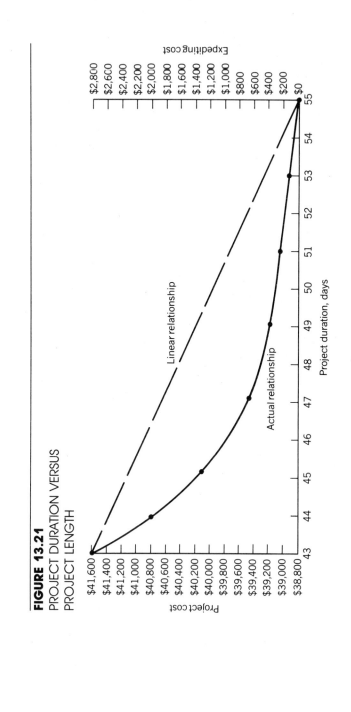

EXPEDITING PROJECTS DIAGRAMMED WITH AON NOTATION

Precedence diagrams can be expedited as described above. Feasible sections can cut through noncritical or crashable task nodes or relationship arrows.

SUMMARY

The method of sections is a practical method for expediting a project at least cost. Before it is used, the diagram should be examined to determine if the desired expediting can be obtained by deleting nonessential logical constraints.

RESOURCE-CONSTRAINED SCHEDULING AND RESOURCE LEVELING

14

OBJECTIVE

The objective of this chapter is to describe the procedures that can be used to perform resource-constrained scheduling and to schedule projects so as to level resource requirements. These resources include people, machines, equipment, and working capital. If some of these resources are in such short supply that normal progress on a project will be impeded, the resulting schedule will be a resource-constrained schedule, and the project duration may be extended beyond what it would have been if there had been no such shortages. If sufficient resources are available, but if there are wide fluctuations in the daily need for these resources, then it may be desirable to perform resource leveling. This latter technique is sometimes termed **manpower leveling** when manpower is the resource involved.

CONSTRAINTS

A constraint is a factor that prevents or delays the initiation or the continuance of work on a task. There are two types of constraints.

Logical Constraints

As indicated in previous chapters, the initiation of work on some of the tasks that make up a project may be constrained by logical relationships between the tasks. Gypsum wallboard cannot be painted until at least some of it is installed. Floor coverings cannot be laid until floor slabs are poured. Finish materials cannot be installed in a building until the building is closed in, that is, until the roof, exterior walls, windows, and doors are installed.

Resource Constraints

This chapter introduces a different type of constraint to the initiation of, and the progress on, tasks, that is, the absence, or the shortage, of resources that are required for progress on the tasks. Painting the wallboard will be constrained if there are no resources (painters and paint) available or if the resources that are available are committed to another task at the same time that they are needed for painting the wallboard. Resources may be categorized as follows:

Labor

Labor resources may be further categorized by craft, such as carpenters, welders, and laborers. There is some interchangeability between kinds of labor resources. An abundance of carpenters may compensate for a shortage of drywall hangers, although the terms of a union contract may preclude such a substitution of skills. In other instances, the substitution of skills may not be feasible. Common laborers cannot be used as welders. It is customary for construction companies to employ some workmen who are "jacks of several trades." This practice reduces delays resulting from a lack of specialized craftsmen and also gives the workforce employment stability and results in increased workforce loyalty.

Even though a labor resource may not be immediately available, it is often possible to recruit workers from other areas, possibly by paying them premium wages or by paying them a commuting or lodging allowance.

Material

Construction material is a resource that is essential to progress on a project. The correct type and proper quantity of materials may not be available because the manager simply failed to order them in time. On other occasions, the shortage may have been beyond the contractor's control. In the spring of 1983, there was a shortage of gypsum wallboard throughout the South Atlantic region, even though plentiful supplies were available in other regions of the country. In this instance, suppliers rationed the amount of wallboard they would deliver to individual customers until additional supplies could be brought in from other regions. A more serious resource shortage occurred in 1973, when there was worldwide shortage of copper electrical wire. The supply of basic copper had been affected by the global energy crisis that was precipitated by the Arab oil embargo. Some manufacturers of copper wire gave priority for delivery to customers who could provide basic copper or scrap copper.

When a commodity is in short supply, federal regulations require that priority for delivery will be given to purposes that are essential to the national defense.

The project manager can reduce the likelihood that materials will become a constraint to project completion by scheduling the material procurement actions just as though they were any other task and then monitoring the delivery of those materials that are most critical. In some situations, with the consent of the owner, it may be feasible to use substitute materials.

Equipment

Lack of construction equipment, either of the correct size and type or in sufficient quantity, may be a constraint to project progress. The project manager can reduce the likelihood of equipment becoming a constraint by advance planning and scheduling. He or she can reduce the impact of a shortage that has developed by substituting other types of equipment or by renting equipment.

Working Capital

In general, a construction contractor must pay for materials soon after they are delivered. He must pay his employees weekly or biweekly. The contractor usually does not receive payment for the work he has performed until some time after he has paid many of these expenses. The difference between a contractor's cumulative income and his or her cumulative expense on a project is termed **project cash flow balance**. If this balance is negative, contractors lacking sufficient working capital to cover the balance and unable to borrow working capital are forced to slow down the delivery of materials and the use of labor. A contractor in this position is suffering a cash flow problem. Chapter 15 covers this topic in detail.

RESOURCE-CONSTRAINED SCHEDULING PROBLEM

This situation is defined as one in which the shortage of some kind, or kinds, of resource is delaying, or will delay, project progress and in which it is impossible to secure additional resources. The project manager's problem, therefore, becomes one of allocating those resources that are available to the tasks in the manner that will result in the least delay of the project completion.

There are several ways to minimize the impact of a resource shortage on project completion. They include the following:

Assignment of Priorities for Allocation of Scarce Resources

It would appear evident that the manager should give priority to assigning limited resources to those tasks that are critical or most nearly critical. This is not always the best solution to the problem. An example that follows illustrates that in a particular instance, another basis for assignment of priority may result in a better solution to a resource-constrained scheduling problem.

Performance of Tasks on a Noncontinuous Basis

Performance on a continuous basis means that once a task is commenced, it must be worked continuously until it is completed. Performance on a noncontinuous basis means that a task can be commenced as soon as all its logical constraints have been satisfied, but performance may be interrupted while scarce resources are diverted to some more critical task. For example, laborers might be used to form and pour sidewalks. If these laborers were required on another, higher-prioirty task, it would be practical to interrupt the sidewalk task while the laborers were diverted to that higher-priority task. It may be impossible or impractical to work some tasks on a noncontinuous basis. For example, a task may require the commitment of two kinds of resources, only one of which is limited in availability, with the other resource being readily available but costly to provide on an interrupted basis. Assume that a task required commitment of a pile driver and an air compressor, with only one air compressor being available. Also assume that the cost of having the pile driver on the job is much greater than the cost of the air compressor. It would be impractical to interrupt the pile driving operation while the air compressor was diverted for an extended period to some other task requiring its use.

Change Level of Resource Commitment to Tasks

Determine whether the impact of constrained resources can be decreased by changing the level of resource commitment to some of the tasks requiring such commitment. Usually, a decrease in resource commitment to a task will extend the duration of that task, and an increase in resource commitment will reduce task duration. The scheduler should be particularly careful to determine whether the scarce resources specified as being necessary for working a task are actually required for the entire duration of the task. If they are not, the task should be subdivided into two or more tasks, with scarce resources being specified as being required only for those subtasks for which they are actually required.

Rules of Thumb for Assigning Priority for Resource Allocation

One such rule was stated earlier, that is, to give priority to the critical, or most nearly critical, tasks. Neither this rule nor any other rule is guaranteed to yield the optimum solution to the resource-constrained scheduling problem. Four such rules are listed below and will be illustrated later in this section. To apply the rules, list the tasks on a bar chart, following the selected rule of thumb to determine their order. Starting at the top of the bar chart, draw the bars for the tasks if sufficient resources are available, if the logical constraints to their initiation have been satisfied, and if initiation of the tasks will not subsequently result in a delay in starting a higher-priority task. Plot the bar for a lower-priority task only when the completion of the task is a logical constraint to starting a higher-priority task.

Rule 1. Give priority to the tasks having the lowest J-node numbers. Schedule these tasks to be performed on a continuous basis. Do not schedule a lower-priority task unless the completion of that task is a logical constraint to an initiation of the higher-priority tasks. If you have observed the convention that nodes be numbered so that all tasks have a higher-numbered node at their J-end than at their I-end and if you list the tasks in order of their J-node numbers, then you will have produced a list in which no task is precedent to another task that occurs earlier in the list. This list is termed a **precedent-ordered list**. It does not follow that a task in such a list is necessarily precedent to every task located lower in the list.

Rule 2. Give priority to the critical, or most nearly critical, task, that is, to those tasks having the lowest total float. Schedule these tasks to be performed on a continuous basis. Do not schedule a task until all higher-priority tasks have been scheduled unless the completion of that task is a logical constraint to initiation of those higher-priority tasks.

Rule 3. Give priority to tasks having the shortest durations, scheduling tasks that have longer durations only if the completion of a low-priority task is a logical constraint to the initiation of a higher-priority task. Schedule these tasks to be performed on a continuous basis.

Rule 4. Follow one of the three rules above, but schedule lower-priority tasks on a noncontinuous basis when insufficient resources are available to start a higher-priority task. Then, interrupt the lower-priority task when such interruption will free resources needed to start a higher-priority task.

Each of the following examples refers to one or more bar charts. The tasks are listed in those bar charts in their order of priority for the allocation of resources, with their priorities being based on the rules of thumb stated above.

Example 1

This concerns a project in which there is a moderate shortage of resources. Figure 14.1*a* depicts a CPM diagram for the project. Tasks A and B both require the

---

FIGURE 14.1*a*

CPM DIAGRAM: UNCONSTRAINED

DURATION = 30 DAYS

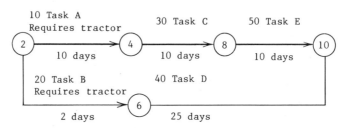

---

use of a tractor, and only one tractor is available. If it were not for the resource constraint (only one tractor is available), tasks A and B could be performed concurrently and the project duration would be 30 days.

Based on Rule 2

Figure 14.1*b* is a bar chart based on the application of rule of thumb 2, that is, the assignment of priority for the allocation of scarce resources to tasks having the least total float. The resource-constrained project duration is 37 days.

Based on Rule 3

Figure 14.1*c* is a bar chart based on the application of rule of thumb 3, that is, the assignment of priority for the allocation of scarce resources to those tasks having the shortest duration. The resource-constrained project duration is 32 days.

The bars on both bar charts were plotted in consideration of all logical constraints. For example, the bar task C was not plotted until after a bar had been

---

FIGURE 14.1*b*

BAR CHART, PRIORITY TO LOW
TOTAL FLOAT TASKS: PROJECT
DURATION = 37 DAYS

Type: Priority to most critical tasks. Project duration is 37 WD

Task	Dur	TF					
A	10	0	XXXXXXXXXX				
B	2	3		XX			
C	10	0		XXXXXXXXXX			
D	25	3		XXXXXXXXXXXXXXXXXXXXXXXXX		
E	10	0			XXXXXXXXXX	

```
                    10        20        30        40        50
                            Workdays
```

(b)

FIGURE 14.1c
BAR CHART, PRIORITY TO LOW
DURATION TASKS: PROJECT
DURATION = 32 DAYS

```
Type: Priority to tasks with shortest duration. Project duration is 32 WD
Task Dur  TF
 B    2    3   XX
 A   10    0   XXXXXXXXXX
 C   10    0             XXXXXXXXXX
 E   10    0                       XXXXXXXXXX
 D   25    3   XXXXXXXXXXXXXXXXXXXXXXXXX
                    10        20        30        40        50
                              Workdays
                                (c)
```

plotted for precedent task A. In this instance, the application of Rule 3 resulted in a shorter project duration than did the application of Rule 2. However, no conclusion can be drawn to the effect that Rule 3 will always yield a better solution than will Rule 2.

Example 2

This concerns a project in which there is a severe shortage of two kinds of resource. The CPM diagram shown in Figure 14.2a indicates the tasks, their logical relationships, their durations, and the number of scarce resources required by each. For example, task A requires the commitment of two type 1 resources and five type 2 resources. If it were not for the resource constraints, this project could be completed in 16 days. Figure 14.2b is a bar chart for this project based upon unlimited resources, that is, there is no upper limit on the number of type

FIGURE 14.2a
CPM DIAGRAM WITH TASK
RESOURCE REQUIREMENTS

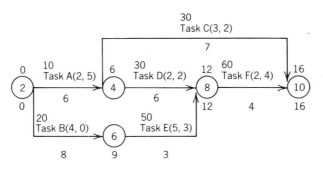

1 and type 2 resources that can be simultaneously committed to the project. For this example, assume that the maximum number of type 1 and type 2 resources that will be available are seven and five, respectively. Hence, the objective of this problem is to schedule the tasks so that the project duration is as close as possible to its resource-unconstrained duration of 16 days without using more than the available number of resources.

Bar charts are presented in Figures 14.2c to 14.2e, which are based upon the rules listed above. The dashed lines to the left of several of the task bars indicate

---

FIGURE 14.2b

NO RESOURCE CONSTRAINTS:
PROJECT DURATION = 16 DAYS

Type: Resource-unconstrained schedule. Project duration is 16 WD

Tsk No.	I-N No.	J-N No.	Dur WD	TF WD	Rsc Rqmts 1	2	Workday 5 10 15 20 25 30 35 40
A	2	4	6	0	2	5	XXXXXX
B	2	6	8	1	4	0	XXXXXXXX
C	4	10	7	3	3	2	XXXXXXX
D	4	8	6	0	2	2	XXXXXX
E	6	8	3	1	5	3	XXX
F	8	10	4	0	2	4	XXXX
Type 1 resources used Maximum daily usage = 10 Total usage = 100 RD							0000000011100000 6666669900055222
Type 2 resources used Maximum daily usage = 7 Total usage = 81 RD							0000000000000000 5555554477746444

FIGURE 14.2c

TWO CONSTRAINED RESOURCES,
PRIORITY TO TASKS WITH LOW-
NUMBERED J-NODES: PROJECT
DURATION = 22 DAYS

Type: Resource-constrained schedule with priority to tasks with the lowest
J-node numbers. Project duration is 22 workdays.
Maximum resources available: Type 1 = 7, Type 2 = 5

Tsk No.	I-N No.	J-N No.	Dur WD	TF WD	Rsc Rqmts 1	2	Workday 5 10 15 20 25 30 35 40
A	2	4	6	0	2	5	XXXXXX
B	2	6	8	1	4	0	XXXXXXXX
D	4	8	6	0	2	2	XXXXXX
E	6	8	3	1	5	3	XXX
C	4	10	7	3	3	2	-----XXXXXXX
F	8	10	4	0	2	4	XXXX
Type 1 Resources Maximum daily usage = 7 Total usage = 100 RD							00000000000000000000000 6666666677753333332222
Type 2 Resources Maximum daily usage = 5 Total usage = 81							00000000000000000000000 5555552255554222224444

FIGURE 14.2*d*

PRIORITY TO TASKS WITH LOWEST
TOTAL FLOAT: PROJECT DURATION
= 23 DAYS

Type: Resource-constrained schedule with priority given to tasks with the
the lowest total float. Project duration is 23 days.
Maximum resources available: Type 1 = 7, Type 2 = 5

Tsk No.	I-N No.	J-N No.	Dur WD	TF WD	Rsc Rqmts 1	2	Workday 5	10	15	20	25	30	35	40
A	2	4	6	0	2	5	XXXXXX							
D	4	8	6	0	2	2	XXXXXX							
F	8	10	4	0	2	4	XXXX							
B	2	6	8	1	4	0	XXXXXXXX							
E	6	8	3	1	5	3	XXX							
C	4	10	7	3	3	2	----------XXXXXXX							
Type 1 Resources							00000000000000000000000							
Maximum daily usage = 7							66666666777222223333333							
Total usage = 100 RD														
Type 2 Resources							00000000000000000000000							
Maximum daily usage = 5							55555522555244442222222							
Total usage = 81 RD														

FIGURE 14.2*e*

NONCONTINUOUS TASK
PERFORMANCE

Type: Resource-constrained schedule with priority given to tasks with the lowest total float. Lower
priority tasks can be scheduled on a noncontinuous basis when resources are available. Task C was
so scheduled.
Project duration = 22 days.
Maximum resources available: Type 1 = 7, Type 2 = 5

Tsk No.	I-N No.	J-N No.	Dur WD	TF WD	Rsc #1	Rqmts #2	Workday 5	10	15	20	25303540
A	2	4	6	0	2	5	XXXXXX				
D	4	8	6	0	2	2	XXXXXX				
F	8	10	4	0	2	4				XXXX	
B	2	6	8	1	4	0	XXXXXXXX				
E	6	8	3	1	5	3	XXX				
C	4	10	7	3	3	2	-----X- ---XXXXXX				
Type 1 resources							0000000000 000 000000000				
Maximum daily usage = 7							66666 66677 752 222333333				
Total Usage = 100 RD											
Type 2 resources							00000 00000 000 000000000				
Maximum daily usage = 5							55555 52255 544 444222222				
Total usage = 81 RD											

that those particular tasks have been delayed only by resource constraints. The resource-constrained project durations are as follows:

Rule 1

Priority to tasks with the smallest J-node numbers. See Figure 14.2c. The tasks are listed in J-node number order. Where two tasks have the same J-node numbers (tasks D and E), they are listed in I-node number. Task C could have been started on the seventh workday (EOD 6), but a shortage of type 1 resources delayed its start until the twelfth workday. The resource-constrained project duration is 22 days.

Rule 2

Priority to tasks with the smallest total float. See Figure 14.2d. The tasks are listed in order of their total float values. Where several tasks have the same total float (A, D, and F), they are listed in J-node order. Logical constraints prevent starting task C until the seventh workday, but an insufficiency of type 1 resources prevented scheduling it until the twelfth workday. At that point, task C could have started, but if it were worked on a continuous basis the start of higher-priority task F would have been delayed starting on the thirteenth day. The resource-constrained project duration is 23 days.

Rule 3

Priority to tasks with the shortest duration. No schedule was prepared based on this rule.

Rule 4

Priority to tasks with the least total float, but lower-priority tasks are scheduled on a noncontinuous basis when logical constraints are satisfied and when resources are available. See Figure 14.2a. In this case, sufficient resources were available to do one day's work on task C on the twelfth day. Task C is to be interrupted as soon as higher-priority task F commences on the thirteenth day. The resource constrained project duration is 22 days.

Comparison of Results

For example 2, the application of Rules 1 and 4 resulted in the shortest project duration. This does not guarantee that someone will not be able to devise other rules of thumb that will result in a smaller resource-constrained project duration for this problem. For most problems, Rule 1 is the simplest and will yield nearly the best results.

Optimum Solution to the Resource-Constrained Scheduling Problem

Finding the optimum solution to the resource-constrained scheduling problem requires testing a great many possible solutions. In fact, it may be impossible to determine the optimum solution for a complex project with many resources constraints, even with sophisticated computer programs. However, finding a solution that is nearly optimum will usually suffice.

It is possible to determine rapidly whether a solution is an optimum or near-optimum solution. To do so, determine the **lower boundary (LB)** of the project duration. It will be equal to the project duration based on no resource constraints, or it will be equal to the time computed by Equation 14.1, whichever is longest. The equation must be applied for each type of scarce resource. There will be no feasible solution with a duration that is shorter than this lower boundary, and there may be no feasible solution that is as short as the lower boundary. The symbol *LB* stands for a trial value for the lower boundary on project duration based on resource requirements and resource availability. The symbol *NR* stands for the number of resources required by a task. The symbol *TD* stands for the duration of the task. The symbol *N* stands for the number of that kind of resource that is available. Determine the lower boundary of the project duration for the project depicted in Figure 14.2*a*:

$$LB = \frac{\Sigma TD \times NR}{N} \qquad (14.1)$$

For the project depicted in Figure 14.2*a*, the lower boundary of task duration is computed as shown below. A trial value for the lower boundary is 16 days based on unlimited resources. Trial values for the lower boundary must be computed based on the task requirements for, and the availability of, type 1 and type 2 resources. The application of Equation 14.1 yields the following trial values:

Type 1 resources:
$$
\begin{array}{ccccccc}
 & (A) & (B) & (C) & (D) & (E) & (F) \\
LB = & 6\times2 & + 8\times4 & + 7\times3 & + 6\times2 & + 3\times5 & + 4\times2 = \dfrac{100}{7} = 14.3 \\
\end{array}
$$

Type 2 resources:
$$
\begin{array}{ccccccc}
 & (A) & (B) & (C) & (D) & (E) & (F) \\
LB = & 6\times5 & + 8\times0 & + 7\times2 & + 6\times2 & + 3\times3 & + 4\times4 = \dfrac{81}{5} = 16.2 \\
\end{array}
$$

Comparison of Lower Boundary to Computed Project Duration

Three trial values were computed for the lower boundary of project duration for the project depicted in Figure 14.2*a*. The largest is selected as the lower boundary. The resource-constrained project duration cannot be less than 16.2 days. The bar charts shown in Figures 14.2*c* to 14.2*e* resulted in a shortest project duration of 22 days, well above the lower boundary. The difference between 22 days and the lower boundary indicates that there may be some other solution with a duration closer to 16.2 days.

RESOURCE LEVELING

The second problem to be addressed in this chapter concerns resource leveling. Figures 14.3a to 14.3c represent three patterns for a project's daily requirements for a certain type of resource. Which pattern will exist depends upon on how the scheduler and the project manager have planned to sequence the tasks and to staff the various work crews. Consider the three patterns of resource requirements and determine which would be most desirable. The total quantity of resources (man-days, tractor-days, etc.) for each figure is equal to the area under the curve. Assume that the three areas are equal.

Resource Requirements

Fluctuating Requirement
See Figure 14.3a. If the resource involved is carpenters, then it is evident that many carpenters will have to be recruited and then furloughed after only a few days' work, and this recruiting–furloughing cycle will be repeated several times during the project duration. If the resource is dozers, then many dozers will have

FIGURE 14.3a
FLUCTUATING REQUIREMENT

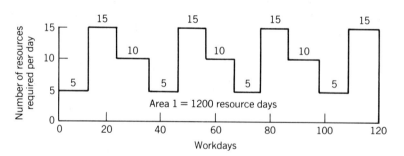

FIGURE 14.3b
LEVEL REQUIREMENT

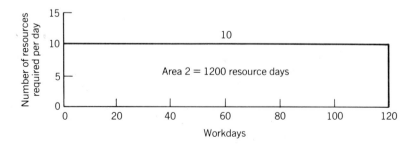

FIGURE 14.3c

VARYING REQUIREMENT

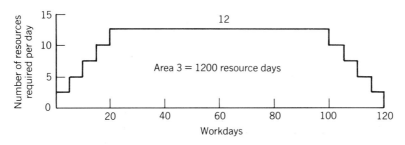

to be brought onto the jobsite and then returned to the equipment yard after only a few days' work. It is difficult to imagine how this pattern of resource utilization could be considered efficient.

Level Requirement

Examine Figure 14.2*b*. At first glance, it would appear that this pattern of resource utilization would be very desirable. The peak number of resources required will be less with this pattern than with either of the other two patterns. However, it will be very difficult to schedule a project so that there will be a level requirement. It will also be very difficult to recruit craftsmen so that the maximum number will be available immediately upon project commencement.

Varying Requirement

Study Figure 14.3*c*. This pattern indicates that there will be a steady buildup in the requirements for a resource (say, laborers) until a certain number is on hand. Then, the requirement will remain constant until near the end of the project, when the requirements will gradually decrease to zero. This pattern is more desirable than the first pattern and is more attainable than the second pattern.

Scheduling the Project to Obtain Desired Pattern

Ideally, one would start all tasks somewhere between their early start time and their late start time, so that project duration would not be extended and would in the process obtain a pattern of the desired type. This can be done by sliding the tasks between the two times and summing the resource requirements on a daily basis. It is very helpful in obtaining the desired pattern to be able to

1. Perform tasks on a noncontinuous basis.

2. Vary the quantity of resources committed to tasks and, therefore, the task durations.

Resource Leveling Example

See Figure 14.4*a* for a CPM diagram that is used for this example. There are 13 task arrows on the diagram. The duration of each task is printed below the arrow, and the number of required resources is enclosed within parentheses above the arrow. The EETs and the LETs are printed above the nodes. The objective of the example is to complete the project in its resource-uncontrained duration of 40 days using the minimum peak resource requirements. Tasks may be performed on a noncontinuous basis, but the level of commitment of resources to a task cannot be changed.

Early Start Project Schedule

See Figure 14.4*b*. The upper bar chart depicts the project schedule if all tasks are started at their early start times. Note that the early start times are expressed as of the beginning of the day, a departure from previous practice. The bars consist of numbers equal to the tasks' resource requirements. This will facilitate calculating the daily resource usage. This format would not have been feasible if there had been more than one constrained resource. The daily usage of the scarce resource is printed at the base of this bar chart. Daily usage varies from 8 to 22, with 22 being the peak daily usage.

Lower Boundary for Peak Daily
Resource Usage (*LB*)

Determine the lower boundary of the peak value of resources required to accomplish the project by using Equation 14.2. Note that *LB* has a different meaning than it did in a previous section. The symbols *TD* and *NR* stand for task duration and task resource requirement, respectively:

$$LB = \frac{TD \times NR}{N} \tag{14.2}$$

For this example, $TD \times NR$ equals 485 resource days and $N = 40$ days; hence, the lower boundary for peak daily resource usage is 12.15. The significance of this lower boundary is that if it were possible to use exactly 12.15 resources every day for 40 days, the utilization pattern would be perfectly level.

In this case, a maximum of 85 resource days can be used during the first 10 days of the project duration and a maximum of 45 resource days can be used during the last 5 days of the task duration. Use Equation 14.2 again to compute a new lower boundary for peak daily resource usage. The new value is 355/25 = 14.2. Any schedule for which peak daily usage is close to 14.2 will be a nearly optimum schedule.

Delay Task Start

Figure 14.4*c* contains a revised schedule. The start of task G was delayed by 5 days. Peak daily utilization of resources is now 17, fairly close to the lower boundary value of 14.2.

FIGURE 14.4a
CPM DIAGRAM WITH RESOURCE REQUIREMENTS

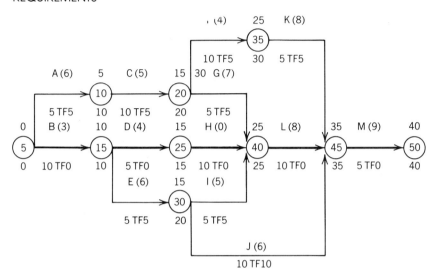

FIGURE 14.4b
EARLY START BAR CHART

Type First try. All tasks scheduled to begin on early start date

Tsk No.	I-N No.	J-N No.	Dur WD	TF WD	Rsc Rqd	ES BOD	LF EOD	Workday 5 10 15 20 25 30 35 40
A	5	10	5	5	6	1	10	66666---->
B	5	15	10	0	3	1	10	3333333333
C	10	20	10	5	5	6	20	5555555555---->
D	15	25	5	0	4	11	15	44444
E	15	30	5	5	6	11	20	66666---->
F	20	25	10	5	4	16	30	4444444444---->
G	20	40	5	5	7	16	25	77777---->
H	25	40	10	0	0	16	25	0000000000
I	30	40	5	5	5	16	25	55555---->
J	30	45	10	10	6	16	35	6666666666--------->
K	35	45	5	5	8	26	35	88888---->
L	40	45	10	0	8	26	35	8888888888
M	45	50	5	0	9	36	40	99999

Constrained resources used
Maximum daily usage = 22
Total usage = 485 RD

```
00000000001111122222111111111110000000000
99999888885555522222000006666688889999
 I    I    I    I    I    I    I    I
<----- 485 RD / 40 days = 12.15 R/D -->
<-- 85 -->< -355 RD/25 = 14.2 R/D ->< 45 >
```

FIGURE 14.4c

EARLY START BAR CHART WITH ONE
TASK DELAYED

Type								Second try. Task G delayed by 5 days to level daily resource usage
Tsk	I-N	J-N	Dur	TF	Rsc	ES	LF	Workday
No.	No.	No.	WD	WD	Rqd	BOD	EOD	5 · 10 · 15 · 20 · 25 · 30 · 35 · 40
A	5	10	5	5	6	1	10	66666---–>
B	5	15	10	0	3	1	10	3333333333
C	10	20	10	5	5	6	20	5555555555---->
D	15	25	5	0	4	11	15	44444
E	15	30	5	5	6	11	20	66666---->
F	20	25	10	5	4	16	30	4444444444---->
G	20	40	5	5	7	16	25	-----77777
H	25	40	10	0	0	16	25	0000000000
I	30	40	5	5	5	16	25	55555---->
J	30	45	10	10	6	16	35	6666666666--------->
K	35	45	5	5	8	26	35	88888---->
L	40	45	10	0	8	26	35	8888888888
M	45	50	5	0	9	36	40	99999
Constrained resources used								00000000001111111111111111111110000000000
Maximum daily usage = 17								99999888885555555555577777666668888899999
Total usage = 485 RD								

Perform Task on a Noncontinuous Basis

Figure 14.4d indicates the performance of work on task J on a noncontinuous basis. The peak daily resource utilization is now 16. This represents very little improvement over the preceding solution. In fact, it is probably not as good a

FIGURE 14.4d

EARLY START BAR CHART WITH
NONCONTINUOUS PERFORMANCE

Type								Third try. Task J performed on a noncontinuous basis
Tsk	I-N	J-N	Dur	TF	Rsc	ES	LF	Workday
No.	No.	No.	WD	WD	Rqd	BOD	EOD	5 · 10 · 15 · 20 · 25 · 30 · 35 · 40
A	5	10	5	5	6	1	10	66666---->
B	5	15	10	0	3	1	10	3333333333
C	10	20	10	5	5	6	20	5555555555---->
D	15	25	5	0	4	11	15	44444
E	15	30	5	5	6	11	20	66666---->
F	20	25	10	5	4	16	30	4444444444---->
G	20	40	5	5	7	16	25	-----77777
H	25	40	10	0	0	16	25	0000000000
I	30	40	5	5	5	16	25	55555---->
J	30	45	10	10	6	16	35	66666 · · 66666
K	35	45	5	5	8	26	35	88888---->
L	40	45	10	0	8	26	35	8888888888
M	45	50	5	0	9	36	40	99999
Constrained resources used								00000000001111111111111111111111100000
Maximum daily usage = 16								99999888885555555555511111666664444499999
Total usage = 485 RD								

solution because the daily utilization pattern now resembles the fluctuating pattern shown in Figure 14.3*a*.

SUMMARY

Resource-leveling and resource-constrained scheduling procedures can be very difficult and time consuming. Except for relatively simple problems, the scheduler cannot be assured that he or she has found the optimum solution. However, a reasonably good solution will be adequate for construction scheduling purposes. Extremely precise solutions to resource-constrained scheduling problems may not be justified considering the inexactitude of the estimates of task duration and task resource requirements.

Before attempting to level resource utilization, the scheduler should ask whether that is a desirable goal. If a contractor is going to build a moon base and only one round trip is allowed for the transportation of resources to the moon, then a level resource requirement may be important. However, at most places here on earth, additional resources can be obtained approximately when they are needed. A more practical goal is to avoid wide fluctuations in daily resource usage.

FIGURE 14.5
CPM DIAGRAM FOR EXERCISE 1

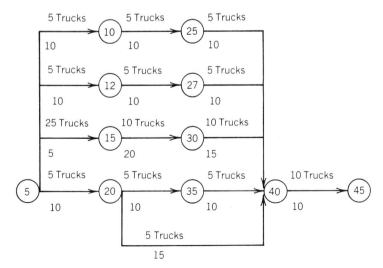

EXERCISES

EXERCISE 14.1

The diagram shown in Figure 14.5 shows the duration of the tasks making up a project and the number of trucks required for each task. A number of trucks will be committed to the project, and this number will remain at the site for the duration of the project. The duration of any task can be decreased by committing more trucks to the task. The duration of any task can be extended by reducing the number of trucks committed to the task. Task durations will be changed in proportion to the change in the number of trucks. For example, doubling the number of trucks will halve the duration, and halving the number of trucks will double the duration. Tasks can be split (worked on a noncontinuous basis). What is the least number of trucks that will be required to accomplish the task in 50 days? *Hint*: Refer to the discussion concerning lower boundaries for daily resource requirements.

CASH FLOW ANALYSIS BASED ON CONSTRUCTION SCHEDULES

15

OBJECTIVE

This chapter describes a procedure by which a contractor can predict his net income on a construction project for future dates. The procedure is presented in the context of a schedule prepared by the Critical Path Method (CPM), but it is also applicable to schedules prepared by the Precedence Method (PM) or to schedules prepared by using only a bar chart. In fact, regardless of which scheduling method is used, the schedule must be converted to a bar chart form to use this procedure. Some construction-oriented, financial management computer programs are available to compute net project income.

ESSENTIAL TERMS

Costs Versus Expenses

To incur a cost is to incur an obligation to pay an expense, either immediately or at some time in the future. An expense is the actual payment of cash (or the issuance of an instrument, such as a check, which can be immediately converted to cash) to satisfy an obligation. The principal components of a construction contractor's costs and expenses result from the use of labor, materials, equipment, and subcontractors. Additional general overhead cost components include taxes, premiums on bonds and insurance, and interest on loans.

The costs and expenses that are incurred for a specific project are termed **direct costs**. Others are termed **general overhead costs**. Some part of the construction company's general overhead costs are allocated to each of the company's projects. The sum of a project's direct costs and its allocated general overhead is termed the **project cost**.

A particular cost component, say, the cost for electrical energy at the project site, may be incurred continuously. Such a cost is a **continuous function**, meaning that the obligation is incurred at a more or less uniform rate over a period of time. Labor costs, equipment usage costs, and most other costs are continuous functions. Some expenses are also incurred as continuous functions. For example, the expenses for the purchase of small quantities of materials using the petty cash fund is a continuous expense function. However, most expenses are paid as **step functions**. The bill for electrical service is received near the end of the month and must be paid within 10 days. Craftsmen and salaried employees are paid at the end of the pay period, usually weekly, biweekly, or monthly.

The payment terms for charge purchases of construction materials determine whether the expense is a step function or a continuous function. If most material costs must be paid by the tenth day of the month following their delivery to the jobsite, then the expense function will be a step function. However, if these materials must be paid for within 20 days after delivery and if materials are being received at a more or less uniform rate, then the expense function is a continuous function.

Earnings Versus Income

An **earning** is an entitlement to immediate or future cash **income**. A contractor earns money when he or she performs work. An earning is usually a continuous function. Under the terms of some contracts, the contractor has earned money when he or she procures material that is to be used on the project and has that material delivered to the jobsite. Some contracts specify that only 50% of the value of such delivered, but not yet installed, material can be credited as earnings.

Income is the actual receipt of cash (or of an instrument, such as a check, which can be immediately converted to cash). The terms of a construction contract usually specify that a contractor may submit a periodic invoice and request for partial payment for the work that he or she performed. The owner will verify that the value of work claimed to have been completed by the contractor is correct, and then will issue a check in the amount of the total value of work performed to date, less a retainage and less previous partial payments.

The retainage (**retained earnings**) is the product of the contractor's cumulative project earnings and the **retained percentage**. The retained percentage is often one value (say, 10%) until the project is 50% complete, and is then reduced to some lesser value (say, 5%) thereafter if the project is on schedule. The lesser value (5%) is termed the **reduced retainage**.

The purpose of the retainage is to protect the owner financially if the contractor fails to perform the work in accordance with the contract. Not all construction contracts will contain the contract terms described above. Some contracts will not contain a retainage provision; others may allow payment in advance of the time that the work is performed. Figure 15.1 illustrates invoices that have been submitted before and after the time that the retainage has to be reduced.

The first invoice in Figure 15.1 is an example of an invoice and request for partial payment that was submitted early in the project duration when the retained percentage of earnings is 10%. The second invoice in Figure 15.1 is an example of an invoice submitted after retainage is reduced to 5%. The contract might specify that retainage would not be reduced if the contract is not on schedule at the time the invoice is submitted.

After a contractor submits an invoice there will be a delay before he or she

---

FIGURE 15.1
INVOICES AND REQUEST FOR
PARTIAL PAYMENT

INVOICE AND REQUEST FOR PARTIAL PAYMENT NUMBER 1

Project: Bilgewater Warehouse   Contract: 85.1
Date of invoice: February 28, 1985 (workdate = 20)
Contract amount: $100,000   Percent complete: 10.0%
Scheduled percent completion: 10.0%
Value of material delivered but not installed: $ 3,000

Earnings: Installed work: $0.10 \times \$100,000 =$ $ 10,000
                 Delivered material $0.5 \times \$3,000 =$ $ 1,500
                 Total earnings $=$ $ 11,500
Less retainage $= 0.10 \times \$11,500$ $=$ $-\$ 1,150$
                                                            $ 10,350

Less previous partial payments $=$ $ 0
Invoiced amount (will be received about Mar. 15) $ 10,350

INVOICE AND REQUEST FOR PARTIAL PAYMENT NUMBER 3

Project: Bilgewater Warehouse   Contract: 85.1
Date of invoice: April 30, 1985 (workdate = 60)
Contract amount: $100,000   Percent complete: 70.0%
Scheduled percentage completion: 70.0%
Value of material delivered but not installed: $ 0

Earnings: Installed work: $0.70 \times \$100,000 =$ $ 70,000
                 Total earnings $=$ $ 70,000
Less retainage $= 0.05 \times \$ 70,000$ $=$ $-\$ 3,500$
                                                            $ 66,500

Less previous partial payments $=$ $ 36,000
Invoiced amount (will be received about May 15) $ 30,500

receives payment. This delay can be decreased if the contractor has the invoice hand-carried to the owner or to the owner's representative.

Cash Flow

Over a long period of time, any business must take in more money than it pays out, otherwise the business will fail. For shorter periods of time, it is acceptable for expenses to exceed income. The difference between project income and project expense is termed **project cash flow**. The difference between a company's total income and its total expense over a period of time is termed the **company cash flow**. If a company has a negative company cash flow, it has a **cash flow problem**.

Declared Values

Usually, shortly after the contract is awarded, the contractor will be required to submit a list of **declared values** for the tasks that make up a project. The sum of these declared values equals the contract amount. Contractors are often tempted to **front load** their declaration of task values. As the computation of total value of work in place will be the basis for partial payments, it is to the contractor's financial advantage to declare that those tasks that will be completed early in the project duration have a greater value than those that will be completed later. In a competitive bidding situation, the contract will usually be awarded to the contractor whose total bid is the least, regardless of the values of the individual tasks. Front loading may backfire on a contractor. The owner may delete some work from the contract, using the declared values as a basis for adjusting the contract amount. If the deleted work has an inflated or front loaded declared value, the contractor will suffer financially.

CASH FLOW AS APPLICABLE TO AN INDIVIDUAL

Income and Expense

Figure 15.2a represents the cash flow functions of an individual who earns a take-home salary of $1000 a month paid at the end of the month. He or she spends money at a uniform rate of $1000 a month. Two curves are shown. One, a step curve, represents the cumulative income received by the individual. It has a **period** of 30 calendar days. The other curve, a continuous curve, represents the cumulative expenses paid by the individual. Note that the ordinates of the expense function are negative, because expense may be considered negative

FIGURE 15.2a
INCOME AND EXPENSE FUNCTION

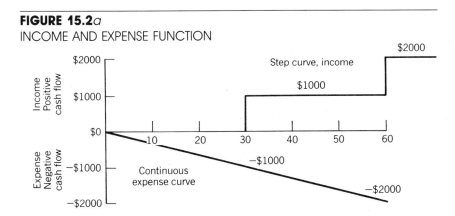

income. At a point in time near the end of the month (say, the twenty-ninth day), the individual's cash flow will be about minus $1000. To have arrived at this cash flow situation, the individual would have had to have charged all costs during the month.

Net Income Function

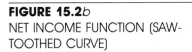

Figure 15.2b combines the income and expense functions into a **saw-toothed** net income function. It represents the net cumulative change in the individual's cash position. Note that the cumulative change ranges from zero, down to minus $1000, back up to zero, down to minus $1000 again, and then back up to zero. At the end of each month, the individual will have a negative cash flow that is

FIGURE 15.2b
NET INCOME FUNCTION (SAW-
TOOTHED CURVE)

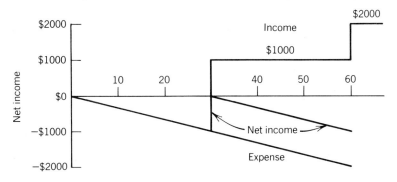

FIGURE 15.2c
CASH BALANCE FUNCTION, BARELY
ADEQUATE RESERVES

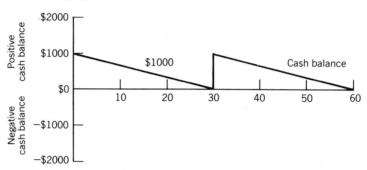

equal to $1000. On receipt of the month's salary, the individual's cash flow will increase to zero.

Figure 15.2c depicts the individual's net cash balance, assuming that he or she commenced employment with a barely adequate cash reserve of $1000. Under these conditions, the individual's cash flow will range from $1000 at the beginning of the month, down to zero at the end of the month, and then back up to $1000 immediately after receipt of his or her salary. This individual will not have to resort to credit charges.

Figure 15.2d is based on the assumption that the individual had a "comfortable" cash reserve of $2000 when commencing employment. Of course, this reserve would not have been comfortable if large and unforeseen expenses occurred during the period or if employment ended during the period.

FIGURE 15.2d
CASH BALANCE FUNCTION,
COMFORTABLE RESERVES

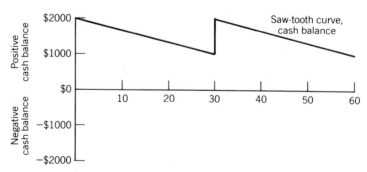

FIGURE 15.3
CPM DIAGRAM WITH TASK VALUES

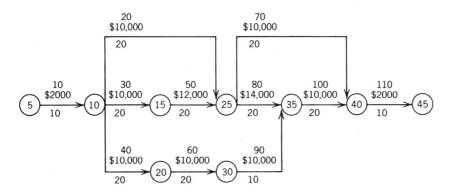

COST FUNCTIONS IN THE CONSTRUCTION INDUSTRY

The Schedule and Cash Flow

Figure 15.3 is the CPM logic diagram for a construction project. The values printed above the arrows on the logic diagram represent the declared values of each task. In Figure 15.4, a list is given of the tasks with the declared value of each broken down into a value per day of estimated task duration.

FIGURE 15.4
CPM SCHEDULE WITH TASK VALUES
IN DOLLARS PER DAY

Task #	Dur	$/Day	ES	EF	LS	LF	TF
10	10	200	0	10	0	10	0
20	20	500	10	30	30	50	20
30	20	500	10	30	10	30	0
40	20	500	10	30	20	40	10
50	20	600	30	50	30	50	0
60	20	500	30	50	40	60	10
70	20	500	50	70	70	90	20
80	20	700	50	70	50	70	0
90	10	1000	50	60	60	70	10
100	20	500	70	90	70	90	0
110	10	200	90	100	90	100	0

FIGURE 15.5

EARLY-START BAR CHART AND
CUMULATIVE EARNINGS

Task	$/Day	Dur	ES	EF					
10	200	10	0	10: XXXXX :	:	:	:	:
20	500	20	10	30:	XXXXXXXXXX :	:	:	:
30	500	20	10	30:	XXXXXXXXXX :	:	:	:
40	500	20	10	30:	XXXXXXXXXX :	:	:	:
50	600	20	30	50:	:	XXXXXXXXXX :	:	:
60	500	20	30	50:	:	XXXXXXXXXX :	:	:
70	500	20	50	70:	:	:	XXXXXXXXXX :	:
80	700	20	50	70:	:	:	XXXXXXXXXX :·	:
90	1000	10	50	60:	:	:	XXXXX :	:
100	500	20	70	90:	:	:	:	XXXXXXXXXX :
110	200	10	90	100:	:	:	:	: XXXXX

```
                    0        20        40        60        80       100
                                     Work Date
                     1         2         3         4         5
                                       Month
```

```
End Of Day    Cumulative Earnings
------  10 --- $    2,000 ---->
------  30 --- $   32,000 -------------->
------  50 --- $   54,000 ---------------------->
------  60 --- $   76,000 ------------------------------->
------  70 --- $   88,000 ------------------------------------->
------  90 --- $   98,000 ------------------------------------------------>
------ 100 --- $  100,000 ------------------------------------------------------->
```

Figure 15.5 is a bar chart schedule for the project based on an early start schedule, meaning that every task will be started at its early start time. The daily task value placement rate is indicated. Figure 15.6 contains the same data based on a late start schedule. Note the arrows beneath the bar charts. They indicate the cumulative value of work that is scheduled to be performed at various dates. The magnitude of the cumulative value depends upon whether all tasks are started on their early start or their late start times. For example, the arrows on the chart in Figure 15.5 indicate that cumulative earnings by the end of the thirtieth workday will be $32,000. These earnings will have accrued when tasks 10, 20, 30, and 40 have been completed. By the end of the fiftieth workday, cumulative earnings of $54,000 will have accrued. The cumulative earnings of $54,000 include the $32,000 earned during the first 30 days.

FIGURE 15.6
LATE-START BAR CHART AND
CUMULATIVE EARNINGS

```
Task $/Day  Dur LS  LF
 10   200   10  0  10:XXXXX    :      :          :         :         :
 20   500   20 30  50:         :      XXXXXXXXXX :         :         :
 30   500   20 10  30: XXXXXXXXXX     :          :         :         :
 40   500   20 20  40: :XXXXXXXXXX    :          :         :         :
 50   600   20 30  50:         :      XXXXXXXXXX :         :         :
 60   500   20 40  60:         :      :XXXXXXXXXX          :         :
 70   500   20 70  90:         :      :          :         XXXXXXXXXX :
 80   700   20 50  70:         :      :          XXXXXXXXXX :         :
 90  1000   10 60  70:         :      :          :XXXXX    :         :
100   500   20 70  90:         :      :          :         XXXXXXXXXX :
110                  :         :      :          :         :         XXXXX
                     0         20     40         60        80        100
                                          Work Date
                          1         2         3         4         5
                                          Month
```

```
End Of Day    Cumulative Earnings
------   10 -- $  2,000  ----->
--------20 -- $  7,000  ---------->
------- 30 -- $ 17,000  --------------->
------- 40 -- $ 33,000  -------------------->
------- 50 -- $ 49,000  ------------------------->
------- 60 -- $ 61,000  ----------------------------->
------- 70 -- $ 78,000  --------------------------------->
------- 90 -- $ 98,000  --------------------------------------------->
-------100 -- $100,000  ------------------------------------------------->
```

Project Status Curves

Figure 15.7 is a plot of project earnings versus time. Two curves are shown, one based on an early start schedule and the other on a late start schedule. The ordinates can be based on dollar values or upon percentage of total project value. If the ordinates of the curves are based on dollars, the curves are **earnings curves**. If the ordinates are percentages of total project earnings, then the curves are **project status curves**, or **project progress curves**. Both sets of ordinates are shown for this example. A third curve is shown; it represents an average of the ordinates of the other two curves and is termed the **estimated progress curve**. Note its S-shape. This shape is typical for construction projects. Note that the progress is slow during the early phases of the project, becomes faster

FIGURE 15.7

PROJECT EARNINGS VERSUS TIME

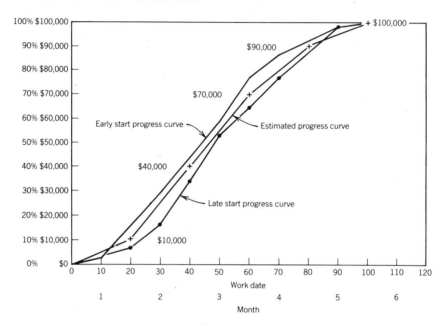

in the middle part of the project, and slows down during the terminal phases of the project.

Project Income Curve

Figure 15.8 is a plot of project income versus time. The curve is based on the estimated schedule, one that is between the early start and the late start schedule, although it could have been based on one or the other of the two schedules. Also shown is the early start earnings curve that was shown on the previous figure. It is assumed that the contractor was permitted to submit a request for partial payment every month. Assume that there are 20 workdays in a month. Further assume that the contractor is paid on the basis of his claimed earnings as of the invoice date, less 10% retainage, with a delay of 10 days after submission of the request. Assume that retainage is reduced to 5% when the project is 50% complete, if the project is on schedule. Note that the income curve is a step curve. The cumulative value of income increases about 10 days after the monthly submission of invoices. The value of the steps is equal to the claimed cumulative earnings times a factor of 0.95 to 0.90, depending upon whether the project was 50% complete and on schedule when the invoice was submitted.

FIGURE 15.8
PROJECT INCOME VERSUS TIME

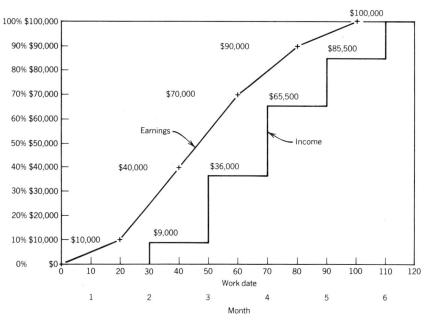

Net Project Income

Figure 15.9 contains several curves. The project income curve from Figure 15.8 is repeated. A cost curve is also shown. Costs are assumed to be incurred as a continuous function starting when the project is commenced. If the contractor will have some "up front" costs, such as payment of bond premiums, the cost function may initially be a step function. For this example, all costs have been lumped together. It is possible to have separate curves for labor, materials, subcontractors, and the like. It is further assumed that there will be a delay of about 10 days between the time that costs are incurred and the time when they must be paid.

The expense curve is the same as the cost curve, except that it has been displaced 10 days to the right. If a separate cost curve had been plotted for subcontractors, then the associated expense curve would have been a step curve. The ordinates of the income curve and the expense curve have been added algebraically, yielding the saw-toothed net project income curve. Note that net project income remains at zero or below zero until the seventieth workday, and even after that date it dips below zero again.

FIGURE 15.9
NET PROJECT INCOME VERSUS TIME

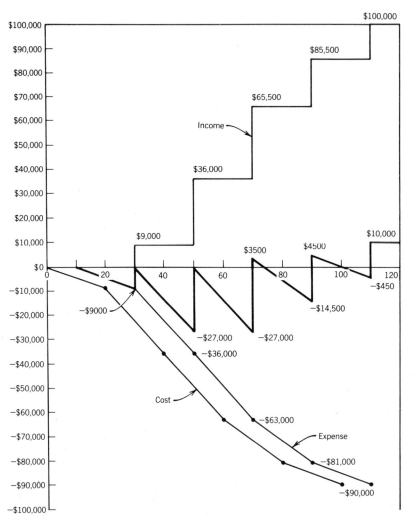

FIGURE 15.10

INVOICES (REQUESTS FOR PARTIAL
PAYMENT)

INVOICE AND REQUEST FOR PARTIAL PAYMENT NUMBER 1

Project: Bilgewater Warehouse   Contract: 85.1
Date of Invoice: February 28, 1985 (Work Date = 20)
Contract Amount: $100,000   Percent Complete: 10.0%
Scheduled Percent Completion   : 10.0%
Value of Material Delivered But Not Installed: $ 3,000

```
Earnings: Installed work: 0.10 x $100,000   =    $ 10,000
          Delivered Material 0.5 x $ 0      =    $      0
          Total Earnings                    =    $ 10,000
Less Retainage = 0.10 x $ 11,500            =   -$      0
                                                 $  9,000


Less Previous partial payments              =    $      0

Invoiced Amount (Will be received about Mar 15) $  9,000
```

INVOICE AND REQUEST FOR PARTIAL PAYMENT NUMBER 3

Project: Bilgewater Warehouse   Contract: 85.1
Date of Invoice: April 30, 1985 (Work Date = 60)
Contract Amount: $100,000   Percent Complete: 70.0%
Scheduled Percentage Completion   : 70.0%
Value of Material Delivered But Not Installed: $ 0

```
Earnings: Installed work: 0.70 x $100,000   =    $ 70,000
          Total Earnings                    =    $ 70,000
Less Retainage = 0.05 x $ 70,000            =   -$  3,500
                                                 $ 66,500

Less Previous partial payments              =    $ 36,000

Invoiced Amount (Will be received about May 15) $ 30,500
```

Impact of Negative Net Project Cash Flow

Figure 15.9 indicates that for most of the duration of this project the contractor will have paid out more cash than was taken in. Unless the contractor had sufficient working capital to cover this negative cash flow, he would have found it necessary to borrow money. The diagrams do not include a factor for the project's indirect costs or contractor general overhead.

The contractor can minimize the impact of the cash flow problem by submitting invoices promptly and as often as the owner will permit (Figure 15.10). The contractor should also consider staggering the times at which he submits invoices for the various projects he is working on. If the contractor can predict that a cash flow problem will occur in the future, he should start making arrangements to borrow before the crisis arrives. Bankers are more sympathetic to loan applicants who present a timely request for a loan than they are to those who are reacting to an emergency.

SUMMARY

During the early part of a project's duration, the predicted project cash balance will usually be negative, meaning that more cash will have been paid out than will have been taken in. If the contractor has sufficient working capital, he may be able to absorb the negative cash flow on the project. Otherwise, he must arrange to borrow more working captial. If he is unable to do so, then he must slow down the rate at which he accomplishes work (and incurs expense) on the project.

The cash flow analyses of all projects, plus an analyses of general overhead cash flow, can be combined so that a contractor can anticipate his overall cash balance at some future date.

EXERCISES

EXERCISE 1
Compute the maximum negative project cash flow that would have occurred if the project described in Figures 15.3 through 15.7 had been accomplished on an early start basis.

EXERCISE 2
Compute the maximum negative project cash flow that would have occurred if the project had been accomplished on a late start basis.

EXERCISE 3

Can you generalize as to whether an early start schedule or a late start schedule results in greater maximum negative project cash flow?

APPLICATION OF COMPUTERS TO SCHEDULING

16

OBJECTIVES

The objectives of this chapter are to briefly describe computer systems and to consider some of the commercially available computer systems and software that may be used to solve scheduling problems.

COMPUTER SYSTEMS

Computers, together with appropriate peripheral equipment, can be used to solve many scheduling problems. A computer is an electronic device that can be programmed to accept input data, perform arithmetic and logical operations on these data, and then output the data in processed form, all in accordance with a set of instructions called a **program**. The input data for a typical scheduling program may include a description of the tasks that make up a project and of the logical relationships between these tasks. The program will contain instructions on how task and event times are to be computed. The output will be a schedule listing the task descriptions and the task times, bar charts, cash flow analyses, and so forth. The program will also allow the user to save the input data and some of the processed data on a data storage device, such as a magnetic disk, so that the data may be recalled at some later time.

Computer and computer systems can be classified by many different criteria. This chapter is based on a computer system that is classified as a microcomputer, or as a microprocessor system. The system will include hardware and software.

Hardware Components

Hardware includes input devices, a Central Processing Unit (CPU), output devices, and data storage devices. The CPU is the "computer" in a computer system. It can be considered the "brain" of the system. Devices that feed data into the CPU are **input devices**. Devices that receive data from the CPU are **output devices**. Data storage devices have the nature of both input and output devices in that they can feed data into the CPU and can accept data from the CPU. Figure 16.1 is a conceptual diagram of the hardware components of a typical computer system. The minimum hardware requirement for a system that is of practical value in scheduling includes at least a CPU with adequate Rapid Access Memory (RAM), a keyboard, a Cathode-Ray Tube display screen (CRT), a printer, and a nonvolatile memory device such as a floppy disk or hard disk drive.

Physical Configuration of a System

The various hardware components of a system may be packaged in a number of modules that are connected by cables. Some systems feature radio wave linkage of their components. Alternatively, several of the components may be enclosed within a single module. A very popular configuration for modern microprocessor systems has the CRT display screen, the CPU, the RAM, and a magnetic disk memory unit all enclosed within a single module, with the terminal keyboard attached by a cable. It is often necessary to physically locate the components at positions that are so far apart that it is not feasible to connect them with cables. In such cases, the components may be linked together by telephone. A modem (modulator/demodulator) unit is required at each end of the telephone circuit to permit this linkage.

Data Input Devices

Data are initially entered into a computer system in the form of decimal numbers and alphabetic characters. The input data must be converted into a form that can be processed by the system. This converted form is based on the binary numerical system, which contains only two digits, zero and 1. Any decimal number or alphabetic character can be represented by a binary number. For example, the decimal numbers 0, 1, 2, 4, and 8 are represented by the binary numbers 0, 1, 10, 100, and 1000. Each digit in a binary number is termed a bit.

The conversion of data into binary numbers takes place in an input device such as a computer terminal. In some systems, the data conversion occurs in a two-step process. Real data are keyed into a card punch or a keypunch device, where they are coded into a form that can be recognized and converted into a binary form by a card reader or a punched-tape reader.

FIGURE 16.1
POSSIBLE HARDWARE COMPONENTS
FOR COMPUTER SYSTEM

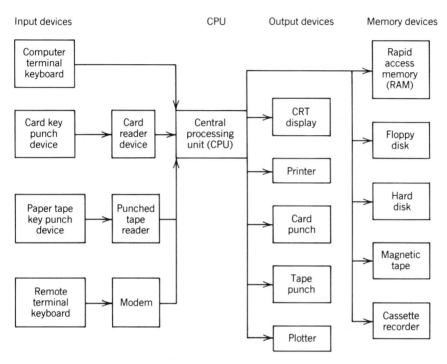

After the data are initially input into the system, they are processed by the CPU. They may then be outputted on a terminal's CRT display screen or on a printer, but they may also be outputted onto a storage device such as a magnetic disk memory unit, a card punch, or paper tape punch. The data may be fed back into the CPU from the magnetic tape memory unit, which will then be functioning as an input device, or through card readers or punched-tape readers. Data are stored on a magnetic disk memory unit in binary form and on cards or tape in coded form.

The Central Processing Unit

The CPU, as previously stated, converts data from real form to binary form. It also performs arithmetic operations on the data and directs the data to an output device or to a data storage device. The CPU performs arithmetic operations, controls the flow of data between the various hardware components of the system, and controls the operation of these other components as specified by a program. Central processing units are termed 8-bit, 16-bit, and 32-bit devices depending upon their design.

Most microprocessors were previously 8-bit devices, but a number of microprocessors are now on the market that are 16-bit devices. A 16-bit device is faster and will control a larger Rapid Access Memory (RAM) than will an 8-bit device. Millions of 8-bit CPUs have been manufactured and are currently in use, and there are many computers programs that will operate on 8-bit machines. However, 16-bit machines are more suitable for scheduling and the purchase of such a machine is recommended. Large mainframe computers and minicomputers are either 16-bit or 32-bit devices. These larger systems are very suitable for scheduling purposes, provided that suitable software is available.

Output Devices

These include CRT display screens, printers, plotters, and card and tape punches. The last two devices could be called data storage devices, because they contain data in a coded form that cannot be directly read but must be converted to a readable form. The CRT displays data on a televisionlike screen. It is possible to use a standard television receiver as a display screen. However, the clarity of the display will be inferior to that which can be expected on a CRT device designed specifically for use in a computer system. CRTs designed for this purpose are termed **monitors**. Both color and nonchrome (white on black, green on white, etc.) monitors are available. The display will be in 12 to 24 lines, with 60 to 80 characters per line. It is advisable to select a CRT device that will display 80 characters per line and 24 lines per screen.

Printers can be line printers, character printers, or dot matrix printers. Line printers are very fast. They are usually available only for large and costly systems. Character printers, sometimes called letter quality printers, use typewriterlike keys or balls, or "daisy wheels." The characters are molded into the keys, balls, or wheels. Many character printers have interchangeable balls, keys, or wheels, permitting the user to select a variety of character styles. Character printers are capable of printing a very high quality of text. Dot matrix printers print dots. The spacing of the dots is controlled so as to form an image of characters. Modern high-quality dot matrix printers can print text that rivals that which is produced by character printers. Furthermore, dot matrix printers can print graphics.

The speed of character and dot matrix printers is less than that of line printers, but printing speeds of 100 characters per second can be readily achieved. Printing speed is an important consideration for a system to be used for scheduling, because the output of scheduling problems is voluminous. **Plotters** are useful for preparing bar charts and logic diagrams. Plotters can also be used to print text but are relatively slow and relatively expensive compared to printers. Multicolor plotters are available.

Data Storage Devices

These include Rapid Access Memories (RAMs), magnetic disks, and magnetic tape devices. Data can be stored on, or retrieved from, a RAM very rapidly, compared to the storage and retrieval rate from other data storage devices. The capacity of a RAM is expressed in kilobytes (thousands of bytes, or K). A byte contains 8 bits of data. A byte may represent an alphabetic character or an integer number of up to 255. It requires 5 bytes to represent integer numbers of up to five digits long and 7 bytes to represent decimal numbers of up to seven digits long. A 64K RAM actually will store 65,536 bytes of data. An 8-bit computer system may have 16K, 32K, 48K, or 64K or RAM. Some of the more recently manufactured 8-bit computer systems may have as much as 512K of installed RAM. The 16-bit and 32-bit systems may have 1024K or more of RAM.

Scheduling problems generally require the entry of a great quantity of data and considerable manipulation of these data. Hence, it is important that as much data as possible be stored in RAM, where it can be rapidly retrieved. The author's experience is that he has never enjoyed the use of a system that has excess RAM. Data in RAM are usually lost if there is even a brief power outage. Important data should be periodically saved in a nonvolatile storage device, such as floppy or hard disk drives.

Magnetic disk units are readily available in two forms: **floppy disks** and **hard disks**. Floppy disks are available in 3½-inch, 5¼-inch, and 8-inch diameters. Some floppy disk units allow recording on one side of the disk, while others allow recording on both sides. The density of recording also varies. A single floppy disk can be used to record from about 100K up to 1000K bytes of data. Hard disk drives can store from about 5 MB (megabytes, or million bytes) up to about 20 MB of data. Hard disk units not only have a greater data storage capacity than floppy disk units, but the rate at which data can be stored and retrieved is much faster than for floppy disk units. Both floppy disk units and hard disk units allow random access to data, that is, data can be stored at, or retrieved from, a specified location on the disk without the necessity to scan the entire disk searching for the desired data.

The last category for data storage device is a **magnetic tape unit**. Magnetic tape units will contain a great quantity of data; however, the time required to store a specific piece of data on a tape or to retrieve it from a tape is much greater than would be required for a magnetic disk storage device. A cassette recorder is an inexpensive device that can be used for data storage. However, the slow speed and the high error rate of cassette recorders make them unsuitable for use in the solution of scheduling problems. Magnetic tape units that have been designed for use in a computer system are faster and more reliable than cassette recorders and are useful for the bulk storage of data.

Modems

These devices are used to connect terminals and input and output devices to CPUs through telephone lines when the devices are physically remote from each other. Modems can be purchased that have transmission rates of 300 to 1200 baud. The term baud means "bits audio." A 1-baud device would transmit one bit per second through the audio channels of a communication circuit. A 300-baud modem will transmit 300 bits (about 35 bytes) of data per second, A 1200-baud modem will transmit data much faster.

SOFTWARE AND FIRMWARE

Software is a term used to describe a set of instructions that will control the operation of a computer system. These instructions are recorded in the form of binary numbers on a magnetic disk or tape. If the instructions are contained in an electronic chip or module that is connected to the CPU, they are termed **firmware**. Three categories of software are described in the discussion that follows.

Operating Systems

These control the operation of a computer system. They cause the CPU to read data from, or to write data to, a memory device. They cause the CRT screen and the printer to perform operations similar to a typewriter, such as line advance, carriage return, back space, and the like.

Language Programs

These are used to convert an operating program written in FORTRAN or BASIC into binary form. These languages are called **high-level languages**. To some extent, the statements of an operating program written in a high-level language resemble normal English language. The CPU is unable to execute the instructions contained in an operating program until they are converted to machine language. An operating program is called a **source program** before it is converted to machine language. Thereafter, it is called an **object program**. Many popular microcomputers are sold with a combination operating system and language program. There are two types of language programs.

Interpreter Programs. These store the operating program as a source program and convert it to machine language, one step at a time, during program execution. If a particular statement must be executed 1000 times during the program execution, then it must be translated to machine language 1000 times. This repeated translation requires time. Hence, interpreter programs are inherently less efficient than the compiler programs described in the next section.

Compiler Programs. These convert the entire source program to machine language. Two versions of the program can be stored: the source version and the object version. However, many vendors of commercial programs will sell only the compiled or machine language versions. Frequently, a compiled program will be usable only on a specific make and model of computer.

Operating Programs

These are written by the user or are purchased from vendors. Operating programs are written in a high-level language but are often available only in a compiled machine language version. Appendix B contains a number of scheduling programs written in BASIC language. These programs can be altered by anyone with a working knowledge of BASIC so that they will run on any microprocessor.

EVALUATION OF A SYSTEM'S CAPABILITY TO SOLVE SCHEDULING PROBLEMS

The number of tasks that make up a project and the number and kind of scheduling problems that can be solved for the project are limited by the computer system's capacity. A given system may be unsuitable for the solution of specified scheduling problems for a project because the system contains insufficient RAM to store all of the descriptive data for the tasks or because the speed of the computer is too slow to solve the problems within an acceptable time.

The available software that will run on the system may not suit the user's needs. As an example of this, consider a scheduling program that requires that data describing tasks be entered into the computer in a precedence-ordered sequence. Further assume that the program allows the use of task numbers and node numbers less than some arbitrary value, say, 200. The persons who write software desire highly structured rules for the inputting of data because such rules simplify the writing of the program and make program execution more efficient. Yet this structuring may be unacceptable to the users. They may find they are spending more time inputting data in a structured form than would have been required to solve the problem manually.

It is suggested that the buyer of computer systems and software require a demonstration by the vendors of their equipment and software. Computers and software are not very expensive compared with the cost of using them. The use of unsatisfactory equipment or software will result in wasted hours.

Commercially Available Scheduling Software

Periodicals like the American Society of Civil Engineers' *Civil Engineer* and the Associated General Contractors of America's *Constructor* occasionally print lists of available construction management software, including scheduling software. These lists briefly describe the software capabilities and may indicate the cost and type of the equipment on which it can be run. Scheduling programs are often part of an integrated system, meaning the data can be transferred back and forth between program modules for cost estimating, scheduling, cost accounting, and other associated function. The concept of integrating such functions is very attractive because there is a great deal of commonality between the data used for each function. The buyer of integrated software should ensure that he is not buying a system that does a great many things, but each very poorly.

THE SCIENTIFIC COST-ESTIMATING METHOD

OBJECTIVE

The objective of this appendix is to briefly describe the scientific cost-estimating method, paticularly as it affects the scheduling process. It is termed the ''scientific'' method because of its structured nature. Other cost-estimating methods are also used in the construction industry. Cost estimating is closely related to scheduling. A project consists of a number of tasks that must be performed in a logical sequence. Therefore, the time that will be required to complete a project, the project duration, depends on the times that will be required to complete these tasks, the task durations. Nearly all tasks have variable durations. They can be completed rapidly if unlimited personnel and equipment resources are used, and less rapidly if limited resources are available.

The commitment of unlimited resources to a task results in a high task cost. The commitment of an inadequate amount of resources will result in long task durations and may also result in increased task costs. For most tasks, there will be a level of resource commitment that will result in a minimum task cost and in a corresponding task duration. This lowest task cost will be termed the **normal task cost**, and the corresponding task duration will be termed the **normal task duration**. The normal task costs and the normal durations are not necessarily the optimal values when considered in respect to the total project costs and duration. It may be cost effective to complete a task in less than its normal duration, and at more than its normal cost, if the result is to reduce total project duration and total project cost.

COMPONENTS OF THE CONTRACTOR'S BID

It will be helpful to look at the big picture before looking at the details of the cost estimation process. Contractors prepare cost estimates for a variety of purposes. A major purpose is to enable the contractor to prepare a **proposal**, or an **offer**, to an owner. In this proposal, the contractor offers to perform certain work for a specified compensation. If the owner accepts this offer, an **agreement** has been reached, agreement being an essential element of a contract. The discussion of cost estimating in this appendix is based on the situation in which an owner has advertised a project. By advertising the project, the owner has requested that qualified contractors submit proposals, or **bids**. The owner will normally accept the proposal that contains the lowest bid price. If the contract is a fixed-cost (lump sum) contract, the bid price of the accepted proposal will become the contract amount, the total amount of compensation that the contractor will receive for performing the work described in the contract documents. The contract amount may be revised if the owner changes the scope of the work to be done or for other reasons.

The components of cost that make up a contractor's bid are categorized in the sections below. Contractors use a variety of cost categorization schemes and terminology. Regardless of the categorization scheme or terminology that is used, it is essential that cost estimates include all costs once, and only once. If a cost element, say, a project superintendent's salary, is omitted from the estimate of total project costs, the contractor's bid will be inadequate for recovering all the costs he or she will incur. The contractor will be required to use a part of the bid price that was intended to be profit to pay that salary. If the salary is included in the estimate twice, say, as a direct cost and also as project overhead, the total project estimate may be so high as to jeopardize the chances of the contractor winning a competitively awarded contract.

Bid Price

The **bid price** (*BP*) is the amount the contractor lists in his or her proposal as being the proposed contract amount. Unless this contract amount is revised by a change in the contract terms (a change order), this amount represents the total compensation the contractor will receive for performing all the work called for in the contract documents. Equation A.1 may be used to calculate the bid price.

$$BP = PC + P \qquad \text{(A.1)}$$

where *PC* stands for the contractor's estimated total project costs and *P* stands for the contractor's expected gross profit. Expected gross profit, being the difference between a contractor's proposed bid price and expected costs, is the reward the contractor expects for exercising his or her skill and for taking the risk that actual costs will be higher than estimated. Contractors increase their profit objective on projects when they face few competitors or when they believe that they have a competitive edge on the other bidders. They will seek more profit on projects when they consider risks to be high than on other projects when they can be relatively certain of their total costs. Gross expected project profit is the difference between the contract amount and the contractor's estimated total project costs as defined below. Net profit is that part of total profit that the contractor will retain after paying income taxes.

Total Estimated Project Costs (*PC*)

This includes the estimated total direct cost (*DC*) that the contractor expects to incur on a project plus a share (*GOH*) of the total general overhead (*GOH-T*) costs that he will incur at his home office while the project is in progress. The calculation of the total estimated direct cost will be covered later. Total estimated project cost may be calculated by Equation A.2:

$$PC = DC + GOH \qquad \text{(A.2)}$$

Allocated General Overhead Costs (*GOH*)

The symbol *GOH* represents the share of a contractor's total general overhead costs that he will allocate to a project for which he is preparing a bid or proposal. Total general overhead costs (*GOH-T*) are those costs that the contractor will incur but that cannot be readily attributed to a particular project. They include: the salaries paid to home office personnel such as company officers, estimators, schedulers, and clerks; costs to own or rent and to maintain and operate the home office building, such as rent or amortization, utilities, and communications; interest paid on borrowed working capital; and all other home office costs that must be incurred so that the contractor can conduct his business. The estimator should not include a cost element in general overhead and also in another cost category.

A method for allocating a part of a contractor's total general overhead costs to a particular project is illustrated in Equations A.3 and A.4. The method involves the determination of an average general overhead rate. The use of such an average general overhead rate is appropriate if all the projects that a contractor accomplishes are similar in respect to the demands they place on the contractor's home office staff and in respect to the demands they make for use of capital. The cost of preparing cost estimates for bidding purposes should be considered general overhead costs. Although the cost of preparing such an estimate is related to a particular job, contractors will only be awarded contracts for a fraction of the projects on which they prepare estimates and submit bids. The general overhead cost that is assigned to a project is sometimes termed a "job indirect."

Average General Overhead Rate (R)

The average general overhead rate is computed by Equation A.3. It will be used for a period of time, usually a fiscal year. The symbol $GOH\text{-}T$ represents the expected total general overhead costs to be incurred during that period of time. The symbol $DC\text{-}T$ represents the expected sum of the direct costs to be incurred on all projects during that period of time:

$$R = \frac{GOH\text{-}T}{DC\text{-}T} \tag{A.3}$$

Allocated General Overhead to a Specific Project (GOH)

The amount of the total general overhead ($GOH\text{-}T$) that should be allocated to a specific project (GOH) can be computed by Equation A.4. This equation is based on the use of the previously computed average general overhead rate R:

$$GOH = R \times DC \tag{A.4}$$

Estimated Direct Costs (DC)

Direct costs will be incurred only if the contractor is awarded a contract and accomplishes the work. The symbol DC stands for the total direct costs to be incurred on a specific project. Direct costs are sometimes termed "job directs." Direct costs include task costs and project overhead costs. The symbol $\Sigma\, TC$ represents the sum of the task costs to be incurred, and $\Sigma\, POH$ represents the sum of the project overhead costs to be incurred on a project. The computation of these values will be covered later.

$$DC = \Sigma\, TC + \Sigma\, POH \tag{A.5}$$

Estimated Task Costs (Σ TC)

The symbol $\Sigma\, TC$ represents the sum of all estimated task costs for a project. The task cost for a specific task is represented by the symbol TC and is computed by Equation A.6. Task costs are costs incurred in completing tasks that involve the performance of measurable work. Examples are: lay 10,000 bricks, excavate 1000 CY of earth, and the like. The symbols M, L, E, and SC stand respectively for the material, labor, equipment, and subcontractor components of the estimated cost for a task.

$$TC = M + L + E + SC \tag{A.6}$$

Project Overhead Costs (Σ POH)

The symbol $\Sigma\, POH$ represents the sum of all the estimated project overhead costs for a project. Project overhead costs are those project costs that will be incurred but that have not been classified as task costs, meaning they do not include the performance of measurable work. POH costs include salaries for the project superintendent, his office engineers, and his clerks. The author trusts that weary project superintendents will forgive him for the implication that superintendents do no measureable work, but it is customary to consider their salaries as project overhead. Other POH costs are: the premiums paid for performance bonds, payment bonds, and for insurance that is applicable only to the specific project; the rental or amortization cost of a field office, plus the utilities and communications costs for that field office; temporary security fences; and portable toilets and trash pickup service. Most project overhead costs are time dependent. If the actual project duration exceeds the scheduled project duration, such time-dependent POH costs will increase proportionally. No equation is offered for computing POH; however, Equation A.6 can be used to estimate these costs.

ESTIMATING TASK COSTS
AND TASK DURATIONS

Tasks are the elements on which project schedules are based. Task costs are direct costs. The components of task costs are: materials cost, labor cost, equipment cost, and subcontractor cost. An accurate and detailed quantity takeoff must be prepared to estimate these cost components. The quantity takeoff is prepared based on the study of the contract plans and specifications. It is essential that the quantity and the exact nature of each kind of material, and the quantity and nature of each type of work, be determined. The materials cost will depend on the quantity, nature, and unit costs of the materials required. The labor and equipment costs will depend upon the amount of work that is to be done, on the labor and equipment resources committed to the accomplishment of the work, on the time of commitment of these resources, and on the hourly costs of those resources. Subcontractor costs are usually based on proposals that potential subcontractors submit to the general contractor.

Materials Cost

Several different kinds of material may be required for the completion of a task. The quantity of each kind of material must be accurately computed during the quantity takeoff process. Quantities must be determined for those materials that will be incorporated into the completed structure, and also for other materials that are required for construction but that will not be a part of the completed structure. Some materials will be consumed during construction (form oil), other materials will be discarded after use (short pieces of lumber used for bracing), and others may be reused a limited number of times on the project or on other projects (form lumber).

The cost of material that is incorporated into the structure or that is consumed, and a part of the cost of the material that will be reused, must be included in the estimation of the task costs. Care should be taken to include all of the materials that will be used: mortar, reinforcement, and anchors for masonry construction, nails and splices for wood construction, bolts, washers, welding rod, and welding gas for steel construction, and so on. An allowance for waste, damage, and pilferage should be included in the estimated materials cost. Waste allowances will range from zero for structural steel members to as much as 10% to 20% for masonry mortar. Some materials are available only in standard lengths (dimensioned lumber) or in standard packages (bricks). If a less-than-standard length or package is required but a standard length or package must be procured, estimators should base their estimate on the costs of the standard length or package. For example, dimensioned lumber is available in lengths that are multiples of 2 feet. The estimator should use the cost of a 10 foot long piece of lumber when the plans call for a 9 foot 6 inch long joist. The estimator should also include delivery costs and sales tax in his estimate of materials cost.

Equation A.7 may be used to estimate the cost of a particular kind of material (*M*):

$$M = Q \times UC + D + T \tag{A.7}$$

where Q represents the quantity of material required, including allowances for waste; UC represents the unit cost; D represents the delivery cost; and T represents sales tax.

Task Duration

The task duration depends on the quantity and nature of the work to be done and on the numbers and the capabilities of the resources committed to its accomplishment. There will usually be a single critical resource for a task, the number and capabilities of that resource being the limiting factor in respect to the time required to complete the task. The critical resource may be a type of craftsman or a type of equipment. The critical resource in a task involving laying bricks will usually be masons, although it could be helpers, mortar mixing machines, or scaffolding. If these resources are not available in adequate amounts to keep up with the masons, one of them may be the critical resource. In an earth-moving task, loading machines or trucks will usually be the critical resource. The objective is to assign a balanced mix of resources to a task, insofar as that is practical. On a masonry job, there should be just enough helpers, just enough mortar mixers, just enough scaffolding, and just enough forklifts and forklift operators to supply the masons with bricks and other materials and services at a rate that will enable them to perform the primary work activity, namely, laying bricks without delay. The example problem on pages 375 to 379 of this appendix illustrates a procedure for determining a balanced mix of resources for commitment to a task.

A task duration that has been estimated on the basis of a balanced assignment of resources is not necessarily the optimum duration. It is uneconomical to assign a large quantity of resources to a task that involves a small amount of work, even if the resources are balanced. It costs time and money to move equipment to the jobsite. It is also costly to hire craftsmen for very brief periods of time because newly recruited employees function at reduced efficiency until they ''learn the ropes.'' For these reasons, it may be more economical to perform a task with a minimum crew, one which may not be balanced. Even the task duration that results from assignment of resources so as to minimize the task cost may not be the optimum duration when the impact of that task duration on total project cost is considered.

Equation A.8 can be used to determine the time t required to complete an amount of work:

$$t = \frac{A}{N \times ROP} \tag{A.8}$$

If that kind of work is the only work making up a task, the time will be the task duration. If several kinds of work must be done, then it will be necessary to analyze the task to determine its duration. The symbol t represents the time required to complete a kind of work included within a task, based on the rate of production of the resource being considered. If several kinds of resources are required to do this work, then this time is the largest time computed based on each of the resources. The symbol A represents the amount of a kind of work activity that is included within a task. The amount of work is determined during the quantity takeoff and is a quantitative task attribute. An example would be laying 10,000 face bricks. There may be instances in which it can be reasonably expected that some of the work will have to be done more than once, for example, cleaning a masonry wall. If that is the case, the total amount of work to be done should be adjusted accordingly. Costs for minor items of work that are related to major items of work (setting up and moving scaffolds for painters) should be estimated separately, unless the production rate defined below allows for such related work. N is the number of resources of a particular kind that are assigned to the task. An example of ROP, the estimated rate of production for a single unit of that kind of resource for that kind of work, would be 100 face bricks per mason man-hour.

The best source of productivity data is an estimator's experience and the records that he or she has made of similar work performed on previous jobs. Reference manuals that list average production rates for many kinds of craftsmen and equipment on various types of work are published. Labor production rates are dependent on the skill of the craftsmen, the quality of supervision, and job conditions. Equipment production rates depend on the type and size of the equipment, operator skill, and job conditions. Job conditions include: temperature, humidity, site congestion, road trafficability, and so forth. The production rate of craftsmen often declines when they are required to work extended hours (more than 8 hours a day or more than 5 days a week). The production rate of equipment is reduced if the jobsite is not laid out efficiently. The estimator allows for such nonproductive time as weather delays, personal breaks, and delays that will result from interference by other crafts.

Labor Cost

During the quantity takeoff, the estimator will have accurately determined the quantity of material that must be installed to complete a task and the quantity of work that must be done. Some work involves the installation of material (laying bricks); other work does not. Examples of work that does not require the installation of material are digging or excavating earth, surveying and layout, and cleaning. In any event, the quantity of work to be done must be accurately determined and the labor resources and the time that they will be required must be estimated. Equation A.9 can be used to estimate the labor cost (L) for a certain kind of craftsman to be used on a task:

$$L = (N \times t \times HC) + F \times t \tag{A.9}$$

where N is the number of that kind of craftsmen to be used. The symbol t represents the time for which the craftsmen must be paid. It may be longer than the time required to do the work if workers must be paid for time to travel to the worksite. HC is the hourly wage cost for craftsmen, including their average wage rates and employer-paid fringe costs such as FICA and unemployment compensation insurance premiums. F is the effective wage rate for the foreman.

Foremen can be working foremen (straw bosses), or they can be full-time supervisors. Working foremen are paid their craft wages plus a supplement for performing supervisory duties. Given the impact that the quality of supervision has on labor production rates, skimping on expenditures for high-quality supervision is counterproductive.

Estimated Equipment Costs

Equipment costs will be incurred on a task when equipment is used to perform the task, regardless of whether the equipment is owned by the contractor or is leased or rented from others. It is customary to estimate the cost of small hand tools as some small percentage of the previously estimated labor costs, say, 1% or 2%. Some contractors will consider all equipment costs as being a part of general overhead and will omit the detailed computation of equipment costs for the specific tasks that make up a project. Such a practice is satisfactory if all projects have similar demands for the use of equipment. However, if some projects require extensive use of equipment and others require little such use, the practice will result in low cost estimates for the first category and high estimates for the latter category. The contractor will find himself winning a disproportionately high percentage of the bids in which he has underestimated total direct costs and a disproportionately low percentage of the bids in which he has overestimated total direct costs. This situation will have an adverse impact on the contractor's financial status. The estimator must estimate the time that each type of equipment will be used on a task. Equation A.8 can be used for that purpose.

Equation A.10 can be used to estimate the cost for the use of a type of equipment on a task. Note that Equation A.10 does not include an allowance for equipment operator wages, those wages having been included as labor costs.

$$E = N \times t \times HC + DAR \qquad (A.10)$$

where E is the estimated cost for using a kind of equipment and N is the number of pieces of that kind of equipment to be used. The time in hours to perform the task is represented by t; HC is the hourly cost of operating a piece of equipment; and DAR is the delivery and return cost for the equipment.

Hourly Equipment Rates

Equation A.11 is appropriate for contractor-owned equipment items. The cost elements that make up the hourly rate are depreciation cost, investment cost, maintainance cost, and operations cost. For rented equipment, the rental rate is substituted for the first three of these four elements. Rental rates depend on the length of the rental period. A typical rate schedule might include an hourly rate and a daily rate that is five times that hourly rate. The weekly rate might be four times the daily rate, and the monthly rate might be three times the weekly rate. The rate schedule may include a rate that applies while the contractor has possession of the rental item and an additional charge for each hour that the item is actually operated or for each mile of operation. Contractors may establish charge schedules in a similar manner for the equipment they own.

$$HC = D + I + MC + OC \qquad (A.11)$$

where HC is the hourly cost of operating an equipment item. This cost does not include the operator's wages, which are treated as a labor cost. D is the hourly depreciation cost of the equipment item. Depreciation is the reduction in the value of an item that occurs as it is used. For cost-estimating purposes, straightline depreciation is an appropriate method. (See Equation A.12 to determine the hourly depreciation cost.) I is the hourly investment cost, the cost per operating hour of owning an equipment item.

The owner of an equipment item must pay interest charges if he has purchased the item with borrowed funds. If he owns an item without encumbrance, then he has lost the opportunity to invest at interest the capital that is tied up in such ownership. The investment cost per operating hour is taken as the annual investment cost divided by the expected number of operating hours per year. The annual investment cost is equal to the product of the item's value and the effective interest rate. The average value can be computed using Equation A.13. The effective interest can be taken as the average rate of interest being paid on outstanding loans, plus a few additional percentage points to cover miscellaneous ownership costs (property taxes, licensing fees, and insurance), which are related to the item's value. See Equations A.13 and A.14 to compute hourly investment cost. MC and OC are respectively the hourly maintenance costs and the hourly operational costs (fuel, lubricants, and the like).

Depreciation Cost

The straightline depreciation cost D per hour of operation is computed by Equation A.12, where IC is the item's initial cost, including delivery and taxes; S is the expected salvage value of the item; n is the item's expected life in years; and h is the expected hours of operation per year:

$$D = \frac{IC - S}{n \times h} \tag{A.12}$$

Average Value

The average value AV of an equipment item must be calculated to compute its hourly investment cost. Use Equation A.13 to compute AV. The terms used in this equation include: n, the expected life of the item in years; IC, the item's initial cost; and S, the item's expected salvage value:

$$AV = \frac{IC \times (n + 1) + S \times (n - 1)}{2 \times n} \tag{A.13}$$

Investment Cost

The hourly investment cost of an equipment item, I, depends on its average value AV, the effective interest rate i, and the expected hours of operation per year, h. The effective interest rate is expressed as a decimal fraction, for example, 10.5% is expressed as 0.105.

$$I = \frac{AV \times i}{h} \tag{A.14}$$

EXAMPLE PROBLEM:
BALANCING RESOURCES

Assume that a task involves the placement of select fill for the base course for a project's roads and parking areas. The fill will be excavated from a borrow pit using a track-mounted power shovel, hauled in dump trucks to the project site, spread by a small-tracked dozer, brought to an optimum moisture content by a water distributor truck, and compacted using a tractor-towed sheepsfoot roller. The problem is to determine how many of each of these equipment items are needed so as to have a balanced mix of resources.

The following abbreviations will be used in this example:

CY	cubic yards
CY-BM	cubic yards, bank measure
CY-LM	cubic yards, loose measure
CY-CM	cubic yards, compacted measure
CYH	cubic yards per hour
CF	cubic foot (feet)
FPM	feet per minute
FT	foot (feet)
GAL	gallon(s)
GPM	gallons per minute
HR	hour(s)
MI	mile(s)
MPH	miles per hour
PCY	pounds per cubic yard
SF	square foot (feet)
SFH	square feet per hour
SY	square yard(s)

The soil will be a sandy clay. The following soil densities are expressed as dry densities, namely, the unit weight of the soil less its free moisture. The soil will exist in three conditions:

1. **Bank Condition.** The unit weight of the soil in its undisturbed condition. Bank measure density = 3200 PCY-BM.

2. **Loose Condition.** The soil will swell by 15% when loaded into the dump trucks. The loose measure density will be 3200/1.15 = 2780 PCY-LM.

3. **Compacted Condition.** Water will be added to the soil as it is spread. It then will be compacted to a compacted density of 3500 PCY-CM.

Any of the three units of measure (BM, LM, CM) can be used as the common unit for the subsequent calculations. Bank measure (BM) will be used in this example.

Equipment Capabilities

Assume that the following data on equipment capabilities have been taken from records that were made on previous jobs. All rates of production are based on the equipment operating 60 minutes per hour.

Loading Equipment

A 2½ CY track-mounted power shovel will be used to load the soil into dump trucks. This shovel is rated at 380 CYH-BM for sandy clay soil when digging into an 8 FT high bank and when it is necessary to swing the dipper only 90° from the bank to the truck. Because the owner of the borrow pit will permit only a 6 FT high cut, the shovel's production has been derated to 320 CYH-BM.

Hauling Equipment

The soil will be hauled in dump trucks having a capacity of 15 CY when heaped full. The capacity of a truck when expressed in bank measure will be 15/1.15 = 13 CY-BM. The trucks will be able to travel at an average speed of 15 MPH when loaded and 25 MPH when empty. The haul distance will be 5 miles each way.

Spreading Equipment

A 250 HP crawler dozer will be used to spread the soil and to mix it before compaction. The dozer has a capacity of 400 CYH-LM = 400/1.15 = 348 CYH-BM under these conditions.

Compaction Equipment

The soil will be spread and then compacted by a tractor-towed sheepsfoot roller. The soil will be spread and compacted in lifts that will be 8 inches thick after compaction. The roller has an effective width of 8 FT and travels at an average speed of 2 MPH. An average of six passes must be made by the roller to attain the required compaction. The roller will cover 2 MPH × 5280 FT/MI × 8 FT = 84,480 SFH for one pass and 84,480/6 = 14,080 SFH for six passes. The rate of compacting soil in 8-inch lifts will be 14,080 × 8 inches/12 inches = 9386 CFH-CM, or 9386/27 = 348 CYH-CM. The production rate expressed in bank measure will be 348 × 3500/3200 = 380 CYH-CM.

Moisture Control Equipment

A 1500 GAL water truck will be used to increase the soil's moisture content for optimum compaction. The moisture content will have to be increased by an average of about 5% of the soil's dry density or by $0.05 \times 3200 = 160$ PCY-BM. This amounts to $160/8.34 = 19$ GAL/CY-BM. The distributor will discharge water at the rate of 100 GPM. It will take about 20 minutes to travel from the jobsite to a reservoir, to fill the tank, and to return to the jobsite. The total time to fill the distributor, discharge its contents, and to return to the reservoir for refilling will be 1500 GAL/100 GPM + 20 = 35 minutes = 35/60 = 0.58 HR. The distributor has a production rate of $1500/0.58 = 2571$ GPH. At 19 GAL/CY-BM, the distributor will be adequate for $2571/19 = 135$ CYH-BM.

Analysis of the Problem

The major item of equipment to be used is the power shovel. Assume that one power shovel will be used and that sufficient trucks, dozers, water distributors, and rollers will be assigned to keep up with the shovel.

Truck Cycle Time

The trucks will be loaded, then they will haul the soil, then they will dump the soil, and then they will return to the shovel. The time required for one truck cycle will be as follows:

$$\text{Load time (LT)} = \frac{\text{truck capacity}}{\text{shovel } ROP}$$

$$= \frac{13 CY}{320 \text{ CYH}} \qquad = 0.04 \text{ HR}$$

$$\text{Haul time } (HT) = \frac{\text{distance}}{\text{truck speed}}$$

$$= \frac{5 \text{ MI}}{15 \text{ MPH}} \qquad = 0.33 \text{ HR}$$

$$\text{Unload time } (UT) = \frac{\text{Assume 2 minutes to}}{\text{position and dump truck}}$$

$$= \frac{2 \text{ MIN}}{60 \text{ MIN/HR}} \qquad = 0.03 \text{ HR}$$

$$\text{Return time } (RT) = \frac{\text{distance}}{\text{truck speed}}$$

$$= \frac{5 \text{ MI}}{25 \text{ MPH}} \qquad = \underline{0.20 \text{ HR}}$$

$$\text{Cycle time} \qquad = 0.60 \text{ HR}$$

Number of Trucks Required

A truck can make one round trip in 0.60 HR. A truck can make 1/0.60 = 1.67 round trips per hour. A truck can haul 1.67 × 13 CY = 21.71 CYH-BM. The number of trucks required to keep up with the shovel is 320 CYH-BM/21.71 CYH-BM = 14.73 trucks. Use 15 trucks.

Balancing Resources

Sufficient trucks have been assigned so that the shovel's production will be the limiting factor. Assign sufficient other resources to keep up with the shovel's production of 320 CYH-BM.

Item	ROP/Unit	No. of Units	Total Production
Shovel	320 CYH-BM	1	320 CYH-BM
Trucks	21.71 CYH-BM	15	* 326 CYH-BM
Dozer	460 CYH-BM	1	* 460 CYH-BM
Roller	380 CYH-BM	1	* 380 CYH-BM
Water truck	135 CYH-BM	3	* 405 CYH-BM

System Rate of Production

The shovel is the limiting factor in the system rate of production. The items marked with an asterisk above will have excess capacity, and it may be possible to find other items that more closely match the production rate of the shovel. The system rate of production is based on operating the equipment for 60 minutes per hour. Assuming that there will only be 50 minutes of productive time per hour, the adjusted system rate of production will be 320 × 50/60 = 267 CYH-BM. The nonproductive time of 10 minutes per hour was assumed to allow for equipment maintenance and for personal breaks for the equipment operators.

Task Duration and Task Cost

Assume that the total amount of soil to be hauled is 20,000 CY-BM. The listed equipment would have to operate for 20,000 CY-BM/267 CYH-BM = 74.9 H (say, 75 HR). See the preceding paragraphs for the procedures to estimate the equipment and the labor costs.

COMPUTER PROGRAMS FOR SCHEDULING

B

OBJECTIVE

The objective of this appendix is to describe several typical computer programs that are useful for scheduling purposes. The description of each program includes a BASIC language program listing, operating instructions for the program, and a discussion of computer hardware requirements. The programs may be typed into any computer that is equipped with a BASIC interpreter and that has sufficient RAM (rapid access memory). It is assumed that readers of this appendix are familiar with the scheduling techniques described in this book.

ABBREVIATED DESCRIPTION OF PROGRAMS

This appendix contains program listings for six scheduling programs and for several utility programs. The scheduling programs have many common features and common program statements. It is feasible to enter one of the programs into computer memory and to then modify that program to the form of another program.

Programs CPM and AON

The two most elaborate programs are programs CPM and AON. They are for the solution of logic diagrams based on the Critical Path Method (CPM) and the

Precedence Method (AON). Both of these programs have the following:

1. Routines for input of data describing the project. These data include node and arrow numbers, task durations and descriptions, and the definition of the relationships between tasks.

2. Routines for saving these data on floppy disks and subsequently retrieving the data for modification and use.

3. Routines to print schedules in work date format.

4. Routines to print bar charts in work date format.

5. Routines to accomplish capabilities 3 and 4 by using calendar date as well as work date format.

6. Routines for periodically updating the projects to reflect the actual status of tasks and to print schedules and bar charts based on this update data.

Programs CPM-MIN and AON-MIN

Programs CPM-MIN and AON-MIN are abridgements of programs CPM and AON. They lack the capabilities in items 4 through 6 in the preceding list. Their listings are provided so that readers can have operating scheduling programs without expending the effort required to enter the complete versions of CPM and AON. It is anticipated that many readers will first try CPM-MIN or AON-MIN and later decide to upgrade the programs to CPM and AON. Readers who make this decision will find that most of the program statements entered for CPM-MIN and AON-MIN are usable for programs CPM and AON.

Programs AOA-PERT and AON-PERT

These programs enable the user to input multiple (optimistic, central, and pessimistic) estimates of task durations (and, for AON-PERT, of relationship lags) and to produce a schedule using the deterministic Program Evaluation Review Technique. They permit the determination of the probability that specified events will occur at particular times using either deterministic or probabilistic methods. They will produce a schedule and a bar chart in work date format. They do not include the capability to update the project. These programs are based on programs CPM and AON and can be created by modifying those two programs.

Utility Programs

Several utility programs are listed. They can be used in connection with the scheduling programs or to produce scheduling-related documents.

Program REGIME can be used to generate a calendar date/work date conversion table for use with either program CPM or program AON. Program REGIME can be incorporated within these two programs for more convenient use, but it is listed as a separate program so as to minimize RAM memory requirements.

Programs RAMTEST1 and RAMTEST2 can be used to automatically generate data files for networks based on Activity On Arrow or on Activity On Node notation. Such data files are useful for determining the maximum size of a project network that the scheduling programs can handle on a particular microcomputer.

Program JULIAN produces a Julian date calendar that is useful when performing calendar date scheduling manually.

HARDWARE AND SOFTWARE REQUIREMENTS

A microcomputer with an appropriate disk operating system, sufficient RAM (rapid access memory), a BASIC interpreter program, a floppy disk system (preferably with two drives), and a printer is required to execute the programs listed in this appendix. The six scheduling programs and the related utility programs have been tested on an IBM-PC computer. Program JULIAN has been tested on an Altair 8080b computer.

Sufficient RAM

Microcomputer systems are labeled as having some specified amount of RAM, with 64K (65,536) bytes being a representative memory. A more significant measure of a system's capacity for executing these scheduling programs is its free RAM after the BASIC interpreter program has been loaded. An IBM-PC has 61,330 bytes free after BASIC is loaded. Another system, one labeled as having 64K of RAM, actually has only about 20,000 bytes free, with about 44,000 bytes of RAM space occupied by the disk operating system and by the BASIC interpreter program. You may test your system for free memory by loading BASIC and entering the command: PRINT FRE(0). The response will tell you how much memory is available for the programs listed hereafter and for their associated data files.

Subsequent sections will list the amount of RAM required for each of the programs. The six scheduling programs require from 6057 bytes (CPM-MIN) to 30,589 bytes (AON) of RAM memory. The size of the project that your system can handle depends on the free RAM after the scheduling program is loaded. For programs CPM and AON, three types of data are required: network data, calendar date data, and update data. Only network data are required for the other four programs. The amount of RAM memory required for network data and update data is approximately a function of the number of tasks in the network being analyzed. The amount of RAM memory required per task depends partly on how many characters are used for the task description. These programs truncate task descriptions that are longer than 24 characters to 24 characters. Hence, a maximum of 24 bytes is required for the description of each task. Additional memory is required for task numbers, task node numbers, task durations, event times, actual start and finish times, and for other input and computed variables. The actual memory required for these numeric variables will range from about 24 to about 60 bytes per task, depending on whether your system stores numbers as 5-byte numbers or as 2-byte string representations of those numbers. Another 5000 bytes is required for storage of a calendar indicating workdates and non-workdates.

Given these imponderables, it is nearly impossible to analytically determine the largest network that can be solved by your particular system. Two of the listed programs, programs RAMTEST1 and RAMTEST2, automatically generate network data files for Activity On Arrow and for Activity On Node networks that contain any desired number of tasks (and, for AON networks, of relationship arrows). It is suggested that you revise the dimension statement in a particular program (statement 50 in program CPM) so that MT (maximum tasks) is equal to the largest network you will analyze. Then use program RAMTEST1 to create a network data file of that size. Create a calendar file using program REGIME if you plan to use calendar dates. Then run your program and load the test network data file and the calendar file. Execute each of the routines in the program. The screen will display free RAM space after these data files have been loaded. If free RAM is never less than about 1000 bytes, then your system will handle a network of the desired size. If a message such as ''OUT OF MEMORY'' is displayed, then you should revise the dimension statement so that MT is equal to some lesser value. Then repeat the test. Entry of actual data representing a large project is very time consuming. It will be very disappointing to enter actual data for a network that is too large for your system.

Printer

An 80-column-wide dot matrix or character printer that will handle fanfold or roll paper is required for the following programs. If your printer is wider, say, 132 characters, then you may revise some of the statements in the programs to utilize this additional paper width.

Terminal Screen

Your terminal screen should display 80 characters wide by 24 lines high. It is possible, although inconvenient, to run the programs on portable personal computers displaying less than 24 lines. It is not feasible to run them using a screen that will display less than 80 characters per line.

PROGRAM CPM (25,967 BYTES)

Program Listing

A complete program listing is provided. The user may desire to run the program with some of its capabilities omitted. For example, if the project updating capability in Program CPM is not desired, then program lines 9000 to 9890 may be omitted. The address 9000 in line 720 should be replaced with the address 500. When run on an IBM-PC, the program will handle projects containing up to 275 tasks with all features operative. Execution time will be reduced if the statement in line 50 is revised so that the maximum number of tasks is reduced. For example, if it is known that a project will consist of no more than 150 tasks, then the statement in line 50 should be revised so that MT = 150. If RAM memory is sufficient to handle the desired number of tasks plus another 4000 bytes, then you should merge Program REGIME into this program for more convenient execution.

Data Elements

Task descriptions can be no longer than 24 characters and they cannot include commas. Task numbers, I-node numbers, and J-node numbers must be positive integers equal to or less than 9999. Durations must be positive integers equal to or less than 999. J-node numbers must be larger than I-node numbers. When entering calendar date data, use the M,D,Y format (1,14,85 = January 14, 1985).

Program Files

Program CPM requires extensive disk file space. It is suggested that the disk operating system files, the BASIC interpreter program, and programs CPM and REGIME be saved on disk drive A. Disk drive B should be reserved for the data files listed below. A particular floppy disk should contain data files for only one project. It is good practice to periodically make backups for these data disks. There are three data files that can be saved on disk.

Network Data Files. This file contains network data (task definitions). Routine 2 permits saving this file on disk. Routine 3 permits retrieval of this file from disk. Always load the netowrk data file before loading the next two files.

Workdate Calendar Files. Routine 8 permits calling up a workdate/ calendar date conversion table if the file has been created using Program REGIME. If REGIME has been merged into Program CPM, then routine 8 permits creation of the workdate calendar data file. Specific days of the week and specific calendar dates may be defined as non-workdates. The first date on such a calendar is the project start date. It is suggested that such calendar files be assigned file names in the format CYYMMDDX. The file name C850114A would be appropriate for a calendar file for a project starting on January 14, 1985. The last character in the eight-character file name is optional. It could be used if there are two calendar files starting on January 14, 1985. Always load the calendar file before loading an update file.

Update Files. Routine 9 permits creation of an update data file, which may be saved on disk. One such file would be created and saved on disk each time the project status is updated. Normally, a project is updated at the end of each month. An appropriate name for the first update file of a project started on January 14, 1985 and initially updated on January 31, 1985 would be U850131. An appropriate name for the second update file for this project (assuming the second update is on February 28, 1985) is U850228. An eighth character may be added to the file name if required. The second and subsequent updates are created by recalling from disk the previous update data file and by revising it to reflect progress since that previous update. The routine also permits printout of update files for use as a worksheet in the preparation of the next update.

Program Execution

Selected screen displays and printout are provided to illustrate the use of the 10 routines making up program CPM. *Screen 1* depicts the master menu. The first four lines of the display indicate the current time (assuming that your computer has a clock) and the elapsed time for executing the last routine called for. The screen also indicates the number of task definitions currently residing in computer memory. The 10 routines are described. To execute a routine, type in the routine number following the question mark prompt at the bottom of the screen. In this instance, routine 1 (review/revise/delete task definitions) has been called for.

Routine 1 Review/Revise/Delete Task Definitions

This routine is used to define tasks and to review or to delete previously entered task definitions. Required input for the definition of a task includes: task number, task I-node number, task J-node number, task duration, and task description. If the task is incorrectly defined, its definition may be deleted. Alternatively, a correct definition may be entered using the same sequence number. Tasks are identified by a task sequence number and by a task number. A task's sequence number may change as a result of a re-sequencing operation (routine 7), because another task has been deleted, or because the task definitions were entered without using all the sequence numbers. On completion of the this routine, the listing of task definitions is automatically closed up so that there are no gaps in the file.

Routines 2 and 3 Network Data File Save and Network Data File Read

These routines permit saving a network data file on disk and then subsequently retrieving it from the disk. The user must specify the disk drive to be used (it was previously suggested that all data files be saved on drive B). Network data file names can be no longer than eight characters. File names should not include spaces, commas, or periods.

Routine 4 Network Analysis

This routine serves two functions. Whenever it is accessed from the main menu, the routine determines operative node numbers. Although task numbers may be as large as 9999, event times are computed for operative node numbers, with only 276 such numbers required for a network with 275 tasks. This feature drastically reduces the need for memory for storage of event times. However, it is a time-consuming process with up to 4 minutes being required for a network of 275 tasks.

Following the determination of operative node numbers, the routine computes task times (early start, early finish, and the like) based on the task data. These task times are saved in memory for future printout. If routine 9 (Update Schedule) is used, then part of routine 4 is used again to compute event times based on update data. The event times are used in routines 5 and 6 to compute revised task times.

Routine 4 should be executed before calling for an analysis based on update data in routine 9, and it should not be run again before printing the schedule and the bar chart. The actual network analysis requires less than a minute for a network with 275 tasks. It is essential that tasks be sequenced in J-node order before running this routine. If the network analysis is made before resequencing tasks in J-node order, computed task times will be incorrect. Skip ahead to the description of routine 7 before studying the description of routine 5.

Routine 5   Display/Print CPM Schedule

The user can specify screen display, printout, or both for all or some of the tasks making up a network. If a calendar date date file has been loaded, the user may specify workdate or calendar date format for the printout. If an update data file has been loaded and the network has been analyzed on the basis of these data, the user may specify that the revised schedule be printed in addition to the original schedule. Skip ahead to the description of routine 9 for updating the project.

Printout of the schedule may be continuous or by pages. A continuous printout will have a single schedule heading followed by the task data for all specified tasks. If page format is specified, the schedule will be printed in as many pages as are required with a heading and data for 17 tasks on each page. Page format is recommended because it permits storage of the printout in folders or binders. *Output 1* illustrates the printout produced by this routine using calendar date format and with the update data reflected. Note that the printout indicates two values for task durations. The upper value is the originally estimated duration. The lower value is the effective duration.

Only workdate or calendar date task times will be displayed on the screen. If calendar date output is specified, without update data, then both the calendar date and the workdate will be on the printed schedule. If update data is specified, then the original and the revised task times will be printed in calendar date format.

Routine 6   Print Gantt Chart

This routine permits printout of a bar chart. Normally this routine will be executed immediately after routine 5, Print Schedule, using the same parameters (calendar date versus work date and page format versus continuous format) that were used for printing the schedule. The bar chart is printed so that one or more sheets of bar chart can be taped to a page of schedule. Visualize the bar chart being as wide as the project duration is long. If the project duration is 300 days, then four sheets of bar chart (each containing a 75-day-wide part of the bar chart) will be required. The bar chart will be in workdate or calendar date format. If update data are included, a separate bar will be printed for the revised schedule. The pages of the bar chart that do not include bars will not be printed. Note on

Output 2 that the bar for the update data for task 15 contains five D's, indicating that the actual task start was delayed five workdays past its early start time. Capital letters are used for the bars for critical tasks. A bar chart for either an early start schedule or a late start schedule can be called for. An ES bar chart was specified in this instance, so all bars start on their tasks' ES dates and end on their EF dates. Periods are plotted at the end of the bars to indicate workdays of float. If an LS bar chart had been specified, then the periods would lead the bars. At the bottom of each page are printed workdays corresponding to the calendar dates at the top of the page.

Routine 7   Resequencing Tasks

The user may specify that tasks be resequenced on the basis of their task numbers, their I-node numbers, their J-node numbers, or their durations. This routine should always be executed before routine 4 so that tasks are listed in a J-node order before the network analysis. After the network analysis (including an analysis that they may be called for from routine 9) is made, the user may again execute this routine to resequence the tasks in any desired order. The user may specify resequencing on the basis of several of these parameters, including task times and task total floats. The resequencing function is based on task times based on the original network data and does not encompass the revised task times or revised task floats computed during the update analysis.

Routine 8   Load Workdate Calendar

This routine will recall from disk a workdate calendar created by Program RE-GIME (or will create, save on disk, and recall from disk a calendar prepared by the routine if Program REGIME has been merged into CPM).

Routine 9   Update Schedule

This routine cannot be executed unless both a network data file and a calendar file are loaded. It enables the user to specify actual and projected start and finish dates for tasks. The update files may be saved on disk for future retrieval and modification. The routine will print out all of the data in an update file. The printout may be used as a worksheet for a subsequent update. On completion of all updating entries, the user should utilize a subroutine calling for a network analysis based on that data. The calendar dates used in this routine must be dates that have not been defined as non-workdates.

An actual start or finish date should be based on data reported by field personnel. The routine will not accept an actual start or finish date that is subsequent to the update date. A projected start or finish date will normally be based on reported data from the field or on the judgment of the scheduler. If an actual start date and percent completion have been entered for a task, the routine will prompt the user to enter a projected finish date and will display suggested projected finish dates based on actual progress on the task and on the original estimate of the task's duration. The user may enter one of those dates or another date as a projected finish date. Similarly, entry of a projected start date will result in a prompt suggesting a projected finish date. The entry of an actual start date will result in the deletion of any previously entered projected start date. The entry of an actual finish date will result in the deletion of any previously entered projected finish date. *Screen 2* illustrates the use of routine 9. The update data file named U850131 has been recalled from disk so as to revise the projected finish date of task 15 from March 4, 1985, to March 8, 1985. Following this change, the revised update data should be saved on disk and a network analysis should be called for using a subroutine of routine 9.

Execution Time

The following times are for a network containing 150 tasks. Approximately four minutes are required to make the network analysis based on the original task data. One minute is required to make the network analysis based on update data. The difference between these two times results from the fact that several error-checking routines and assignment of operative node numbers must be done for the first of these operations but not for the second. The time for printing schedules is about 15 seconds per task. Similarly, the time for printing bar charts is about 15 seconds per task. The time required to input task definition data and update data is about 30 seconds per task.

PROGRAM AON (30,589 BYTES)

Program Listing

A complete program listing is provided. The program has the same capabilities as program CPM. Program REGIME can be merged into program AON. The program will handle 175 tasks nodes and 300 relationship arrows when run on an IBM-PC computer. The program has a limited capability of handling double-headed arrows.

Data Elements

Task numbers must be positive integers equal to or less than 9999. Relationship numbers must be positive integers equal to or less than 32,567. Durations must be positive integers equal to or less than 999. Lags can be zero or positive or negative integers can be equal to or less than 999.

Program Files

The program data files include two network data files (one for task nodes and one for relationship arrows), a workdate/calendar date conversion file (generated by Program REGIME), and an update data file. It is suggested that all data files be saved on disk drive B and the program (and Program REGIME) be saved on disk drive A. When saving network data files on disk, the user must limit the length of the file name to seven characters. The program saves the task definition data under that name and saves the relationship data under the same name with an A appended as the eighth character of the file name.

Program Execution

The tasks must be sorted in task number order before making a network analysis. They can be resequenced in any other desired order after the network analysis has been made (and after the network analysis based on update data has been made). The routines have generally the same functions as the corresponding routines in program CPM. Refer to the discussion of the CPM routines.

Routine 1   Review/Revise/Delete Network Data

This routine allows the user to define tasks (task number, task duration, and task description) and to define logical relationships (arrow number, lag, I-node, J-node, and type of relationship). To define a double-headed arrow, define two single-headed arrows. They may have the same or different arrow numbers. The program will not handle networks in which more than one double-headed arrow is attached to either side (right side or left side) of a task node.

Assume that a double-headed arrow connects the right side of task node 10 to the left side of task node 20. The first arrow would be an end-to-start type with an I-node of 10 and a J-node of 20. The second arrow would be a start-to-end type with an I-node of 20 and a J-node of 10. The two arrows could have the same or different arrow numbers. The lags for double-headed arrows must be zero.

Routines 2 and 3   Network Data Save and
Network Data Read

These routines are similar to the coresponding CPM routines. Network data file names can be no longer than seven characters. Although there are two network data files (one for task data and one for relationship data), the user need enter only a single seven-character maximum file name. These routines automatically append an A to that name to access or to retrieve the second file.

Routine 4   Network Analysis

This routine is functionally similar to the corresponding CPM routine. The routine determines the precedence of logical relationship arrows. If a logic loop exists, or if excessive double-headed arrows have been specified, a screen display will indicate the arrows that may be causing the trouble. Determination of arrow precedence is very time consuming. If the network data are saved on disk after the precedence of arrows has been determined, then determination of their precedence will be much faster in subsequent sessions. After the precedence determination is completed, the network analysis will be made. A part of this routine will be used when called for from routine 9, Update Schedule. When accessed from routine 9, the part of this routine that determines arrow precedence will be skipped over. Hence, it is essential that this program be accessed from the main menu before it is accessed from routine 9.

Routine 5   Print Schedule

This routine is similar to the corresponding CPM routine. A subroutine permits calling for a printout of logical relationships. The printout will indicate the total float of the arrows. *Output 1* and *Output 2* illustrate the printout obtainable from this routine. The project involved is identical to that used for the CPM example illustrated in *Output 1*, and the AON logic diagram is logically identical to the CPM diagram used for that previous example. In this instance, revised task times are shown only for tasks having no actual or projected finish times. The tasks are listed in a different order than in this previous example, but could have been placed in the same order by using routine 7. Revised task times based on update data can only be printed, not displayed.

Routine 6   Print Gantt Chart

This routine is similar to the corresponding CPM routine. A bar chart identical to that shown in *Output 2* can be produced by this routine.

Routine 7   Resequence Tasks

This routine is similar to the corresponding CPM routine.

Routine 8   Read Workdate/Calendardate
Conversion Data

This routine is identical to the coresponding routine in program CPM.

Routine 9   Update Schedule

This routine is similar to the corresponding routine in program CPM.

Routine 10   End Execution

A prompt requesting confirmation will be displayed before execution terminates.

PROGRAM REGIME (3905 BYTES)

This program computes a three-year long calendar with specified days of the week and calendar dates designated as non-workdates. The calendar can be printed out, and it can be saved as a data file on a floppy disk. The data file can be accessed by programs CPM and AON when the calendar date format is desired. The statement numbers for program REGIME are compatible with those of programs CPM and AON. Hence, Program REGIME can be merged into programs CPM and AON. *Screen 3* illustrates the use of program REGIME.

CPM-MIN: A MINIMAL CPM
PROGRAM (6057 BYTES)

This program lacks bar charting, calendar dating, and updating capabilities. It can be upgraded to program CPM. The program was written on an IBM-PC computer. It should run on any computer equipped with a BASIC interpreter program. The program includes five major routines: data input, data save on disk, data retrieval from disk, network analysis, and display or printout of the schedule. The first three of these routines are nearly identical to the first three routines of Program CPM listed in a subsequent section.

Program Capacity

The IBM-PC BASIC interpreter language is in firmware (a computer chip); hence, 61,598 bytes of RAM are available for the program and data. The program uses 6065 bytes, leaving about 55,000 bytes for data. This is sufficient for a network containing over 1000 tasks. The output routine of the program is formatted so that task numbers cannot exceed four digits and node numbers cannot exceed three digits. The listed program is set up for 999 tasks. The limit of 999 for node numbers was established because the scheduling algorithm requires that two memory spaces of 5 bytes be reserved for the early event and the late event times for each possible node number. Hence, about 10,000 bytes of memory are required just for these two values. If some of your system's RAM is utilized for the BASIC interpreter program and the disk operating system program, then your system will handle less than 999 tasks. To determine the actual capacity of your system, use program RAMTEST1 as described in a subsequent section.

Conventions

The following conventions must be used with this program.

1. Node numbers must be positive integers equal or less than 999.
2. No two nodes may have the same node number.
3. Task numbers must be positive integers equal to or less than 9999.
4. The node number at an arrow's J-end must be larger than the node number at its I-end. This convention precludes creation of logic loops.
5. Task descriptions cannot exceed 24 characters in length. If any task description exceeds this permissible length, it will automatically be truncated to 24 characters.

AON-MIN: A MINIMAL PRECEDENCE METHOD PROGRAM (13,661 BYTES)

The statements in this program are compatible with those in Program AON. The user may desire to first load AON-MIN and later upgrade it to AON. AON-MIN lacks calendar dating and project updating capabilities. It will not produce a bar chart. The variables used for task times are double-subscripted so as to facilitate upgrading the program to program AON. The limitations for data elements are the same as those for program AON.

AOA-PERT: A PROGRAM EVALUATION REVIEW TECHNIQUE (15,641 BYTES)

This program is for Activity On Arrow networks such as CPM. It accepts optimistic, most likely, and pessimistic estimates of task duration. It computes and prints the project schedule and bar chart using workdate format and Program Evaluation Review Technique (PERT) procedures. It also will perform a probabilistic analysis of selected event times using the Monte Carlo technique, that is, repetitive analysis of the network with task times varying in a random manner. The output of this program has been illustrated in the text. The program statements are very compatible with those of program CPM.

AON-PERT: A PERT AND MONTE CARLO PROGRAM (22,393 BYTES)

This program is similar to AOA-PERT except that it is to be used for networks diagrammed with activity on node conventions. Multiple estimates of relationship lag values as well as task duration values are used. The program statements are somewhat compatible with those of program AON.

JULIAN: A JULIAN DATE CALENDAR PROGRAM

This program produces a Julian date calendar for use in manual scheduling based on calendar date format.

RAMTEST1 AND RAMTEST2: NETWORK DATA FILE GENERATOR PROGRAMS (1010 AND 1880 BYTES)

These programs automatically generate network data files that can be read by the appropriate routines in programs CPM, AON, CPM-MIN, AON-MIN, CPM-PERT, and AON-PERT. The size of the network (number of nodes and arrows) that any of the scheduling programs will handle depends on a number of factors, including computer memory and average length of task descriptions. Integer numbers may be stored in RAM as numbers requiring 5 bytes of memory, or as string representations of numbers, requiring only two bytes of memory. These programs will automatically generate appropriate network data files to test a computer's capacity to handle a network of a given size. It is recommended that all of the programs be tested on your computer system using programs RAMTEST1 or RAMTEST2, before data are loaded for an actual project.

DISCLAIMER

Both the publisher and the author disclaim any responsiblity for damages incurred as a result of the use of these programs.

AVAILABILITY OF PROGRAMS IN FLOPPY DISK FORMAT

Readers desiring to purchase 5.25-inch floppy disks containing these programs should contact the author, care of the College of Engineering, University of North Carolina at Charlotte, Charlotte, NC 28223.

```
CPM                                                        Page  1 of 12
10 REM PROGRAM CPM
20 SCREEN 0:CLS:KEY OFF:IW=75
30 REM PROGRAM IS FORMATTED FOR 80 COLUMN TERMINAL SCREEN AND PRINTER
40 DEFINT A-P:DEFSTR R-T:DEFINT U-Z:DEFSNG Q
50 MT=276:MN=277:REM MT=MAX NBR OF TASKS. MN=MAX NBR OF NODES. YOU MAY REVISE.
60 DIM I(MT),J(MT),D(MT),T(MT),ES(MT),EF(MT),LS(MT),LF(MT),FT(MT),FF(MT)
70 DIM A(MT),FI(MT),E(MN),L(MN)
80 DIM NS(MN+1),IO(MN),JO(MN)
90 DIM DS(1100),DM(12),Q(1100),DD(75),MM(75),YY(75),SM(12),CW(75)
100 DIM U(MT,6)
110 SD(0)="0":SD(1)="1":SD(2)="2":SD(3)="3":SD(4)="4":SD(5)="5"
120 SD(6)="6":SD(7)="7":SD(8)="8":SD(9)="9"
130 SM(1)="JAN":SM(2)="FEB":SM(3)="MAR":SM(4)="APR"
140 SM(5)="MAY":SM(6)="JUN":SM(7)="JUL":SM(8)="AUG"
150 SM(9)="SEP":SM(10)="OCT":SM(11)="NOV":SM(12)="DEC"
160 BEEP:PRINT"SET TERMINAL IN UPPERCASE MODE"
500 REM ******** MAIN MENU ROUTINE ********************************************
510 CLS
520 PRINT"LAST ROUTINE EXECUTED WAS:";:PRINT USING"##";LX
530 PRINT"CURRENT TIME IS      :";:PRINT USING"!";"";:PRINT TIME$
540 PRINT"LAST ROUTINE STARTED:";:PRINT USING"!";"";:PRINT TZ$
550 PRINT"ELAPSED TIME (SECONDS)   :";:PRINT USING"########";TIMER-QX
560 BEEP:PRINT"******** MAIN MENU ********"
570 NT=0:FOR N=1 TO MT:IF A(N)>0 THEN NT=NT+1
580 NEXT N:PRINT"NBR TASKS =";:PRINT NT;:PRINT USING"!";""
590 PRINT"FREE RAM SPACE=";:PRINT FRE(0)
600 PRINT"1 - REVIEW/REVISE/DELETE NETWORK DATA"
610 PRINT"2 - SAVE DATA IN RANDOM FORMAT ON DISK."
620 PRINT"3 - READ DATA FROM DISK"
630 PRINT"4 - ANALYZE NETWORK"
640 PRINT"5 - PRINT SCHEDULE"
650 PRINT"6 - PRINT GANTT CHART"
660 PRINT"7 - RESEQUENCE TASKS"
670 PRINT"8 - READ WORKDATE/CALENDARDATE CONVERSION DATA"
680 PRINT"9 - UPDATE SCHEDULE"
690 PRINT"10 - END EXECUTION"
700 INPUT "SELECT OPTION?";O
710 TZ$=TIME$:LX=0:QX=TIMER
720 ON O GOTO 1000,2000,3000,4000,5000,6000,7000,8000,9000,10000
730 GOTO 560
1000 REM **** REVIEW/REVISE/DELETE NETWORK DATA ROUTINE  *****************
1010 CLS
1020 TD="SEQ TASK# I-# J-# DUR DESCRIPTION              ES  EF  LS  L"
1030 TD=TD+"F   TF  FF  IF"
1040 INPUT"REVIEW/REVISE TASKS STARTING WITH SEQUENCE NUMBER?";IN
1050 IF IN<1 THEN 1040 ELSE IF IN >MT-14 THEN IN=MT-14
1060 REM *** DISPLAY TASK DATA SUBROUTINE *****
1070 CLS:PRINT TD
1080 FOR N=IN TO IN+14
1090 GOSUB 1100:GOTO 1170
1100 PRINT USING"###";N;:PRINT USING"######";A(N);
1110 PRINT USING"####";I(N),J(N),D(N);
1120 IF T(N)="" THEN T(N)="blank"
1130 PRINT USING"!";"";:PRINT USING"\            \";T(N);
1140 IF RD="R"THEN PRINT
1150 IF RD="R"THEN RETURN
1160 PRINT USING"####";ES(N),EF(N),LS(N),LF(N),FT(N),FF(N),FI(N):RETURN
1170 NEXT N
1180 INPUT"ENTER R-REVISE D-DELETE N-NEXT PAGE X-EXIT?";R
1190 IF R="R" THEN RD="R"ELSE RD=""
```

```
CPM                                                        Page  2 of 12
1200 IF R="R"THEN 1230 ELSE IF R="D"THEN 1340 ELSE IF R="N"THEN 1390
1210 IF R="X"THEN 1410 ELSE 1180
1220 REM **** REVISE TASK DATA SUBROUTINE *****
1230 INPUT"REVISE DATA FOR SEQUENCE NUMBER?(0 TO EXIT)";NR:IF NR=0 THEN 1180
1240 PRINT TD:N=NR:GOSUB 1100
1250 PRINT"ENTER VALUES FOR TASK#, I-#, J-#, AND DURATION, SEPARATED BY"
1260 INPUT"COMMAS (ENTER 4 ZEROES IF DATA IS OKAY)";A1,A2,A3,A4
1270 IF A3>A2 THEN 1290
1280 BEEP:BEEP:PRINT"J-NODE NUMBER MUST BE > I-NODE NUMBER":GOTO 1180
1290 A(N)=A1:I(N)=A2:J(N)=A3:D(N)=A4
1300 INPUT"ENTER TASK DESCRIPTION (CARRIAGE RETURN IF DATA IS OKAY)";TT
1310 IF TT="" THEN 1070 ELSE T(N)=LEFT$(TT,24)
1320 GOTO 1070
1330 REM **** DELETE TASK DATA SUBROUTINE ********
1340 INPUT"ENTER SEQUENCE NUMBER OF TASK TO BE DELETED (0 TO EXIT)";ND
1350 IF ND=0 THEN 1180
1360 N=ND:A(N)=0:I(N)=0:J(N)=0:T(N)="blank":D(N)=0:ES(N)=0:EF(N)=0
1370 LS(N)=0:LF(N)=0:FT(N)=0:FF(N)=0:FI(N)=0:GOTO 1070
1380 REM **** DISPLAY NEXT SCREEN SUBROUTINE ***
1390 IN=IN+15:IF IN+14>MT THEN IN=MT-14
1400 GOTO 1070
1410 REM *** CLOSE GAPS IN DATA FILE SUBROUTINE *****
1420 PRINT"NT=";:PRINT NT
1430 BT=0:NT=0:FOR N=1 TO MT:IF A(N)>0 THEN NT=NT+1
1440 IF A(N)>0 THEN BT=N
1450 NEXT N
1460 IF BT=NT THEN 500
1470 PRINT"CLOSING GAPS IN DATA FILE"
1480 N=0
1490 N=N+1
1500 IF A(N)>0 THEN 1570
1510 NX=N
1520 NX=NX+1:IF A(NX)=0 THEN 1520
1530 A(N)=A(NX):A(NX)=0:I(N)=I(NX):I(NX)=0:J(N)=J(NX):J(NX)=0
1540 D(N)=D(NX):D(NX)=0:T(N)=T(NX):T(NX)="":ES(N)=ES(NX):ES(NX)=0
1550 EF(N)=EF(NX):EF(NX)=0:LS(N)=LS(NX):LS(NX)=0:LF(N)=LF(NX):LF(NX)=0
1560 FT(N)=FT(NX):FT(NX)=0:FF(N)=FF(NX):FF(NX)=0:FI(N)=FI(NX):FI(NX)=0
1570 IF N=NT THEN 500 ELSE 1490
1580 GOTO 500
2000 REM ****** SAVE DATA ON DISK IN RANDOM FORMAT *****************************
2010 INPUT"ENTER NAME OF FILE TO BE SAVED (8 CHARACTERS MAX)";SF$
2020 INPUT"SAVE ON DRIVE (A,B,C,ETC)?";SD$
2030 SS$=SD$+":"+SF$
2040 OPEN SS$ AS #1 LEN=32
2050 FOR N=1 TO NT
2060 FIELD #1,2 AS S1,2 AS S2,2 AS S3,2AS S4,24 AS S5
2070 LSET S1=MKI$(A(N)):LSET S2=MKI$(I(N)):LSET S3=MKI$(J(N))
2080 LSET S4=MKI$(D(N)):LSET S5=T(N)
2090 PUT #1
2100 NEXT N
2110 CLOSE #1:GOTO 500
2120 REM ****** THE FOLLOWING STATEMENTS MAY BE USED IN LIEU OF 2040-2100
2130 REM TO SAVE DATA IN SEQUENTIAL FORMAT.
2140 OPEN "O",#1,SS$
2150 FOR N=1 TO NT:WRITE #1,A(N),I(N),J(N),D(N),T(N):NEXT N:CLOSE #1:GOTO 500
3000 REM **** READ DATA FROM DISK ROUTINE *********************************
3010 INPUT"ENTER NAME OF FILE TO BE READ FROM DISK";RF$
3020 INPUT"ENTER DRIVE FROM WHICH FILE IS TO BE READ (A,B,C,ETC)";RD$
3030 SS$=RD$+":"+RF$
3040 OPEN SS$ AS #1 LEN=32
```

```
CPM                                                          Page  3 of 12
3050 N=1
3060 FIELD #1,2 AS S1,2 AS S2,2 AS S3,2AS S4,24 AS S5
3070 GET #1:NT=N
3080 A(N)=CVI(S1):I(N)=CVI(S2):J(N)=CVI(S3):D(N)=CVI(S4):T(N)=S5
3090 IF EOF(1) THEN 3110
3100 N=N+1:GOTO 3060
3110 CLOSE #1:GOTO 500
3120 REM ********** THE FOLLOWING STATEMENTS MAY BE USED IN LIEU 3040-3110
3130 REM TO READ A SEQUENTIAL FORMAT DATA FILE.
3140 OPEN "I",#1,SS$:N=0
3150 N=N+1:INPUT #1,A(N),I(N),J(N),D(N),T(N):IF EOF(1) THEN 3160 ELSE 3150
3160 CLOSE #1:GOTO 500
4000 REM ****** NETWORK ANALYSIS ROUTINE ************
4010 LN=32746:FOR N=1 TO NT:IF A(N)=0 THEN 4030
4020 IF I(N)<LN THEN LN=I(N)
4030 NEXT N
4040 NS(1)=LN:PRINT"PLEASE ALLOW UP TO 5 MINUTES"
4050 FOR N=1 TO NT:IF A(N)=0 THEN 4060 ELSE NS(N+1)=J(N)
4060 NEXT N:NM=NT+1:GOSUB 4090
4070 FOR M=2 TO NT+1:IF NS(M)=NS(M-1) THEN NS(M)=32567
4080 NEXT M:NM=NT+1:GOSUB 4090:GOTO 4240
4090 MM=NM
4100 MM=INT(MM/2)
4110 IF MM=0 THEN RETURN ELSE 4120
4120 KK=NM-MM
4130 JJ=1
4140 II=JJ
4150 LL=II+MM
4160 IF NS(II)>NS(LL)THEN 4170 ELSE 4220
4170 IT=NS(II)
4180 NS(II)=NS(LL)
4190 NS(LL)=IT
4200 II=II-MM
4210 IF II>=1 THEN 4150 ELSE 4220
4220 JJ=JJ+1
4230 IF JJ>KK THEN 4100 ELSE 4140
4240 FOR N=1 TO NT:IF A(N)=0 THEN 4260 ELSE NQ=J(N)
4250 GOSUB 4270:JO(N)=IT:NQ=I(N):GOSUB 4270:IO(N)=IT
4260 NEXT N:GOTO 4340
4270 IV=1:JV=NM
4280 IT=(IV+JV)/2:IA=IT-1:IB=IT:IC=IT+1
4290 IF NS(IA)=NQ THEN IT=IA ELSE IF NS(IB)=NQ THEN IT=IB
4300 IF NS(IC)=NQ THEN IT=IC
4310 IF NS(IT)=NQ THEN RETURN
4320 IF NS(IT)>NQ THEN JV=IT ELSE IV=IT
4330 GOTO 4280
4340 PRINT"OPERATIVE NODE NUMBERS ASSIGNED. STARTING ANALYSIS"
4600 FOR M=1 TO MN:E(M)=0:L(M)=9999:NEXT M
4610 GOSUB 4620:GOSUB 4720:GOSUB 4760:GOSUB 4820:BT=BV:GOTO 500
4620 FOR N=1 TO NT
4630 IF A(N)=0 THEN 4710
4640 IF TU<>"Y" THEN 4690
4650 IF U(N,2)>0 THEN 4660 ELSE IF U(N,4)>0 THEN 4670 ELSE 4680
4660 D(N)=U(N,2)-E(IO(N)):GOTO 4690
4670 D(N)=U(N,4)-E(IO(N)):GOTO 4690
4680 D(N)=U(N,6)
4690 KV=E(IO(N))+D(N)
4700 IF KV>E(JO(N))THEN E(JO(N))=KV
4710 NEXT N:RETURN
4720 BV=0:FOR N=1 TO NT
```

```
4730 IF A(N)=0 THEN 4750
4740 IF E(JO(N))>BV THEN BV=E(JO(N))
4750 NEXT N:RETURN
4760 FOR M=1 TO MN:L(JO(M))=BV:NEXT M
4770 FOR N=NT TO 1 STEP-1
4780 IF A(N)=0 THEN 4810
4790 KV=L(JO(N))-D(N)
4800 IF KV<L(IO(N)) THEN L(IO(N))=KV
4810 NEXT N:RETURN
4820 FOR N=1 TO NT
4830 IF A(N)=0 THEN 4860
4840 ES(N)=E(IO(N)):EF(N)=ES(N)+D(N):LF(N)=L(JO(N)):LS(N)=LF(N)-D(N)
4850 FT(N)=LF(N)-EF(N):FF(N)=E(JO(N))-E(IO(N))-D(N):FI(N)=FT(N)-FF(N)
4860 NEXT N:RETURN
5000 REM ********* DISPLAY/PRINT SCHEDULE ROUTINE ****************************
5010 INPUT"S=SCREEN DISPLAY, H=HARDCOPY , B=BOTH.    WHICH?";R
5020 IF R="S"THEN PM=1 ELSE IF R="H"THEN PM=2 ELSE IF R="B"THEN PM=3 ELSE 5010
5030 IF Q(1)>0 THEN INPUT"C=CALENDAR DATE FORMAT, W=WORKDATE FORMAT.WHICH?";R
5040 CF=1:IF Q(1)>0 AND R="C" THEN CF=2
5050 UP=1:IF TU="Y"THEN INPUT"USE UPDATE DATA Y OR N?";R
5060 IF TU="Y" AND R="Y" THEN UP =2 ELSE UP=1
5070 IF UP=1 THEN 5090 ELSE INPUT"M,D,Y OF UPDATE?";M,D,Y
5080 GOSUB 9095:UD=IT
5090 INPUT"C=PRINT SCHEDULE CONTINUOUSLY, P=PRINT SCHEDULE BY PAGES. WHICH?";R
5100 IF R="C"THEN PL=300 ELSE PL=17
5110 INPUT"PRINT/DISPLAY TASKS WITH SEQUENCE NUMBERS I TO J?    I,J=?";IX,JX
5120 IF IX<1 THEN 5110 ELSE IF JX>MT THEN 5110 ELSE IF IX>JX THEN 5110
5130 IF PM=1 THEN 5160 ELSE INPUT"ENTER ONE LINE PROJECT TITLE";TP
5140 IF LEN(TP)=<80 THEN 5160
5150 TP=LEFT$(TP,80):PRINT TP:INPUT"OK";R:IF R="Y"THEN 5160 ELSE 5130
5160 S1="TSK# I-N# J-N# DUR DESCRIPTIO":S2=S1
5170 IF CF=2 THEN 5180 ELSE 5200
5180 S1=S1+"N              ES(BD) EF(ED) LS(BD) LF(ED)   TF    FF"
5190 GOTO 5210
5200 S1=S1+"N              ES(ED) EF(ED) LS(ED) LF(ED)   TF    FF"
5210 S2=S2+"N              ES/RVS EF/RVS LS/RVS LF/RVS   TF    FF"
5220 ST$="\              \":SD="":FOR K=1 TO 15:SD=SD+"     -":NEXT K
5230 S0$="!" :LV=0:P=0
5240 FOR N=IX TO JX:IF A(N)=0 THEN 5270
5250 LV=LV+1:IF LV=1 THEN GOSUB 5300
5260 GOSUB 5420:IF LV=PL THEN LV=0
5270 NEXT N:IF PM<>1 THEN LPRINT CHR$(12)
5280 IF PM<>2 THEN INPUT "CARRIAGE RETURN TO RETURN TO MAIN MENU";R
5290 GOTO 500
5300 P=P+1:IF PM=1 THEN 5370
5310 IF P>1 THEN LPRINT CHR$(12)
5320 LPRINT"Page No.";:LPRINT USING"###";P;
5330 IF UP=1 THEN LPRINT
5340 IF UP=1 THEN 5360
5350 LPRINT USING"\            \";"";:LPRINT"UDATED";:LPRINT USING"#######";Q(DS(UD))
5360 LPRINT:LPRINT TP:LPRINT
5370 IF PM<>2 THEN PRINT S1
5380 IF PM<>1 AND UP=1 THEN LPRINT S1
5390 IF PM<>1 AND UP=2 THEN LPRINT S2
5400 IF PM<>1 THEN LPRINT SD
5410 RETURN
5420 VA=A(N):VB=I(N):VC=J(N):VD=D(N):VE=ES(N):VF=EF(N):VG=LS(N):VH=LF(N)
5430 VI=FT(N):VJ=FF(N):IF CF=1 THEN 5510
5440 QA=Q(DS(VE+1)):QB=Q(DS(VF)):QC=Q(DS(VG+1)):QD=Q(DS(VH)):IF UP=1 THEN 5510
5450 GOSUB 5460:GOTO 5510
```

```
5460 VP=U(N,6):VK=E(IO(N)):VL=VK+VP:VN=L(JO(N)):VM=VN-VP:VO=U(N,2)-U(N,1)
5470 VQ=VN-VL:VR=E(JO(N))-E(IO(N))-VP:VT=U(N,5)
5480 VS=100*(UD-VE)/VD:IF VS>100 THEN VS=100 ELSE IF VS<0 THEN VS=0
5490 QE=Q(DS(U(N,1))):QF=Q(DS(U(N,2))):QG=Q(DS(U(N,3))):QH=Q(DS(U(N,4)))
5500 QI=Q(DS(VK+1)):QJ=Q(DS(VL)):QK=Q(DS(VM+1)):QL=Q(DS(VN))  :RETURN
5510 IF PM<>2 AND CF=1 THEN GOSUB 5570
5520 IF PM<>2 AND CF=2 THEN GOSUB 5600
5530 IF PM<>1 AND CF=1 THEN GOSUB 5630
5540 IF PM<>1 AND CF=2 AND UP=1 THEN GOSUB 5670
5550 IF PM<>1 AND CF=2 AND UP=2 THEN GOSUB 5720
5560 RETURN
5570 PRINT USING"####";VA;:PRINT USING"#####";VB,VC;
5580 PRINT USING"####";VD;:PRINT USING S0$;"";:PRINT USING ST$;T(N);
5590 PRINT USING"#######";VE,VF,VG,VH;:PRINT USING"####";VI,VJ:RETURN
5600 PRINT USING"####";VA;:PRINT USING"#####";VB,VC;
5610 PRINT USING"####";VD;:PRINT USING S0$;"";:PRINT USING ST$;T(N);
5620 PRINT USING"#######";QA,QB,QC,QD;:PRINT USING"####";VI,VJ:RETURN
5630 LPRINT USING"####";VA;:LPRINT USING"#####";VB,VC;
5640 LPRINT USING"####";VD;:LPRINT USING S0$;"";:LPRINT USING ST$;T(N);
5650 LPRINT USING"#######";VE,VF,VG,VH;:LPRINT USING"####";VI,VJ
5660 LPRINT:LPRINT SD:RETURN
5670 LPRINT USING"####";VA;:LPRINT USING"#####";VB,VC;
5680 LPRINT USING"####";VD;:LPRINT USING S0$;"";:LPRINT USING ST$;T(N);
5690 LPRINT USING"#######";QA,QB,QC,QD;:LPRINT USING"####";VI,VJ
5700 LPRINT USING"\                             \";"";
5710 LPRINT USING"#######";VE,VF,VG,VH:LPRINT SD:RETURN
5720 LPRINT USING"####";VA;:LPRINT USING"#####";VB,VC;
5730 LPRINT USING"####";VD;:LPRINT USING S0$;"";:LPRINT USING ST$;T(N);
5740 LPRINT USING"#######";QA,QB,QC,QD;:LPRINT USING"####";VI,VJ
5750 IF U(N,2)=0 AND U(N,4)=0 THEN Z=0 ELSE Z=1
5760 LPRINT USING"\             \";"";
5770 IF Z=1 THEN LPRINT USING"####";VP; ELSE LPRINT USING"\        \";"";
5780 SA="":SB="":IF U(N,1)>0 THEN SA="AS=" ELSE IF U(N,3)>0 THEN SA="PS="
5790 IF U(N,2)>0 THEN SB="AF=" ELSE IF U(N,4)>0 THEN SB="PF="
5800 QM=0:QN=0:IF U(N,1)>0 THEN QM=QE ELSE IF U(N,3)>0 THEN QM=QG
5810 IF U(N,2)>0 THEN QN=QF ELSE IF U(N,4)>0 THEN QN=QH
5820 LPRINT USING"!";"";:LPRINT USING"\      \";
5830 IF SA="" THEN LPRINT USING"\      \";""; ELSE LPRINT USING"######";QM;
5840 LPRINT USING"!";"";:LPRINT USING"\ \";SB;
5850 IF SB="" THEN LPRINT USING"\      \";""; ELSE LPRINT USING"######";QN;
5860 LPRINT USING"\    \";"";
5870 LPRINT USING"#######";QI,QJ,QK,QL;:LPRINT USING"####";VQ,VR
5880 SA="SCH%=":SB="ACT%=":IF VS=0 AND VT=0 THEN LPRINT SD
5890 IF VS=0 AND VT=0 THEN RETURN
5900 LPRINT USING"\                    \";"";:LPRINT SA;:LPRINT USING"####";VS;
5910 LPRINT USING"!";"";:LPRINT SB;:LPRINT USING"####";VT:RETURN
6000 REM ********** PRINT GANTT CHART ROUTINE ******************************
6005 IW=75:S5="N":INPUT"USE SAME PARAMETERS AS USED FOR SCHEDULE? Y OR N";S5
6010 IF S5="Y"THEN 6020
6015 INPUT "GANTT CHART FOR SEQUENCE NBRS I TO J. ENTER I,J",IX,JX
6020 IF IX<1 THEN IX=1
6025 IF JX>NT THEN JX=NT
6030 BF =0:SP="":FOR K=1 TO 15:SP=SP+"    +":NEXT K
6035 FOR K=IX TO JX:IF LF(K)>BF THEN BF=LF(K)
6040 NEXT K :IF UP=1 THEN 6055
6045 FOR K=IX TO JX:IF E(JO(K))>BF THEN BF=E(JO(K))
6050 NEXT K
6055 IF S5="Y" THEN 6070
6060 INPUT"WORKDAY (W) OR CALENDARDAY (C) FORMAT?";R
6065 IF R="C" THEN CF=2 ELSE IF R="W" THEN CF=1 ELSE 6060
```

```
6070 IF CF=2 AND S5<>"Y" THEN 6075 ELSE 6090
6075 INPUT"UPDATE DATA DESIRED? Y OR N?";R:UP=1:IF R="Y"THEN UP=2
6080 IF UP=2 THEN INPUT"DATE OF UPDATE? M,D,Y?";M,D,Y:GOSUB 9095:UD=IT
6085 IF IT=0 THEN 6075
6090 QU=Q(DS(UD)):INPUT"1- ES SCHEDULE   , 2- LS SCHEDULE. WHICH?";KS
6095 IF CF=1 THEN 6100 ELSE 6305
6100 REM **** BAR CHART IN WORKDATE FORMAT **************
6105 SX=" ":SX=STRING$(75,SX)
6110 NH=(JX-IX+1)/PL:IF JX-IX+1>NH*PL THEN NH=NH+1
6115 IV=IX:JV=JX:GOSUB 6165:P1=INT((IR-1)/75)+1:P2=INT((JR-1)/75)+1
6120 FOR P=P1 TO P2:S1$="":S2$="":S3$=""
6125 ID=1+IW*(P-1):JD=ID+IW-1:DD=ID-1
6130 FOR II=ID TO JD:KH=INT(II/100):S1$=S1$+SD(KH):NEXT II
6135 FOR II=ID TO JD:KH=INT(II/100):KT=INT((II-100*KH)/10)
6140 S2$=S2$+SD(KT):NEXT II
6145 FOR II=ID TO JD:KH=INT(II/100):KT=INT((II-100*KH)/10)
6150 KU=INT(II-100*KH-10*KT):S3$=S3$+SD(KU):NEXT II
6155 FOR PP=1 TO NH:IV=IX+PL*(PP-1):JV=IV+PL-1:IF JV>JX THEN JV=JX
6160 GOSUB 6165:GOTO 6185
6165 IR=9999:JR=0:FOR N=IV TO JV:IF A(N)=0 THEN 6180
6170 IF ES(N)+1<IR THEN IR=ES(N)+1
6175 IF LF(N)>JR THEN JR=LF(N)
6180 NEXT N:RETURN
6185 IF JR<ID THEN 6275 ELSE IF IR>JD THEN 6275
6190 PRINT CHR$(12):GOSUB 6290:FOR N=IV TO JV
6195 IF A(N)=0 THEN 6270
6200 SB=SX:IF D(N)=0 THEN 6265
6205 EB=ES(N)+1-DD:EC=EB+D(N)-1:LC=LF(N)-DD:LB=LC-D(N)+1
6210 IF FT(N)=0 THEN 6215 ELSE 6220
6215 S$="C":IC=EB:JC=LC:GOSUB 6240:GOTO 6265
6220 S$=".":IC=EB:JC=LC:GOSUB 6240
6225 IF KS=1 THEN 6230 ELSE 6235
6230 S$="e":IC=EB:JC=EC:GOSUB 6240:GOTO 6265
6235 S$="l":IC=LB:JC=LC:GOSUB 6240:GOTO 6265
6240 IF IC>75 THEN RETURN
6245 IF JC<1 THEN RETURN
6250 IF IC<1 THEN IC=1
6255 IF JC>75 THEN JC=75
6260 L=JC-IC+1:S$=STRING$(L,S$):MID$(SB,IC,L)=S$:RETURN
6265 LPRINT SP:LPRINT SB:LPRINT
6270 NEXT N:LPRINT SP:LPRINT CHR$(12)
6275 NEXT PP
6280 NEXT P
6285 GOTO 500
6290 LPRINT"PAGE NO.";:LPRINT USING"###";PP;:LPRINT USING"!";"";
6295 LPRINT "SHEET NO.";:LPRINT USING"###";P
6300 LPRINT S1$:LPRINT S2$:LPRINT S3$:RETURN
6305 REM **** BAR CHART IN CALENDARDATE FORMAT ********
6310 SX=" ":SX=STRING$(75,SX):GOTO 6335
6315 FOR N=IV TO JV:IF A(N)=0 THEN 6330
6320 IF E(IO(N))+1<IR THEN IR=E(IO(N))+1
6325 IF L(JO(N))>JR THEN JR=L(JO(N))
6330 NEXT N:RETURN
6335 IV=IX:JV=JX:GOSUB 6165:IF UP=2 THEN GOSUB 6315
6340 IR=DS(IR):JR=DS(JR):P1=INT((IR-1)/75)+1:P2=INT((JR-1)/75)+1
6345 NH=(JX-IX+1)/PL:IF JX-IX+1>NH*PL THEN NH=NH+1
6350 FOR P=P1 TO P2:DD=75*(P-1)
6355 REM ***** CONSTRUCTS HEADINGS ***************
6360 S1$=SX:S2$=SX:S3$=SX:SP=SX:S4$=SX:S5$=SX:S6$=SX
6365 OD=0:FOR N=0 TO DD:IF Q(N)>0 THEN OD=OD+1
```

```
6370 NEXT N:FOR K=1 TO 75:KK=K+DD:IF Q(KK)<0 THEN 6385 ELSE OD =OD+1
6375 VH=INT(OD/100):VT=INT((OD-100*VH)/10):VU=OD-100*VH-10*VT
6380 MID$(S4$,K,1)=SD(VH):MID$(S5$,K,1)=SD(VT):MID$(S6$,K,1)=SD(VU)
6385 NEXT K
6390 FOR K=1 TO 75:N=K+DD:QQ=ABS(Q(N)):YY(K)=INT(QQ/10000)
6395 IF Q(N)<0 THEN MID$(SP,K,1)="-"
6400 MM(K)=INT((QQ-10000*YY(K))/100):DD(K)=QQ-10000*YY(K)-100*MM(K)
6405 NEXT K:FOR K=1 TO 71 STEP 10:MID$(S1$,K,3)=SM(MM(K+2)):NEXT K
6410 FOR K=4 TO 74 STEP 10:N1=INT(YY(K-1)/10):N2=YY(K-1)-10*N1
6415 SA=SD(N1)+SD(N2):MID$(S1$,K,2)=SA:NEXT K
6420 FOR K=1 TO 75:MID$(S2$,K,1)=SD(INT(DD(K)/10))
6425 MID$(S3$,K,1)=SD(INT(DD(K) MOD 10)):NEXT K
6430 FOR PP=1 TO NH:IV=IX+PL*(PP-1):JV=IV+PL-1:IF JV>JX THEN JV=JX
6435 GOSUB 6165:IF UP=2 THEN GOSUB 6315
6440 IR=DS(IR):JR=DS(JR):IF JR=<DD THEN 6725 ELSE IF IR>DD+75 THEN 6725
6445 GOSUB 6735
6450 REM ****** CONSTRUCTS BARS BASED ON ORIGINAL DATA ********
6455 FOR N=IV TO JV:SB=SX:SC=SX:IF A(N)=0 THEN 6720
6460 IF D(N)=0 THEN 6715
6465 A1=DS(ES(N)+1):A2=DS(EF(N)):A3=DS(LS(N)+1):A4=DS(LF(N))
6470 IF A1>JR THEN 6535 ELSE IF A4<IR THEN 6535
6475 A1=A1-DD:A2=A2-DD:A3=A3-DD:A4=A4-DD
6480 IF FT(N)=0 THEN 6485 ELSE 6490
6485 S$="C":IC=A1:JC=A2:GOSUB 6510:GOSUB 6540:GOTO 6535
6490 S$=".":IC=A1:JC=A4:GOSUB 6510
6495 IF KS=1 THEN 6500 ELSE 6505
6500 S$="e":IC=A1:JC=A2:GOSUB 6510:GOSUB 6540:GOTO 6535
6505 S$="l":IC=A3:JC=A4:GOSUB 6510:GOSUB 6540:GOTO 6535
6510 IF IC>75 THEN RETURN
6515 IF JC<1 THEN RETURN
6520 IF IC<1 THEN IC=1
6525 IF JC>75 THEN JC=75
6530 L=JC-IC+1:S$=STRING$(L,S$):MID$(SB,IC,L)=S$:RETURN
6535 IF UP=1 THEN 6715 ELSE 6550
6540 FOR K=1 TO 75:IF MID$(SP,K,1)="-" THEN MID$(SB,K,1)=" "
6545 NEXT K:RETURN
6550 REM ******** CONSTRUCTS BARS FOR UPDATE DATA ************
6555 FV=L(JO(N))-E(IO(N))-U(N,6):DD=75*(P-1):F1=DS(UD+1)-DD
6560 T1="D":T2="A":T3="P":T4="R":IF FV=0 THEN 6570
6565 T1="d":T2="a":T3="p":T4="r"
6570 D1=DS(E(IO(N))+1)-DD:D2=DS(E(IO(N))+U(N,6))-DD
6575 D3=DS(L(JO(N))-U(N,6)+1)-DD:D4=DS(L(JO(N)))-DD
6580 U1=DS(U(N,1))-DD:U2=DS(U(N,2))-DD:U3=DS(U(N,3))-DD
6585 U4=DS(U(N,4))-DD:UU=DS(UD)-DD:IF U(N,1)>0 THEN JA=DS(U(N,1)-1)-DD
6590 IF U(N,3)>0 THEN JB=DS(U(N,3)-1)-DD
6595 IF FV=0 THEN 6605
6600 S$=".":IC=D1:JC=D4:GOSUB 6670
6605 IF U(N,2)>0 THEN 6615 ELSE IF U(N,1)>0 AND U(N,4)>0 THEN 6625
6610 IF U(N,3)>0 AND U(N,4)>0 THEN 6650 ELSE 6655
6615 S$=T1:IC=D1:JC=JA:GOSUB 6670 :REM ACTUALLY FINISHED
6620 S$=T2:IC=U1:JC=U2:GOSUB 6670:GOTO 6705
6625 S$=T1:IC=D1:JC=JA:GOSUB 6670:REM ACTUAL START & PROJECTED FINISH
6630 IF UU<1 THEN 6640 ELSE IF UU>75 THEN 6640
6635 S$=T2:IC=U1:JC=UU:GOSUB 6670:S$=T3:IC=F1:JC=U4:GOSUB 6670:GOTO 6705
6640 S$=T3:IC=1:JC=U4:GOSUB 6670:GOTO 6705
6645 REM PROJECTED START AND FINISH
6650 S$=T1:IC=D1:JC=JB:GOSUB 6670:S$=T3:IC=U3:JC=U4:GOSUB 6670:GOTO 6705
6655 S$=T4:IF KS=1 THEN 6660 ELSE 6665:REM NO ACTUAL OR PROJECTED DATES
6660 IC=D1:JC=D2:GOSUB 6670:GOTO 6705
6665 IC=D3:JC=D4:GOSUB 6670: GOTO 6705
```

```
6670 IF IC>75 THEN RETURN :REM SUBROUTINE FOR  BAR CONSTRUCTION
6675 IF JC<IC THEN RETURN
6680 IF JC<1 THEN RETURN
6685 IF IC<1 THEN IC=1
6690 IF JC>75 THEN JC=75
6695 L=JC-IC+1:IF L<1 THEN RETURN ELSE S$=STRING$(L,S$)
6700 MID$(SC,IC,L)=S$:RETURN
6705 FOR K=1 TO 75:IF MID$(SP,K,1)="-" THEN MID$(SC,K,1)=" "
6710 NEXT K
6715 LPRINT SP:LPRINT SB:LPRINT SC
6720 NEXT N:LPRINT SP:LPRINT S4$:LPRINT S5$:LPRINT S6$:LPRINT CHR$(12)
6725 NEXT PP
6730 NEXT P :GOTO 500
6735 LPRINT"PAGE NO.";:LPRINT USING"###";PP;:LPRINT USING"!";"";
6740 LPRINT "SHEET NO.";:LPRINT USING"###";P;:IF UP=1 THEN LPRINT
6745 IF UP=1 THEN 6755 ELSE LPRINT USING"!";" ";
6750 LPRINT"UPDATED ";:LPRINT USING"########";Q(DS(UD))
6755 LPRINT TP
6760 LPRINT S1$:LPRINT S2$:LPRINT S3$:RETURN
7000 REM ************** RESEQUENCE TASKS ROUTINE *****************************
7010 PRINT"BEFORE RESEQUENCING, YOU SHOULD ELIMINATE UNUSED SEQUENCE"
7020 PRINT"NUMBERS. TO DO SO, EXIT FROM THIS ROUTINE AND SAVE DATA"
7030 INPUT"ON DISK AND THEN READ IT BACK. DO YOU WANT TO EXIT? Y OR N ?";R
7040 IF R="Y"THEN 500
7050 PRINT"PARAMETER 1 - TASK NUMBERS"
7060 PRINT"PARAMETER 2 - I-NODE NUMBERS"
7070 PRINT"PARAMETER 3 - J-NODE NUMBERS"
7080 PRINT"PARAMETER 4 - TASK DURATIONS"
7090 PRINT"PARAMETER 5 - EARLY START TIME"
7100 PRINT"PARAMETER 6 - EARLY FINISH TIME"
7110 PRINT"PARAMETER 7 - LATE START TIME"
7120 PRINT"PARAMETER 8 - LATE FINISH TIME"
7130 PRINT"PARAMETER 9 - TOTAL FLOAT"
7140 INPUT"HOW MANY PARAMETERS FOR SORTING";NP:IF NP>9 THEN 7140
7150 PRINT"ENTER PARAMETER CODES WITH MOST SIGNIFICANT PARAMETER FIRST"
7160 FOR L=1 TO NP
7170 INPUT"PARAMETER NBR?";PL(L)
7180 NEXT L
7190 MM=NT
7200 MM=INT(MM/2)
7210 IF MM=0 THEN 7610 ELSE 7220
7220 KK=NT-MM
7230 JJ=1
7240 II=JJ
7250 LL=II+MM
7260 FOR L=1 TO NP
7270 IF PL(L)=1 THEN 7320 ELSE IF PL(L)=2 THEN 7330
7280 IF PL(L)=3 THEN 7340 ELSE IF PL(L)=4 THEN 7350
7290 IF PL(L)=5 THEN 7360 ELSE IF PL(L)=6 THEN 7370
7300 IF PL(L)=7 THEN 7380 ELSE IF PL(L)=8 THEN 7390
7310 IF PL(L)=9 THEN 7400
7320 VI=A(II):VL=A(LL):GOTO 7410
7330 VI=I(II):VL=I(LL):GOTO 7410
7340 VI=J(II):VL=J(LL):GOTO 7410
7350 VI=D(II):VL=D(LL):GOTO 7410
7360 VI=ES(II):VL=ES(LL):GOTO 7410
7370 VI=EF(II):VL=EF(LL):GOTO 7410
7380 VI=LS(II):VL=LS(LL):GOTO 7410
7390 VI=LF(II):VL=LF(LL):GOTO 7410
7400 VI=FT(II):VL=FT(LL):GOTO 7410
```

```
CPM                                                              Page  9 of 12
7410 IF VI>VL THEN 7440 ELSE IF VI=VL THEN 7420 ELSE 7590
7420 NEXT L
7430 GOTO 7590
7440 AT=A(II):IT=I(II):JT=J(II):DT=D(II):TT=T(II)
7450 C1=ES(II):C2=EF(II):C3=LS(II):C4=LF(II):C5=FT(II):C6=FF(II):C7=FI(II)
7460 A(II)=A(LL):I(II)=I(LL):J(II)=J(LL):D(II)=D(LL):T(II)=T(LL)
7470 ES(II)=ES(LL):EF(II)=EF(LL):LS(II)=LS(LL):LF(II)=LF(LL)
7480 FF(II)=FF(LL):FT(II)=FT(LL):FI(II)=FI(LL)
7490 A(LL)=AT:I(LL)=IT:J(LL)=JT:D(LL)=DT:T(LL)=TT
7500 ES(LL)=C1:EF(LL)=C2:LS(LL)=C3:LF(LL)=C4:FT(LL)=C5:FF(LL)=C6:FI(LL)=C7
7510 IF TU<>"Y" THEN 7570
7520 U1=U(II,1):U2=U(II,2):U3=U(II,3):U4=U(II,4):U5=U(II,5):U6=U(II,6)
7530 U(II,1)=U(LL,1):U(II,2)=U(LL,2):U(II,3)=U(LL,3):U(II,4)=U(LL,4)
7540 U(II,5)=U(LL,5):U(II,6)=U(LL,6)
7550 U(LL,1)=U1:U(LL,2)=U2:U(LL,3)=U3:U(LL,4)=U4:U(LL,5)=U5:U(LL,6)=U6
7560 OI=IO(II):OJ=JO(II):IO(II)=IO(LL):JO(II)=JO(LL):IO(LL)=OI:JO(LL)=OJ
7570 II=II-MM
7580 IF II=>1 THEN 7250 ELSE 7590
7590 JJ=JJ+1
7600 IF JJ>KK THEN 7200 ELSE 7240
7610 GOTO 500
8000 REM ******* READ WORKDAY REGIME FROM DISK ROUTINE ********************
8010 GOTO 8080
8020 REM***** MAKE WORKDAY/CALENDAR DAY CONVERSION ************
8030 PRINT"PLEASE WAIT ABOUT A MINUTE"
8040 N=0:FOR K=1 TO 1097:IF Q(K)>0 THEN N=N+1
8050 IF Q(K)>0 THEN DS(N)=K
8060 NEXT K:NI=N
8070 GOTO 500
8080 REM **** READ CALENDAR DATA FROM DISK ROUTINE *****************
0090 INPUT"ENTER NAME OF CALENDAR FILE TO BE READ FROM DISK";RF$
8100 INPUT"ENTER DRIVE FROM WHICH FILE IS TO BE READ (A,B,C,ETC)";RD$
8110 SS$=RD$+":"+RF$:SZ="Y"
8120 OPEN SS$ AS #1 LEN=16
8130 FOR NI=1 TO 1093 STEP 4
8140 FIELD #1,4 AS S1,4 AS S2,4 AS S3,4 AS S4
8150 GET #1
8160 Q(NI)=CVS(S1):Q(NI+1)=CVS(S2):Q(NI+2)=CVS(S3):Q(NI+3)=CVS(S4)
8170 IF EOF(1) THEN 8190
8180 NEXT NI
8190 CLOSE #1:GOTO 8020
9000 REM ************* UPDATE SCHEDULE ROUTINE  ***********************
9005 IF Q(DS(1))<>0 THEN 9015
9010 BEEP:PRINT"A WORK DAY/CALENDARDAY FILE MUST BE LOADED TO RUN THIS ROUTINE"
9015 IF A(1)>0 THEN 9030
9020 BEEP:PRINT"A PROJECT DATA FILE NUST BE LOADED TO RUN THIS ROUTINE"
9025 INPUT"UNDERSTAND? Y OR N";R:IF R="Y"THEN 500 ELSE 9010
9030 TD="SEQ TASK# I-# J-# DUR DESCRIPTION                           AS       A"
9035 TD=TD+"F       PS      PF STAT":SU$="":RU$=""
9040 PRINT"UPDATE FILE READ:";:PRINT USING"\          \";RU$;
9045 PRINT"UPDATE FILE SAVED:";:PRINT SU$
9050 PRINT"UPDATED ON";:PRINT USING "########";Q(DS(UD))
9055 PRINT"YOU MAY: 1 - READ AN UPDATE FILE FROM DISK"
9060 PRINT"         2 - SAVE THIS UPDATE FILE ON DISK"
9065 PRINT"         3 - REVIEW AND REVISE THE FILE "
9070 PRINT"         4 - MAKE A NETWORK ANALYSIS BASED ON UPDATE DATA."
9075 PRINT"         5 - PRINT UPDATE DATA"
9080 PRINT"         0 - EXIT TO MAIN MENU"
9085 INPUT"WHICH?";A:ON A GOTO 9680,9620,9160,9755,9825
9090 IF A =0 THEN 500 ELSE 9040
```

```
9095 QV=10000*Y+100*M+D:IV=1:JV=NI:IF QV=0 THEN IT=0
9100 IF QV=0 THEN RETURN
9105 IT=INT((IV+JV)/2):Q2=Q(DS(IT)):Q1=Q(DS(IV)):Q3=Q(DS(JV))
9110 IF QV=Q1 THEN 9130 ELSE IF QV=Q2 THEN 9145 ELSE IF QV=Q3 THEN 9135
9115 IF JV-IV<3 THEN 9150 ELSE IT=(IV+JV)/2
9120 IF QV>Q2 THEN IV=IT ELSE JV =IT
9125 GOTO 9105
9130 IT=IV:GOTO 9145
9135 IT=JV:GOTO 9145
9140 GOTO 9105
9145 PRINT USING"######";QV;:PRINT"= WORKDAY";:PRINT IT:RETURN
9150 PRINT USING"###";M,D,Y;:PRINT USING"!";"";:PRINT"IS NOT A WORKDAY"
9155 BEEP:INPUT"UNDERSTAND ?Y OR N?";RR:IT=0:RETURN
9160 REM **** REVIEW AND REVISE UPDATE DATA SUBROUTINE ***************
9165 INPUT"ENTER DATE OF UPDATE. M,D,Y";M,D,Y:GOSUB 9095:IF IT>0 THEN 9175
9170 BEEP:PRINT"ALL DATES ENTERED MUST BE WORKDATES":GOTO 9000
9175 UD=IT
9180 INPUT"REVIEW/REVISE TASK STATUS STARTING WITH SEQUENCE NUMBER?";IN
9185 IF IN<1 THEN IN=1 ELSE IF IN >MT-14 THEN IN=MT-14
9190 REM *** DISPLAY TASK STATUS DATA SUBROUTINE *****
9195 CLS:PRINT TD
9200 N1=IN:N2=N1+14:GOSUB 9210:GOTO 9245
9205 PRINT"UPDATE:";:PRINT Q(DS(UD)):PRINT TD:GOSUB 9210:GOTO 9305
9210 FOR K=N1 TO N2:IF A(K)=0 THEN 9240 ELSE PRINT USING"###";K;
9215 PRINT USING"######";A(K);
9220 PRINT USING"####";I(K),J(K),D(K);
9225 PRINT USING"!";"";:PRINT USING"\              \";T(K);
9230 FOR DQ=1 TO 4:QD(DQ)=Q(DS(U(K,DQ))):NEXT DQ
9235 PRINT USING"#######";QD(1),QD(2),QD(3),QD(4);:PRINT USING"####";U(K,5)
9240 NEXT K :RETURN
9245 INPUT"ENTER R-REVISE, N-NEXT PAGE, X-EXIT?";R
9250 IF R="R"THEN 9260 ELSE IF R="N"THEN IN=IN+15
9255 IF R="X"THEN 9040 ELSE 9185
9260 REM **** REVISE TASK UPDATE DATA SUBROUTINE *****
9265 INPUT"CHANGE UPDATE DATA FOR SEQUENCE NBR?";N
9270 N1=N:N2=N:PRINT TD:GOSUB 9205
9275 FOR K=1 TO NT:E(JO(K))=0:NEXT K
9280 FOR K=1 TO NT:IF U(K,2)>0 THEN 9285 ELSE IF U(K,4)>0 THEN 9295 ELSE 9300
9285 IF U(K,2)>E(JO(K)) THEN E(JO(K))=U(K,2)
9290 GOTO 9300
9295 IF U(K,4)>E(JO(K)) THEN E(JO(K))=U(K,4)
9300 NEXT K
9305 PRINT"CHANGE: 1-ACTUAL START      2-ACTUAL FINISH      3-PROJECTED START"
9310 PRINT"         4-PROJECTED FINISH  5-PERCENT COMPLETE   6-DELETE ENTRY"
9315 INPUT"         0-NO MORE CHANGES                       WHICH?";A
9320 ON A GOTO 9330,9375,9405,9465,9545,9575
9325 GOTO 9195
9330 INPUT"ACTUAL START DATE? M,D,Y ?";M,D,Y:GOSUB 9095:IF IT>0 THEN 9340
9335 BEEP:PRINT"DATE IS NOT A WORKDATE. ENTRY REJECTED":GOTO 9205
9340 IF ES(N)=0 THEN 9360 ELSE IF IT>E(IO(N)) THEN 9360
9345 BEEP:PRINT"NO ACTUAL COMPLETION DATE REPORTED FOR A PRECEDENT TASK"
9350 PRINT"OR ELSE A PRECEDENT TASK HAS AN ACTUAL FINISH = OR > THAN THIS DATE"
9355 INPUT"CANCEL ENTRY? Y OR N?";R:IF R="Y"THEN 9205
9360 IF IT=<UD THEN 9370 ELSE BEEP
9365 INPUT"DATE IS AFTER UPDATE. CANCEL ENTRY? Y OR N?";R:IF R="Y"THEN 9205
9370 U(N,1)=IT:U(N,3)=0:PRINT TD:GOSUB 9210:GOTO 9545
9375 IF U(N,1)>0 THEN 9385 ELSE BEEP
9380 PRINT"YOU MUST ENTER ACTUAL START BEFORE ACTUAL FINISH":GOTO 9570
9385 INPUT"ACTUAL FINISH DATE. M,D,Y?";M,D,Y:GOSUB 9095:IF IT=0 THEN 9335
9390 IF IT=<UD THEN 9400 ELSE BEEP
```

```
CPM                                                        Page 11 of 12
9395 INPUT"DATE IS AFTER UPDATE. CANCEL ENTRY? Y OR N?";R:IF R="Y"THEN 9205
9400 U(N,2)=IT:U(N,5)=100:E(JO(N))=IT:L(JO(N))=IT:U(N,4)=0:GOTO 9205
9405 IF U(N,1)=0 THEN 9415 ELSE BEEP
9410 PRINT"YOU HAVE ALREADY ENTERED AN ACTUAL START DATE.":GOTO 9205
9415 INPUT"ENTER PROJECTED START DATE. M,D,Y?";M,D,Y:GOSUB 9095
9420 IF IT>0 THEN 9335
9425 IF IT>UD THEN 9445 ELSE BEEP
9430 PRINT USING"#######";Q(DS(IT))::PRINT USING"!";"";
9435 INPUT"IS BEFORE UPDATE DATE. DO YOU WANT TO CANCEL ENTRY? Y OR N";R
9440 IF R="Y" THEN 9205
9445 IF IT>E(IO(N)) AND IT>L(IO(N)) THEN 9460 ELSE BEEP
9450 INPUT"A PRECEDENT TASK HAS NO ACTUAL OR PROJECTED FINISH. CANCEL ENTRY?";R
9455 IF R="Y" THEN 9205
9460 U(N,3)=IT:PRINT TD:GOSUB 9210:GOTO 9465
9465 IF U(N,1)>0 THEN 9475 ELSE IF U(N,3)>0 THEN 9495 ELSE BEEP
9470 PRINT"ENTER ACTUAL OR PROJECTED START BEFORE PROJECTED FINISH":GOTO 9205
9475 PRINT"BASED ON PROGRESS SINCE START,PROJECTED FINISH IS:";
9480 PRINT USING"#######";Q(DS(INT(U(N,1)-1+100*(UD-U(N,1)+1)/U(N,5))))
9485 PRINT"BASED ON ESTIMATED DURATION, PROJECTED FINISH IS:";
9490 PRINT USING"#######";Q(DS(U(N,1)-1+D(N))):GOTO 9505
9495 PRINT"BASED ON ESTIMATED DURATION, PROJECTED FINISH IS:";
9500 PRINT USING"#######";Q(DS(U(N,3)-1+D(N)))
9505 INPUT"ENTER PROJECTED FINISH DATE. M,D,Y?";M,D,Y:GOSUB 9095
9510 IF IT=0 THEN 9335
9515 IF U(N,1)>0 THEN 9530
9520 IF IT>=U(N,1) THEN 9540 ELSE BEEP
9525 PRINT"PROJECTED FINISH MUST BE = OR > ACTUAL START":GOTO 9205
9530 IF IT=>U(N,3) THEN 9540 ELSE BEEP
9535 PRINT"PROJECTED FINISH MUST BE= OR > PROJECTED START":GOTO 9205
9540 U(N,4)=IT:L(JO(N))=IT:GOTO 9205
9545 IF U(N,1)>0 THEN 9555 ELSE BEEP
9550 PRINT"ENTER ACTUAL START DATE BEFORE ENTERING PERCENT COMPLETE":GOTO 9205
9555 INPUT"ENTER PERCENT COMPLETION AS OF UPDATE DATE";A:IF A=100 THEN 9375
9560 IF A>0 AND A<100 THEN 9570 ELSE BEEP
9565 PRINT"PERCENT COMPLETION MUST BE BETWEEN 0 AND 100":GOTO 9555
9570 U(N,5)=A:PRINT TD:GOSUB 9210:GOTO 9465
9575 INPUT"DELETE ITEM NBR ?";A:IF A<1 THEN 9195 ELSE IF A>5 THEN 9195
9580 ON A GOTO 9585,9595,9600,9610,9615
9585 U(N,1)=0:U(N,5)=0:U(N,2)=0:IF U(N,3)=0 THEN U(N,4)=0
9590 PRINT TD:GOSUB 9210:GOTO 9575
9595 U(N,2)=0:PRINT TD:GOSUB 9210:GOTO 9545
9600 U(N,3)=0:IF U(N,1)=0 THEN U(N,4)=0
9605 PRINT TD:GOSUB 9210:GOTO 9575
9610 U(N,4)=0:PRINT TD:GOSUB 9210:GOTO 9575
9615 U(N,1)=0:U(N,5)=0:U(N,1)=0:PRINT TD:GOSUB 9210:GOTO 9575
9620 REM **** SAVE DATA ON DISK IN RANDOM FORMAT **************
9625 INPUT"ENTER NAME OF UPDATE FILE TO BE SAVED (8 CHARACTERS MAX)";SF$
9630 INPUT"SAVE ON DRIVE (A,B,C,ETC)?";SD$
9635 SS$=SD$+":"+SF$:SU$=SF$
9640 OPEN SS$ AS #1 LEN=12
9645 FOR N=1 TO NT:IF U(N,2)+U(N,4)=0 THEN 9670 ELSE IF A(N)=0 THEN 9670
9650 FIELD #1,2 AS S1,2 AS S2,2 AS S3,2 AS S4,2 AS S5, 2 AS S6
9655 LSET S1=MKI$(A(N)):LSET S2=MKI$(U(N,1)):LSET S3=MKI$(U(N,2))
9660 LSET S4=MKI$(U(N,3)):LSET S5=MKI$(U(N,4)):LSET S6=MKI$(U(N,5))
9665 PUT #1
9670 NEXT N
9675 CLOSE #1:GOTO 9040
9680 REM **** READ DATA FROM DISK ROUTINE *****************
9685 INPUT"ENTER NAME OF FILE TO BE READ FROM DISK";RF$
9690 INPUT"ENTER DRIVE FROM WHICH FILE IS TO BE READ (A,B,C,ETC)";RD$
```

```
CPM
9695 SS$=RD$+":"+RF$:RU$=RF$
9700 OPEN SS$ AS #1 LEN=12
9705 FIELD #1,2 AS S1,2 AS S2,2 AS S3,2 AS S4,2 AS S5,2 AS S6
9710 GET #1:AV=CVI(S1):PRINT"AV=";:PRINT AV;:IF AV=0 THEN 9735
9715 U1=CVI(S2):U2=CVI(S3):U3=CVI(S4):U4=CVI(S5)
9720 U5=CVI(S6):GOSUB 9740:PRINT NN:A(NN)=AV:N=NN:U(N,1)=U1:U(N,2)=U2
9725 U(N,3)=U3:U(N,4)=U4:U(N,5)=U5
9730 IF EOF(1) THEN 9735 ELSE 9705
9735 CLOSE #1:GOTO 9040
9740 REM *** SUBROUTINE FOR FINDING TASKS WITH SPECIFIED TASK NUMBER ***
9745 NN=0
9750 NN=NN+1:IF A(NN)=AV THEN RETURN ELSE 9750
9755 REM ****** NETWORK ANAYLSIS BASED ON UPDATE DATA ROUTINE **********
9760 TU="Y":FOR M=1 TO MN:E(M)=0:NEXT M
9765 FOR N=1 TO NT:IF A(N)=0 THEN 9785
9770 IF U(N,2)>E(JO(N)) THEN E(JO(N))=U(N,2)
9775 IF U(N,2)>0 THEN 9785
9780 IF U(N,4)>E(JO(N)) THEN E(JO(N))=U(N,4)
9785 NEXT N
9790 GOSUB 9795:GOSUB 4620:GOSUB 4720:BU=BV:GOSUB 4760:GOSUB 9795:GOTO 9040
9795 FOR N=1 TO NT:IF A(N)=0 THEN 9805
9800 IT=D(N):D(N)=U(N,6):U(N,6)=IT
9805 NEXT N:RETURN
9825 REM ***** PRINT UPDATE DATA ROUTINE *************
9830 QU=Q(DS(UD)):IF QU>0 THEN 9840
9835 THEN INPUT"UPDATE DATE? M,D,Y?";M,D,Y:QU=10000*Y+100*M+D
9840 LPRINT TAB(40) "LAST UPDATE/NEXT UPDATE";:LPRINT USING"########";QU;
9845 LPRINT"/":LPRINT:LPRINT TD
9850 FOR N=1 TO MT
9855 IF A(N)=0 THEN 9890 ELSE LPRINT USING"###";N;
9860 LPRINT USING"#####"; A(N);
9865 LPRINT USING"####";I(N),J(N),D(N);
9870 LPRINT USING"!";"";:LPRINT USING"\                    \";T(N);
9875 FOR DQ=1 TO 4:QD(DQ)=Q(DS(U(N,DQ))):NEXT DQ
9880 LPRINT USING"#######";QD(1),QD(2),QD(3),QD(4);:LPRINT USING"####";U(N,5)
9885 LPRINT
9890 NEXT N:LPRINT CHR$(12):GOTO 9040
10000 INPUT"ARE YOU SURE? Y OR N?";R:IF R<>"Y" THEN 500
```

```
AON                                                      Page  1 of 14
10 REM PROGRAM AON by E.M. Willis. University of North Carolina at Charlotte
20 SCREEN 0 : CLS : KEY OFF
30 DEFINT A-P:DEFSTR R-T:DEFINT U-Z:DEFSNG Q
40 PW=90:REM PRINTER WIDTH-REVISE IF NECESSARY
50 MT=160:MR=320
60 DIM A(MT),J(MR),I(MR),D(MT),R(MR),T(MT),FT(MT,2),AN(MR),IO(MR)
70 DIM ES(MT,2),EF(MT,2),LS(MT,2),LF(MT,2),L(MR),NL(MR),NR(MR)
80 DIM AP(MR),AF(MR,2),JO(MR)
90 DIM DM(12),DS(1100),Q(1100),DD(75),MM(75),YY(75),SM(12)
100 DIM U(MT,6)
110 SD(0)="0":SD(1)="1":SD(2)="2":SD(3)="3":SD(4)="4":SD(5)="5"
120 SD(6)="6":SD(7)="7":SD(8)="8":SD(9)="9"
130 SM(1)="JAN":SM(2)="FEB":SM(3)="MAR":SM(4)="APR"
140 SM(5)="MAY":SM(6)="JUN":SM(7)="JUL":SM(8)="AUG"
150 SM(9)="SEP":SM(10)="OCT":SM(11)="NOV":SM(12)="DEC"
160 BEEP:PRINT"SET TERMINAL IN UPPERCASE MODE"
500 REM ******** MAIN MENU ROUTINE ****************************************
510 CLS
520 PRINT"LAST ROUTINE EXECUTED WAS:";:PRINT USING"##";LX
530 PRINT"CURRENT TIME IS     :";:PRINT USING"!";"";:PRINT TIME$
540 PRINT"LAST ROUTINE STARTED:";:PRINT USING"!";"";:PRINT TZ$
550 PRINT"ELAPSED TIME (SECONDS)    :";:PRINT USING"########";TIMER-QX
560 BEEP:PRINT"******** MAIN MENU ********"
565 FOR N=1 TO MT:IF A(N)>NT THEN NT=N
570 NEXT N:FOR A=1 TO MR:IF AN(A)<>0 THEN NR=A
575 NEXT A:
580 PRINT"NUMBER OF TASKS :";:PRINT USING"###";NT
585 PRINT"NUMBER OF ARROWS:";:PRINT USING"###";NR
590 PRINT"FREE RAM SPACE=";:PRINT FRE(0)
600 PRINT"1 - REVIEW/REVISE/DELETE NETWORK DATA"
610 PRINT"2 - SAVE DATA IN RANDOM FORMAT ON DISK."
620 PRINT"3 - READ DATA FROM DISK"
630 PRINT"4 - ANALYZE NETWORK"
640 PRINT"5 - PRINT SCHEDULE"
650 PRINT"6 - PRINT GANTT CHART"
660 PRINT"7 - RESEQUENCE TASKS"
670 PRINT"8 - READ WORKDATE/CALENDARDATE CONVERSION DATA"
680 PRINT"9 - UPDATE SCHEDULE"
690 PRINT"10 - END EXECUTION"
700 INPUT "SELECT OPTION?";O
710 TZ$=TIME$:LX=O:QX=TIMER
720 ON O GOTO 1000,2000,3000,4000,5000,6000,7000,8000,9000,10000
730 GOTO 560
1000 REM **** REVIEW/REVISE/DELETE NETWORK DATA ROUTINE  *****************
1010 CLS:INPUT"1=ARROWS, 2=TASKS. WHICH?",A: IF A=1 1590
1020 TD="SEQ TASK# DUR DESCRIPTION              ES    EF    LS    L"
1030 TD=TD+"F    TF"
1040 INPUT"REVIEW/REVISE TASKS STARTING WITH SEQUENCE NUMBER?";IN
1050 IF IN<1 THEN 1040 ELSE IF IN >MT-14 THEN IN=MT-14
1060 REM *** DISPLAY TASK DATA SUBROUTINE *****
1070 CLS:PRINT TD
1080 FOR N=IN TO IN+14
1090 GOSUB 1100:GOTO 1170
1100 PRINT USING"###";N;:PRINT USING"######";A(N);:PRINT USING"####";D(N);
1110 PRINT USING"!";"";:PRINT USING"\                    \";T(N);
1140 IF RD="R"THEN PRINT
1150 IF RD="R"THEN RETURN
1160 PRINT USING"####";ES(N,1),EF(N,1),LS(N,1),LF(N,1);
1165 PRINT USING "####"; FT(N,1):RETURN
1170 NEXT N
1180 INPUT"ENTER R-REVISE D-DELETE N-NEXT PAGE X-EXIT?";R
```

```
1190 IF R="R" THEN RD="R"ELSE RD=""
1200 IF R="R"THEN 1230 ELSE IF R="D"THEN 1340 ELSE IF R="N"THEN 1390
1210 IF R="X"THEN 1410 ELSE 1180
1220 REM **** REVISE TASK DATA SUBROUTINE *****
1230 INPUT"REVISE DATA FOR SEQUENCE NUMBER?(0 TO EXIT)";NR:IF NR=0 THEN 1180
1240 PRINT TD:N=NR:GOSUB 1100
1250 INPUT"TASK#, DUR ?";A(N),D(N):INPUT"TASK DESCRIPTION (CR IF OK)?";TT
1260 IF TT=""THEN 1070
1270 T(N)=LEFT$(TT,24):GOTO 1070
1330 REM **** DELETE TASK DATA SUBROUTINE ********
1340 INPUT"ENTER SEQUENCE NUMBER OF TASK TO BE DELETED (0 TO EXIT)";ND
1350 IF ND=0 THEN 1180
1360 N=ND:A(N)=0:D(N)=0:T(N)="blank":GOTO 1070
1380 REM **** DISPLAY NEXT SCREEN SUBROUTINE ***
1390 IN=IN+15:IF IN+14>MT THEN IN=MT-14
1400 GOTO 1070
1410 REM *** CLOSE GAPS IN DATA FILE SUBROUTINE *****
1420 PRINT"NT=";:PRINT NT
1430 BT=0:NT=0:FOR N=1 TO MT:IF A(N)>0 THEN NT=NT+1
1440 IF A(N)>0 THEN BT=N
1450 NEXT N
1460 IF BT=NT THEN 500
1470 PRINT"CLOSING GAPS IN DATA FILE"
1480 N=0
1490 N=N+1
1500 IF A(N)>0 THEN 1570
1510 NX=N
1520 NX=NX+1:IF A(NX)=0 THEN 1520
1530 A(N)=A(NX):A(NX)=0
1540 D(N)=D(NX):D(NX)=0:T(N)=T(NX):T(NX)="blank"
1570 IF N=NT THEN 500 ELSE 1490
1580 GOTO 500
1590 REM ***************REVIEW/REVISE ARROWS ROUTINE*************
1595 GOTO 1615
1600 PRINT:PRINT"SEQ ARROW# TYPE    LAG I-NODE# J-NODE#        TF":RETURN
1605 ER=0:IF A<1 THEN GOSUB 1030 ELSE IF A>MR THEN GOSUB 1030
1610 RETURN
1615 INPUT"REVIEW/REVISE ARROWS STARTING WITH SEQUENCE NBR: ?";A
1620 GOSUB 1605:IF ER=1 THEN 1615 ELSE AI=A
1625 IF AI>MR -14 THEN AI=MR-14
1630 AJ=AI+14
1635 GOSUB 1600
1640 FOR A=AI TO AJ:GOSUB 1645:GOTO 1660
1645 PRINT USING"###";A;:PRINT USING"#######";AN(A);
1650 PRINT USING"\ \";"";:PRINT USING"\\";R(A);:PRINT USING"#####";L(A);
1655 PRINT USING"#########";I(A),J(A),AF(A,1):RETURN
1660 NEXT A
1665 PRINT
1670 INPUT"R=REVISE, D=DELETE, N=NEXT SCREEN, I=INSERT ,X=EXIT?";R
1675 IF R="R" THEN 1805 ELSE IF R="D" THEN 1685 ELSE IF R="I" THEN 1705
1680 IF R="X"THEN 1705  ELSE IF R="N" THEN 1700 ELSE 1635
1685 INPUT"SEQUENCE NUMBER TO BE DELETED?";A:GOSUB 1605
1690 IF ER=0 THEN 1695 ELSE 1635
1695 AN(A)=0: L(A)=0:J(A)=0:I(A)=0:R(A)="":GOTO 1635
1700 AI=AI+15:GOTO 1625
1705 NR=0:FOR A1=1 TO MR:IF AN(A)>0 THEN BA=A
1710 IF AN(A)>0 THEN NR=NR+1
1715 NEXT A:IF BA=NR AND R="X" THEN 500
1720 IF BA=NR AND R="I"THEN GOSUB 1765
1725 IF BA=NR AND R="I" THEN 1635
```

```
AON                                                    Page  3 of 14
1730 PRINT"CLOSING GAPS IN FILE"
1735 FOR A=1 TO NR:IF AN(A)>0 THEN 1755 ELSE AA=A
1740 AA=AA+1: IF AN(AA)=0 THEN 1740
1745 I(A)=I(AA):J(A)=J(AA):AN(A)=AN(AA):R(A)=R(AA):L(A)=L(AA)
1750 I(AA)=0:J(AA)=0:L(AA)=0:AN(AA)=0:R(AA)=""
1755 NEXT A:IF R="X" THEN 500
1760 PRINT"GAPS CLOSED. RE-SPECIFY INSERT OPTION":GOTO 1635
1765 INPUT"OPEN A SPACE BEFORE SEQUENCE NUMBER N, ENTER N?";N
1770 IF N=0 THEN 1635
1775 BA=0:FOR A=1 TO MR:IF AN(A)>0 THEN BA=A
1780 NEXT A
1785 FOR A=BA+1 TO N+1 STEP-1
1790 L(A)=L(A-1):I(A)=I(A-1):J(A)=J(A-1):R(A)=R(A-1):AN(A)=AN(A-1)
1795 NEXT A
1800 L(N)=0:I(N)=0:J(N)=0:R(N)="":AN(N)=0:GOTO 1625
1805 INPUT"SEQUENCE NUMBER TO BE REVISED?";A:GOSUB 1605
1810 IF ER=1 THEN 1635
1815 GOSUB 1600:GOSUB 1645
1820 INPUT"ARROW NBR, LAG, I-NODE#, J-NODE #?";AN(A),L(A),I(A),J(A)
1825 INPUT"ENTER TYPE OF ARROW: SS, SE, ES, EE";R(A)
1830 IF R(A)<>"SS" AND R(A)<>"SE" AND R(A)<>"ES" AND R(A)<>"EE"THEN 1825
1835 GOTO 1635
2000 REM **** SAVE DATA ON DISK IN RANDOM FORMAT ***************************
2010 INPUT"ENTER NAME OF FILE TO BE SAVED (7 CHARACTERS MAX)";SF$
2020 IF LEN(SF$)>7 THEN 2010
2030 INPUT"SAVE ON DRIVE (A,B,C,ETC)?";SD$
2040 SS$=SD$+":"+SF$:SA$=SS$+"A"
2050 OPEN SS$ AS #1 LEN=28
2060 FOR N=1 TO NT:FIELD #1,2 AS S1,2 AS S2,24 AS S3
2070 LSET S1=MKI$(A(N)):LSET S2=MKI$(D(N)):LSET S3=T(N):PUT #1
2080 NEXT N:CLOSE #1
2090 OPEN SA$ AS #2 LEN=10
2100 FOR A=1 TO NR:FIELD #2,2 AS S1,2 AS S2,2 AS S3, 2 AS S4, 2 AS S5
2110 LSET S1=MKI$(AN(A)):LSET S2=MKI$(L(A)):LSET S3=MKI$(I(A))
2120 LSET S4=MKI$(J(A)):LSET S5=R(A):PUT #2:NEXT A:CLOSE #2:GOTO 500
3000 REM **** READ DATA FROM DISK ROUTINE ******************************
3010 INPUT"ENTER NAME OF FILE TO BE READ FROM DISK";RF$
3020 INPUT"ENTER DRIVE FROM WHICH FILE IS TO BE READ (A,B,C,ETC)";RD$
3030 SS$=RD$+":"+RF$:SA$=SS$+"A"
3040 OPEN SS$ AS # 1 LEN=28:N=1
3050 FIELD # 1,2 AS S1,2 AS S2,24 AS S3:GET #1:NI=N
3060 A(N)=CVI(S1):D(N)=CVI(S2):T(N)=S3
3070 IF EOF(1) THEN 3090
3080 N=N+1:GOTO 3050
3090 CLOSE #1
3100 OPEN SA$ AS #2 LEN=10:A=1
3110 FIELD #2, 2 AS S1, 2 AS S2, 2 AS S3, 2 AS S4, 2 AS S5:GET #2:NR=A
3120 AN(A)=CVI(S1):L(A)=CVI(S2):I(A)=CVI(S3):J(A)=CVI(S4):R(A)=S5
3130 IF EOF(2) THEN 3150
3140 A=A+1:GOTO 3110
3150 CLOSE #2:GOTO 500
4000 REM ****** NETWORK ANALYSIS ROUTINE ************
4005 PRINT"TO RUN THIS ROUTINE, TASKS MUST BE SEQUENCED IN TASK NUMBER ORDER."
4010 INPUT"DO YOU WANT TO RESEQUENCE TASKS? Y OR N?";R:IF R="Y" THEN 7000
4015 M=1:IF R="N"THEN 4065 ELSE 4005
4020 REM****SUBROUTINE FOR FINDING TASKS WITH SPECIFIED TASK NBRS*****
4025 IX=1:JX=NT
4030 MX=INT((IX+JX)/2):IF A(MX)=NV THEN RETURN
4035 IF A(MX)>NV THEN JX=MX ELSE IX=MX
4040 IF A(IX)=NV THEN MX=IX ELSE IF A(JX)=NV THEN MX=JX
4045 IF A(IX)=NV THEN RETURN ELSE IF A(JX)=NV THEN RETURN
```

```
4050 IF JX=IX+1 AND A(IX)<>NV THEN MX=0
4055 IF MX=0 THEN RETURN ELSE 4030
4060 REM*****END OF SUBROUTINE************
4065 PRINT"CHECKING THAT NO TASKS HAVE DUPLICATE NODE NUMBERS."
4070 DT=0:FOR N=1 TO NT-1:IF A(N)<>A(N+1) THEN 4085
4075 PRINT "TASK SEQUENCE NUMBERS";:PRINT USING"######";N,N+1;
4080 PRINT USING"!";"";:PRINT"HAVE DUPLICATE TASK NUMBERS":DT=1
4085 NEXT N:IF DT=0 THEN 4100
4090 PRINT"YOU MUST CORRECT BEFORE PROCEEDING. DO YOU UNDERSTAND? Y OR N?"
4095 INPUT"?";R:IF R="Y"THEN 500 ELSE 4090
4100 FOR N=1 TO NT:NL(N)=0:NR(N)=0:NEXT N
4105 PRINT"CHECKING THAT I AND J NODES OF ARROWS ARE DEFINED TASKS"
4110 FOR A=1 TO NR:AP(A)=0:IF R(A)="" THEN 4170
4115 NV=I(A):GOSUB 4025:IF MX<>0 THEN 4140
4120 PRINT"ARROW #";:PRINT USING"#####";AN(A);:PRINT USING"!";"";
4125 PRINT"DOES NOT CONNECT TO A DEFINED TASK AT ITS I END"
4130 INPUT"CARRIAGE RETURN TO CONTINUE";ZZ
4135 GOTO 500
4140 IO(A)=MX:NV=J(A):GOSUB 4025:IF MX<>0 THEN 4160
4145 PRINT "ARROW #";:PRINT USING"####";AN(A);:PRINT USING"!";"";
4150 PRINT "DOES NOT CONNECT TO A DEFINED TASK AT ITS J END"
4155 INPUT"CARRIAGE RETURN TO CONTINUE";ZZZ:GOTO 500
4160 JO(A)=MX:IF RIGHT$(R(A),1)="S" THEN NL(MX)=NL(MX)+1
4165 IF RIGHT$(R(A),1)="E"THEN NR(MX)=NR(MX)+1
4170 NEXT A
4175 PRINT"DETERMINING ARROW SEQUENCE NUMBERS"
4180 FOR A=1 TO NR:AP(A)=0:NEXT A:PN=0
4185 CV=0:PRINT"EXAMINING SINGLE-HEADED ARROWS"
4190 FOR A=1 TO NR:IF AP(A)>0 THEN 4245
4195 IF R(A)="ES"THEN 4205 ELSE IF R(A)="SS"THEN 4215
4200 IF R(A)="EE"THEN 4225 ELSE 4235
4205 IF NL(IO(A))>0 THEN 4245 ELSE IF NR(IO(A))>0 THEN 4245
4210 PN=PN+1:AP(A)=PN:NL(JO(A))=NL(JO(A))-1:CV=1:GOTO 4245
4215 IF NL(IO(A))>0 THEN 4245
4220 PN=PN+1:AP(A)=PN:NL(JO(A))=NL(JO(A))-1:CV=1:GOTO 4245
4225 IF NL(IO(A))>0 THEN 4245 ELSE IF NR(IO(A))>0 THEN 4245
4230 PN=PN+1:AP(A)=PN:NR(JO(A))=NR(JO(A))-1:CV=1:GOTO 4245
4235 IF NL(IO(A))>0 THEN 4245
4240 PN=PN+1:AP(A)=PN:NR(JO(A))=NR(JO(A))-1:CV=1:GOTO 4245
4245 NEXT A:IF PN=NR THEN 4420
4250 IF CV>0 THEN 4185
4255 CV=0:PRINT"SEARCHING FOR DOUBLE-HEADED ARROWS"
4260 FOR A=1 TO NR:IF AP(A)>0 THEN 4385
4265 IF CV=1 THEN 4385
4270 FOR B=1 TO NR:IF AP(B)>0 THEN 4380 ELSE IF A=B THEN 4380
4275 IF CV=1 THEN 4380
4280 IA=IO(A):IB=IO(B):JA=JO(A):JB=JO(B)
4285 IF IA<> JB THEN 4380
4290 IF R(A)="SS" AND R(B)="SS"THEN 4310
4295 IF R(A)="EE" AND R(B)="EE"THEN 4325
4300 IF R(A)="ES" AND R(B)="SE" THEN 4340 ELSE 4360
4305 IF R(A)="SE" AND R(B)="ES" THEN 4360 ELSE 4380
4310 IF NL(IA)>1 THEN 4380 ELSE IF NL(JA)>1 THEN 4380
4315 PN=PN+1:AP(A)=PN:PN=PN+1:AP(B)=PN:CV=1
4320 NL(IA)=NL(IA)-1:NL(JA)=NL(JA)-1:GOTO 4380
4325 IF NL(IA)=0 AND NL(JA)=0 AND NR(IA)=1 AND NR(JA)=1 THEN 4330 ELSE 4380
4330 PN=PN+1:AP(A)=PN:PN=PN+1:AP(B)=PN:CV=1:NR(IA)=NR(IA)-1:NR(JA)=NR(JA)-1
4335 GOTO 4380
4340 IF NL(JA)>0 THEN 4380 ELSE IF NR(IA)>1 THEN 4380
4345 IF NL(JA)>1 THEN 4380
4350 PN=PN+1:AP(A)=PN:PN=PN+1:AP(B)=PN:CV=1
```

```
AON
4355 NR(IA)=NR(IA)-1:NL(JA)=NL(JA)-1:GOTO 4380
4360 IF NL(JA)>0 THEN 4380 ELSE IF NR(JA)>1 THEN 4380
4365 IF NL(IA)>1 THEN 4380
4370 PN=PN+1:AP(A)=PN:PN=PN+1:AP(B)=PN:CV=1
4375 NR(JA)=NR(JA)-1:NL(IA)=NL(IA)-1
4380 NEXT B
4385 NEXT A
4390 IF PN=NR THEN 4420 ELSE IF CV=1 THEN 4185
4395 PRINT"YOU HAVE A LOGIC LOOP OR TOO MANY DOUBLE-HEADED ARROWS"
4400 PRINT"SEQUENCE NUMBERS OF SUSPECT ARROWS ARE:"
4405 FOR A=1 TO NR:IF AP(A)=0 THEN PRINT USING"####";A:
4410 NEXT A
4415 INPUT"UNDERSTAND? Y OR NO:";R:IF R="Y" THEN 500 ELSE 4415
4420 PRINT"RESEQUENCING ARROWS"
4425 NN=NR
4430 MM=NN
4435 MM=INT(MM/2)
4440 IF MM=0 THEN 4520 ELSE 4445
4445 KK=NN-MM
4450 JJ=1
4455 II=JJ
4460 LL=II+MM
4465 IF AP(II) > AP(LL) THEN 4470 ELSE 4510
4470 AT=AN(II):LT=L(II):IT=IO(II):JT=JO(II):RT=R(II):KQ=AP(II)
4475 IH=I(II):JH=J(II)
4480 AN(II)=AN(LL):L(II)=L(LL):IO(II)=IO(LL):JO(II)=JO(LL):R(II)=R(LL)
4485 AP(II)=AP(LL):I(II)=I(LL):J(II)=J(LL)
4490 AN(LL)=AT:L(LL)=LT:IO(LL)=IT:JO(LL)=JT:R(LL)=RT:I(LL)=IH:J(LL)=JH
4495 AP(LL)=KQ
4500 II=II-MM
4505 IF II>=1 THEN 4460 ELSE 4510
4510 JJ=JJ+1
4515 IF JJ>KK THEN 4435 ELSE 4455
4520 PRINT"SUGGEST YOU SAVE THIS ON DISK. UNLESS YOU ADD OR REVISE ARROWS, YOU"
4525 INPUT"CAN DO THIS FASTER IN SUBSEQUENT RUNS. UNDERSTAND? Y OR N?";R
4530 IF R<>"Y"THEN 4520
4600 PRINT"MAKING NETWORK ANALYSIS":IF M=2 THEN 4615
4605 M=1:KA=0:FOR N=1 TO NT:ES(N,M)=0
4610 EF(N,M)=D(N):NEXT N:GOSUB 4615:GOTO 500
4615 FOR A=1 TO NR:II=IO(A):JJ=JO(A):IF M=1 THEN 4625
4620 IF U(JJ,2)>0 THEN 4675 ELSE IF U(JJ,4)>0 THEN 4675
4625 IF R(A)="SS" THEN 4635 ELSE IF R(A)="EE" THEN 4645
4630 IF R(A)="ES" THEN 4650 ELSE 4660
4635 MS=ES(II,M)+L(A)
4640 MF=MS+D(JJ):GOTO 4665
4645 MF=EF(II,M)+L(A):MS=0:GOTO 4665
4650 MS=EF(II,M)+L(A)
4655 MF=MS+D(JJ):GOTO 4665
4660 MF=ES(II,M)+L(A):MS=0
4665 IF MS>ES(JJ,M) THEN ES(JJ,M)=MS
4670 IF MF>EF(JJ,M) THEN EF(JJ,M)=MF
4675 NEXT A
4680 BF=0
4685 FOR N=1 TO NT:IF EF(N,M)>BF THEN BF=EF(N,M)
4690 NEXT N
4695 FOR N=1 TO NT:LF(N,M)=BF
4700 LS(N,M)=LF(N,M)-D(N):NEXT N
4705 FOR A=NR TO 1 STEP-1:II=IO(A):JJ=JO(A)
4710 IF R(A)="SS"THEN 4720 ELSE IF R(A)="EE" THEN 4725
4715 IF R(A)= "ES"THEN 4735 ELSE 4745
4720 MS= LS(JJ,M)-L(A):MF=9999:GOTO 4750
```

```
4725 MF=LF(JJ,M)-L(A)
4730 MS=MF-D(II):GOTO 4750
4735 MF=LS(JJ,M)-L(A)
4740 MS=MF-D(II):GOTO 4750
4745 MS=LF(JJ,M)-L(A):MF=9999
4750 IF MS<LS(II,M) THEN LS(II,M)=MS
4755 IF MF<LF(II,M) THEN LF(II,M)=MF
4760 NEXT A
4765 FOR N=1 TO NT:FT(N,M)=LF(N,M)-ES(N,M)-D(N):NEXT N
4770 FOR A=1 TO NR:AF(A,M)=0
4775 IF R(A)="ES"THEN AF(A,M)=LS(JO(A),M)-EF(IO(A),M)-L(A) ELSE 4785
4780 GOTO 4810
4785 IF R(A)="SS" THEN AF(A,M)=LS(JO(A),M)-ES(IO(A),M)-L(A) ELSE 4795
4790 GOTO 4810
4795 IF R(A)="EE" THEN AF(A,M)=LF(JO(A),M)-EF(IO(A),M)-L(A) ELSE 4805
4800 GOTO 4810
4805 IF R(A)="SE" THEN AF(A,M)=LF(JO(A),M)-ES(IO(A),M)-L(A)
4810 NEXT A
4815 RETURN
5000 REM ******** DISPLAY/PRINT SCHEDULE ROUTINE ***************************
5010 INPUT"S=SCREEN DISPLAY, H=HARDCOPY , B=BOTH.    WHICH?";R
5020 IF R="S"THEN PM=1 ELSE IF R="H"THEN PM=2 ELSE IF R="B"THEN PM=3 ELSE 5010
5030 IF Q(1)>0 THEN INPUT"C=CALENDAR DATE FORMAT, W=WORKDATE FORMAT.WHICH?";R
5040 CF=1:IF Q(1)>0 AND R="C" THEN CF=2
5050 UP=1:IF TU="Y"THEN INPUT"USE UPDATE DATA Y OR N?";R
5060 IF TU="Y" AND R="Y" THEN UP =2 ELSE UP=1
5070 IF UP=1 THEN 5090 ELSE INPUT"M,D,Y OF UPDATE?";M,D,Y
5080 GOSUB 9095:UD=IT
5090 INPUT"C=PRINT SCHEDULE CONTINUOUSLY, P=PRINT SCHEDULE BY PAGES. WHICH?";R
5100 IF R="C"THEN PL=300 ELSE PL=17
5110 INPUT"PRINT/DISPLAY TASKS WITH SEQUENCE NUMBERS I TO J?    I,J=?";IX,JX
5120 IF IX<1 THEN 5110 ELSE IF JX>MT THEN 5110 ELSE IF IX>JX THEN 5110
5130 IF PM=1 THEN 5155 ELSE INPUT"ENTER ONE LINE PROJECT TITLE";TP
5140 IF LEN(TP)=<80 THEN 5155
5150 TP=LEFT$(TP,80):PRINT TP:INPUT"OK";R:IF R="Y"THEN 5155 ELSE 5130
5155 SX="TSK# DUR DESCRIPTIO"
5160 S1=SX+"N               ES(ED) EF(ED) LS(ED) LF(ED)    TF"
5165 S2=SX+"N               ES(BD) EF(BD) LS(BD) LF(BD)    TF"
5180 S3=SX+"N               ES/RVS EF/RVS LS/RVS LF/RVS    TF"
5185 ST$="\              \":SD="":FOR K=1 TO 15:SD=SD+"    -":NEXT K
5190 SF=" -":FOR K=1 TO 9:SF=SF+"    -":NEXT K
5195 S0$="!" :LV=0:P=0
5200 FOR N=IX TO JX:IF A(N)=0 THEN 5215
5205 LV=LV+1:IF LV=1 THEN GOSUB 5230
5210 GOSUB 5290:IF LV=PL THEN LV=0
5215 NEXT N:IF PM<>1 THEN LPRINT CHR$(12)
5220 IF PM<>2 THEN INPUT "CARRIAGE RETURN TO RETURN TO MAIN MENU";R
5225 GOTO 5555
5230 P=P+1:IF PM=1 THEN 5265
5235 IF P>1 THEN LPRINT CHR$(12)
5240 LPRINT"Page No.";:LPRINT USING"###";P;
5245 IF UP=1 THEN LPRINT
5250 IF UP=1 THEN 5260
5255 LPRINT USING"\        \";"";:LPRINT"UDATED";:LPRINT USING"#######";Q(DS(UD))
5260 LPRINT:LPRINT TP:LPRINT
5265 IF PM<>2 AND CF=1 THEN PRINT S1 ELSE IF PM<>2 THEN PRINT S2
5266 IF PM=1 THEN RETURN
5270 IF CF=1 THEN LPRINT S1 ELSE IF CF=2 AND UP=1 THEN LPRINT S2
5275 IF UP=2 THEN LPRINT S3
5280 IF PM<>1 THEN LPRINT SD
```

```
AON                                                          Page  7 of 14
5285 RETURN
5290 VA=A(N):VD=D(N):VE=ES(N,1):VF=EF(N,1)
5295 VG=LS(N,1):VH=LF(N,1)
5300 VI=FT(N,1):IF CF=1 THEN 5340
5305 QA=Q(DS(VE+1)):QB=Q(DS(VF)):QC=Q(DS(VG+1)):QD=Q(DS(VH)):IF UP=1 THEN 5340
5310 GOSUB 5315:GOTO 5340
5315 VP=U(N,2)-U(N,1)+1:VK=ES(N,2):VL=EF(N,2):VM=LS(N,2):VN=LF(N,2)
5320 VQ=FT(N,2):VT=U(N,5)
5325 VS=100*(UD-VE)/VD:IF VS>100 THEN VS=100 ELSE IF VS<0 THEN VS=0
5330 QE=Q(DS(U(N,1))):QF=Q(DS(U(N,2))):QG=Q(DS(U(N,3))):QH=Q(DS(U(N,4)))
5335 QI=Q(DS(VK+1)):QJ=Q(DS(VL)):QK=Q(DS(VM+1)):QL=Q(DS(VN))  :RETURN
5340 IF PM<>2 AND CF=1 THEN GOSUB 5370
5345 IF PM<>2 AND CF=2 THEN GOSUB 5385
5350 IF PM<>1 AND CF=1 THEN GOSUB 5400
5355 IF PM<>1 AND CF=2 AND UP=1 THEN GOSUB 5420
5360 IF PM<>1 AND CF=2 AND UP=2 THEN GOSUB 5445
5365 RETURN
5370 PRINT USING"####";VA;
5375 PRINT USING"####";VD;:PRINT USING S0$;"";:PRINT USING ST$;T(N);
5380 PRINT USING"#######";VE,VF,VG,VH;:PRINT USING"####";VI:RETURN
5385 PRINT USING"####";VA;
5390 PRINT USING"####";VD;:PRINT USING S0$;"";:PRINT USING ST$;T(N);
5395 PRINT USING"#######";QA,QB,QC,QD;:PRINT USING"####";VI:RETURN
5400 LPRINT USING"####";VA;
5405 LPRINT USING"####";VD;:LPRINT USING S0$;"";:LPRINT USING ST$;T(N);
5410 LPRINT USING"#######";VE,VF,VG,VH;:LPRINT USING"####";VI
5415 LPRINT:LPRINT SD:RETURN
5420 LPRINT USING"####";VA;
5425 LPRINT USING"####";VD;:LPRINT USING S0$;"";:LPRINT USING ST$;T(N);
5430 LPRINT USING"#######";QA,QB,QC,QD;:LPRINT USING"####";VI
5435 LPRINT USING"\                    \";"";
5440 LPRINT USING"#######";VE,VF,VG,VH:LPRINT SD:RETURN
5445 LPRINT USING"####";VA;
5450 LPRINT USING"####";VD;:LPRINT USING S0$;"";:LPRINT USING ST$;T(N);
5455 LPRINT USING"#######";QA,QB,QC,QD;:LPRINT USING"####";VI
5460 IF U(N,2)=0 THEN Z=0 ELSE Z=1
5465 LPRINT USING"\   \";"";
5470 IF Z=1 THEN LPRINT USING"####";VP; ELSE LPRINT USING"\   \";"";
5475 SA="":SB="":IF U(N,1)>0 THEN SA="AS=" ELSE IF U(N,3)>0 THEN SA="PS="
5480 IF U(N,2)>0 THEN SB="AF=" ELSE IF U(N,4)>0 THEN SB="PF="
5485 QM=0:QN=0:IF U(N,1)>0 THEN QM=QE ELSE IF U(N,3)>0 THEN QM=QG
5490 IF U(N,2)>0 THEN QN=QF ELSE IF U(N,4)>0 THEN QN=QH
5495 LPRINT USING"!";"";:LPRINT USING"\ \";SA;
5500 IF SA="" THEN LPRINT USING"\     \";""; ELSE LPRINT USING"######";QM;
5505 LPRINT USING"!";"";:LPRINT USING"\ \";SB;
5510 IF SB="" THEN LPRINT USING"\     \";""; ELSE LPRINT USING"######";QN;
5515 IF U(N,2)=0 AND U(N,4)=0 THEN 5525
5520 LPRINT:GOTO 5535
5525 LPRINT USING"\   \";"";
5530 LPRINT USING"#######";QI,QJ,QK,QL;:LPRINT USING"####";VQ
5535 SA="SCH%=":SB="ACT%=":IF VS=0 AND VT=0 THEN LPRINT SD
5540 IF VS=0 AND VT=0 THEN RETURN
5545 LPRINT USING"\     \";"";:LPRINT SA;:LPRINT USING"####";VS;
5550 LPRINT USING"!";"";:LPRINT SB;:LPRINT USING"####";VT;:LPRINT SF:RETURN
5555 IF RM="S"THEN 500
5560 BEEP:INPUT"DO YOU WANT A LISTING OF LOGICAL RELATIONSHIPS? Y OR ?";R
5565 IF R="N" THEN 500 ELSE IF R="Y" THEN 5570 ELSE 5560
5570 SR="SEQ RLTSHP#  LAG  I-N#   J-N#  TYPE  AF":SR=SR+"     "+SR
5575 LPRINT"LOGICAL RELATIONSHIPS":LPRINT TP:LPRINT SR
5580 NL=NR/2:IF 2*NL<NR THEN NL=NL+1
5585 FOR N=1 TO NL:A=N:GOSUB 5595:A=NL+N:GOSUB 5595:LPRINT
```

```
5590 NEXT N:LPRINT CHR$(12):GOTO 500
5595 LPRINT USING"###";A;:LPRINT USING"########";AN(A);
5600 LPRINT USING"#####";L(A);:LPRINT USING"######";I(A),J(A);
5605 LPRINT USING"\";"";:LPRINT R(A);:LPRINT USING"#####";AF(A,1);
5610 LPRINT USING"\    \";"";:RETURN
6000 REM ********** PRINT GANTT CHART ROUTINE ******************************
6005 IW=75:S5="N":INPUT"USE SAME PARAMETERS AS USED FOR SCHEDULE? Y OR N";S5
6010 IF S5="Y"THEN 6020
6015 INPUT "GANTT CHART FOR SEQUENCE NBRS I TO J. ENTER I,J",IX,JX
6020 IF IX<1 THEN IX=1
6025 IF JX>NT THEN JX=NT
6030 BF =0:SP="":FOR K=1 TO 15:SP=SP+"    +":NEXT K
6035 FOR K=IX TO JX:IF LF(K,1)>BF THEN BF=LF(K,1)
6040 NEXT K :IF UP=1 THEN 6055
6045 FOR K=IX TO JX:IF LF(K,2)>BF THEN BF=LF(K,2)
6050 NEXT K
6055 IF S5="Y" THEN 6070
6060 INPUT"WORKDAY (W) OR CALENDARDAY (C) FORMAT?";R
6065 IF R="C" THEN CF=2 ELSE IF R="W" THEN CF=1 ELSE 6060
6070 IF CF=2 AND S5<>"Y" THEN 6075 ELSE 6090
6075 INPUT"UPDATE DATA DESIRED? Y OR N?";R:UP=1:IF R="Y"THEN UP=2
6080 IF UP=2 THEN INPUT"DATE OF UPDATE? M,D,Y?";M,D,Y:GOSUB 9095:UD=IT
6085 IF IT=0 THEN 6075
6090 QU=Q(DS(UD)):INPUT"1- ES SCHEDULE  , 2- LS SCHEDULE. WHICH?";KS
6095 IF CF=1 THEN 6100 ELSE 6305
6100 REM **** BAR CHART IN WORKDATE FORMAT **************
6105 SX=" ":SX=STRING$(75,SX)
6110 NH=(JX-IX+1)/PL:IF JX-IX+1>NH*PL THEN NH=NH+1
6115 IV=IX:JV=JX:GOSUB 6165:P1=INT((IR-1)/75)+1:P2=INT((JR-1)/75)+1
6120 FOR P=P1 TO P2:S1$="":S2$="":S3$=""
6125 ID=1+IW*(P-1):JD=ID+IW-1:DD=ID-1
6130 FOR II=ID TO JD:KH=INT(II/100):S1$=S1$+SD(KH):NEXT II
6135 FOR II=ID TO JD:KH=INT(II/100):KT=INT((II-100*KH)/10)
6140 S2$=S2$+SD(KT):NEXT II
6145 FOR II=ID TO JD:KH=INT(II/100):KT=INT((II-100*KH)/10)
6150 KU=INT(II-100*KH-10*KT):S3$=S3$+SD(KU):NEXT II
6155 FOR PP=1 TO NH:IV=IX+PL*(PP-1):JV=IV+PL-1:IF JV>JX THEN JV=JX
6160 GOSUB 6165:GOTO 6185
6165 IR=9999:JR=0:FOR N=IV TO JV:IF A(N)=0 THEN 6180
6170 IF ES(N,1)+1<IR THEN IR=ES(N,1)+1
6175 IF LF(N,1)>JR THEN JR=LF(N,1)
6180 NEXT N:RETURN
6185 IF JR<ID THEN 6275 ELSE IF IR>JD THEN 6275
6190 PRINT CHR$(12):GOSUB 6290:FOR N=IV TO JV
6195 IF A(N)=0 THEN 6270
6200 SB=SX:IF D(N)=0 THEN 6265
6205 EB=ES(N,1)+1-DD:EC=EF(N,1)-DD:LC=LF(N,1)-DD:LB=LS(N,1)-DD
6210 IF FT(N,1)=0 THEN 6215 ELSE 6220
6215 S$="C":IC=EB:JC=LC:GOSUB 6240:GOTO 6265
6220 S$=".":IC=EB:JC=LC:GOSUB 6240
6225 IF KS=1 THEN 6230 ELSE 6235
6230 S$="e":IC=EB:JC=EC:GOSUB 6240:GOTO 6265
6235 S$="1":IC=LB:JC=LC:GOSUB 6240:GOTO 6265
6240 IF IC>75 THEN RETURN
6245 IF JC<1 THEN RETURN
6250 IF IC<1 THEN IC=1
6255 IF JC>75 THEN JC=75
6260 L=JC-IC+1:S$=STRING$(L,S$):MID$(SB,IC,L)=S$:RETURN
6265 LPRINT SP:LPRINT SB:LPRINT
6270 NEXT N:LPRINT SP:LPRINT CHR$(12)
6275 NEXT PP
```

```
AON                                                      Page  9 of 14
6280 NEXT P
6285 GOTO 500
6290 LPRINT"PAGE NO.";:LPRINT USING"###";PP;:LPRINT USING"!";"";
6295 LPRINT "SHEET NO.";:LPRINT USING"###";P :LPRINT TP
6300 LPRINT S1$:LPRINT S2$:LPRINT S3$:RETURN
6305 REM **** BAR CHART IN CALENDARDATE FORMAT ********
6310 SX=" ":SX=STRING$(75,SX):GOTO 6335
6315 FOR N=IV TO JV:IF A(N)=0 THEN 6330
6320 IF ES(N,1)+1<IR THEN IR=ES(N,1)+1
6325 IF LF(N,1)>JR THEN JR=LF(N,1)
6330 NEXT N:RETURN
6335 IV=IX:JV=JX:GOSUB 6165:IF UP=2 THEN GOSUB 6315
6340 IR=DS(IR):JR=DS(JR):P1=INT((IR-1)/75)+1:P2=INT((JR-1)/75)+1
6345 NH=(JX-IX+1)/PL:IF JX-IX+1>NH*PL THEN NH=NH+1
6350 FOR P=P1 TO P2:DD=75*(P-1)
6355 REM ***** CONSTRUCTS HEADINGS ****************
6360 S1$=SX:S2$=SX:S3$=SX:SP=SX:S4$=SX:S5$=SX:S6$=SX
6365 OD=0:FOR N=0 TO DD:IF Q(N)>0 THEN OD=OD+1
6370 NEXT N:FOR K=1 TO 75:KK=K+DD:IF Q(KK)<0 THEN 6385 ELSE OD =OD+1
6375 VH=INT(OD/100):VT=INT((OD-100*VH)/10):VU=OD-100*VH-10*VT
6380 MID$(S4$,K,1)=SD(VH):MID$(S5$,K,1)=SD(VT):MID$(S6$,K,1)=SD(VU)
6385 NEXT K
6390 FOR K=1 TO 75:N=K+DD:QQ=ABS(Q(N)):YY(K)=INT(QQ/10000)
6395 IF Q(N)<0 THEN MID$(SP,K,1)="-"
6400 MM(K)=INT((QQ-10000*YY(K))/100):DD(K)=QQ-10000*YY(K)-100*MM(K)
6405 NEXT K:FOR K=1 TO 71 STEP 10:MID$(S1$,K,3)=SM(MM(K+2)):NEXT K
6410 FOR K=4 TO 74 STEP 10:N1=INT(YY(K-1)/10):N2=YY(K-1)-10*N1
6415 SA=SD(N1)+SD(N2):MID$(S1$,K,2)=SA:NEXT K
6420 FOR K=1 TO 75:MID$(S2$,K,1)=SD(INT(DD(K)/10))
6425 MID$(S3$,K,1)=SD(INT(DD(K) MOD 10)):NEXT K
6430 FOR PP=1 TO NH:IV=IX+PL*(PP-1):JV=IV+PL-1:IF JV>JX THEN JV=JX
6435 GOSUB 6165:IF UP=2 THEN GOSUB 6315
6440 IR=DS(IR):JR=DS(JR):IF JR=<DD THEN 6725 ELSE IF IR>DD+75 THEN 6725
6445 GOSUB 6735
6450 REM ****** CONSTRUCTS BARS BASED ON ORIGINAL DATA ********
6455 FOR N=IV TO JV:SB=SX:SC=SX:IF A(N)=0 THEN 6720
6460 IF D(N)=0 THEN 6715
6465 A1=DS(ES(N,1)+1):A2=DS(EF(N,1)):A3=DS(LS(N,1)+1):A4=DS(LF(N,1))
6470 IF A1>JR THEN 6535 ELSE IF A4<IR THEN 6535
6475 A1=A1-DD:A2=A2-DD:A3=A3-DD:A4=A4-DD
6480 IF FT(N,1)=0 THEN 6485 ELSE 6490
6485 S$="C":IC=A1:JC=A2:GOSUB 6510:GOSUB 6540:GOTO 6535
6490 S$=".":IC=A1:JC=A4:GOSUB 6510
6495 IF KS=1 THEN 6500 ELSE 6505
6500 S$="e":IC=A1:JC=A2:GOSUB 6510:GOSUB 6540:GOTO 6535
6505 S$="1":IC=A3:JC=A4:GOSUB 6510:GOSUB 6540:GOTO 6535
6510 IF IC>75 THEN RETURN
6515 IF JC<1 THEN RETURN
6520 IF IC<1 THEN IC=1
6525 IF JC>75 THEN JC=75
6530 L=JC-IC+1:S$=STRING$(L,S$):MID$(SB,IC,L)=S$:RETURN
6535 IF UP=1 THEN 6715 ELSE 6550
6540 FOR K=1 TO 75:IF MID$(SP,K,1)="-" THEN MID$(SB,K,1)=" "
6545 NEXT K:RETURN
6550 REM ******** CONSTRUCTS BARS FOR UPDATE DATA ************
6555 FV=FT(N,2):DD=75*(P-1):F1=DS(UD+1)-DD
6560 T2="A":T3="P":T4="R":IF FV=0 THEN 6570
6565 T2="A":T3="p":T4="r"
6570 D1=DS(ES(N,2)+1)-DD:D2=DS(EF(N,2))-DD
6575 D3=DS(LS(N,2)+1)-DD:D4=DS(LF(N,2))-DD
6580 U1=DS(U(N,1))-DD:U2=DS(U(N,2))-DD:U3=DS(U(N,3))-DD
```

```
6585 U4=DS(U(N,4))-DD:UU=DS(UD)-DD:IF U(N,1)>0 THEN JA=DS(U(N,1)-1)-DD
6590 IF U(N,3)>0 THEN JB=DS(U(N,3)-1)-DD
6595 IF FV=0 THEN 6605 ELSE IF U(N,2)>0 THEN 6605 ELSE IF U(N,4)>0 THEN 6605
6600 S$=".":IC=D1:JC=D4:GOSUB 6670
6605 IF U(N,2)>0 THEN 6615 ELSE IF U(N,1)>0 AND U(N,4)>0 THEN 6625
6610 IF U(N,3)>0 AND U(N,4)>0 THEN 6650 ELSE 6655
6615 REM ACTUALLY FINISHED
6620 S$=T2:IC=U1:JC=U2:GOSUB 6670:GOTO 6705
6625 REM ACTUAL START & PROJECTED FINISH
6630 IF UU<1 THEN 6640 ELSE IF UU>75 THEN 6640
6635 S$=T2:IC=U1:JC=UU:GOSUB 6670:S$=T3:IC=F1:JC=U4:GOSUB 6670:GOTO 6705
6640 S$=T3:IC=1:JC=U4:GOSUB 6670:GOTO 6705
6645 REM PROJECTED START AND FINISH
6650 S$=T3:IC=U3:JC=U4:GOSUB 6670:GOTO 6705
6655 S$=T4:IF KS=1 THEN 6660 ELSE 6665:REM NO ACTUAL OR PROJECTED DATES
6660 IC=D1:JC=D2:GOSUB 6670:GOTO 6705
6665 IC=D3:JC=D4:GOSUB 6670: GOTO 6705
6670 IF IC>75 THEN RETURN :REM SUBROUTINE FOR  BAR CONSTRUCTION
6675 IF JC<IC THEN RETURN
6680 IF JC<1 THEN RETURN
6685 IF IC<1 THEN IC=1
6690 IF JC>75 THEN JC=75
6695 L=JC-IC+1:IF L<1 THEN RETURN ELSE S$=STRING$(L,S$)
6700 MID$(SC,IC,L)=S$:RETURN
6705 FOR K=1 TO 75:IF MID$(SP,K,1)="-" THEN MID$(SC,K,1)=" "
6710 NEXT K
6715 LPRINT SP:LPRINT SB:LPRINT SC
6720 NEXT N:LPRINT SP:LPRINT S4$:LPRINT S5$:LPRINT S6$:LPRINT CHR$(12)
6725 NEXT PP
6730 NEXT P :GOTO 500
6735 LPRINT"PAGE NO.";:LPRINT USING"###";PP:LPRINT USING"!";"";
6740 LPRINT "SHEET NO.";:LPRINT USING"###";P;:IF UP=1 THEN LPRINT
6745 IF UP=1 THEN 6755 ELSE LPRINT USING"!";" ";
6750 LPRINT"UPDATED ";:LPRINT USING"########";Q(DS(UD))
6755 LPRINT TP
6760 LPRINT S1$:LPRINT S2$:LPRINT S3$:RETURN
7000 REM ************* RESEQUENCE TASKS ROUTINE ****************************
7010 PRINT"BEFORE RESEQUENCING, YOU SHOULD ELIMINATE UNUSED SEQUENCE"
7020 PRINT"NUMBERS. TO DO SO, EXIT FROM THIS ROUTINE AND SAVE DATA"
7030 INPUT"ON DISK AND THEN READ IT BACK. DO YOU WANT TO EXIT? Y OR N ?";R
7040 IF R="Y"THEN 500
7050 PRINT"PARAMETER 1 - TASK NUMBERS"
7080 PRINT"PARAMETER 4 - TASK DURATIONS"
7090 PRINT"PARAMETER 5 - EARLY START TIME"
7100 PRINT"PARAMETER 6 - EARLY FINISH TIME"
7110 PRINT"PARAMETER 7 - LATE START TIME"
7120 PRINT"PARAMETER 8 - LATE FINISH TIME"
7130 PRINT"PARAMETER 9 - TOTAL FLOAT"
7140 INPUT"HOW MANY PARAMETERS FOR SORTING";NP:IF NP>9 THEN 7140
7150 PRINT"ENTER PARAMETER CODES WITH MOST SIGNIFICANT PARAMETER FIRST"
7160 FOR L=1 TO NP
7170 INPUT"PARAMETER NBR?";PL(L):IF PL(L)>1 AND PL(L)<4 THEN 7170
7180 NEXT L
7190 MM=NT
7200 MM=INT(MM/2)
7210 IF MM=0 THEN 7610 ELSE 7220
7220 KK=NT-MM
7230 JJ=1
7240 II=JJ
7250 LL=II+MM
7260 FOR L=1 TO NP
```

```
7270 IF PL(L)=1 THEN 7320
7280 IF PL(L)=4 THEN 7350
7290 IF PL(L)=5 THEN 7360 ELSE IF PL(L)=6 THEN 7365
7300 IF PL(L)=7 THEN 7370 ELSE IF PL(L)=8 THEN 7375
7310 IF PL(L)=9 THEN 7380
7320 VI=A(II):VL=A(LL):GOTO 7410
7350 VI=D(II):VL=D(LL):GOTO 7410
7360 VI=ES(II,1):VL=ES(LL,1):GOTO 7410
7365 VI=EF(II,1):VL=EF(LL,1):GOTO 7410
7370 VI=LS(II,1):VL=LS(LL,1):GOTO 7410
7375 VI=LF(II,1):VL=LF(LL,1):GOTO 7410
7380 VI=FT(II,1):VL=FT(LL,1):GOTO 7410
7410 IF VI>VL THEN 7440 ELSE IF VI=VL THEN 7420 ELSE 7590
7420 NEXT L
7430 GOTO 7590
7440 AT= A(II):DT=D(II):TT=T(II):FQ=FT(II,1)
7445 E1=ES(II,1):E2=EF(II,1):L1=LS(II,1):L2=LF(II,1)
7450 ES(II,1)=ES(LL,1):EF(II,1)=EF(LL,1):LS(II,1)=LS(LL,1):LF(II,1)=LF(LL,1)
7455 A(II)=A(LL):D(II)=D(LL):T(II)=T(LL):FT(II,1)=FT(LL,1)
7460 ES(LL,1)=E1:EF(LL,1)=E2:LS(LL,1)=L1:LF(LL,1)=L2 :FT(LL,1)=FQ
7465 A(LL)=AT:D(LL)=DT:T(LL)=TT
7470 IF TU<>"Y" THEN 7570
7475 U1=U(II,1):U2=U(II,2):U3=U(II,3):U4=U(II,4):U5=U(II,5):U6=U(II,6)
7480 U(II,1)=U(LL,1):U(II,2)=U(LL,2):U(II,3)=U(LL,3):U(II,4)=U(LL,4)
7485 U(II,5)=U(LL,5):U(II,6)=U(LL,6)
7490 U(LL,1)=U1:U(LL,2)=U2:U(LL,3)=U3:U(LL,4)=U4:U(LL,5)=U5:U(LL,6)=U6
7495 E1=ES(II,2):E2=EF(II,2):L1=LS(II,2):L2=LF(II,2):FQ=FT(II,2)
7500 ES(II,2)=ES(LL,2):EF(II,2)=EF(LL,2):LS(II,2)=LS(LL,2):LF(II,2)=LF(LL,2)
7505 FT(II,2)=FT(LL,2)
7510 ES(LL,2)=E1:EF(LL,2)=E2:LS(LL,2)=L1:LF(LL,2)=L2 :FT(LL,2)=FQ
7570 II=II-MM
7580 IF II=>1 THEN 7250 ELSE 7590
7590 JJ=JJ+1
7600 IF JJ>KK THEN 7200 ELSE 7240
7610 GOTO 500
8000 REM ******* READ WORKDAY REGIME FROM DISK ROUTINE *********************
8010 GOTO 8080
8020 REM***** MAKE WORKDAY/CALENDAR DAY CONVERSION ************
8030 PRINT"PLEASE WAIT ABOUT A MINUTE"
8040 N=0:FOR K=1 TO 1097:IF Q(K)>0 THEN N=N+1
8050 IF Q(K)>0 THEN DS(N)=K
8060 NEXT K:NI=N
8070 GOTO 500
8080 REM **** READ CALENDAR DATA FROM DISK ROUTINE *****************
8090 INPUT"ENTER NAME OF CALENDAR FILE TO BE READ FROM DISK";RF$
8100 INPUT"ENTER DRIVE FROM WHICH FILE IS TO BE READ (A,B,C,ETC)";RD$
8110 SS$=RD$+":"+RF$:SZ="Y"
8120 OPEN SS$ AS #1 LEN=16
8130 FOR NI=1 TO 1093 STEP 4
8140 FIELD #1,4 AS S1,4 AS S2,4 AS S3,4 AS S4
8150 GET #1
8160 Q(NI)=CVS(S1):Q(NI+1)=CVS(S2):Q(NI+2)=CVS(S3):Q(NI+3)=CVS(S4)
8170 IF EOF(1) THEN 8190
8180 NEXT NI
8190 CLOSE #1:GOTO 8020
9000 REM ************* UPDATE SCHEDULE ROUTINE  **********************
9005 IF Q(DS(1))<>0 THEN 9015
9010 BEEP:PRINT"A WORK DAY/CALENDARDAY FILE MUST BE LOADED TO RUN THIS ROUTINE"
9015 IF A(1)>0 THEN 9030
9020 BEEP:PRINT"A PROJECT DATA FILE NUST BE LOADED TO RUN THIS ROUTINE"
9025 INPUT"UNDERSTAND? Y OR N";R:IF R="Y"THEN 500 ELSE 9010
```

```
AON                                                        Page 12 of 14
9030 TD="TASK-# DUR DESCRIPTION                    AS      A"
9035 TD=TD+"F        PS      PF STAT":SU$="":RU$=""
9040 PRINT"UPDATE FILE READ:";:PRINT USING"\          \";RU$;
9045 PRINT"UPDATE FILE SAVED:";:PRINT SU$
9050 PRINT"UPDATED ON";:PRINT USING "#######";Q(DS(UD))
9055 PRINT"YOU MAY: 1 - READ AN UPDATE FILE FROM DISK"
9060 PRINT"         2 - SAVE THIS UPDATE FILE ON DISK"
9065 PRINT"         3 - REVIEW AND REVISE THE FILE "
9070 PRINT"         4 - MAKE A NETWORK ANALYSIS BASED ON UPDATE DATA."
9075 PRINT"         5 - PRINT UPDATE DATA"
9080 PRINT"         0 - EXIT TO MAIN MENU"
9085 INPUT"WHICH?";A:ON A GOTO 9680,9620,9160,9755,9825
9090 IF A =0 THEN 500 ELSE 9040
9095 QV=10000*Y+100*M+D:IV=1:JV=NI:IF QV=0 THEN IT=0
9100 IF QV=0 THEN RETURN
9105 IT=INT((IV+JV)/2):Q2=Q(DS(IT)):Q1=Q(DS(IV)):Q3=Q(DS(JV))
9110 IF QV=Q1 THEN 9130 ELSE IF QV=Q2 THEN 9145 ELSE IF QV=Q3 THEN 9135
9115 IF JV-IV<3 THEN 9150 ELSE IT=(IV+JV)/2
9120 IF QV>Q2 THEN IV=IT ELSE JV =IT
9125 GOTO 9105
9130 IT=IV:GOTO 9145
9135 IT=JV:GOTO 9145
9140 GOTO 9105
9145 PRINT USING"######";QV;:PRINT"= WORKDAY";:PRINT IT:RETURN
9150 PRINT USING"###";M,D,Y;:PRINT USING"!";"";:PRINT"IS NOT A WORKDAY"
9155 BEEP:INPUT"UNDERSTAND ?Y OR N?";RR:IT=0:RETURN
9160 REM **** REVIEW AND REVISE UPDATE DATA SUBROUTINE ***************
9165 INPUT"ENTER DATE OF UPDATE. M,D,Y";M,D,Y:GOSUB 9095:IF IT>0 THEN 9175
9170 BEEP:PRINT"ALL DATES ENTERED MUST BE WORKDATES":GOTO 9000
9175 UD=IT
9180 INPUT"REVIEW/REVISE TASK STATUS STARTING WITH SEQUENCE NUMBER?";IN
9185 IF IN<1 THEN IN=1 ELSE IF IN >MT-14 THEN IN=MT-14
9190 REM *** DISPLAY TASK STATUS DATA SUBROUTINE *****
9195 CLS:PRINT TD
9200 N1=IN:N2=N1+14:GOSUB 9210:GOTO 9245
9205 PRINT"UPDATE:";:PRINT Q(DS(UD)):PRINT TD:GOSUB 9210:GOTO 9305
9210 FOR K=N1 TO N2:IF A(K)=0 THEN 9240 ELSE PRINT USING"###";K;
9215 PRINT USING"######";A(K);
9220 PRINT USING"####";D(K);
9225 PRINT USING"!";"";:PRINT USING"\                        \";T(K);
9230 FOR DQ=1 TO 4:QD(DQ)=Q(DS(U(K,DQ))):NEXT DQ
9235 PRINT USING"#######";QD(1),QD(2),QD(3),QD(4);:PRINT USING"####";U(K,5)
9240 NEXT K :RETURN
9245 INPUT"ENTER R-REVISE, N-NEXT PAGE, X-EXIT?";R
9250 IF R="R"THEN 9260 ELSE IF R="N"THEN 9675
9255 IF R="X"THEN 9040 ELSE 9245
9260 REM **** REVISE TASK UPDATE DATA SUBROUTINE *****
9265 INPUT"CHANGE UPDATE DATA FOR SEQUENCE NBR?";N
9270 N1=N:N2=N:PRINT TD:GOSUB 9205
9300 NEXT K
9305 PRINT"CHANGE: 1-ACTUAL START       2-ACTUAL FINISH      3-PROJECTED START"
9310 PRINT"        4-PROJECTED FINISH  5-PERCENT COMPLETE   6-DELETE ENTRY"
9315 INPUT"        0-NO MORE CHANGES                        WHICH?";A
9320 ON A GOTO 9330,9375,9405,9465,9545,9575
9325 GOTO 9195
9330 INPUT"ACTUAL START DATE? M,D,Y ?";M,D,Y:GOSUB 9095:IF IT>0 THEN 9340
```

```
9335 BEEP:PRINT"DATE IS NOT A WORKDATE. ENTRY REJECTED":GOTO 9205
9360 IF IT=<UD THEN 9370 ELSE BEEP
9365 INPUT"DATE IS AFTER UPDATE. CANCEL ENTRY? Y OR N?";R:IF R="Y"THEN 9205
9370 U(N,1)=IT:U(N,3)=0:PRINT TD:GOSUB 9210:GOTO 9545
9375 IF U(N,1)>0 THEN 9385 ELSE BEEP
9380 PRINT"YOU MUST ENTER ACTUAL START BEFORE ACTUAL FINISH":GOTO 9570
9385 INPUT"ACTUAL FINISH DATE. M,D,Y?";M,D,Y:GOSUB 9095:IF IT=0 THEN 9335
9390 IF IT=<UD THEN 9400 ELSE BEEP
9395 INPUT"DATE IS AFTER UPDATE. CANCEL ENTRY? Y OR N?";R:IF R="Y"THEN 9205
9400 U(N,2)=IT:U(N,5)=100:U(N,4)=0:GOTO 9205
9405 IF U(N,1)=0 THEN 9415 ELSE BEEP
9410 PRINT"YOU HAVE ALREADY ENTERED AN ACTUAL START DATE.":GOTO 9205
9415 INPUT"ENTER PROJECTED START DATE. M,D,Y?";M,D,Y:GOSUB 9095
9420 IF IT=0 THEN 9335
9425 IF IT>UD THEN 9445 ELSE BEEP
9430 PRINT USING"#######";Q(DS(IT))::PRINT USING"!";"";
9435 INPUT"IS BEFORE UPDATE DATE. DO YOU WANT TO CANCEL ENTRY? Y OR N";R
9440 IF R="Y" THEN 9205
9460 U(N,3)=IT:PRINT TD:GOSUB 9210:GOTO 9465
9465 IF U(N,1)>0 THEN 9475 ELSE IF U(N,3)>0 THEN 9495 ELSE BEEP
9470 PRINT"ENTER ACTUAL OR PROJECTED START BEFORE PROJECTED FINISH":GOTO 9205
9475 PRINT"BASED ON PROGRESS SINCE START,PROJECTED FINISH IS:";
9480 PRINT USING"########";Q(DS(INT(U(N,1)-1+100*(UD-U(N,1)+1)/U(N,5))))
9485 PRINT"BASED ON ESTIMATED DURATION, PROJECTED FINISH IS:";
9490 PRINT USING"########";Q(DS(U(N,1)-1+D(N))):GOTO 9505
9495 PRINT"BASED ON ESTIMATED DURATION, PROJECTED FINISH IS:";
9500 PRINT USING"########";Q(DS(U(N,3)-1+D(N)))
9505 INPUT"ENTER PROJECTED FINISH DATE. M,D,Y?";M,D,Y:GOSUB 9095
9510 IF IT=0 THEN 9335
9515 IF U(N,1)>0 THEN 9530
9520 IF IT>=U(N,1) THEN 9540 ELSE BEEP
9525 PRINT"PROJECTED FINISH MUST BE = OR > ACTUAL START":GOTO 9205
9530 IF IT=>U(N,3) THEN 9540 ELSE BEEP
9535 PRINT"PROJECTED FINISH MUST BE= OR > PROJECTED START":GOTO 9205
9540 U(N,4)=IT:GOTO 9205
9545 IF U(N,1)>0 THEN 9555 ELSE BEEP
9550 PRINT"ENTER ACTUAL START DATE BEFORE ENTERING PERCENT COMPLETE":GOTO 9205
9555 INPUT"ENTER PERCENT COMPLETION AS OF UPDATE DATE";A:IF A=100 THEN 9375
9560 IF A>0 AND A<100 THEN 9570 ELSE BEEP
9565 PRINT"PERCENT COMPLETION MUST BE BETWEEN 0 AND 100":GOTO 9555
9570 U(N,5)=A:PRINT TD:GOSUB 9210:GOTO 9465
9575 INPUT"DELETE ITEM NBR ?";A:IF A<1 THEN 9195 ELSE IF A>5 THEN 9195
9580 ON A GOTO 9585,9595,9600,9610,9615
9585 U(N,1)=0:U(N,5)=0:U(N,2)=0:IF U(N,3)=0 THEN U(N,4)=0
9590 PRINT TD:GOSUB 9210:GOTO 9575
9595 U(N,2)=0:PRINT TD:GOSUB 9210:GOTO 9545
9600 U(N,3)=0:IF U(N,1)=0 THEN U(N,4)=0
9605 PRINT TD:GOSUB 9210:GOTO 9575
9610 U(N,4)=0:PRINT TD:GOSUB 9210:GOTO 9575
9615 U(N,1)=0:U(N,5)=0:U(N,1)=0:PRINT TD:GOSUB 9210:GOTO 9575
9620 REM **** SAVE DATA ON DISK IN RANDOM FORMAT **************
9625 INPUT"ENTER NAME OF UPDATE FILE TO BE SAVED (8 CHARACTERS MAX)";SF$
9630 INPUT"SAVE ON DRIVE (A,B,C,ETC)?";SD$
9635 SS$=SD$+":"+SF$:SU$=SF$
```

```
9640 OPEN SS$ AS #1 LEN=12
9645 FOR N=1 TO NT:IF U(N,2)+U(N,4)=0 THEN 9670 ELSE IF A(N)=0 THEN 9670
9650 FIELD #1,2 AS S1,2 AS S2,2 AS S3,2 AS S4,2 AS S5, 2 AS S6
9655 LSET S1=MKI$(A(N)):LSET S2=MKI$(U(N,1)):LSET S3=MKI$(U(N,2))
9660 LSET S4=MKI$(U(N,3)):LSET S5=MKI$(U(N,4)):LSET S6=MKI$(U(N,5))
9665 PUT #1
9670 NEXT N
9675 CLOSE #1:GOTO 9040
9680 REM **** READ DATA FROM DISK ROUTINE *****************
9685 INPUT"ENTER NAME OF FILE TO BE READ FROM DISK";RF$
9690 INPUT"ENTER DRIVE FROM WHICH FILE IS TO BE READ (A,B,C,ETC)";RD$
9695 SS$=RD$+":"+RF$:RU$=RF$
9700 OPEN SS$ AS #1 LEN=12
9705 FIELD #1,2 AS S1,2 AS S2,2 AS S3,2 AS S4,2 AS S5,2 AS S6
9710 GET #1:AV=CVI(S1):PRINT"AV=";:PRINT AV;:IF AV=0 THEN 9735
9715 U1=CVI(S2):U2=CVI(S3):U3=CVI(S4):U4=CVI(S5)
9720 U5=CVI(S6):GOSUB 9740:PRINT NN:A(NN)=AV:N=NN:U(N,1)=U1:U(N,2)=U2
9725 U(N,3)=U3:U(N,4)=U4:U(N,5)=U5
9730 IF EOF(1) THEN 9735 ELSE 9705
9735 CLOSE #1:GOTO 9040
9740 REM *** SUBROUTINE FOR FINDING TASKS WITH SPECIFIED TASK NUMBER ***
9745 NN=0
9750 NN=NN+1:IF A(NN)=AV THEN RETURN ELSE 9750
9755 REM ****** NETWORK ANAYLSIS BASED ON UPDATE DATA ROUTINE **********
9760 IF UD>0 THEN 9770
9765 INPUT"ENTER UPDATE DATE. M,D,Y?";M,D,Y:GOSUB 9095:IF IT=0 THEN 9040
9770 TU="Y":FOR N=1 TO MT:ES(N,2)=0:EF(N,2)=0:LS(N,2)=0:LF(N,2)=0:NEXT N
9775 FOR N=1 TO NT:IF U(N,2)>0 THEN 9785 ELSE IF U(N,4)>0 THEN 9790
9780 U(N,6)=D(N):EF(N,2)=D(N):GOTO 9800
9785 ES(N,2)=U(N,1)-1:EF(N,2)=U(N,2):U(N,6)=0:GOTO 9800
9790 EF(N,2)=U(N,4):U(N,6)=0
9795 IF U(N,1)>0 THEN ES(N,2)=U(N,1)-1 ELSE ES(N,2)=U(N,3)-1
9800 NEXT N:M=2:GOSUB 9810:GOSUB 4600:GOSUB 9810:GOTO 9040
9805 GOSUB 9810:GOSUB 4600:GOSUB 9810:GOTO 9040
9810 FOR N=1 TO NT:IF A(N)=0 THEN 9820
9815 IT=D(N):D(N)=U(N,6):U(N,6)=IT
9820 NEXT N:RETURN
9825 REM **** PRINT UPDATA DATA SUBROUTINE ****
9830 INPUT"UPDATE DATE? M,D,Y";M,D,Y:QU=10000*Y+100*M+D:LPRINT TP
9835 LPRINT TAB(40) "LAST UPDATE/NEXT UPDATE";:LPRINT USING"########";QU;
9840 LPRINT"/":LPRINT:LPRINT TD
9845 FOR N=1 TO MT
9850 IF A(N)=0 THEN 9880 ELSE LPRINT USING"###";N;
9855 LPRINT USING"######"; A(N);
9860 LPRINT USING"!";"":LPRINT USING"\                    \";T(N);
9865 FOR DQ=1 TO 4:QD(DQ)=Q(DS(U(N,DQ))):NEXT DQ
9870 LPRINT USING"#######";QD(1),QD(2),QD(3),QD(4);:LPRINT USING"####";U(N,5)
9875 LPRINT
9880 NEXT N:LPRINT CHR$(12):GOTO 9040
10000 INPUT"ARE YOU SURE? Y OR N?";R:IF R<>"Y" THEN 500
```

```
10 REM PROGRAM REGIME
20 SCREEN 0:CLS:KEY OFF:IW=75
40 DEFINT A-P:DEFSTR R-T:DEFINT U-Z:DEFSNG Q
90 DIM DS(1100),DM(12),Q(1100),DD(75),MM(75),YY(75),SM(12),CW(75)
100 DIM U(MT,6):PRINT FRE(0)
110 SD(0)="0":SD(1)="1":SD(2)="2":SD(3)="3":SD(4)="4":SD(5)="5"
120 SD(6)="6":SD(7)="7":SD(8)="8":SD(9)="9"
130 BEEP:PRINT"SET TERMINAL IN UPPERCASE MODE"
8000 REM ****** DEFINITION OF WORKDAY REGIME ROUTINE **************************
8010 DM(1)=31:DM(2)=28:DM(3)=31:DM(4)=30:DM(5)=31:DM(6)=30:DW=3
8020 DM(7)=31:DM(8)=31:DM(9)=30:DM(10)=31:DM(11)=30:DM(12)=31
8030 SM(1)="JAN":SM(2)="FEB":SM(3)="MAR":SM(4)="APR":SM(5)="MAY":SM(6)="JUN"
8040 SM(7)="JUL":SM(8)="AUG":SM(9)="SEP":SM(10)="OCT":SM(11)="NOV":SM(12)="DEC"
8050 DM(2)=25:DW=2
8060 SW(1)="SUN":SW(2)="MON":SW(3)="TUE":SW(4)="WED":SW(5)="THU":SW(6)="FRI"
8070 SW(7)="SAT":SZ="N"
8080 PRINT"YOU MAY: 1 - RECALL SAVED CALENDAR DATA FROM DISK"
8090 PRINT"          2 - DEFINE A WORKDAY CALENDAR"
8100 S$="!"
8110 INPUT"WHICH?";K:IF K=2 THEN 8120 ELSE IF K=1 THEN 8870 ELSE 8070
8120 PRINT"YOU MAY DESIGNATE ANY NUMBER OF DAYS OF THE WEEK AS NON-WORK"
8130 PRINT"DAYS AND ANY CALENDAR DATE AS NON-WORK DATES. USE THE"
8140 PRINT"M,D,Y FORMAT WHEN DESIGNATING CALENDAR DATES AS NON-WORK DATES."
8150 REM **** FIND DAY OF WEEK OF PROJECT START ********
8160 DW=2:INPUT"PROJECT START DATE (M,D,Y EXAMPLE 2,3,86)?";MI,DI,YI
8170 FOR Y=85 TO YI:IF Y MOD 4 =0 THEN DM(2)=29 ELSE DM(2)=28
8180 IF Y=YI THEN MF=MI ELSE MF=12
8190 FOR M=1 TO MF
8200 IF Y=YI AND M=MI THEN DF=DI ELSE DF=DM(M)
8210 FOR D-1 TO DF
8220 DW=DW+1:IF DW=8 THEN DW=1
8230 NEXT D
8240 NEXT M
8250 NEXT Y
8260 PRINT USING"###";MI,DI,YI;:PRINT USING S$;"";:PRINT"IS A";
8270 PRINT USING S$;"";:PRINT SW(DW) :FD=DW:INPUT"OK- Y OR N?";R
8280 IF R<>"Y"THEN 8160
8290 PRINT"PLEASE WAIT ABOUT A MINUTE FOR CALENDAR CONSTRUCTION"
8300 REM ****** CONSTRUCT CALENDAR **********
8310 DW=FD-1:N=0:IF DW=0 THEN DW=7
8320 FOR Y=YI TO YI+3:IF Y MOD 4 = 0 THEN DM(2)=29 ELSE DM(2)=28
8330 IF Y=YI THEN MB=MI ELSE MB=1
8340 IF Y=YI+3 THEN MF=MI ELSE MF=12
8350 FOR M=MB TO MF
8360 IF Y=YI AND M=MI THEN DB=DI ELSE DB=1
8370 FOR D=DB TO DM(M):N=N+1:IF N>1097 THEN 8400
8380 DW=DW+1:IF DW=8 THEN DW=1
8390 Q(N)=Y*10000+M*100+D
8400 NEXT D
8410 NEXT M
8420 NEXT Y
8430 REM ****** ENTER NONWORK DAYS OF WEEK  ******
8440 SZ="N":FOR K=1 TO 7:BEEP
8450 PRINT SW(K);:PRINT USING"!";"";:INPUT"IS THIS A WORKDAY? Y OR N?";R
```

```
8460 IF R<>"N" THEN 8500
8470 IK=K-FD+1:IF IK<1 THEN IK=IK+7
8480 IF IK<0 THEN IK=IK+7
8490 FOR N=IK TO 1097 STEP 7:Q(N)=-Q(N):NEXT N
8500 NEXT K
8510 REM******** ENTER NONWORK CALENDAR DATES **********
8520 BEEP:INPUT"ENTER NON-WORK CALENDAR DATES (M,D,Y)?";MX,DX,YX
8530 IF MX+DX+YX = 0 THEN 8610
8540 N=0:KV=0:QT=YX*10000+MX*100+DX
8550 N=N+1
8560 IF QT=ABS(Q(N))THEN KV=1
8570 IF KV=0 AND N<1097 THEN 8550
8580 IF KV=1 THEN Q(N)=-ABS(Q(N))
8590 IF KV=1 THEN 8520
8600 BEEP:BEEP:PRINT"NO SUCH DATE IN THIS CALENDAR":GOTO 8520
8610 REM***** MAKE WORKDAY/CALENDAR DAY CONVERSION ************
8620 PRINT"PLEASE WAIT ABOUT A MINUTE"
8630 N=0:FOR K=1 TO 1097:IF Q(K)>0 THEN N=N+1
8640 IF Q(K)>0 THEN DS(N)=K
8650 NEXT K:NI=N
8660 REM ***** PRINT WORKDAY/CALENDARDAY CONVERSIONS *********
8670 BEEP:PRINT"THERE ARE";:PRINT USING"#####";NI;:PRINT USING S$;"";
8680 INPUT"WORKDATES IN THIS CALENDAR. LINE PRINT X WD/CD VALUES? X=";KP
8690 IF KP=0 THEN 8730
8700 FOR N=1 TO KP:LPRINT USING"#####";N;:LPRINT USING S$;"=";
8710 LPRINT USING"######";Q(DS(N));:IF N MOD 6=0 THEN LPRINT
8720 NEXT N:LPRINT CHR$(12)
8730 REM **** SAVE CALENDAR DATA ON DISK IN RANDOM FORMAT **************
8740 IF SZ="Y" THEN 500
8750 INPUT"Y TO SAVE ON DISK, N TO RETURN TO MAIN MENU?";R
8760 IF R="Y" THEN 8770 ELSE IF R="N" THEN 500 ELSE 8750
8770 INPUT"ENTER NAME OF CALENDAR FILE TO BE SAVED (8 CHARACTERS MAX)";SF$
8780 INPUT"SAVE ON DRIVE (A,B,C,ETC)?";SD$
8790 SS$=SD$+":"+SF$
8800 OPEN SS$ AS #1 LEN=16
8810 FOR N=1 TO 1096 STEP 4
8820 FIELD #1,4 AS S1,4 AS S2,4 AS S3,4 AS S4
8830 LSET S1=MKS$(Q(N)):LSET S2=MKS$(Q(N+1)):LSET S3=MKS$(Q(N+2))
8840 LSET S4=MKS$(Q(N+3)):PUT #1
8850 NEXT N
8860 CLOSE #1:GOTO 500
8870 REM **** READ CALENDAR DATA FROM DISK ROUTINE *****************
8880 INPUT"ENTER NAME OF CALENDAR FILE TO BE READ FROM DISK";RF$
8890 INPUT"ENTER DRIVE FROM WHICH FILE IS TO BE READ (A,B,C,ETC)";RD$
8900 SS$=RD$+":"+RF$:SZ="Y"
8910 OPEN SS$ AS #1 LEN=16
8920 FOR NI=1 TO 1093 STEP 4
8930 FIELD #1,4 AS S1,4 AS S2,4 AS S3,4 AS S4
8940 GET #1
8950 Q(NI)=CVS(S1):Q(NI+1)=CVS(S2):Q(NI+2)=CVS(S3):Q(NI+3)=CVS(S4)
8960 IF EOF(1) THEN 8980
8970 NEXT NI
8980 CLOSE #1:GOTO 8610
```

```
10 REM PROGRAM CPM-MIN: E.M. Willis. University of North Carolina at Charlotte
20 SCREEN 0:CLS:KEY OFF:IW=75
30 REM PROGRAM IS FORMATTED FOR 80 COLUMN TERMINAL SCREEN AND PRINTER
40 DEFINT A-P:DEFSTR R-T:DEFINT U-Z:DEFSNG Q
50 MT=999:MN=MT+1:REM MT=MAX NBR OF TASKS. MN=MAX NBR OF NODES
60 DIM I(MT),J(MT),D(MT),T(MT),ES(MT),EF(MT),LS(MT),LF(MT),FT(MT),FF(MT)
70 DIM A(MT),E(MN),L(MN)
130 BEEP:PRINT"SET TERMINAL IN UPPERCASE MODE"
500 REM ******** MAIN MENU ROUTINE ****************************************
510 CLS
520 PRINT"LAST ROUTINE EXECUTED WAS:";:PRINT USING"##";LX
530 PRINT"CURRENT TIME IS      :";:PRINT USING"!";"";:PRINT TIME$
540 PRINT"LAST ROUTINE STARTED:";:PRINT USING"!";"";:PRINT TZ$
550 PRINT"ELAPSED TIME (SECONDS)   :";:PRINT USING"########";TIMER-QX
560 BEEP:PRINT"******** MAIN MENU ********"
570 NT=0:FOR N=1 TO MT:IF A(N)>0 THEN NT=NT+1
580 NEXT N:PRINT"NBR TASKS =";:PRINT NT;:PRINT USING"!";""
590 PRINT"FREE RAM SPACE=";:PRINT FRE(0)
600 PRINT"1 - REVIEW/REVISE/DELETE TASK DEFINITIONS"
610 PRINT"2 - SAVE DATA IN RANDOM FORMAT ON DISK."
620 PRINT"3 - READ DATA FROM DISK"
630 PRINT"4 - ANALYZE NETWORK"
640 PRINT"5 - PRINT SCHEDULE"
690 PRINT"10 - END EXECUTION"
700 INPUT "SELECT OPTION?";O
710 TZ$=TIME$:LX=0:QX=TIMER
720 ON O GOTO 1000,2000,3000,4000,5000,500,500,500,500,10000
730 GOTO 500
1000 REM **** REVIEW/REVISE/DELETE TASK DATA ROUTINE  ***********************
1010 CLS
1020 TD="SEQ TASK# I-# J-# DUR DESCRIPTION              ES EF LS L"
1030 TD=TD+"F  TF  FF"
1040 INPUT"REVIEW/REVISE TASKS STARTING WITH SEQUENCE NUMBER?";IN
1050 IF IN<1 THEN 1040 ELSE IF IN >MT-14 THEN IN=MT-14
1060 REM *** DISPLAY TASK DATA SUBROUTINE *****
1070 CLS:PRINT TD
1080 FOR N=IN TO IN+14
1090 GOSUB 1100:GOTO 1170
1100 PRINT USING"###";N;:PRINT USING"######";A(N);
1110 PRINT USING"####";I(N),J(N),D(N);
1120 IF T(N)="" THEN T(N)="blank"
1130 PRINT USING"!";"";:PRINT USING"\                    \";T(N);
1140 IF RD="R"THEN PRINT
1150 IF RD="R"THEN RETURN
1160 PRINT USING"####";ES(N),EF(N),LS(N),LF(N),FT(N),FF(N):RETURN
1170 NEXT N
1180   INPUT"ENTER R-REVISE D-DELETE N-NEXT PAGE X-EXIT?";R
1190 IF R="R" THEN RD="R"ELSE RD=""
1200 IF R="R"THEN 1230 ELSE IF R="D"THEN 1340 ELSE IF R="N"THEN 1390
1210 IF R="X"THEN 1410 ELSE 1180
1220 REM **** REVISE TASK DATA SUBROUTINE *****
1230 INPUT"REVISE TASK DATA FOR SEQUENCE NUMBER?(0 TO EXIT)";NR:IF NR=0 THEN 1180
1240 PRINT TD:N=NR:GOSUB 1100
1250 PRINT"ENTER VALUES FOR TASK#, I-#, J-#, AND DURATION, SEPARATED BY"
1260 INPUT"COMMAS (ENTER 4 ZEROES IF DATA IS OKAY)";A1,A2,A3,A4
1270 IF A3>A2 THEN 1290
```

```
1280 BEEP:BEEP:PRINT"J-NODE NUMBER MUST BE > I-NODE NUMBER":GOTO 1180
1290 A(N)=A1:I(N)=A2:J(N)=A3:D(N)=A4
1292 IF A1<32578 AND A2<1000 AND A3<1000 AND A4<1000 THEN 1300
1294 BEEP:PRINT"TASKS NUMBERS MUST BE LESS THAN 32,568"
1296 PRINT"NODE NUMBERS AND DURATIONS MUST BE LESS THAN 1000"
1300 INPUT"ENTER TASK DESCRIPTION (CARRIAGE RETURN IF DATA IS OKAY)";TT
1310 IF TT="" THEN 1070 ELSE T(N)=LEFT$(TT,24)
1320 GOTO 1070
1330 REM **** DELETE TASK DATA SUBROUTINE ********
1340 INPUT"ENTER SEQUENCE NUMBER OF TASK TO BE DELETED (0 TO EXIT)";ND
1350 IF ND=0 THEN 1180
1360 N=ND:A(N)=0:I(N)=0:J(N)=0:T(N)="blank":D(N)=0:ES(N)=0:EF(N)=0
1370 LS(N)=0:LF(N)=0:FT(N)=0:FF(N)=0:GOTO 1070
1380 REM **** DISPLAY NEXT SCREEN SUBROUTINE ***
1390 IN=IN+15:IF IN+14>MT THEN IN=MT-14
1400 GOTO 1070
1410 REM *** CLOSE GAPS IN DATA FILE SUBROUTINE *****
1420 PRINT"NI=";:PRINT NT
1430 BT=0:NT=0:FOR N=1 TO MT:IF A(N)>0 THEN NT=NT+1
1440 IF A(N)>0 THEN BT=N
1450 NEXT N
1460 IF BT=NT THEN 500
1470 PRINT"CLOSING GAPS IN DATA FILE"
1480 N=0
1490 N=N+1
1500 IF A(N)>0 THEN 1570
1510 NX=N
1520 NX=NX+1:IF A(NX)=0 THEN 1520
1530 A(N)=A(NX):A(NX)=0:I(N)=I(NX):I(NX)=0:J(N)=J(NX):J(NX)=0
1540 D(N)=D(NX):D(NX)=0:T(N)=T(NX):T(NX)="":ES(N)=ES(NX):ES(NX)=0
1550 EF(N)=EF(NX):EF(NX)=0:LS(N)=LS(NX):LS(NX)=0:LF(N)=LF(NX):LF(NX)=0
1560 FT(N)=FT(NX):FT(NX)=0:FF(N)=FF(NX):FF(NX)=0:FI(N)=FI(NX):FI(NX)=0
1570 IF N=NT THEN 500 ELSE 1490
1580 GOTO 500
2000 REM **** SAVE DATA ON DISK IN RANDOM FORMAT ****************************
2010 INPUT"ENTER NAME OF FILE TO BE SAVED (8 CHARACTERS MAX)";SF$
2020 INPUT"SAVE ON DRIVE (A,B,C,ETC)?";SD$
2030 SS$=SD$+":"+SF$
2040 OPEN SS$ AS #1 LEN=32
2050 FOR N=1 TO NT
2060 FIELD #1,2 AS S1,2 AS S2,2 AS S3,2AS S4,24 AS S5
2070 LSET S1=MKI$(A(N)):LSET S2=MKI$(I(N)):LSET S3=MKI$(J(N))
2080 LSET S4=MKI$(D(N)):LSET S5=T(N)
2090 PUT #1
2100 NEXT N
2110 CLOSE #1:GOTO 500
2120 REM ****** THE FOLLOWING STATEMENTS MAY BE USED IN LIEU OF 2040-2100
2130 REM TO SAVE DATA IN SEQUENTIAL FORMAT.
2140 OPEN "O",#1,SS$
2150 FOR N=1 TO NT:WRITE #1,A(N),I(N),J(N),D(N),T(N):NEXT N:CLOSE #1:GOTO 500
3000 REM **** READ DATA FROM DISK ROUTINE *********************************
3010 INPUT"ENTER NAME OF FILE TO BE READ FROM DISK";RF$
3020 INPUT"ENTER DRIVE FROM WHICH FILE IS TO BE READ (A,B,C,ETC)";RD$
3030 SS$=RD$+":"+RF$
3040 OPEN SS$ AS #1 LEN=32
3050 N=1
3060 FIELD #1,2 AS S1,2 AS S2,2 AS S3,2 AS S4,24 AS S5
3070 GET #1:NT=N
```

```
3080 A(N)=CVI(S1):I(N)=CVI(S2):J(N)=CVI(S3):D(N)=CVI(S4):T(N)=S5
3090 IF EOF(1) THEN 3110
3100 N=N+1:GOTO 3060
3110 CLOSE #1:GOTO 500
3120 REM ********** THE FOLLOWING STATEMENTS MAY BE USED IN LIEU 3040-3110
3130 REM TO READ A SEQUENTIAL FORMAT DATA FILE.
3140 OPEN "I",#1,SS$:N=0
3150 N=N+1:INPUT #1,A(N),I(N),J(N),D(N),T(N):IF EOF(1) THEN 3160 ELSE 3150
3160 CLOSE #1:GOTO 500
4000 REM *** NETWORK ANALYSIS ROUTINE ****************
4010 RS="N":FOR N=1 TO NT-1:IF J(N+1)<J(N) THEN RS="Y"
4020 NEXT N
4030 IF RS="N" THEN 4180
4040 PRINT"RESEQUENCING TASK DATA IN J-NODE ORDER"
4050 MM=NT
4060 MM=INT(MM/2):IF MM=0 THEN 4180
4070 KK=NT-MM:JJ=1
4080 II=JJ
4090 LL=II+MM
4100 IF J(II)>J(LL) THEN 4110 ELSE 4160
4110 X1=A(II):X2=I(II):X3=J(II):X4=D(II):TX=T(II)
4120 A(II)=A(LL):I(II)=I(LL):J(II)=J(LL):D(II)=D(LL):T(II)=T(LL)
4130 A(LL)=X1:I(LL)=X2:J(LL)=X3:D(LL)=X4:T(LL)=TX
4140 II=II-MM
4150 IF II>=1 THEN 4090
4160 JJ=JJ+1
4170 IF JJ>KK THEN 4060 ELSE 4080
4180 FOR M=1 TO MN:E(M)=0:NEXT M
4190 FOR N=1 TO NT:VT=E(I(N))+D(N)
4200 IF VT>E(J(N)) THEN E(J(N))=VT
4210 NEXT N
4220 BV=0:FOR M=1 TO MN:IF E(M)>BV THEN BV=E(M)
4230 NEXT M
4240 FOR M=1 TO MN:L(M)=BV:NEXT M
4250 FOR N=NT TO 1 STEP-1:VT=L(J(N))-D(N)
4260 IF VT<L(I(N))THEN L(I(N))=VT
4270 NEXT N
4280 FOR N=1 TO NT:ES(N)=E(I(N)):LF(N)=L(J(N)):EF(N)=ES(N)+D(N)
4290 LS(N)=LF(N)-D(N):FT(N)=LF(N)-EF(N):FF(N)=E(J(N))-E(I(N))-D(N)
4300 NEXT N:GOTO 500
5000 REM ******* PRINT SCHEDULE ROUTINE *******************************
5010 TP="TASK# I-# J-# DUR DESCRIPTION                    ES   EF   LS   L"
5020 TP=TP+"F   TF   FF"
5030 INPUT"POSITION PAPER AND DEPRESS P";R:IF R<>"P"THEN 500
5040 PRINT"YOU MAY ENTER ANY NUMBER OF LINES TO DESCRIBE SCHEDULE (X TO EXIT)"
5050 INPUT"?";ST:IF ST="X" THEN 5070
5060 LPRINT ST:GOTO 5050
5070 LPRINT TP:LPRINT:FOR N=1 TO NT
5080 LPRINT USING "#####";A(NN);:LPRINT USING"####";I(N),J(N),D(N);
5090 LPRINT USING"!";"";:LPRINT USING"\                      \";T(N);
5100 LPRINT USING"####";ES(N),EF(N),LS(N),LF(N),FT(N),FF(N)
5110 NEXT N:GOTO 500
10000 END
```

```
10 REM PROGRAM AON-MIN E.M. Willis. University of North Carolina at Charlotte
20 SCREEN 0 : CLS : KEY OFF
30 DEFINT A-P:DEFSTR R-T:DEFINT U-Z:DEFSNG Q
40 PW=80:REM PRINTER WIDTH-REVISE IF NECESSARY
50 MT=160:MR=320
60 DIM A(MT),J(MR),I(MR),D(MT),R(MR),T(MT),FT(MT,2),AN(MR),IO(MR)
70 DIM ES(MT,2),EF(MT,2),LS(MT,2),LF(MT,2),L(MR),NL(MR),NR(MR)
80 DIM AP(MR),AF(MR,2),JO(MR)
160 BEEP:PRINT"SET TERMINAL IN UPPERCASE MODE"
500 REM ******** MAIN MENU ROUTINE ******************************************
510 CLS
520 PRINT"LAST ROUTINE EXECUTED WAS:";:PRINT USING"##";LX
530 PRINT"CURRENT TIME IS     :";:PRINT USING"!";"";:PRINT TIME$
540 PRINT"LAST ROUTINE STARTED:";:PRINT USING"!";"";:PRINT TZ$
550 PRINT"ELAPSED TIME (SECONDS)   :";:PRINT USING"########";TIMER-QX
560 BEEP:PRINT"******** MAIN MENU ********"
565 FOR N=1 TO MT:IF A(N)>NT THEN NT=N
570 NEXT N:FOR A=1 TO MR:IF AN(A)<>0 THEN NR=A
575 NEXT A:
580 PRINT"NUMBER OF TASKS :";:PRINT USING"###";NT
585 PRINT"NUMBER OF ARROWS:";:PRINT USING"###";NR
590 PRINT"FREE RAM SPACE=";:PRINT FRE(0)
600 PRINT"1 - REVIEW/REVISE/DELETE NETWORK DATA"
610 PRINT"2 - SAVE DATA IN RANDOM FORMAT ON DISK."
620 PRINT"3 - READ DATA FROM DISK"
630 PRINT"4 - ANALYZE NETWORK"
640 PRINT"5 - PRINT SCHEDULE"
690 PRINT"10 - END EXECUTION"
700 INPUT "SELECT OPTION?";O
710 TZ$=TIME$:LX=O:QX=TIMER
720 ON O GOTO 1000,2000,3000,4000,5000,500,500,500,5000,10000
730 GOTO 560
1000 REM **** REVIEW/REVISE/DELETE NETWORK DATA ROUTINE  *****************
1010 CLS:INPUT"1=ARROWS, 2=TASKS. WHICH?",A: IF A=1 THEN 1590
1020 TD="SEQ TASK# DUR DESCRIPTION              ES    EF   LS   L"
1030 TD=TD+"F    TF"
1040 INPUT"REVIEW/REVISE TASKS STARTING WITH SEQUENCE NUMBER?";IN
1050 IF IN<1 THEN 1040 ELSE IF IN >MT-14 THEN IN=MT-14
1060 REM *** DISPLAY TASK DATA SUBROUTINE *****
1070 CLS:PRINT TD
1080 FOR N=IN TO IN+14
1090 GOSUB 1100:GOTO 1170
1100 PRINT USING"###";N;:PRINT USING"######";A(N);:PRINT USING"####";D(N);
1110 PRINT USING"!";"";:PRINT USING"\                    \";T(N);
1140 IF RD="R"THEN PRINT
1150 IF RD="R"THEN RETURN
1160 PRINT USING"####";ES(N,1),EF(N,1),LS(N,1),LF(N,1);
1165 PRINT USING "####"; FT(N,1):RETURN
1170 NEXT N
1180 INPUT"ENTER R-REVISE D-DELETE N-NEXT PAGE X-EXIT?";R
1190 IF R="R" THEN RD="R"ELSE RD=""
1200 IF R="R"THEN 1230 ELSE IF R="D"THEN 1340 ELSE IF R="N"THEN 1390
1210 IF R="X"THEN 1410 ELSE 1180
1220 REM **** REVISE TASK DATA SUBROUTINE *****
1230 INPUT"REVISE DATA FOR SEQUENCE NUMBER?(0 TO EXIT)";NR:IF NR=0 THEN 1180
1240 PRINT TD:N=NR:GOSUB 1100
```

```
1250 INPUT"TASK#, DUR ?";A(N),D(N):INPUT"TASK DESCRIPTION (CR IF OK)?";TT
1260 IF TT=""THEN 1070
1270 T(N)=LEFT$(TT,24):GOTO 1070
1330 REM **** DELETE TASK DATA SUBROUTINE ********
1340 INPUT"ENTER SEQUENCE NUMBER OF TASK TO BE DELETED (0 TO EXIT)";ND
1350 IF ND=0 THEN 1180
1360 N=ND:A(N)=0:D(N)=0:T(N)="blank":GOTO 1070
1380 REM **** DISPLAY NEXT SCREEN SUBROUTINE ***
1390 IN=IN+15:IF IN+14>MT THEN IN=MT-14
1400 GOTO 1070
1410 REM *** CLOSE GAPS IN DATA FILE SUBROUTINE *****
1420 PRINT"NT=";:PRINT NT
1430 BT=0:NT=0:FOR N=1 TO MT:IF A(N)>0 THEN NT=NT+1
1440 IF A(N)>0 THEN BT=N
1450 NEXT N
1460 IF BT=NT THEN 500
1470 PRINT"CLOSING GAPS IN DATA FILE"
1480 N=0
1490 N=N+1
1500 IF A(N)>0 THEN 1570
1510 NX=N
1520 NX=NX+1:IF A(NX)=0 THEN 1520
1530 A(N)=A(NX):A(NX)=0
1540 D(N)=D(NX):D(NX)=0:T(N)=T(NX):T(NX)="blank"
1570 IF N=NT THEN 500 ELSE 1490
1580 GOTO 500
1590 REM *************REVIEW/REVISE ARROWS ROUTINE*************
1595 GOTO 1615
1600 PRINT:PRINT"SEQ ARROW# TYPE   LAG I-NODE# J-NODE#        TF":RETURN
1605 ER=0:IF A<1 THEN GOSUB 1030 ELSE IF A>MR THEN GOSUB 1030
1610 RETURN
1615 INPUT"REVIEW/REVISE ARROWS STARTING WITH SEQUENCE NBR: ?";A
1620 GOSUB 1605:IF ER=1 THEN 1615 ELSE AI=A
1625 IF AI>MR -14 THEN AI=MR-14
1630 AJ=AI+14
1635 GOSUB 1600
1640 FOR A=AI TO AJ:GOSUB 1645:GOTO 1660
1645 PRINT USING"###";A;:PRINT USING"#######";AN(A);
1650 PRINT USING"\ \";"";:PRINT USING"\\";R(A);:PRINT USING"#####";L(A);
1655 PRINT USING"########";I(A),J(A),AF(A,1):RETURN
1660 NEXT A
1665 PRINT
1670 INPUT"R=REVISE, D=DELETE, N=NEXT SCREEN, I=INSERT ,X=EXIT?";R
1675 IF R="R" THEN 1805 ELSE IF R="D" THEN 1685 ELSE IF R="I" THEN 1705
1680 IF R="X"THEN 1705   ELSE IF R="N" THEN 1700 ELSE 1635
1685 INPUT"SEQUENCE NUMBER TO BE DELETED?";A:GOSUB 1605
1690 IF ER=0 THEN 1695 ELSE 1635
1695 AN(A)=0: L(A)=0:J(A)=0:I(A)=0:R(A)="":GOTO 1635
1700 AI=AI+15:GOTO 1625
1705 NR=0:FOR A=1 TO MR:IF AN(A)>0 THEN BA=A
1710 IF AN(A)>0 THEN NR=NR+1
1715 NEXT A:IF BA=NR AND R="X" THEN 500
1720 IF BA=NR AND R="I"THEN GOSUB 1765
1725 IF BA=NR AND R="I" THEN 1635
1730 PRINT"CLOSING GAPS IN FILE"
1735 FOR A=1 TO NR:IF AN(A)>0 THEN 1755 ELSE AA=A
```

```
1740 AA=AA+1: IF AN(AA)=0 THEN 1740
1745 I(A)=I(AA):J(A)=J(AA):AN(A)=AN(AA):R(A)=R(AA):L(A)=L(AA)
1750 I(AA)=0:J(AA)=0:L(AA)=0:AN(AA)=0:R(AA)=""
1755 NEXT A:IF R="X" THEN 500
1760 PRINT"GAPS CLOSED. RE-SPECIFY INSERT OPTION":GOTO 1635
1765 INPUT"OPEN A SPACE BEFORE SEQUENCE NUMBER N, ENTER N?";N
1770 IF N=0 THEN 1635
1775 BA=0:FOR A=1 TO MR:IF AN(A)>0 THEN BA=A
1780 NEXT A
1785 FOR A=BA+1 TO N+1 STEP-1
1790 L(A)=L(A-1):I(A)=I(A-1):J(A)=J(A-1):R(A)=R(A-1):AN(A)=AN(A-1)
1795 NEXT A
1800 L(N)=0:I(N)=0:J(N)=0:R(N)="":AN(N)=0:GOTO 1625
1805 INPUT"SEQUENCE NUMBER TO BE REVISED?";A:GOSUB 1605
1810 IF ER=1 THEN 1635
1815 GOSUB 1600:GOSUB 1645
1820 INPUT"ARROW NBR, LAG, I-NODE#, J-NODE #?";AN(A),L(A),I(A),J(A)
1825 INPUT"ENTER TYPE OF ARROW: SS, SE, ES, EE";R(A)
1830 IF R(A)<>"SS" AND R(A)<>"SE" AND R(A)<>"ES" AND R(A)<>"EE"THEN 1825
1835 GOTO 1635
2000 REM **** SAVE DATA ON DISK IN RANDOM FORMAT *****************************
2010 INPUT"ENTER NAME OF FILE TO BE SAVED (7 CHARACTERS MAX)";SF$
2020 IF LEN(SF$)>7 THEN 2010
2030 INPUT"SAVE ON DRIVE (A,B,C,ETC)?";SD$
2040 SS$=SD$+":"+SF$:SA$=SS$+"A"
2050 OPEN SS$ AS #1 LEN=28
2060 FOR N=1 TO NT:FIELD #1,2 AS S1,2 AS S2,24 AS S3
2070 LSET S1=MKI$(A(N)):LSET S2=MKI$(D(N)):LSET S3=T(N):PUT #1
2080 NEXT N:CLOSE #1
2090 OPEN SA$ AS #2 LEN=10
2100 FOR A=1 TO NR:FIELD #2,2 AS S1,2 AS S2,2 AS S3, 2 AS S4, 2 AS S5
2110 LSET S1=MKI$(AN(A)):LSET S2=MKI$(L(A)):LSET S3=MKI$(I(A))
2120 LSET S4=MKI$(J(A)):LSET S5=R(A):PUT #2:NEXT A:CLOSE #2:GOTO 500
3000 REM **** READ DATA FROM DISK ROUTINE *****************************
3010 INPUT"ENTER NAME OF FILE TO BE READ FROM DISK";RF$
3020 INPUT"ENTER DRIVE FROM WHICH FILE IS TO BE READ (A,B,C,ETC)";RD$
3030 SS$=RD$+":"+RF$:SA$=SS$+"A"
3040 OPEN SS$ AS # 1 LEN=28:N=1
3050 FIELD # 1,2 AS S1,2 AS S2,24 AS S3:GET #1:NI=N
3060 A(N)=CVI(S1):D(N)=CVI(S2):T(N)=S3
3070 IF EOF(1) THEN 3090
3080 N=N+1:GOTO 3050
3090 CLOSE #1
3100 OPEN SA$ AS #2 LEN=10:A=1
3110 FIELD #2, 2 AS S1, 2 AS S2, 2 AS S3, 2 AS S4, 2 AS S5:GET #2:NR=A
3120 AN(A)=CVI(S1):L(A)=CVI(S2):I(A)=CVI(S3):J(A)=CVI(S4):R(A)=S5
3130 IF EOF(2) THEN 3150
3140 A=A+1:GOTO 3110
3150 CLOSE #2:GOTO 500
4000 REM ****** NETWORK ANALYSIS ROUTINE ************
4005 GOSUB 7000:GOTO 4065
4010 INPUT"DO YOU WANT TO RESEQUENCE TASKS? Y OR N?";R:IF R="Y" THEN 7000
4015 M=1:IF R="N"THEN 4065 ELSE 4005
4020 REM****SUBROUTINE FOR FINDING TASKS WITH SPECIFIED TASK NBRS*****
4025 IX=1:JX=NT
4030 MX=INT((IX+JX)/2):IF A(MX)=NV THEN RETURN
```

```
4035 IF A(MX)>NV THEN JX=MX ELSE IX=MX
4040 IF A(IX)=NV THEN MX=IX ELSE IF A(JX)=NV THEN MX=JX
4045 IF A(IX)=NV THEN RETURN ELSE IF A(JX)=NV THEN RETURN
4050 IF JX=IX+1 AND A(IX)<>NV THEN MX=0
4055 IF MX=0 THEN RETURN ELSE 4030
4060 REM*****END OF SUBROUTINE************
4065 PRINT"CHECKING THAT NO TASKS HAVE DUPLICATE NODE NUMBERS."
4070 DT=0:FOR N=1 TO NT-1:IF A(N)<>A(N+1) THEN 4085
4075 PRINT "TASK SEQUENCE NUMBERS";:PRINT USING"######";N,N+1;
4080 PRINT USING"!";"";:PRINT"HAVE DUPLICATE TASK NUMBERS":DT=1
4085 NEXT N:IF DT=0 THEN 4100
4090 PRINT"YOU MUST CORRECT BEFORE PROCEEDING. DO YOU UNDERSTAND? Y OR N?"
4095 INPUT"?";R:IF R="Y"THEN 500 ELSE 4090
4100 FOR N=1 TO NT:NL(N)=0:NR(N)=0:NEXT N
4105 PRINT"CHECKING THAT I AND J NODES OF ARROWS ARE DEFINED TASKS"
4110 FOR A=1 TO NR:AP(A)=0:IF R(A)="" THEN 4170
4115 NV=I(A):GOSUB 4025:IF MX<>0 THEN 4140
4120 PRINT"ARROW #";:PRINT USING"#####";AN(A);:PRINT USING"!";"";
4125 PRINT"DOES NOT CONNECT TO A DEFINED TASK AT ITS I END"
4130 INPUT"CARRIAGE RETURN TO CONTINUE";ZZ
4135 GOTO 500
4140 IO(A)=MX:NV=J(A):GOSUB 4025:IF MX<>0 THEN 4160
4145 PRINT "ARROW #";:PRINT USING"####";AN(A);:PRINT USING"!";"";
4150 PRINT "DOES NOT CONNECT TO A DEFINED TASK AT ITS J END"
4155 INPUT"CARRIAGE RETURN TO CONTINUE";ZZZ:GOTO 500
4160 JO(A)=MX:IF RIGHT$(R(A),1)="S" THEN NL(MX)=NL(MX)+1
4165 IF RIGHT$(R(A),1)="E"THEN NR(MX)=NR(MX)+1
4170 NEXT A
4175 PRINT"DETERMINING ARROW SEQUENCE NUMBERS"
4180 FOR A=1 TO NR:AP(A)=0:NEXT A:PN=0
4185 CV=0:PRINT"EXAMINING SINGLE-HEADED ARROWS"
4190 FOR A=1 TO NR:IF AP(A)>0 THEN 4245
4195 IF R(A)="ES"THEN 4205 ELSE IF R(A)="SS"THEN 4215
4200 IF R(A)="EE"THEN 4225 ELSE 4235
4205 IF NL(IO(A))>0 THEN 4245 ELSE IF NR(IO(A))>0 THEN 4245
4210 PN=PN+1:AP(A)=PN:NL(JO(A))=NL(JO(A))-1:CV=1:GOTO 4245
4215 IF NL(IO(A))>0 THEN 4245
4220 PN=PN+1:AP(A)=PN:NL(JO(A))=NL(JO(A))-1:CV=1:GOTO 4245
4225 IF NL(IO(A))>0 THEN 4245 ELSE IF NR(IO(A))>0 THEN 4245
4230 PN=PN+1:AP(A)=PN:NR(JO(A))=NR(JO(A))-1:CV=1:GOTO 4245
4235 IF NL(IO(A))>0 THEN 4245
4240 PN=PN+1:AP(A)=PN:NR(JO(A))=NR(JO(A))-1:CV=1:GOTO 4245
4245 NEXT A:IF PN=NR THEN 4420
4250 IF CV>0 THEN 4185
4255 CV=0:PRINT"SEARCHING FOR DOUBLE-HEADED ARROWS"
4260 FOR A=1 TO NR:IF AP(A)>0 THEN 4385
4265 IF CV=1 THEN 4385
4270 FOR B=1 TO NR:IF AP(B)>0 THEN 4380 ELSE IF A=B THEN 4380
4275 IF CV=1 THEN 4380
4280 IA=IO(A):IB=IO(B):JA=JO(A):JB=JO(B)
4285 IF IA<> JB THEN 4380
4290 IF R(A)="SS" AND R(B)="SS"THEN 4310
4295 IF R(A)="EE" AND R(B)="EE"THEN 4325
4300 IF R(A)="ES" AND R(B)="SE" THEN 4340 ELSE 4360
4305 IF R(A)="SE" AND R(B)="ES" THEN 4360 ELSE 4380
4310 IF NL(IA)>1 THEN 4380 ELSE IF NL(JA)>1 THEN 4380
```

```
4315 PN=PN+1:AP(A)=PN:PN=PN+1:AP(B)=PN:CV=1
4320 NL(IA)=NL(IA)-1:NL(JA)=NL(JA)-1:GOTO 4380
4325 IF NL(IA)=0 AND NL(JA)=0 AND NR(IA)=1 AND NR(JA)=1 THEN 4330 ELSE 4380
4330 PN=PN+1:AP(A)=PN:PN=PN+1:AP(B)=PN:CV=1:NR(IA)=NR(IA)-1:NR(JA)=NR(JA)-1
4335 GOTO 4380
4340 IF NL(IA)>0 THEN 4380 ELSE IF NR(IA)>1 THEN 4380
4345 IF NL(JA)>1 THEN 4380
4350 PN=PN+1:AP(A)=PN:PN=PN+1:AP(B)=PN:CV=1
4355 NR(IA)=NR(IA)-1:NL(JA)=NL(JA)-1:GOTO 4380
4360 IF NL(JA)>0 THEN 4380 ELSE IF NR(JA)>1 THEN 4380
4365 IF NL(IA)>1 THEN 4380
4370 PN=PN+1:AP(A)=PN:PN=PN+1:AP(B)=PN:CV=1
4375 NR(JA)=NR(JA)-1:NL(IA)=NL(IA)-1
4380 NEXT B
4385 NEXT A
4390 IF PN=NR THEN 4420 ELSE IF CV=1 THEN 4185
4395 PRINT"YOU HAVE A LOGIC LOOP OR TOO MANY DOUBLE-HEADED ARROWS"
4400 PRINT"SEQUENCE NUMBERS OF SUSPECT ARROWS ARE:"
4405 FOR A=1 TO NR:IF AP(A)=0 THEN PRINT USING"####";A:
4410 NEXT A
4415 INPUT"UNDERSTAND? Y OR NO:";R:IF R="Y" THEN 500 ELSE 4415
4420 PRINT"RESEQUENCING ARROWS"
4425 NN=NR
4430 MM=NN
4435 MM=INT(MM/2)
4440 IF MM=0 THEN 4520 ELSE 4445
4445 KK=NN-MM
4450 JJ=1
4455 II=JJ
4460 LL=II+MM
4465 IF AP(II) > AP(LL) THEN 4470 ELSE 4510
4470 AT=AN(II):LT=L(II):IT=IO(II):JT=JO(II):RT=R(II):KQ=AP(II)
4475 IH=I(II):JH=J(II)
4480 AN(II)=AN(LL):L(II)=L(LL):IO(II)=IO(LL):JO(II)=JO(LL):R(II)=R(LL)
4485 AP(II)=AP(LL):I(II)=I(LL):J(II)=J(LL)
4490 AN(LL)=AT:L(LL)=LT:IO(LL)=IT:JO(LL)=JT:R(LL)=RT:I(LL)=IH:J(LL)=JH
4495 AP(LL)=KQ
4500 II=II-MM
4505 IF II>=1 THEN 4460 ELSE 4510
4510 JJ=JJ+1
4515 IF JJ>KK THEN 4435 ELSE 4455
4520 PRINT"SUGGEST YOU SAVE THIS ON DISK. UNLESS YOU ADD OR REVISE ARROWS, YOU"
4525 INPUT"CAN DO THIS FASTER IN SUBSEQUENT RUNS. UNDERSTAND? Y OR N?";R
4530 IF R<>"Y"THEN 4520
4600 PRINT"MAKING NETWORK ANALYSIS":IF M=2 THEN 4615
4605 M=1:KA=0:FOR N=1 TO NT:ES(N,M)=0
4610 EF(N,M)=D(N):NEXT N:GOSUB 4615:GOTO 500
4615 FOR A=1 TO NR:II=IO(A):JJ=JO(A):IF M=1 THEN 4625
4620 IF U(JJ,2)>0 THEN 4675 ELSE IF U(JJ,4)>0 THEN 4675
4625 IF R(A)="SS" THEN 4635 ELSE IF R(A)="EE" THEN 4645
4630 IF R(A)="ES" THEN 4650 ELSE 4660
4635 MS=ES(II,M)+L(A)
4640 MF=MS+D(JJ)+L(A):GOTO 4665
4645 MF=EF(II,M)+L(A):MS=0:GOTO 4665
4650 MS=EF(II,M)+L(A)
4655 MF=MS+D(JJ):GOTO 4665
```

```
4660 MF=ES(II,M)+L(A):MS=0
4665 IF MS>ES(JJ,M) THEN ES(JJ,M)=MS
4670 IF MF>EF(JJ,M) THEN EF(JJ,M)=MF
4675 NEXT A
4680 BF=0
4685 FOR N=1 TO NT:IF EF(N,M)>BF THEN BF=EF(N,M)
4690 NEXT N
4695 FOR N=1 TO NT:LF(N,M)=BF
4700 LS(N,M)=LF(N,M)-D(N):NEXT N
4705 FOR A=NR TO 1 STEP-1:II=IO(A):JJ=JO(A)
4710 IF R(A)="SS"THEN 4720 ELSE IF R(A)="EE" THEN 4725
4715 IF R(A)= "ES"THEN 4735 ELSE 4745
4720 MS= LS(JJ,M)-L(A):MF=9999:GOTO 4750
4725 MF=LF(JJ,M)-L(A)
4730 MS=MF-D(II):GOTO 4750
4735 MF=LS(JJ,M)-L(A)
4740 MS=MF-D(II):GOTO 4750
4745 MS=LF(JJ,M)-L(A):MF=9999
4750 IF MS<LS(II,M) THEN LS(II,M)=MS
4755 IF MF<LF(II,M) THEN LF(II,M)=MF
4760 NEXT A
4765 FOR N=1 TO NT:FT(N,M)=LF(N,M)-ES(N,M)-D(N):NEXT N
4770 FOR A=1 TO NR:AF(A,M)=0
4775 IF R(A)="ES"THEN AF(A,M)=LS(JO(A),M)-EF(IO(A),M)-L(A) ELSE 4785
4780 GOTO 4810
4785 IF R(A)="SS" THEN AF(A,M)=LS(JO(A),M)-ES(IO(A),M)-L(A) ELSE 4795
4790 GOTO 4810
4795 IF R(A)="EE" THEN AF(A,M)=LF(JO(A),M)-EF(IO(A),M)-L(A) ELSE 4805
4800 GOTO 4810
4805 IF R(A)="SE" THEN AF(A,M)=LF(JO(A),M)-ES(IO(A),M)-L(A)
4810 NEXT A
4815 RETURN
5000 REM ******** DISPLAY/PRINT SCHEDULE ROUTINE *****************************
5010 INPUT"S=SCREEN DISPLAY, H=HARDCOPY , B=BOTH.    WHICH?";R
5020 IF R="S"THEN PM=1 ELSE IF R="H"THEN PM=2 ELSE IF R="B"THEN PM=3 ELSE 5010
5030 CF=1:UP=1:TU="N"
5090 INPUT"C=PRINT SCHEDULE CONTINUOUSLY, P=PRINT SCHEDULE BY PAGES. WHICH?";R
5100 IF R="C"THEN PL=300 ELSE PL=17
5110 INPUT"PRINT/DISPLAY TASKS WITH SEQUENCE NUMBERS I TO J?    I,J=?";IX,JX
5120 IF IX<1 THEN 5110 ELSE IF JX>MT THEN 5110 ELSE IF IX>JX THEN 5110
5130 IF PM=1 THEN 5160 ELSE INPUT"ENTER ONE LINE PROJECT TITLE";TP
5140 IF LEN(TP)=<80 THEN 5155
5150 TP=LEFT$(TP,80):PRINT TP:INPUT"OK";R:IF R="Y"THEN 5155 ELSE 5130
5155 S1="TSK# DUR DESCRIPTIO"
5175 S1=S1+"N              ES(ED) EF(ED) LS(ED) LF(ED)  TF":GOTO 5185
5185 ST$="\              \":SD="":FOR K=1 TO 15:SD=SD+"   -":NEXT K
5190 SF=" -":FOR K=1 TO 9:SF=SF+"   -":NEXT K
5195 S0$="!" :LV=0:P=0
5200 FOR N=IX TO JX:IF A(N)=0 THEN 5215
5205 LV=LV+1:IF LV=1 THEN GOSUB 5230
5210 GOSUB 5290:IF LV=PL THEN LV=0
5215 NEXT N:IF PM<>1 THEN LPRINT CHR$(12)
5220 IF PM<>2 THEN INPUT "CARRIAGE RETURN TO RETURN TO MAIN MENU";R
5225 GOTO 5555
5230 P=P+1:IF PM=1 THEN 5265
5235 IF P>1 THEN LPRINT CHR$(12)
```

```
5240 LPRINT"Page No.";:LPRINT USING"###";P;
5245 IF UP=1 THEN LPRINT
5260 LPRINT:LPRINT TP:LPRINT
5265 IF PM<>2 THEN PRINT S1
5270 IF PM<>1 AND UP=1 THEN LPRINT S1
5280 IF PM<>1 THEN LPRINT SD
5285 RETURN
5290 VA=A(N):VD=D(N):VE=ES(N,1):VF=EF(N,1)
5295 VG=LS(N,1):VH=LF(N,1)
5300 VI=FT(N,1):IF CF=1 THEN 5340
5340 IF PM<>2 AND CF=1 THEN GOSUB 5370
5350 IF PM<>1 AND CF=1 THEN GOSUB 5400
5365 RETURN
5370 PRINT USING"####";VA;
5375 PRINT USING"####";VD;:PRINT USING S0$;"";:PRINT USING ST$;T(N);
5380 PRINT USING"#######";VE,VF,VG,VH;:PRINT USING"####";VI:RETURN
5400 LPRINT USING"####";VA;
5405 LPRINT USING"####";VD;:LPRINT USING S0$;"";:LPRINT USING ST$;T(N);
5410 LPRINT USING"#######";VE,VF,VG,VH;:LPRINT USING"####";VI
5415 LPRINT SD:RETURN
5555 IF RM="S"THEN 500
5560 BEEP:INPUT"DO YOU WANT A LISTING OF LOGICAL RELATIONSHIPS? Y OR ?";R
5565 IF R="N" THEN 500 ELSE IF R="Y" THEN 5570 ELSE 5560
5570 SR="SEQ RLTSHP#  LAG   I-N#  J-N# TYPE  AF":SR=SR+"       "+SR
5575 LPRINT"LOGICAL RELATIONSHIPS":LPRINT TP:LPRINT SR
5580 NL=NR/2:IF 2*NL<NR THEN NL=NL+1
5585 FOR N=1 TO NL:A=N:GOSUB 5595:A=NL+N:GOSUB 5595:LPRINT
5590 NEXT N:LPRINT CHR$(12):GOTO 500
5595 LPRINT USING"###";A;:LPRINT USING"########";AN(A);
5600 LPRINT USING"#####";L(A);:LPRINT USING"######";I(A),J(A);
5605 LPRINT USING"\\";"";:LPRINT R(A);:LPRINT USING"#####";AF(A,1);
5610 LPRINT USING"\  \";"";:RETURN
7000 REM ****** RESEQUENCE TASKS SUBROUTINE ROUTINE ************************
7010 AA=0:FOR N=2 TO NT:IF A(N)>A(N-1) THEN 7020 ELSE AA=1
7020 NEXT N:IF AA=0 THEN RETURN
7030 PRINT"RESEQUENCING TASKS IN TASK NUMBER ORDER"
7190 MM=NT
7200 MM=INT(MM/2)
7210 IF MM=0 THEN 7610 ELSE 7220
7220 KK=NT-MM
7230 JJ=1
7240 II=JJ
7250 LL=II+MM
7320 VI=A(II):VL=A(LL):GOTO 7410
7410 IF VI>VL THEN 7440 ELSE IF VI=VL THEN 7420 ELSE 7590
7430 GOTO 7590
7440 AT=A(II):DT=D(II):TT=T(II):FQ=FT(II,1)
7445 E1=ES(II,1):E2=EF(II,1):L1=LS(II,1):L2=LF(II,1)
7450 ES(II,1)=ES(LL,1):EF(II,1)=EF(LL,1):LS(II,1)=LS(LL,1):LF(II,1)=LF(LL,1)
7455 A(II)=A(LL):D(II)=D(LL):T(II)=T(LL):FT(II,1)=FT(LL,1)
7460 ES(LL,1)=E1:EF(LL,1)=E2:LS(LL,1)=L1:LF(LL,1)=L2 :FT(LL,1)=FQ
7465 A(LL)=AT:D(LL)=DT:T(LL)=TT
7570 II=II-MM
7580 IF II=>1 THEN 7250 ELSE 7590
7590 JJ=JJ+1
7600 IF JJ>KK THEN 7200 ELSE 7240
7610 RETURN
10000 INPUT"ARE YOU SURE? Y OR N?";R:IF R<>"Y" THEN 500
```

```
10 REM PROGRAM AOA-PERT: E.M. Willis, University of North Carolina at Charlotte
20 SCREEN 0:CLS:KEY OFF:IW=75
30 REM PROGRAM IS FORMATTED FOR 80 COLUMN TERMINAL SCREEN AND PRINTER
40 DEFSNG A-Q:DEFSTR R-T:DEFSNG U-V:DEFINT X-Y:DEFSNG Z
50 MT=276:MN=277:REM MT=MAX NBR OF TASKS. MN=MAX NBR OF NODES
60 DIM I(MT),J(MT),D(MT,5),T(MT),ES(MT),EF(MT),LS(MT),LF(MT),FT(MT)
70 DIM AN(MT),E(MN),L(MN),NS(MN+1),IO(MN),JO(MN)
90 DIM MC(100),EM(MN),CT(50)
110 SD(0)="0":SD(1)="1":SD(2)="2":SD(3)="3":SD(4)="4":SD(5)="5"
120 SD(6)="6":SD(7)="7":SD(8)="8":SD(9)="9"
130 BEEP:PRINT"SET TERMINAL IN UPPERCASE MODE"
500 REM ******** MAIN MENU ROUTINE ******************************************
510 CLS:PRINT"LAST ROUTINE EXECUTED WAS:";:PRINT USING"##";LX
530 PRINT"CURRENT TIME IS    :";:PRINT USING"!";"";:PRINT TIME$
540 PRINT"LAST ROUTINE STARTED:";:PRINT USING"!";"";:PRINT TZ$
550 PRINT"ELAPSED TIME (SECONDS)   :";:PRINT USING"########";TIMER-QX
560 BEEP:PRINT"******** MAIN MENU ********"
570 NT=0:FOR N=1 TO MT:IF AN(N)>0 THEN NT=NT+1
580 NEXT N:PRINT"NBR TASKS =";:PRINT NT;:PRINT USING"!";""
590 PRINT"FREE RAM SPACE=";:PRINT FRE(0)
600 PRINT"1 - REVIEW/REVISE/DELETE TASK DEFINITIONS"
610 PRINT"2 - SAVE DATA IN RANDOM FORMAT ON DISK."
620 PRINT"3 - READ DATA FROM DISK"
630 PRINT"4 - ANALYZE PERT NETWORK"
640 PRINT"5 - PRINT PERT SCHEDULE"
650 PRINT"6 - PRINT PERT GANTT CHART"
660 PRINT"7 - RESEQUENCE TASKS"
670 PRINT"8 - PERT/MONTE CARLO ROUTINES"
690 PRINT"10 - END EXECUTION"
700 INPUT "SELECT OPTION?";O
710 TZ$=TIME$:LX=O:QX=TIMER
720 ON O GOTO 1000,2000,3000,4000,5000,6000,7000,8000,500,10000
730 GOTO 560
1000 REM **** REVIEW/REVISE/DELETE TASK DATA ROUTINE  ************************
1010 CLS
1020 TD="SEQ TSK#  I-#  J-#  DURATIONS        DESCRIPTIO"
1030 TD=TD+"N              ES   EF   LS   LF   TF" :PRINT TD
1032 TX="                         OPT MED PES EFF"
1040 INPUT"REVIEW/REVISE TASKS STARTING WITH SEQUENCE NUMBER?";IN
1050 IF IN<1 THEN 1040 ELSE IF IN >MT-14 THEN IN=MT-14
1060 REM *** DISPLAY TASK DATA SUBROUTINE *****
1070 CLS:PRINT TD,TX
1080 FOR N=IN TO IN+14
1090 GOSUB 1100:GOTO 1170
1100 PRINT USING"###";N;:PRINT USING"#####";AN(N);
1110 PRINT USING"#####";I(N),J(N);:D(N,4)=(D(N,1)+4*D(N,2)+D(N,3))/6
1120 PRINT USING"####";D(N,1),D(N,2),D(N,3),D(N,4);
1130 PRINT USING"!";"";:PRINT USING"\                      \";T(N);
1140 IF RD="R"THEN PRINT
1150 IF RD="R"THEN RETURN
1160 PRINT USING"####";ES(N),EF(N),LS(N),LF(N),FT(N):RETURN
1170 NEXT N
1180   INPUT"ENTER R-REVISE D-DELETE N-NEXT PAGE X-EXIT?";R
1190 IF R="R" THEN RD="R"ELSE RD=""
1200 IF R="R"THEN 1230 ELSE IF R="D"THEN 1340 ELSE IF R="N"THEN 1390
1210 IF R="X"THEN 1410 ELSE 1180
1220 REM **** REVISE TASK DATA SUBROUTINE *****
1230 INPUT"REVISE DATA FOR SEQUENCE NUMBER?(0 TO EXIT)";NR:IF NR=0 THEN 1180
1240 PRINT TD:N=NR:GOSUB 1100
1250 PRINT"ENTER VALUES FOR TASK#, I-#, J-#, AND OPT, MED, PESS DURATIONS"
1260 INPUT"SEPARATE VALUES WITH COMMAS ?";A1,A2,A3,A4,A5,A6
```

```
1270 IF A3>A2 THEN 1290
1280 BEEP:BEEP:PRINT"J-NODE NUMBER MUST BE > I-NODE NUMBER":GOTO 1180
1290 AN(N)=A1:I(N)=A2:J(N)=A3:D(N,1)=A4:D(N,2)=A5:D(N,3)=A6
1300 INPUT"ENTER TASK DESCRIPTION (CARRIAGE RETURN IF DATA IS OKAY)";TT
1310 IF TT="" THEN 1070 ELSE T(N)=LEFT$(TT,24)
1320 GOTO 1070
1330 REM **** DELETE TASK DATA SUBROUTINE ********
1340 INPUT"ENTER SEQUENCE NUMBER OF TASK TO BE DELETED (0 TO EXIT)";ND
1350 IF ND=0 THEN 1180
1360 N=ND:AN(N)=0:I(N)=0:J(N)=0:T(N)="":D(N,1)=0:D(N,2)=0:ES(N)=0:EF(N)=0
1370 D(N,3)=0:D(N,4)=0:LS(N)=0:LF(N)=0:FT(N)=0:GOTO 1070
1380 REM **** DISPLAY NEXT SCREEN SUBROUTINE ***
1390 IN=IN+15:IF IN+14>MT THEN IN=MT-14
1400 GOTO 1070
1410 REM *** CLOSE GAPS IN DATA FILE SUBROUTINE *****
1420 PRINT"NT=";:PRINT NT
1430 DT=0:NT=0:FOR N=1 TO MT:IF AN(N)>0 THEN NT=NT+1
1440 IF AN(N)>0 THEN BT=N
1450 NEXT N
1460 IF BT=NT THEN 500
1470 PRINT"CLOSING GAPS IN DATA FILE"
1480 N=0
1490 N=N+1
1500 IF AN(N)>0 THEN 1570
1510 NX=N
1520 NX=NX+1:IF AN(NX)=0 THEN 1520
1530 AN(N)=AN(NX):AN(NX)=0:I(N)=I(NX):I(NX)=0:J(N)=J(NX):J(NX)=0
1532 D(N,1)=D(NX,1):D(NX,1)=0:D(N,2)=D(NX,2):D(NX,2)=0:D(N,3)=D(NX,3):D(NX,3)=0
1540 D(N,4)=D(NX,4):D(NX,4)=0:T(N)=T(NX):T(NX)="":ES(N)=ES(NX):ES(NX)=0
1550 EF(N)=EF(NX):EF(NX)=0:LS(N)=LS(NX):LS(NX)=0:LF(N)=LF(NX):LF(NX)=0
1560 FT(N)=FT(NX):FT(NX)=0
1570 IF N=NT THEN 500 ELSE 1490
1580 GOTO 500
2000 REM **** SAVE DATA ON DISK IN RANDOM FORMAT ****************************
2010 INPUT"ENTER NAME OF FILE TO BE SAVED (8 CHARACTERS MAX)";SF$
2020 INPUT"SAVE ON DRIVE (A,B,C,ETC)?";SD$
2030 SS$=SD$+":"+SF$
2040 OPEN SS$ AS #1 LEN=36
2050 FOR N=1 TO NT
2060 FIELD #1,2 AS S1,2 AS S2,2 AS S3,2AS S4,2 AS S5,2 AS S6,24 AS S7
2070 LSET S1=MKI$(AN(N)):LSET S2=MKI$(I(N)):LSET S3=MKI$(J(N))
2080 LSET S4=MKI$(D(N,1)):LSET S5=MKI$(D(N,2)):LSET S6=MKI$(D(N,3))
2090 LSET S7=T(N):PUT #1
2100 NEXT N
2110 CLOSE #1:GOTO 500
3000 REM **** READ DATA FROM DISK ROUTINE ********************************
3010 INPUT"ENTER NAME OF FILE TO BE READ FROM DISK";RF$
3020 INPUT"ENTER DRIVE FROM WHICH FILE IS TO BE READ (A,B,C,ETC)";RD$
3030 SS$=RD$+":"+RF$
3040 OPEN SS$ AS #1 LEN=36
3050 N=1
3060 FIELD #1,2 AS S1,2 AS S2,2 AS S3,2AS S4,2 AS S5,2 AS S6,24 AS S7
3070 GET #1:NT=N
3080 AN(N)=CVI(S1):I(N)=CVI(S2):J(N)=CVI(S3):D(N,1)=CVI(S4):T(N)=S7
3082 D(N,2)=CVI(S5):D(N,3)=CVI(S6)
3090 IF EOF(1) THEN 3110
3100 N=N+1:GOTO 3060
3110 CLOSE #1:GOTO 500
4000 REM ****** NETWORK ANALYSIS ROUTINE ************
4001 GOTO 4010
4010 LN=32746:FOR N=1 TO NT:IF AN(N)=0 THEN 4030
4020 IF I(N)<LN THEN LN=I(N)
```

```
4030 NEXT N
4040 NS(1)=LN:PRINT"PLEASE ALLOW UP TO 5 MINUTES"
4050 FOR N=1 TO NT:IF AN(N)=0 THEN 4060 ELSE NS(N+1)=J(N)
4060 NEXT N:NM=NT+1:GOSUB 4090
4070 FOR M=2 TO NT+1:IF NS(M)=NS(M-1) THEN NS(M)=32567
4080 NEXT M:NM=NT+1:GOSUB 4090
4082 MN=0:FOR M=1 TO NT+1:IF NS(M)>0 AND NS(M)<32567 THEN MN=MN+1
4084 NEXT M:GOTO 4240
4090 MM=NM
4100 MM=INT(MM/2)
4110 IF MM=0 THEN RETURN ELSE 4120
4120 KK=NM-MM
4130 JJ=1
4140 II=JJ
4150 LL=II+MM
4160 IF NS(II)>NS(LL)THEN 4170 ELSE 4220
4170 IT=NS(II)
4180 NS(II)=NS(LL)
4190 NS(LL)=IT
4200 II=II-MM
4210 IF II>=1 THEN 4150 ELSE 4220
4220 JJ=JJ+1
4230 IF JJ>KK THEN 4100 ELSE 4140
4240 FOR N=1 TO NT:IF AN(N)=0 THEN 4260 ELSE NQ=J(N)
4250 GOSUB 4270:JO(N)=IT:NQ=I(N):GOSUB 4270:IO(N)=IT
4260 NEXT N:GOTO 4340
4270 IV=1:JV=MN
4280 IT=(IV+JV)/2:IA=IT-1:IB=IT:IC=IT+1
4290 IF NS(IA)=NQ THEN IT=IA ELSE IF NS(IB)=NQ THEN IT=IB
4300 IF NS(IC)=NQ THEN IT=IC
4310 IF NS(IT)=NQ THEN RETURN
4320 IF NS(IT)>NQ THEN JV=IT ELSE IV=IT
4330 GOTO 4280
4340 PRINT"OPERATIVE NODE NUMBERS ASSIGNED.  STARTING ANALYSIS"
4350 FOR M=1 TO MN:E(M)=0:L(M)=9999:NEXT M
4360 GOSUB 4370:GOSUB 4470:GOSUB 4510:GOSUB 4570:BT=BV:GOTO 500
4370 UP=1:CF=1:FOR N=1 TO NT
4380 IF AN(N)=0 THEN 4460
4390 D(N,4)=(D(N,1)+4*D(N,2)+D(N,3))/6
4440 KV=E(IO(N))+D(N,4)
4450 IF KV>E(JO(N))THEN E(JO(N))=KV
4460 NEXT N:RETURN
4470 BV=0:FOR N=1 TO NT
4480 IF AN(N)=0 THEN 4500
4490 IF E(JO(N))>BV THEN BV=E(JO(N))
4500 NEXT N:RETURN
4510 FOR M=1 TO MN:L(JO(M))=BV:NEXT M
4520 FOR N=NT TO 1 STEP-1
4530 IF AN(N)=0 THEN 4560
4540 KV=L(JO(N))-D(N,4)
4550 IF KV<L(IO(N)) THEN L(IO(N))=KV
4560 NEXT N:RETURN
4570 FOR N=1 TO NT
4580 IF AN(N)=0 THEN 4610
4590 ES(N)=E(IO(N)):EF(N)=ES(N)+D(N,4):LF(N)=L(JO(N)):LS(N)=LF(N)-D(N,4)
4600 FT(N)=LF(N)-EF(N):IF ABS(FT(N))<.01 THEN FT(N)=0
4610 NEXT N:RETURN
5000 REM ***** DISPLAY/PRINT SCHEDULE ROUTINE ************
5002 TX="":TX="TSK#  I-#  J-#     DURATIONS      DESCRIPTIO"
5004 TX=TX+"N              ES   EF  LS  LF   TF"
5006 S2="              OPT MED PES      EFF"
5010 INPUT"S=SCREEN DISPLAY, H=HARDCOPY , B=BOTH.   WHICH?";R
```

```
AOA-PERT                                                    Page 4 of 7
5020 IF R="S"THEN PM=1 ELSE IF R="H"THEN PM=2 ELSE IF R="B"THEN PM=3 ELSE 5010
5040 CF=1:UP=1
5090 INPUT"C=PRINT SCHEDULE CONTINUOUSLY, P=PRINT SCHEDULE BY PAGES. WHICH?";R
5100 IF R="C"THEN PL=300 ELSE PL=25
5110 INPUT"PRINT/DISPLAY TASKS WITH SEQUENCE NUMBERS I TO J?    I,J=?";IX,JX
5120 IF IX<1 THEN 5110 ELSE IF JX>MT THEN 5110 ELSE IF IX>JX THEN 5110
5130 IF PM=1 THEN 5220 ELSE INPUT"ENTER ONE LINE PROJECT TITLE";TP
5140 IF LEN(TP)=<80 THEN 5220
5150 TP=LEFT$(TP,80):PRINT TP:INPUT"OK";R:IF R="Y"THEN 5220 ELSE 5130
5220 ST$="\                   \":SD="":FOR K=1 TO 14:SD=SD+"   -":NEXT K
5230 S0$="!" :LV=0:P=0
5240 FOR N=IX TO JX:IF AN(N)=0 THEN 5270
5250 LV=LV+1:IF LV=1 THEN GOSUB 5300
5260 GOSUB 5420:IF LV=PL THEN LV=0
5270 NEXT N:IF PM<>1 THEN LPRINT CHR$(12)
5280 IF PM<>2 THEN INPUT "CARRIAGE RETURN TO RETURN TO MAIN MENU";R
5290 GOTO 500
5300 P=P+1:IF PM=1 THEN 5370
5310 IF P>1 THEN LPRINT CHR$(12)
5320 LPRINT"Page No.";:LPRINT USING"###";P;
5330 IF UP=1 THEN LPRINT
5360 LPRINT:LPRINT TP:LPRINT
5370 IF PM<>2 THEN PRINT TX
5380 IF PM<>2 THEN PRINT S2
5400 IF PM<>1 THEN LPRINT TX
5402 IF PM<>1 THEN LPRINT S2
5410 RETURN
5420 VA=AN(N):VB=I(N):VC=J(N):VD=D(N,4):VE=ES(N):VF=EF(N):VG=LS(N):VH=LF(N)
5430 V1=D(N,1):V2=D(N,2):V3=D(N,3):VI=FT(N)
5510 IF PM<>2 AND CF=1 THEN GOSUB 5570
5530 IF PM<>1 AND CF=1 THEN GOSUB 5630
5560 RETURN
5570 PRINT USING"####";VA;:PRINT USING"#####";VB,VC;
5572 PRINT USING"####";V1,V2,V3;:PRINT USING"####.#";VD;
5580 PRINT USING S0$;"";:PRINT USING ST$;T(N);
5590 PRINT USING"####";VE,VF,VG,VH;:PRINT USING"####";VI:RETURN
5630 LPRINT SD:LPRINT USING"####";VA;:LPRINT USING"#####";VB,VC;
5640 LPRINT USING"####";V1,V2,V3;:LPRINT USING"####.#";VD;
5650 LPRINT USING S0$;"";:LPRINT USING ST$;T(N);
5660 LPRINT USING"####";VE,VF,VG,VH,VI:RETURN
6000 REM ********** PRINT GANTT CHART ROUTINE ***************************
6005 IW=75:IF PL=0 THEN PL=17
6015 INPUT "GANTT CHART FOR SEQUENCE NBRS I TO J. ENTER I,J?",IX,JX
6020 IF IX<1 THEN IX=1
6025 IF JX>NT THEN JX=NT
6030 BF =0:SP="":FOR K=1 TO 15:SP=SP+"    +":NEXT K
6035 FOR K=IX TO JX:IF LF(K)>BF THEN BF=LF(K)
6040 NEXT K
6100 REM **** BAR CHART IN WORKDATE FORMAT **************
6105 SX=" ":SX=STRING$(75,SX)
6110 NH=INT((JX-IX+1)/PL):IF JX-IX+1>INT(NH*PL) THEN NH=NH+1
6115 IV=IX:JV=JX:GOSUB 6165:P1=INT((IR-1)/75)+1:P2=INT((JR-1)/75)+1
6120 FOR P=P1 TO P2:S1$="":S2$="":S3$=""
6125 ID=1+IW*(P-1):JD=ID+IW-1:DD=ID-1
6130 FOR II=ID TO JD:KH=INT(II/100):S1$=S1$+SD(KH):NEXT II
6135 FOR II=ID TO JD:KH=INT(II/100):KT=INT((II-100*KH)/10)
6140 S2$=S2$+SD(KT):NEXT II
6145 FOR II=ID TO JD:KH=INT(II/100):KT=INT((II-100*KH)/10)
6150 KU=INT(II-100*KH-10*KT):S3$=S3$+SD(KU):NEXT II
6155 FOR PP=1 TO NH:IV=IX+PL*(PP-1):JV=IV+PL-1:IF JV>JX THEN JV=JX
6160 GOSUB 6165:GOTO 6185
6165 IR=9999:JR=0:FOR N=IV TO JV:IF AN(N)=0 THEN 6180
```

```
6170 IF ES(N)+1<IR THEN IR=ES(N)+1
6175 IF LF(N)>JR THEN JR=LF(N)
6180 NEXT N:RETURN
6185 IF JR<ID THEN 6275 ELSE IF IR>JD THEN 6275
6190 PRINT CHR$(12):GOSUB 6290:FOR N=IV TO JV
6195 IF AN(N)=0 THEN 6270
6200 SB=SX:IF D(N,4)=0 THEN 6265
6205 EB=ES(N)+1-DD:EC=EF(N)-DD:LC=LF(N)-DD:LB=LS(N)+1-DD
6210 IF FT(N)=0 THEN 6215 ELSE 6220
6215 S$="C":IC=EB:JC=LC:GOSUB 6240:GOTO 6265
6220 S$=".":IC=EB:JC=LC:GOSUB 6240
6230 S$="e":IC=EB:JC=EC:GOSUB 6240:GOTO 6265
6240 IF IC>75 THEN RETURN
6245 IF JC<1 THEN RETURN
6250 IF IC<1 THEN IC=1
6255 IF JC>75 THEN JC=75
6260 L=JC-IC+1:S$=STRING$(L,S$):MID$(SB,IC,L)=S$:RETURN
6265 LPRINT SP:LPRINT SB
6270 NEXT N:LPRINT SP:LPRINT CHR$(12)
6275 NEXT PP
6280 NEXT P
6285 GOTO 500
6290 LPRINT"PAGE NO.";:LPRINT USING"###";PP;:LPRINT USING"!";"";
6295 LPRINT"SHEET NO.";:LPRINT USING"###";P:LPRINT:LPRINT TP:LPRINT
6300 LPRINT S1$:LPRINT S2$:LPRINT S3$:RETURN
7000 REM ************* RESEQUENCE TASKS ROUTINE ****************************
7010 PRINT"BEFORE RESEQUENCING, YOU SHOULD ELIMINATE UNUSED SEQUENCE"
7020 PRINT"NUMBERS. TO DO SO, EXIT FROM THIS ROUTINE AND SAVE DATA"
7030 INPUT"ON DISK AND THEN READ IT BACK. DO YOU WANT TO EXIT? Y OR N ?";R
7040 IF R="Y"THEN 500
7050 PRINT"PARAMETER 1 - TASK NUMBERS"
7060 PRINT"PARAMETER 2 - I-NODE NUMBERS"
7070 PRINT"PARAMETER 3 - J-NODE NUMBERS"
7080 PRINT"PARAMETER 4 - EFFECTIVE TASK DURATIONS"
7090 PRINT"PARAMETER 5 - EARLY START TIME"
7100 PRINT"PARAMETER 6 - EARLY FINISH TIME"
7110 PRINT"PARAMETER 7 - LATE START TIME"
7120 PRINT"PARAMETER 8 - LATE FINISH TIME"
7130 PRINT"PARAMETER 9 - TOTAL FLOAT"
7140 INPUT"HOW MANY PARAMETERS FOR SORTING";NP:IF NP>9 THEN 7140
7150 PRINT"ENTER PARAMETER CODES WITH MOST SIGNIFICANT PARAMETER FIRST"
7160 FOR L=1 TO NP
7170 INPUT"PARAMETER NBR?";PL(L)
7180 NEXT L
7190 MM=NT
7200 MM=INT(MM/2)
7210 IF MM=0 THEN 7600 ELSE 7220
7220 KK=NT-MM
7230 JJ=1
7240 II=JJ
7250 LL=II+MM
7260 FOR L=1 TO NP
7270 IF PL(L)=1 THEN 7320 ELSE IF PL(L)=2 THEN 7330
7280 IF PL(L)=3 THEN 7340 ELSE IF PL(L)=4 THEN 7350
7290 IF PL(L)=5 THEN 7360 ELSE IF PL(L)=6 THEN 7370
7300 IF PL(L)=7 THEN 7380 ELSE IF PL(L)=8 THEN 7390
7310 IF PL(L)=9 THEN 7400
7320 IF  AN(II)> AN(LL) THEN 7430 ELSE IF  AN(II)= AN(LL) THEN 7410 ELSE 7580
7330 IF  I(II)> I(LL) THEN 7430 ELSE IF  I(II)= I(LL) THEN 7410 ELSE 7580
7340 IF  J(II)> J(LL) THEN 7430 ELSE IF  J(II)= J(LL) THEN 7410 ELSE 7580
7350 IF D(II,4)> D(LL,4) THEN 7430 ELSE IF D(II,4)= D(LL,4) THEN 7410 ELSE 7580
7360 IF ES(II)>ES(LL) THEN 7430 ELSE IF ES(II)=ES(LL) THEN 7410 ELSE 7580
```

```
AOA-PERT                                                     Page 6 of 7
7370 IF EF(II)>EF(LL) THEN 7430 ELSE IF EF(II)=EF(LL) THEN 7410 ELSE 7580
7380 IF LS(II)>LS(LL) THEN 7430 ELSE IF LS(II)=LS(LL) THEN 7410 ELSE 7580
7390 IF LF(II)>LF(LL) THEN 7430 ELSE IF LF(II)=LF(LL) THEN 7410 ELSE 7580
7400 IF FT(II)>FT(LL) THEN 7430 ELSE IF FT(II)=FT(LL) THEN 7410 ELSE 7580
7410 NEXT L
7420 GOTO 7580
7430 AT= AN(II):IT=I(II):JT=J(II):DT=D(II,4):TT=T(II)
7432 A1=D(II,1):D(II,1)=D(LL,1):D(LL,1)=A1:A2=D(II,2):D(II,2)=D(LL,2)
7434 D(LL,2)=A2:A3=D(II,3):D(II,3)=D(LL,3):D(LL,3)=A3
7440 C1=ES(II):C2=EF(II):C3=LS(II):C4=LF(II):C5=FT(II):C6=FF(II):C7=FI(II)
7450 AN(II)=AN(LL):I(II)=I(LL):J(II)=J(LL):D(II,4)=D(LL,4):T(II)=T(LL)
7460 ES(II)=ES(LL):EF(II)=EF(LL):LS(II)=LS(LL):LF(II)=LF(LL)
7470 FF(II)=FF(LL):FT(II)=FT(LL):FI(II)=FI(LL)
7480 AN(LL)=AT:I(LL)=IT:J(LL)=JT:D(LL,4)=DT:T(LL)=TT
7490 ES(LL)=C1:EF(LL)=C2:LS(LL)=C3:LF(LL)=C4:FT(LL)=C5:FF(LL)=C6:FI(LL)=C7
7550 OI=IO(II):OJ=JO(II):IO(II)=IO(LL):JO(II)=JO(LL):IO(LL)=OI:JO(LL)=OJ
7560 II=II-MM
7570 IF II=>1 THEN 7250 ELSE 7580
7580 JJ=JJ+1
7590 IF JJ>KK THEN 7200 ELSE 7240
7600 GOTO 500
8000 REM ****** PERT/MONTE CARLO ROUTINE ************
8010 GOTO 8100
8020 AQ=0:NN=0
8030 NN=NN+1:IF AN(NN)=AV THEN AQ=NN
8040 IF AQ>0 THEN RETURN ELSE IF NN<NT THEN 8030
8050 BEEP:PRINT"NO TASK HAS THIS NUMBER":RETURN
8060 BN=0:NN=0
8070 NN=NN+1:IF NS(NN)=NI THEN BN=NN
8080 IF BN>0 THEN RETURN ELSE IF NN<NM THEN 8070
8090 BEEP:PRINT"NO NODE HAS THIS NUMBER" :RETURN
8100 S1="  0%  5% 10% 15% 20% 25% 30% 40% 50% 60% 70% 75% 80% 85"
8110 S1=S1+"% 90% 95% 100%"
8120 PRINT"THIS ROUTINE ENABLES YOU TO DETERMINE THE EET FOR A NODE"
8130 PRINT"CORRESPONDING TO VARIOUS PROBABILITIES OF ATTAINMENT"
8140 INPUT"ENTER NODE NUMBER FOR DESIRED EVENT (0 TO EXIT)?";NI
8150 IF NI=0 THEN LPRINT CHR$(12)
8160 IF NI=0 THEN 500 ELSE GOSUB 8060
8170 IF BN>0 THEN 8190 ELSE BEEP
8180 PRINT"UNDERSTAND? Y OR N?";R:IF R="Y"THEN 8140 ELSE 8170
8190 PRINT"1-USE PERT METHOD, 2-USE MONTE CARLO METHOD, 3-USE BOTH METHODS"
8200 INPUT"WHICH?";MU:IF MU<1 THEN 8190 ELSE IF MU>3 THEN 8190
8210 LPRINT"NODE NUMBER:";LPRINT USING"#####";NI;:LPRINT USING"!";"":
8220 FOR KK=1 TO 2
8230 FOR M=1 TO MN:EM(M)=0:NEXT M
8240 FOR N=1 TO NT
8250 IF KK=1 THEN DD=D(N,1) ELSE DD=D(N,3)
8260 KV=EM(IO(N))+DD:IF KV>EM(JO(N)) THEN EM(JO(N))=KV
8270 NEXT N
8280 IF KK=1 THEN MC(1)=EM(BN) ELSE MC(2)=EM(BN)
8290 NEXT KK
8300 LPRINT"SMALLEST AND LARGEST POSSIBLE EET'S FOR NODE ARE:";
8310 PRINT"SMALLEST AND LARGEST POSSIBLE EET'S FOR NODE ARE:";
8320 PRINT USING"#####";MC(1),MC(2)
8330 LPRINT USING"#####";MC(1),MC(2)
8340 IF MU=2 THEN 8570
8350 REM ********** PERT SUBROUTINE **********
8360 LPRINT"***** PROBABILITY ANALYSIS BY PERT METHOD *******"
8370 INPUT"HOW MANY ARROWS ON PATH LEADING TO NODE OF INTEREST?";KA
8380 A=0:IF KA=0 THEN 8140 ELSE CV=0
8390 A=A+1:PRINT USING"##";A;:PRINT USING"!";"";:
8400 INPUT"ENTER ARROW NBR?";AV:GOSUB 8020:IF AQ>0 THEN 8430
```

```
AOA-PERT                                                    Page 7 of 7
8410 INPUT"R=RE-ENTER ARROW NUMBER, X=EXIT";R:IF R="R" THEN 8400
8420 IF R="X" THEN 8140 ELSE 8410
8430 VT=((D(AQ,3)-D(AQ,1))/6)^2:CV=CV+VT
8440 LPRINT"TASK NBR";:LPRINT USING"######";AV;:LPRINT USING"!";"";
8450 LPRINT"VARIANCE=";:LPRINT USING"####.##";VT;:LPRINT USING"!";"";:
8460 LPRINT"CUMULATIVE VARIANCE=";:LPRINT USING"######.##";CV
8470 IF A<KA THEN 8390
8480 LPRINT"COMPUTED EVENT DEVIATION=";:LPRINT USING"####.##"; CV^.5
8490 LPRINT"COMPUTED EET'S ROUNDED OFF TO NEAREST WHOLE NUMBER"
8500 LPRINT"PERT PROBABILITY"
8510 LPRINT S1:LT=E(BN):AD=CV^.5
8520 LPRINT USING"####";LT-3*AD,LT-1.645*AD,LT-1.282*AD,LT-1.033*AD;
8530 LPRINT USING"####";LT-.842*AD,LT-.675*AD,LT-.525*AD;
8540 LPRINT USING"####";LT-.253*AD,LT,LT+.253*AD,LT+.525*AD;
8550 LPRINT USING"####";LT+.675*AD,LT+.842*AD,LT+1.033*AD;
8560 LPRINT USING"####";LT+1.282*AD,LT+1.645*AD,LT+3*AD
8570 REM ***** MONTE CARLO ROUTINE *******
8580 IF MU=1 THEN 8000 ELSE INPUT"HOW MANY CYCLES FOR MONTE CARLO ANALYSIS?";X
8590 IF X=0 THEN 8000  ELSE IF X>100 THEN 8580
8600 LPRINT"******** PROBABILITY ANALYSIS BY MONTE CARLO METHOD ******"
8610 LPRINT"PROBABILITY BASED ON";:LPRINT USING"####";X;:LPRINT USING"!";"";
8620 LPRINT"MONTE CARLO SIMULATIONS":LPRINT S1:NA=0
8630 INPUT"ENTER RANDOM NUMBER BETWEEN 0.001 AND .999";XX
8640 FOR N= 1 TO N:IF J(N)>0 AND J(N)=<NI THEN NA=N
8650 NEXT N
8660 FOR K=1 TO X
8670 FOR N=1 TO NA:EM(JO(N))=0:NEXT N
8680 FOR N=1 TO NA:DD=0:OT=D(N,1):MT=D(N,2):PT=D(N,3):IF PT-OT=0 THEN DD=OT
8690 IF PT-OT=0 THEN 8720
8700 AO=(MT-OT)/(PT-OT):Z=RND(XX):IF Z<AO THEN DD=OT+(MT-OT)*((Z/AO)^.5)
8710 IF Z=>AO THEN DD=PT-(PT-MT)*(((1-Z)/(1-AO))^.5)
8720 KV=EM(IO(N))+DD
8730 IF KV>EM(JO(N)) THEN EM(JO(N))=KV
8740 NEXT N
8750 MC(K)=EM(BN):PRINT"CYCLE NBR=";
8760 PRINT USING"####";K;:PRINT USING"!";"";:PRINT"EET=";:PRINT MC(K)
8770 NEXT K:MM=X:PRINT"SORTING VALUES"
8780 MM=INT(MM/2)
8790 IF MM=0 THEN 8860 ELSE 8800
8800 KK=X-MM:JJ=1
8810 II=JJ
8820 LL=II+MM
8830 IF MC(II)>MC(LL) THEN 8840 ELSE 8850
8840 IT=MC(II):MC(II)=MC(LL):MC(LL)=IT:II=II-MM:IF II=>1 THEN 8820 ELSE 8850
8850 JJ=JJ+1:IF JJ>KK THEN 8780 ELSE 8810
8860 LPRINT USING"####";MC(1),MC(.05*X),MC(.1*X),MC(.15*X),MC(.2*X);
8870 LPRINT USING"####";MC(.25*X),MC(.3*X),MC(.4*X),MC(.5*X);
8880 LPRINT USING"####";MC(.6*X),MC(.7*X),MC(.8*X);
8890 LPRINT USING"####";MC(.85*X),MC(.9*X),MC(.95*X),MC(X)
8900 LPRINT"OF EET FOR NODE BEING EQUAL OR LESS THAN ABOVE TIMES."
8910 INPUT"DESIRE COMPLETE LIST OF COMPUTED DURATIONS? Y OR N";R
8920 IF R<>"Y" THEN 8960 ELSE LPRINT"COMPUTED EARLY EVENT TIMES"
8930 FOR K=1 TO X
8940 LPRINT USING"####.##";MC(K);:IF K MOD 10 =0 THEN LPRINT
8950 NEXT K:LPRINT:LPRINT
8960 AA=0:KK=0:AS=99999!:AB=0
8970 FOR K=1 TO X:AA=MC(K)+AA:IF MC(K)<AS THEN AS=MC(K)
8980 IF MC(K)>AB THEN AB=MC(K)
8990 NEXT K
9000 LPRINT"SMALLEST, MEAN, AND MAXIMUM VALUES ARE:";
9010 LPRINT USING"#######.##";AS,AA/X,AB:GOTO 8000
10000 END
```

```
AON-PERT                                          Page  1 of 10
10 REM PROGRAM AON-PERT E.M. Willis. University of North Carolina at Charlotte
20 SCREEN Ø : CLS : KEY OFF
30 DEFSNG A-P:DEFSTR R-T:DEFSNG U-Z
40 PW=80:REM PRINTER WIDTH-REVISE IF NECESSARY
50 MT=125:MR=250
60 DIM A(MT),J(MR),I(MR),D(MT),R(MR),T(MT),FT(MT,2),AN(MR),IO(MR)
70 DIM ES(MT,2),EF(MT,2),LS(MT,2),LF(MT,2),L(MR),NL(MR),NR(MR)
80 DIM AP(MR),AF(MR,2),JO(MR)
90 DIM MC(100),DM(MT,3),LM(MR,3)
110 SD(Ø)="Ø":SD(1)="1":SD(2)="2":SD(3)="3":SD(4)="4":SD(5)="5"
120 SD(6)="6":SD(7)="7":SD(8)="8":SD(9)="9"
500 BEEP:PRINT"LAST ROUTINE EXECUTED WAS :";:PRINT USING"##";LX
510 PRINT"CURRENT TIME IS              :";:PRINT TIME$
520 PRINT"LAST ROUTINE STARTED         :";:PRINT TZ$
530 PRINT"ELAPSED TIME (SECONDS)       :";:PRINT USING"######";TIMER-QX
540 FOR N=1 TO MT:IF A(N)>NT THEN NT=N
550 NEXT N:FOR A=1 TO MR:IF AN(A)<>Ø THEN NR=A
560 NEXT A:
570 PRINT"NUMBER OF TASKS :";:PRINT USING"###";NT
580 PRINT"NUMBER OF ARROWS:";:PRINT USING"###";NR
590 PRINT"FREE RAM SPACE:";:PRINT FRE(Ø)
600 PRINT"1-REVIEW/REVISE TASKS        2-REVIEW/REVISE ARROWS"
610 PRINT"3-SAVE ON DISK               4-READ NETWORK DATA FROM DISK"
620 PRINT"5-ANALYZE NETWORK BY PERT    6-DISPLAY/PRINT PERT SCHEDULE"
630 PRINT"7-PRINT PERT GANTT CHART     8-RESEQUENCE ARROWS"
640 PRINT"9-RESEQUENCE TASKS          10-PERT/MONTE CARLO ROUTINE"
650 PRINT"11-NOT USED                 12-END EXECUTION"
660 INPUT"WHICH OPTION?";O:TZ$=TIME$:LX=O:QX=TIMER
670 ON O GOTO 1000,2000,3000,4000,5000,6000,7000,8000,9000,10000,500,12000
1000 REM******** REVIEW/REVISE TASK ROUTINE***************
1010 GOTO 1060
1020 PRINT:PRINT"SEQ#    TASK#        DURATIONS        DESCRIPTION"
1022 PRINT"                      OPT  MED PESS  EFF"
1024 PRINT:RETURN
1030 ER=1:BEEP:PRINT"SEQUENCE NUMBER IS OUTSIDE THE ALLOWABLE RANGE":RETURN
1040 ER=0:IF N<1 THEN GOSUB 1030 ELSE IF N>MT THEN GOSUB 1030
1050 RETURN
1060 INPUT"REVIEW/REVISE TASKS STARTING WITH SEQUENCE NBR?";N
1070 GOSUB 1040:IF ER=1 THEN 1060 ELSE NI=N
1080 NJ=NI+14:IF NJ>MT THEN NJ=MT
1090 NI=NJ-14
1100 GOSUB 1020
1110 FOR N=NI TO NJ
1120 PRINT USING"####";N;:PRINT USING"########";A(N);
1122 PRINT USING"####";DM(N,1);
1130 PRINT USING"#####";DM(N,2),DM(N,3);:PRINT USING"###.##";D(N);
1132 PRINT USING"!";"";:PRINT T(N)
1140 NEXT N:PRINT:INPUT"R-REVISE, D-DELETE, N-NEXT PAGE, X-EXIT. WHICH";R
1150 IF R="R"THEN 1280 ELSE IF R="D" THEN 1250 ELSE IF R="X" THEN 1180
1160 IF R="N" THEN 1170 ELSE 1100
1170 NI=NI+15:GOTO 1080
1180 NT=0:FOR N=1 TO MT:IF A(N)>0 THEN  BT=N
1190 IF A(N)>0 THEN NT=NT+1
1200 NEXT N:IF BT=NT THEN 500
1210 FOR N=1 TO NT:NN=N:IF A(N)>0 THEN 1240
1220 NN=NN+1:IF A(NN)=0 THEN 1220
1230 A(N)=A(NN):D(N)=D(NN):T(N)=T(NN):A(NN)=0:D(NN)=0:T(NN)=""
1232 D(N)=D(NN):DM(N,1)=DM(NN,1):DM(N,2)=DM(NN,2):DM(N,3)=DM(NN,3)
1240 NEXT N:GOTO 500
1250 INPUT"ENTER SEQUENCE NUMBER OF TASK TO BE DELETED";N:GOSUB 1040
1260 IF ER=1 THEN 1100
```

```
AON-PERT                                                    Page  2 of 10
1270 A(N)=0:D(N)=0:DM(N,1)=0:DM(N,2)=0:DM(N,3)=0:T(N)="":GOTO 1100
1280 INPUT"ENTER SEQUENCE NBR OF TASK TO BE REVISED";N:GOSUB 1040
1290 IF ER=1 THEN 1100 ELSE GOSUB 1020
1300 PRINT USING"####";N;:PRINT USING"########";A(N);
1302 PRINT USING"####";DM(N,1);
1304 PRINT USING"#####";DM(N,2),DM(N,3);:PRINT USING"###.##";D(N)
1306 PRINT USING"!";"";:PRINT T(N)
1310 INPUT"TASK#, OPT DUR, MED DUR, PESS DUR";A(N),DM(N,1),DM(N,2),DM(N,3)
1312 D(N)=(DM(N,1)+4*DM(N,2)+DM(N,3))/6:INPUT"TASK DESCRIPTION (CR IF OK)?";TT
1320 IF TT=""THEN 1100
1330 T(N)=LEFT$(TT,24):GOTO 1100
2000 REM *************REVIEW/REVISE ARROWS ROUTINE*************
2010 GOTO 2050
2020 PRINT
2022 PRINT"SEQ ARROW# TYPE   RELATIONSHIP LAGS   I-NODE# J-NODE#        TF"
2024 PRINT"                  OPT   MED  PESS  EFF"
2026 RETURN
2030 ER=0:IF A<1 THEN GOSUB 1030 ELSE IF A>MR THEN GOSUB 1030
2040 RETURN
2050 INPUT"REVIEW/REVISE ARROWS STARTING WITH SEQUENCE NBR: ?";A
2060 GOSUB 2030:IF ER=1 THEN 2050 ELSE AI=A
2070 IF AI>MR -14 THEN AI=MR-14
2080 AJ=AI+14
2090 GOSUB 2020
2100 FOR A=AI TO AJ:GOSUB 2110:GOTO 2140
2110 PRINT USING"###";A;:PRINT USING"########";AN(A);
2120 PRINT USING"\ \";" ";:PRINT USING"\\";R(A);
2122 PRINT USING"#####";LM(A,1),LM(A,2),LM(A,3);:PRINT USING"#####.#";L(A);
2130 PRINT USING"########";I(A),J(A),AF(A,1):RETURN
2140 NEXT A
2150 PRINT
2160 INPUT"R=REVISE, D=DELETE, N=NEXT SCREEN, I=INSERT ,X=EXIT?";R
2170 IF R="R" THEN 2430 ELSE IF R="D" THEN 2190 ELSE IF R="I" THEN 2230
2180 IF R="X"THEN 2230  ELSE IF R="N" THEN 2220 ELSE 2090
2190 INPUT"SEQUENCE NUMBER TO BE DELETED?";A:GOSUB 2030
2200 IF ER=0 THEN 2210 ELSE 2090
2210 AN(A)=0:LM(A,1)=0:LM(A,2)=0:LM(A,3)=0:L(A)=0:J(A)=0:I(A)=0:R(A)=""
2212 GOTO 2090
2220 AI=AI+15:GOTO 2070
2230 NR=0:FOR A=1 TO MR:IF AN(A)>0 THEN BA=A
2240 IF AN(A)>0 THEN NR=NR+1
2250 NEXT A:IF BA=NR AND R="X" THEN 500
2260 IF BA=NR AND R="I"THEN GOSUB 2350
2270 IF BA=NR AND R="I" THEN 2090
2280 PRINT"CLOSING GAPS IN FILE"
2290 FOR A=1 TO NR:IF AN(A)>0 THEN 2330 ELSE AA=A
2300 AA=AA+1: IF AN(AA)=0 THEN 2300
2310 I(A)=I(AA):J(A)=J(AA):AN(A)=AN(AA):R(A)=R(AA):L(A)=L(AA)
2312 LM(A,1)=LM(AA,1):LM(A,2)=LM(AA,2):LM(A,3)=LM(AA,3)
2320 I(AA)=0:J(AA)=0:L(AA)=0:AN(AA)=0:R(AA)=""
2322 LM(AA,1)=0:LM(AA,2)=0:LM(AA,3)=0
2330 NEXT A:IF R="X" THEN 500
2340 PRINT"GAPS CLOSED. RE-SPECIFY INSERT OPTION":GOTO 2090
2350 INPUT"OPEN A SPACE BEFORE SEQUENCE NUMBER N, ENTER N?";N
2360 IF N=0 THEN 2090
2370 BA=0:FOR A=1 TO MR:IF AN(A)>0 THEN BA=A
2380 NEXT A
2390 FOR A=BA+1 TO N+1 STEP-1
2400 L(A)=L(A-1):I(A)=I(A-1):J(A)=J(A-1):R(A)=R(A-1):AN(A)=AN(A-1)
2402 LM(A,1)=LM(A-1,1):LM(A,2)=LM(A-1,2):LM(A,3)=LM(A-1,3)
2410 NEXT A
```

```
AON-PERT                                          Page  3 of 10
2420 L(N)=0:I(N)=0:J(N)=0:R(N)="":AN(N)=0
2422 LM(N,1)=0:LM(N,2)=0:LM(N,3)=0:GOTO 2070
2430 INPUT"SEQUENCE NUMBER TO BE REVISED?";A:GOSUB 2030
2440 IF ER=1 THEN 2090
2450 GOSUB 2020:GOSUB 2110
2460 PRINT"ENTER ARROW NBR, OPT LAG, MED LAG, PESS LAG, I-NODE#, J-NODE #?"
2462 INPUT AN(A),LM(A,1),LM(A,2),LM(A,3),I(A),J(A)
2464 L(A)=(LM(A,1)+4*LM(A,2)+LM(A,3))/6
2470 INPUT"ENTER TYPE OF ARROW: SS, SE, ES, EE";R(A)
2480 IF R(A)<>"SS" AND R(A)<>"SE" AND R(A)<>"ES" AND R(A)<>"EE"THEN 2470
2490 GOTO 2090
3000 REM **** SAVE DATA ON DISK IN RANDOM FORMAT ************************
3010 INPUT"ENTER NAME OF FILE TO BE SAVED (7 CHARACTERS MAX)";SF$
3020 IF LEN(SF$)>7 THEN 3010
3030 INPUT"SAVE ON DRIVE (A,B,C,ETC)?";SD$
3040 SS$=SD$+":"+SF$:SA$=SS$+"A"
3050 OPEN SS$ AS #1 LEN=32
3060 FOR N=1 TO NT:FIELD #1,2 AS S1,2 AS S2,2 AS S3,2 AS S4, 24 AS S5
3070 LSET S1=MKI$(A(N)):LSET S2=MKI$(DM(N,1)):LSET S3=MKI$(DM(N,2))
3080 LSET S4=MKI$(DM(N,3)):LSET S5=T(N):PUT #1:NEXT N:CLOSE #1
3090 OPEN SA$ AS #2 LEN=14
3092 FOR A=1 TO NR
3100 FIELD #2,2 AS S1,2 AS S2,2 AS S3, 2 AS S4, 2 AS S5, 2 AS S6, 2 AS S7
3110 LSET S1=MKI$(AN(A)):LSET S2=MKI$(LM(A,1)):LSET S3=MKI$(LM(A,2))
3112 LSET S4=MKI$(LM(A,3)):LSET S5=MKI$(I(A)):LSET S6=MKI$(J(A))
3120 LSET S7=R(A):PUT #2:NEXT A:CLOSE #2:GOTO 500
4000 REM **** READ DATA FROM DISK ROUTINE ***********************
4010 INPUT"ENTER NAME OF FILE TO BE READ FROM DISK";RF$
4020 INPUT"ENTER DRIVE FROM WHICH FILE IS TO BE READ (A,B,C,ETC)";RD$
4030 SS$=RD$+":"+RF$:SA$=SS$+"A"
4040 OPEN SS$ AS # 1 LEN=32:N=1
4050 NT=N:FIELD # 1,2 AS S1,2 AS S2,2 AS S3, 2 AS S4, 24 AS S5:GET #1:NI=N
4060 A(N)=CVI(S1):DM(N,1)=CVI(S2):DM(N,2)=CVI(S3):DM(N,3)=CVI(S4):T(N)=S5
4070 IF EOF(1) THEN 4090
4080 N=N+1:GOTO 4050
4090 CLOSE #1
4100 OPEN SA$ AS #2 LEN=14:A=1
4110 FIELD #2, 2 AS S1, 2 AS S2, 2 AS S3, 2 AS S4, 2 AS S5, 2 AS S6, 2 AS S7
4112 GET #2:NR=A
4120 AN(A)=CVI(S1):LM(A,1)=CVI(S2):LM(A,2)=CVI(S3):LM(A,3)=CVI(S4)
4122 I(A)=CVI(S5):J(A)=CVI(S6):R(A)=S7
4130 IF EOF(2) THEN 4150
4140 A=A+1:GOTO 4110
4150 CLOSE #2
4160 FOR N=1 TO NT:D(N)=(DM(N,1)+4*DM(N,2)+DM(N,3))/6:NEXT N
4170 FOR A=1 TO NR:L(A)=(LM(A,1)+4*LM(A,2)+LM(A,3))/6:NEXT A
4180 GOTO 500
5000 REM ***************NETWORK ANALYSIS ROUTINE **************
5010 M=1:INPUT"HAVE YOU RESEQUENCED ARROWS?Y OR N?";R:IF R<>"Y" THEN 500
5020 GOSUB 5030:GOTO 500
5030 FOR N=1 TO NT:ES(N,M)=0:EF(N,M)=D(N):NEXT N
5040 FOR A=1 TO NR:II=IO(A):JJ=JO(A):IF M=1 THEN 5050
5050 IF R(A)="SS" THEN 5070 ELSE IF R(A)="EE" THEN 5090
5060 IF R(A)="ES" THEN 5100 ELSE 5120
5070 MS=ES(II,M)+L(A)
5080 MF=MS+D(JJ):GOTO 5130
5090 MF=EF(II,M)+L(A):MS=0:GOTO 5130
5100 MS=EF(II,M)+L(A)
5110 MF=MS+D(JJ):GOTO 5130
5120 MF=ES(II,M)+L(A):MS=0
5130 IF MS>ES(JJ,M) THEN ES(JJ,M)=MS
```

```
5140 IF MF>EF(JJ,M) THEN EF(JJ,M)=MF
5150 NEXT A:IF M=2 THEN RETURN
5160 BF=0
5170 FOR N=1 TO NT:IF EF(N,M)>BF THEN BF=EF(N,M)
5180 NEXT N
5190 FOR N=1 TO NT:LF(N,M)=BF
5200 LS(N,M)=LF(N,M)-D(N):NEXT N
5210 FOR A=NR TO 1 STEP-1:II=IO(A):JJ=JO(A)
5220 IF R(A)="SS"THEN 5240 ELSE IF R(A)="EE" THEN 5250
5230 IF R(A)= "ES"THEN 5270 ELSE 5290
5240 MS= LS(JJ,M)-L(A):MF=9999:GOTO 5300
5250 MF=LF(JJ,M)-L(A)
5260 MS=MF-D(II):GOTO 5300
5270 MF=LS(JJ,M)-L(A)
5280 MS=MF-D(II):GOTO 5300
5290 MS=LF(JJ,M)-L(A):MF=9999
5300 IF MS<LS(II,M) THEN LS(II,M)=MS
5310 IF MF<LF(II,M) THEN LF(II,M)=MF
5320 NEXT A
5330 FOR N=1 TO NT:FT(N,M)=LF(N,M)-ES(N,M)-D(N):NEXT N
5340 FOR A=1 TO NR:AF(A,M)=0
5350 IF R(A)="ES"THEN AF(A,M)=LS(JO(A),M)-EF(IO(A),M)-L(A) ELSE 5370
5360 GOTO 5420
5370 IF R(A)="SS" THEN AF(A,M)=LS(JO(A),M)-ES(IO(A),M)-L(A) ELSE 5390
5380 GOTO 5420
5390 IF R(A)="EE" THEN AF(A,M)=LF(JO(A),M)-EF(IO(A),M)-L(A) ELSE 5410
5400 GOTO 5420
5410 IF R(A)="SE" THEN AF(A,M)=LF(JO(A),M)-ES(IO(A),M)-L(A)
5420 NEXT A
5430 RETURN
6000 REM ********* DISPLAY/PRINT SCHEDULE ROUTINE ****************************
6005 INPUT"S=SCREEN DISPLAY, H=HARDCOPY , B=BOTH.   WHICH?";R
6010 IF R="S"THEN PM=1 ELSE IF R="H"THEN PM=2 ELSE IF R="B"THEN PM=3 ELSE 6005
6015 CF=1:UP=1
6045 INPUT"C=PRINT SCHEDULE CONTINUOUSLY, P=PRINT SCHEDULE BY PAGES. WHICH?";R
6050 IF R="C"THEN PL=300 ELSE PL=25
6055 INPUT"PRINT/DISPLAY TASKS WITH SEQUENCE NUMBERS I TO J?    I,J=?";IX,JX
6060 IF IX<1 THEN 6055 ELSE IF JX>MT THEN 6055 ELSE IF IX>JX THEN 6055
6065 IF PM=1 THEN 6080 ELSE INPUT"ENTER ONE LINE PROJECT TITLE";TP
6070 IF LEN(TP)=<80 THEN 6080
6075 TP=LEFT$(TP,80):PRINT TP:INPUT"OK";R:IF R="Y"THEN 6080 ELSE 6065
6080 S1="TSK#      DURATIONS          DESCRIPTIO"
6100 S1=S1+"N            ES(ED)  EF(ED) LS(ED) LF(ED) TF"
6102 S2="         OPT MED PESS EFF"
6110 ST$="\                            \":SD="":FOR K=1 TO 15:SD=SD+"   -":NEXT K
6120 S0$="!" :LV=0:P=0
6125 FOR N=IX TO JX:IF A(N)=0 THEN 6140
6130 LV=LV+1:IF LV=1 THEN GOSUB 6155
6135 GOSUB 6215:IF LV=PL THEN LV=0
6140 NEXT N:IF PM<>1 THEN LPRINT CHR$(12)
6145 IF PM<>2 THEN INPUT "CARRIAGE RETURN TO RETURN TO MAIN MENU";R
6150 GOTO 6480
6155 P=P+1:IF PM=1 THEN 6190
6160 IF P>1 THEN LPRINT CHR$(12)
6165 LPRINT"Page No.";:LPRINT USING"###";P;
6185 LPRINT:LPRINT TP:LPRINT
6190 IF PM<>2 THEN PRINT S1
6192 IF PM<>2 THEN PRINT S2
6195 IF PM<>1 AND UP=1 THEN LPRINT S1
6197 IF PM<>1 THEN LPRINT S2
6205 IF PM<>1 THEN LPRINT SD
```

```
6210 RETURN
6215 VA=A(N):VD=D(N):VE=ES(N,1):VF=EF(N,1)
6220 VG=LS(N,1):VH=LF(N,1)
6225 VI=FT(N,1):IF CF=1 THEN 6265
6265 IF PM<>2 AND CF=1 THEN GOSUB 6295
6275 IF PM<>1 AND CF=1 THEN GOSUB 6325
6290 RETURN
6295 PRINT USING"####";VA,DM(N,1),DM(N,2),DM(N,3);
6300 PRINT USING"####";VD;:PRINT USING S0$;"";:PRINT USING ST$;T(N);
6305 PRINT USING"#######";VE,VF,VG,VH;:PRINT USING"####";VI:RETURN
6310 PRINT USING"####";VA,DM(N,1),DM(N,2),DM(N,3);
6315 PRINT USING"####";VD;:PRINT USING S0$;"";:PRINT USING ST$;T(N);
6320 PRINT USING"#######";QA,QB,QC,QD;:PRINT USING"####";VI:RETURN
6325 LPRINT USING"####";VA,DM(N,1),DM(N,2),DM(N,3);
6330 LPRINT USING"####";VD;:LPRINT USING S0$;"";:LPRINT USING ST$;T(N);
6335 LPRINT USING"########";VE,VF,VG,VH;:LPRINT USING"####";VI
6340 LPRINT SD:RETURN
6480 IF RM="S"THEN 500
6485 BEEP:INPUT"DO YOU WANT A LISTING OF LOGICAL RELATIONSHIPS? Y OR ?";R
6490 IF R="N" THEN 500 ELSE IF R="Y" THEN 6495 ELSE 6485
6495 SR="SEQ RLN#      LAGS      I-N# J-N# TYPE AF":SR=SR+"     "+SR
6497 SS="          OPT MED PES            ":SS=SS+"     "+SS
6500 LPRINT SR:LPRINT SS
6505 NL=INT(NR/2):IF 2*NL<NR THEN NL=NL+1
6510 FOR N=1 TO NL:A=N:GOSUB 6520:A=NL+N:GOSUB 6520:LPRINT
6515 NEXT N:LPRINT CHR$(12):GOTO 500
6520 LPRINT USING"###";A;:LPRINT USING"#####";AN(A);
6522 LPRINT USING"####";LM(A,1),LM(A,2),LM(A,3);
6525 LPRINT USING"#####";I(A),J(A);
6530 LPRINT USING"\\";"";:LPRINT R(A);:LPRINT USING"####";AF(A,1);
6535 LPRINT USING"\ \";"";:RETURN
7000 REM ********** PRINT GANTT CHART ROUTINE *****************************
7005 IW=75
7015 INPUT "GANTT CHART FOR SEQUENCE NBRS I TO J. ENTER I,J",IX,JX
7020 IF IX<1 THEN IX=1
7025 IF JX>NT THEN JX=NT
7030 BF =0:SP="":FOR K=1 TO 15:SP=SP+"     +":NEXT K
7035 FOR K=IX TO JX:IF LF(K,1)>BF THEN BF=LF(K,1)
7040 NEXT K
7090 INPUT"1- ES SCHEDULE   , 2- LS SCHEDULE. WHICH?";KS
7100 REM **** BAR CHART IN WORKDATE FORMAT **************
7105 SX=" ":SX=STRING$(75,SX)
7110 NH=INT((JX-IX+1)/PL):IF JX-IX+1>NH*PL THEN NH=NH+1
7115 IV=IX:JV=JX:GOSUB 7165:P1=INT((IR-1)/75)+1:P2=INT((JR-1)/75)+1
7120 FOR P=P1 TO P2:S1$="":S2$="":S3$=""
7125 ID=1+IW*(P-1):JD=ID+IW-1:DD=ID-1
7130 FOR II=ID TO JD:KH=INT(II/100):S1$=S1$+SD(KH):NEXT II
7135 FOR II=ID TO JD:KH=INT(II/100):KT=INT((II-100*KH)/10)
7140 S2$=S2$+SD(KT):NEXT II
7145 FOR II=ID TO JD:KH=INT(II/100):KT=INT((II-100*KH)/10)
7150 KU=INT(II-100*KH-10*KT):S3$=S3$+SD(KU):NEXT II
7155 FOR PP=1 TO NH:IV=IX+PL*(PP-1):JV=IV+PL-1:IF JV>JX THEN JV=JX
7160 GOSUB 7165:GOTO 7185
7165 IR=9999:JR=0:FOR N=IV TO JV:IF AN(N)=0 THEN 7180
7170 IF ES(N,1)+1<IR THEN IR=ES(N,1)+1
7175 IF LF(N,1)>JR THEN JR=LF(N,1)
7180 NEXT N:RETURN
7185 IF JR<ID THEN 7275 ELSE IF IR>JD THEN 7275
7190 PRINT CHR$(12):GOSUB 7290:FOR N=IV TO JV
7195 IF A(N)=0 THEN 7270
7200 SB=SX:IF D(N)=0 THEN 7265
```

```
7205 EB=ES(N,1)+1-DD:EC=EF(N,1)-DD:LC=LF(N,1)-DD:LB=LS(N,1)-DD
7210 IF ABS(FT(N,1))<.01 THEN 7215 ELSE 7220
7215 S$="C":IC=EB:JC=LC:GOSUB 7240:GOTO 7265
7220 S$=".":IC=EB:JC=LC:GOSUB 7240
7225 IF KS=1 THEN 7230 ELSE 7235
7230 S$="e":IC=EB:JC=EC:GOSUB 7240:GOTO 7265
7235 S$="l":IC=LB:JC=LC:GOSUB 7240:GOTO 7265
7240 IF IC>75 THEN RETURN
7245 IF JC<1 THEN RETURN
7250 IF IC<1 THEN IC=1
7255 IF JC>75 THEN JC=75
7260 L=JC-IC+1:S$=STRING$(L,S$):MID$(SB,IC,L)=S$:RETURN
7265 LPRINT SP:LPRINT SB
7270 NEXT N:LPRINT SP:LPRINT CHR$(12)
7275 NEXT PP
7280 NEXT P
7285 GOTO 500
7290 LPRINT"PAGE NO.";:LPRINT USING"###";PP;:LPRINT USING"!";"";
7295 LPRINT "SHEET NO.";:LPRINT USING"###";P :LPRINT TP
7300 LPRINT S1$:LPRINT S2$:LPRINT S3$:RETURN
8000 REM************** RESEQUENCE ARROWS ROUTINE  ****************
8005 PRINT"TO RUN THIS ROUTINE, TASKS MUST BE SEQUENCED IN TASK NUMBER ORDER.
8010 INPUT"DO YOU WANT TO RESEQUENCE TASKS? Y OR N?";R:IF R="Y" THEN 9000
8015 IF R="N"THEN 8065 ELSE 8005
8020 REM****SUBROUTINE FOR FINDING TASKS WITH SPECIFIED TASK NBRS*****
8025 IX=1:JX=NT
8030 MX=INT((IX+JX)/2):IF A(MX)=NV THEN RETURN
8035 IF A(MX)>NV THEN JX=MX ELSE IX=MX
8040 IF A(IX)=NV THEN MX=IX ELSE IF A(JX)=NV THEN MX=JX
8045 IF A(IX)=NV THEN RETURN ELSE IF A(JX)=NV THEN RETURN
8050 IF JX=IX+1 AND A(IX)<>NV THEN MX=0
8055 IF MX=0 THEN RETURN ELSE 8030
8060 REM*****END OF SUBROUTINE************
8065 PRINT"CHECKING THAT NO TASKS HAVE DUPLICATE NODE NUMBERS."
8070 DT=0:FOR N=1 TO NT-1:IF A(N)<>A(N+1) THEN 8085
8075 PRINT "TASK SEQUENCE NUMBERS";:PRINT USING"######";N,N+1;
8080 PRINT USING"!";"";:PRINT"HAVE DUPLICATE TASK NUMBERS":DT=1
8085 NEXT N:IF DT=0 THEN 8100
8090 PRINT"YOU MUST CORRECT BEFORE PROCEEDING. DO YOU UNDERSTAND? Y OR N?"
8095 INPUT"?";R:IF R="Y"THEN 500 ELSE 8090
8100 FOR N=1 TO NT:NL(N)=0:NR(N)=0:NEXT N
8105 PRINT"CHECKING THAT I AND J NODES OF ARROWS ARE DEFINED TASKS"
8110 FOR A=1 TO NR:AP(A)=0:IF R(A)="" THEN 8170
8115 NV=I(A):GOSUB 8025:IF MX<>0 THEN 8140
8120 PRINT"ARROW #";:PRINT USING"#####";AN(A);:PRINT USING"!";"";
8125 PRINT"DOES NOT CONNECT TO A DEFINED TASK AT ITS I END"
8130 INPUT"CARRIAGE RETURN TO CONTINUE";ZZ
8135 GOTO 500
8140 IO(A)=MX:NV=J(A):GOSUB 8025:IF MX<>0 THEN 8160
8145 PRINT "ARROW #";:PRINT USING"####";AN(A);:PRINT USING"!";"";
8150 PRINT "DOES NOT CONNECT TO A DEFINED TASK AT ITS J END"
8155 INPUT"CARRIAGE RETURN TO CONTINUE";ZZZ:GOTO 500
8160 JO(A)=MX:IF RIGHT$(R(A),1)="S" THEN NL(MX)=NL(MX)+1
8165 IF RIGHT$(R(A),1)="E"THEN NR(MX)=NR(MX)+1
8170 NEXT A
8175 PRINT"DETERMINING ARROW SEQUENCE NUMBERS"
8180 FOR A=1 TO NR:AP(A)=0:NEXT A:PN=0
8185 CV=0:PRINT"EXAMINING SINGLE-HEADED ARROWS"
8190 FOR A=1 TO NR:IF AP(A)>0 THEN 8245
8195 IF R(A)="ES"THEN 8205 ELSE IF R(A)="SS"THEN 8215
8200 IF R(A)="EE"THEN 8225 ELSE 8235
```

```
8205 IF NL(IO(A))>0 THEN 8245 ELSE IF NR(IO(A))>0 THEN 8245
8210 PN=PN+1:AP(A)=PN:NL(JO(A))=NL(JO(A))-1:CV=1:GOTO 8245
8215 IF NL(IO(A))>0 THEN 8245
8220 PN=PN+1:AP(A)=PN:NL(JO(A))=NL(JO(A))-1:CV=1:GOTO 8245
8225 IF NL(IO(A))>0 THEN 8245 ELSE IF NR(IO(A))>0 THEN 8245
8230 PN=PN+1:AP(A)=PN:NR(JO(A))=NR(JO(A))-1:CV=1:GOTO 8245
8235 IF NL(IO(A))>0 THEN 8245
8240 PN=PN+1:AP(A)=PN:NR(JO(A))=NR(JO(A))-1:CV=1:GOTO 8245
8245 NEXT A:IF PN=NR THEN 8420
8250 IF CV>0 THEN 8185
8255 CV=0:PRINT"SEARCHING FOR DOUBLE-HEADED ARROWS"
8260 FOR A=1 TO NR:IF AP(A)>0 THEN 8385
8265 IF CV=1 THEN 8385
8270 FOR B=1 TO NR:IF AP(B)>0 THEN 8380 ELSE IF A=B THEN 8380
8275 IF CV=1 THEN 8380
8280 IA=IO(A):IB=IO(B):JA=JO(A):JB=JO(B)
8285 IF IA<> JB THEN 8380
8290 IF R(A)="SS" AND R(B)="SS"THEN 8310
8295 IF R(A)="EE" AND R(B)="EE"THEN 8325
8300 IF R(A)="ES" AND R(B)="SE" THEN 8340 ELSE 8360
8305 IF R(A)="SE" AND R(B)="ES" THEN 8360 ELSE 8380
8310 IF NL(IA)>1 THEN 8380 ELSE IF NL(JA)>1 THEN 8380
8315 PN=PN+1:AP(A)=PN:PN=PN+1:AP(B)=PN:CV=1
8320 NL(IA)=NL(IA)-1:NL(JA)=NL(JA)-1:GOTO 8380
8325 IF NL(IA)=0 AND NL(JA)=0 AND NR(IA)=1 AND NR(JA)=1 THEN 8330 ELSE 8380
8330 PN=PN+1:AP(A)=PN:PN=PN+1:AP(B)=PN:CV=1:NR(IA)=NR(IA)-1:NR(JA)=NR(JA)-1
8335 GOTO 8380
8340 IF NL(IA)>0 THEN 8380 ELSE IF NR(IA)>1 THEN 8380
8345 IF NL(JA)>1 THEN 8380
8350 PN=PN+1:AP(A)=PN:PN=PN+1:AP(B)=PN:CV=1
8355 NR(IA)=NR(IA)-1:NL(JA)=NL(JA)-1:GOTO 8380
8360 IF NL(JA)>0 THEN 8380 ELSE IF NR(JA)>1 THEN 8380
8365 IF NL(IA)>1 THEN 8380
8370 PN=PN+1:AP(A)=PN:PN=PN+1:AP(B)=PN:CV=1
8375 NR(JA)=NR(JA)-1:NL(IA)=NL(IA)-1
8380 NEXT B
8385 NEXT A
8390 IF PN=NR THEN 8420 ELSE IF CV=1 THEN 8185
8395 PRINT"YOU HAVE A LOGIC LOOP OR TOO MANY DOUBLE-HEADED ARROWS"
8400 PRINT"SEQUENCE NUMBERS OF SUSPECT ARROWS ARE:"
8405 FOR A=1 TO NR:IF AP(A)=0 THEN PRINT USING"####";A:
8410 NEXT A
8415 INPUT"UNDERSTAND? Y OR NO:";R:IF R="Y" THEN 500 ELSE 8415
8420 PRINT"RESEQUENCING ARROWS"
8425 NN=NR
8430 MM=NN
8435 MM=INT(MM/2)
8440 IF MM=0 THEN 8520 ELSE 8445
8445 KK=NN-MM
8450 JJ=1
8455 II=JJ
8460 LL=II+MM
8465 IF AP(II) > AP(LL) THEN 8470 ELSE 8510
8470 AT=AN(II):LT=L(II):IT=IO(II):JT=JO(II):RT=R(II):KQ=AP(II)
8472 L1=LM(II,1):L2=LM(II,2):L3=LM(II,3)
8475 IH=I(II):JH=J(II)
8480 AN(II)=AN(LL):L(II)=L(LL):IO(II)=IO(LL):JO(II)=JO(LL):R(II)=R(LL)
8482 LM(II,1)=LM(LL,1):LM(II,2)=LM(LL,2):LM(II,3)=LM(LL,3)
8485 AP(II)=AP(LL):I(II)=I(LL):J(II)=J(LL)
8490 AN(LL)=AT:L(LL)=LT:IO(LL)=IT:JO(LL)=JT:R(LL)=RT:I(LL)=IH:J(LL)=JH
8492 LM(LL,1)=L1:LM(LL,2)=L2:LM(LL,3)=L3
```

```
8495 AP(LL)=KQ
8500 II=II-MM
8505 IF II>=1 THEN 8460 ELSE 8510
8510 JJ=JJ+1
8515 IF JJ>KK THEN 8435 ELSE 8455
8520 PRINT"SUGGEST YOU SAVE THIS ON DISK. UNLESS YOU ADD OR REVISE ARROWS, YOU"
8525 INPUT"CAN DO THIS FASTER IN SUBSEQUENT RUNS. UNDERSTAND? Y OR N?";R
8530 IF R="Y"THEN 500 ELSE 8525
9000 REM ************* RESEQUENCE TASKS ROUTINE *****************
9050 PRINT"ENTRY OF ZERO FOR NBR OF PARAMETERS OR PARAMETER NBR RETURNS TO MAIN
MENU"
9060 PRINT"PARAMETER 1 - TASK NUMBERS"
9070 PRINT"PARAMETER 5 - EARLY START TIME"
9080 PRINT"PARAMETER 6 - EARLY FINISH TIME"
9090 PRINT"PARAMETER 7 - LATE START TIME"
9100 PRINT"PARAMETER 8 - LATE FINISH TIME"
9110 PRINT"PARAMETER 9 - TOTAL FLOAT"
9120 INPUT"HOW MANY PARAMETERS FOR SORTING";NP:IF NP>9 THEN 9120
9130 IF NP=0 THEN 500
9140 PRINT"ENTER PARAMETER CODES WITH MOST SIGNIFICANT PARAMETER FIRST"
9150 FOR L=1 TO NP
9160 INPUT"PARAMETER NBR?";PL(L)
9170 IF PL(L)>1 THEN IF PL(L)<5 THEN PRINT"NOT ALLOWED - RE-ENTER"
9180 IF PL(L)>1 THEN IF PL(L)<5 THEN 9160
9190 IF PL(L)=0 THEN 500
9200 NEXT L
9210 MM=NT
9220 MM=INT(MM/2)
9230 IF MM=0 THEN 9630 ELSE 9240
9240 KK=NT-MM
9250 JJ=1
9260 II=JJ
9270 LL=II+MM
9280 FOR L=1 TO NP
9290 IF PL(L)=1 THEN 9340 ELSE IF PL(L)=2 THEN 9350
9310 IF PL(L)=5 THEN 9380 ELSE IF PL(L)=6 THEN 9390
9320 IF PL(L)=7 THEN 9400 ELSE IF PL(L)=8 THEN 9410
9330 IF PL(L)=9 THEN 9420
9340 VI=A(II):VL=A(LL):GOTO 9425
9380 VI=ES(II,1):VL=ES(LL,1):GOTO 9425
9390 VI=EF(II,1):VL=EF(LL,1):GOTO 9425
9400 VI=LS(II,1):VL=LS(LL,1):GOTO 9425
9410 VI=LF(II,1):VL=LF(LL,1):GOTO 9425
9420 VI=FT(II,1):VL=FT(LL,1:GOTO 9425
9425 IF VI>VL THEN 9440 ELSE IF VI=VL THEN 9430 ELSE 9610
9430 NEXT L
9440 AT= A(II):DT=D(II):TT=T(II):FQ=FT(II,1)
9450 E1=ES(II,1):E2=EF(II,1):L1=LS(II,1):L2=LF(II,1)
9460 ES(II,1)=ES(LL,1):EF(II,1)=EF(LL,1):LS(II,1)=LS(LL,1):LF(II,1)=LF(LL,1)
9470 A(II)=A(LL):D(II)=D(LL):T(II)=T(LL):FT(II,1)=FT(LL,1)
9480 ES(LL,1)=E1:EF(LL,1)=E2:LS(LL,1)=L1:LF(LL,1)=L2 :FT(LL,1)=FQ
9490 A(LL)=AT:D(LL)=DT:T(LL)=TT
9492 D1=DM(II,1):D2=DM(II,2):D3=DM(II,3)
9494 DM(II,1)=DM(LL,1):DM(II,2)=DM(LL,2):DM(II,3)=DM(LL,3)
9496 DM(LL,1)=D1:DM(LL,2)=D2:DM(LL,3)=D3
9590 II=II-MM
9600 IF II=>1 THEN 9270 ELSE 9610
9610 JJ=JJ+1
9620 IF JJ>KK THEN 9220 ELSE 9260
```

```
9630 GOTO 500
10000 REM ****** PERT/MONTE CARLO ROUTINE ************
10010 GOTO 10100
10020 AQ=0:NN=0
10030 NN=NN+1:IF AN(NN)=AV THEN AQ=NN
10040 IF AQ>0 THEN RETURN ELSE IF NN<NR THEN 10030
10050 BEEP:PRINT"NO ARROW HAS THIS NUMBER":RETURN
10060 BN=0:NN=0
10070 NN=NN+1:IF A(NN)=NI THEN BN=NN
10080 IF BN>0 THEN RETURN ELSE IF NN<NT THEN 10070
10090 BEEP:PRINT"NO TASK NODE HAS THIS NUMBER" :RETURN
10100 S1="  0%   5% 10% 15% 20% 25% 30% 40% 50% 60% 70% 75% 80% 85"
10110 S1=S1+"% 90% 95% 100%"
10120 PRINT"THIS ROUTINE ENABLES YOU TO DETERMINE THE EF FOR A TASK"
10130 PRINT"CORRESPONDING TO VARIOUS PROBABILITIES OF ATTAINMENT"
10140 INPUT"ENTER TASK NUMBER FOR ANALYSIS (0 TO EXIT)?";NI:NX=NI
10150 IF NI=0 THEN LPRINT CHR$(12)
10160 IF NI=0 THEN M=1
10170 IF NI=0 THEN 500 ELSE GOSUB 10060
10180 IF BN>0 THEN 10200 ELSE BEEP
10190 INPUT"UNDERSTAND? Y OR N?";R:IF R="Y"THEN 10140 ELSE 10180
10200 PRINT"1-USE PERT METHOD, 2-USE MONTE CARLO METHOD, 3-USE BOTH METHODS"
10210 INPUT"WHICH?";MU:IF MU<1 THEN 10200 ELSE IF MU>3 THEN 10200
10220 LPRINT"TASK NUMBER:";:LPRINT USING"#####";NI:M=2
10230 FOR KK=1 TO 2
10240 FOR N=1 TO NT:D(N)=DM(N,1):NEXT N
10250 FOR A=1 TO NR:L(A)=LM(A,1):NEXT A:GOSUB 5030:MC(1)=EF(BN,2)
10260 FOR N=1 TO NT:D(N)=DM(N,3):NEXT N
10270 FOR A=1 TO NR:L(A)=LM(A,3):NEXT A:GOSUB 5030:MC(2)=EF(BN,2)
10280 FOR N=1 TO NT:D(N)=(DM(N,1)+4*DM(N,2)+DM(N,3))/6:NEXT N
10290 FOR A=1 TO NR:L(A)=(LM(A,1)+4*LM(A,2)+LM(A,3))/6:NEXT A:GOSUB 5030
10300 NEXT KK
10310 LPRINT"SMALLEST AND LARGEST POSSIBLE EF TIMES FOR TASK ARE:";
10320 PRINT"SMALLEST AND LARGEST POSSIBLE EF TIMES FOR TASK ARE:";
10330 PRINT USING"#####";MC(1),MC(2)
10340 LPRINT USING"#####";MC(1),MC(2)
10350 IF MU=2 THEN 10710
10360 REM *********** PERT SUBROUTINE ************
10370 LPRINT"***** PROBABILITY ANALYSIS BY PERT METHOD *******"
10380 INPUT"HOW MANY ARROWS ON PATH LEADING TO TASK NODE OF INTEREST?";KA
10390 A=0:CV=0:IF KA=0 THEN 10450
10400 A=A+1:PRINT USING"##";A;:PRINT USING"!";"";:
10410 INPUT"ENTER ARROW NBR?";AV:GOSUB 10020:IF AQ>0 THEN 10440
10420 INPUT"R=RE-ENTER ARROW NUMBER, X=EXIT";R:IF R="R" THEN 10410
10430 IF R="X" THEN 10140 ELSE 10420
10440 GOSUB 10530:IF A<KA THEN 10400
10450 PRINT"HOW MANY NODES ON PATH LEADING TO TASK NODE OF INTEREST?"
10460 INPUT"INCLUDE THE NODE OF INTEREST?";KN
10470 A=0:IF KN=0 THEN 10140
10480 A=A+1:PRINT USING"##";A;:PRINT USING"!";"";:
10490 INPUT"ENTER TASK NBR?";NI:GOSUB 10060:IF BN>0 THEN 10520
10500 INPUT"R=RE-ENTER TASK NUMBER, X=EXIT";R:IF R="R" THEN 10480
10510 IF R="X" THEN 10140 ELSE 10480
10520 GOSUB 10570:IF A<KN THEN 10480 ELSE 10610
10530 VA=((LM(AQ,3)-LM(AQ,1))/6)^2:CV=CV+VA
10540 LPRINT"ARROW NBR";:LPRINT USING"######";AV;:LPRINT USING"!";"";
10550 LPRINT"VARIANCE=";:LPRINT USING"####.##";VA;:LPRINT USING"!";"";:
10560 LPRINT"CUMULATIVE VARIANCE=";:LPRINT USING"######.##";CV:RETURN
10570 VT=((DM(BN,3)-DM(BN,1))/6)^2:CV=CV+VT
10580 LPRINT"TASK NBR";:LPRINT USING"######";NI;:LPRINT USING"!";"";
10590 LPRINT"VARIANCE=";:LPRINT USING"####.##";VT;:LPRINT USING"!";"";:
```

```
10600 LPRINT"CUMULATIVE VARIANCE=";:LPRINT USING"######.##";CV:RETURN
10610 NI=NX:GOSUB 10060
10620 LPRINT"COMPUTED EVENT DEVIATION=";:LPRINT USING"####.##"; CV^.5
10630 LPRINT"COMPUTED EF TIMES ROUNDED OFF TO NEAREST WHOLE NUMBER"
10640 LPRINT"PERT PROBABILITY"
10650 LPRINT S1:LT=EF(BN,2):AD=CV^.5
10660 LPRINT USING"####";LT-3*AD,LT-1.645*AD,LT-1.282*AD;
10670 LPRINT USING"####";LT-.842*AD,LT-.675*AD,LT-.525*AD;
10680 LPRINT USING"####";LT-.253*AD,LT,LT+.253*AD,LT+.525*AD;
10690 LPRINT USING"####";LT+.675*AD,LT+.842*AD,LT+1.033*AD;
10700 LPRINT USING"####";LT+1.282*AD,LT+1.645*AD,LT+3*AD
10710 REM ***** MONTE CARLO ROUTINE *******
10720 IF MU=1 THEN 10000 ELSE INPUT"HOW MANY CYCLES FOR MONTE CARLO ANALYSIS?";X
10730 IF X=0 THEN 10000  ELSE IF X>100 THEN 10720
10740 LPRINT"******** PROBABILITY ANALYSIS BY MONTE CARLO METHOD ******"
10750 LPRINT"PROBABILITY BASED ON";:LPRINT USING"####";X;:LPRINT USING"!";"";
10760 LPRINT"MONTE CARLO SIMULATIONS":LPRINT S1:NA=0
10770 INPUT"ENTER RANDOM NUMBER BETWEEN 0.001 AND .999";XX
10780 FOR K=1 TO X
10790 FOR N=1 TO NT:ES(N,2)=0:EF(N,2)=0:NEXT N
10800 FOR N=1 TO NT:OT=DM(N,1):CT=DM(N,2):PT=DM(N,3):IF PT-OT<>0 THEN 10820
10810 D(N)=OT:GOTO 10840
10820 AO=(CT-OT)/(PT-OT):Z=RND(XX):IF Z<AO THEN D(N)=OT+(CT-OT)*((Z/AO)^.5)
10830 IF Z=>AO THEN D(N)=PT-(PT-CT)*(((1-Z)/(1-AO))^.5)
10840 NEXT N
10850 FOR A=1 TO NR:OT=LM(N,1):CT=LM(N,2):PT=LM(N,3):IF PT-OT<>0 THEN 10870
10860 L(A)=OT:GOTO 10890
10870 AO=(CT-OT)/(PT-OT):Z=RND(XX):IF Z<AO THEN L(A)=OT+(CT-OT)*((Z/AO)^.5)
10880 IF Z=>AO THEN L(A)=PT-(PT-CT)*(((1-Z)/(1-AO))^.5)
10890 NEXT A
10900 GOSUB 5030:MC(K)=EF(BN,2)
10910 PRINT"CYCLE NBR=";
10920 PRINT USING"####";K;:PRINT USING"!";"";:PRINT"EF=";:PRINT MC(K)
10930 NEXT K:MM=X:PRINT"SORTING VALUES"
10940 MM=INT(MM/2)
10950 IF MM=0 THEN 11020 ELSE 10960
10960 KK=X-MM:JJ=1
10970 II=JJ
10980 LL=II+MM
10990 IF MC(II)>MC(LL) THEN 11000 ELSE 11010
11000 IT=MC(II):MC(II)=MC(LL):MC(LL)=IT:II=II-MM:IF II=>1 THEN 10980 ELSE 11010
11010 JJ=JJ+1:IF JJ>KK THEN 10940 ELSE 10970
11020 LPRINT USING"####";MC(1),MC(.05*X),MC(.1*X),MC(.15*X),MC(.2*X);
11030 LPRINT USING"####";MC(.25*X),MC(.3*X),MC(.4*X),MC(.5*X);
11040 LPRINT USING"####";MC(.6*X),MC(.7*X),MC(.75*X),MC(.8*X);
11050 LPRINT USING"####";MC(.85*X),MC(.9*X),MC(.95*X),MC(X)
11060 LPRINT"OF EF TIME BEING EQUAL OR LESS THAN ABOVE TIMES."
11070 INPUT"DESIRE COMPLETE LIST OF COMPUTED DURATIONS? Y OR N";R
11080 IF R<>"Y" THEN 11120 ELSE LPRINT"COMPUTED EARLY EVENT TIMES"
11090 FOR K=1 TO X
11100 LPRINT USING"####.##";MC(K);:IF K MOD 10 =0 THEN LPRINT
11110 NEXT K:LPRINT:LPRINT
11120 AA=0:KK=0:AS=99999!:AB=0
11130 FOR K=1 TO X:AA=MC(K)+AA:IF MC(K)<AS THEN AS=MC(K)
11140 IF MC(K)>AB THEN AB=MC(K)
11150 NEXT K
11160 LPRINT"SMALLEST, MEAN, AND MAXIMUM VALUES ARE:";
11170 LPRINT USING"#######.##";AS,AA/X,AB
11180 FOR N=1 TO NT:D(N)=(DM(N,1)+4*DM(N,2)+DM(N,3))/6:NEXT N
11190 FOR A=1 TO NR:L(A)=(LM(A,1)+4*LM(A,2)+LM(A,3))/6:NEXT A:GOTO 10000
12000 END:REM ***************** END EXECUTUION *************************
```

```
RAMTEST1 and RAMTEST2                                    Page 1 of 1
10 REM RAMTEST1 - FILE GENERATOR PROGRAM FOR AOA NETWORKS
20 DEFINT A-P:DEFSTR R-T:DEFSNG Q:DEFINT U-Z
30 S$="A":S$=STRING$(24,S$):INPUT "NBR OF TASKS?";NT
40 INPUT"ENTER NAME OF FILE TO BE SAVED (8 CHARACTERS MAX)";SF$
50 IF LEN(SF$)>8 THEN 40 ELSE INPUT"SAVE ON DRIVE (A,B,C,ETC)?";SD$
60 SS$=SD$+":"+SF$
70 INPUT"S=SINGLE TASK DURATION, M=MULTIPLE TASK DURATIONS?";R
80 IF R="S"THEN 90 ELSE IF R="M" THEN 150 ELSE 70
90 DIM A(NT),I(NT),J(NT),D(NT),T(NT)
100 FOR N=1 TO NT:I(N)=N:J(N)=N+1:D(N)=1:T(N)=S$:A(N)=N :NEXT N
110 OPEN SS$ AS #1 LEN=32:FOR N=1 TO NT
120 FIELD #1,2 AS S1,2 AS S2,2 AS S3,2 AS S4,24 AS S5
130 LSET S1=MKI$(A(N)):LSET S2=MKI$(I(N)):LSET S3=MKI$(J(N))
140 LSET S4=MKI$(D(N)):LSET S5=T(N):PUT #1:NEXT N:CLOSE #1:GOTO 230
150 DIM A(NT),I(NT),J(NT),D(NT,3),T(NT)
160 FOR N=1 TO NT:I(N)=N:J(N)=N+1:T(N)=S$:A(N)=N
170 D(N,1)=1:D(N,2)=2:D(N,3)=3:NEXT N
180 OPEN SS$ AS #1 LEN=36:FOR N=1 TO NT
190 FIELD #1,2 AS S1,2 AS S2,2 AS S3,2 AS S4,2 AS S5, 2 AS S6,24 AS S7
200 LSET S1=MKI$(A(N)):LSET S2=MKI$(I(N)):LSET S3=MKI$(J(N))
210 LSET S4=MKI$(D(N,1)):LSET S5=MKI$(D(N,2)):LSET S6=MKI$(D(N,3)):LSET S7=T(N)
220 PUT #1:NEXT N:CLOSE #1
230 END
10 REM PROGRAM RAMTEST2 - FILE GENERATOR FOR ACTIVITY ON NODE NETWORKS
20 DEFINT A-P:DEFSTR R-W:T$="A":S$=STRING$(24,T$)
30 INPUT"NUMBER OF TASKS,NUMBER OF ARROWS";MT,MR:IF MR>MT THEN AA=MT-1 ELSE 30
40 INPUT"ENTER NAME OF FILE TO BE SAVED (7 CHARACTERS MAX)";SF$
50 IF LEN(SF$)>7 THEN 40 ELSE INPUT"SAVE ON DRIVE (A,B,C,ETC)?";SD$
60 SS$=SD$+":"+SF$:SA$=SS$+"A"
70 INPUT"DURATIONS AND LAGS: S=SINGLE VALUES, M=MULTIPLE VALUES?";R
80 IF R="S" THEN 90 ELSE IF R="M" THEN 220 ELSE 70
90 DIM A(MT),D(MT),AN(MR),L(MR),I(MR),J(MR),R(MR),T(MT)
100 FOR N=1 TO MT:A(N)=N:D(N)=1:T(N)=S$:NEXT N
110 FOR A=1 TO MT-1:AN(A)=A:L(A)=1:I(A)=A:J(A)=A+1:R(A)="ES":NEXT A :K=0
120 K=K+1:A=K+AA:AN(A)=A:I(A)=K:J(A)=K+1:L(A)=1
130 IF A MOD 2=0 THEN R(A)="SS" ELSE R(A)="EE"
140 IF A>=MR THEN 160 ELSE IF K<MT-1 THEN 120
150 K=0:AA=AA+MT-1:PRINT"AA=";:PRINT AA:GOTO 120
160 OPEN SS$ AS #1 LEN=28:FOR N=1 TO MT:FIELD #1,2 AS S1,2 AS S2,24 AS S3
170 LSET S1=MKI$(A(N)):LSET S2=MKI$(D(N)):LSET S3=T(N):PUT #1
180 NEXT N:CLOSE #1:OPEN SA$ AS #2 LEN=10
190 FOR A=1 TO MR:FIELD #2,2 AS S1,2 AS S2,2 AS S3, 2 AS S4, 2 AS S5
200 LSET S1=MKI$(AN(A)):LSET S2=MKI$(L(A)):LSET S3=MKI$(I(A))
210 LSET S4=MKI$(J(A)):LSET S5=R(A):PUT #2:NEXT A:CLOSE #2:GOTO 390
220 DIM A(MT),D(MT,3),AN(MR),L(MR,3),I(MR),J(MR),R(MR),T(MT)
230 FOR N=1 TO MT:A(N)=N:D(N,1)=1:D(N,2)=2:D(N,3)=3:T(N)=S$:NEXT N
240 FOR A=1 TO MT-1:AN(A)=A:L(A,1)=1:L(A,2)=2:L(A,3)=3:I(A)=A:J(A)=A+1
250 R(A)="ES":NEXT A:K=0
260 K=K+1:A=K+AA:AN(A)=A:I(A)=K:J(A)=K+1:L(A,1)=1:L(A,2)=2:L(A,3)=3
270 IF A MOD 2=0 THEN R(A)="SS" ELSE R(A)="EE"
280 IF A=MR THEN 300 ELSE IF K<MT-1 THEN 260
290 K=0:AA=AA+MT-1:GOTO 260
300 OPEN SS$ AS #1 LEN=32
310 FOR N=1 TO MT:FIELD #1,2 AS S1,2 AS S2,2 AS S3,2 AS S4,24 AS S5
320 LSET S1=MKI$(A(N)):LSET S2=MKI$(D(N,1)):LSET S3=MKI$(D(N,2))
330 LSET S4=MKI$(D(N,3)):LSET S5=T(N):PUT #1:NEXT N:CLOSE #1
340 OPEN SA$ AS #2 LEN=14:FOR A=1 TO MR
350 FIELD #2,2 AS S1,2 AS S2,2 AS S3,2 AS S4,2 AS S5,2 AS S6,2 AS S7
360 LSET S1=MKI$(AN(A)):LSET S2=MKI$(L(A,1)):LSET S3=MKI$(L(A,2))
370 LSET S4=MKI$(L(A,3)):LSET S5=MKI$(I(A))
380 LSET S6=MKI$(J(A)):LSET S7=R(A):PUT #2:NEXT A:CLOSE #2:GOTO 390
390 END
```

Program listing for Program JULIAN   Page 1 of 1

```
10 CLEAR 10000
20 DEFINT I:DEFINT K:DEFINT M-N:DEFINT Y:DEFINT D
30 DEFSTR W:DEFSTR L:DEFSTR J:DEFSTR V
40 DIM W(7),J(12,31),L(12),V(11),K(12)
50 V(0)="0":V(1)="1":V(2)="2":V(3)="3":V(4)="4":V(5)="5":V(6)="6"
60 V(7)="7":V(8)="8":V(9)="9"
70 W(0)=" "
80 W(1)="S":W(2)="M":W(3)="T":W(4)="W":W(5)="T":W(6)="F":W(7)="S"
90 L(1)="JAN":L(2)="FEB":L(3)="MAR":L(4)="APR":L(5)="MAY":L(6)="JUN"
100 L(7)="JUL":L(8)="AUG":L(9)="SEP":L(10)="OCT":L(11)="NOV":L(12)="DEC"
110 K(1)=31:K(2)=28:K(3)=31:K(4)=30:K(5)=31:K(6)=30
120 K(7)=31:K(8)=31:K(9)=30:K(10)=31:K(11)=30:K(12)=31
130 INPUT"ENTER YEAR FOR WHICH JULIAN CALENDAR IS DESIRED";Y
140 PRINT"ENTER DAY OF WEEK (SUNDAY =1) FOR JANUARY 1,";
150 PRINT USING"####";Y
160 INPUT ID
170 IF ID>7 THEN 140 ELSE IF ID<1 THEN 140
180 IF INT(Y/4)=Y/4 THEN K(2)=29 ELSE K(2)=28
190 IJ=1
200 FOR M=1 TO 12
210 FOR D=1 TO K(M)
220 J(M,D)="     "
230 NEXT D
240 NEXT M
250 FOR M=1 TO 12
260 FOR D=1 TO K(M)
270 D1=INT(IJ/100):D2=INT((IJ-100*D1)/10):D3=IJ-100*D1-10*D2
280 J(M,D)=W(ID)+V(D1)+V(D2)+V(D3)
290 IJ=IJ+1:ID=ID+1:IF ID>7 THEN ID=1
300 NEXT D
310 NEXT M
320 N=1
330 LPRINT
340 LPRINT" DAY OF WEEK AND JULIAN DATE FOR CALENDAR YEAR",Y
350 IF N=1 THEN LPRINT
360 LPRINT"DOM";:LPRINT USING"®®";"    ";
370 FOR M=1 TO 12:LPRINT USING"®     ®";L(M);:NEXT M:LPRINT
380 FOR D=1 TO 31
390 IF N=1 THEN LPRINT
400 LPRINT USING"###";D;:LPRINT USING"!";" ";
410 FOR M=1 TO 12
420 LPRINT USING"®     ®";J(M,D);
430 NEXT M
440 LPRINT
450 N=N+1:IF N>5 THEN N=1
460 NEXT D
470 GOTO 130
```

```
LAST ROUTINE EXECUTED WAS: 3
CURRENT TIME IS     : 01:04:11
LAST ROUTINE STARTED: 01:04:03
ELAPSED TIME (SECONDS)   :        9
******** MAIN MENU ********
NBR TASKS = 6
FREE RAM SPACE= 13911
1 - REVIEW/REVISE/DELETE NETWORK DATA
2 - SAVE DATA IN RANDOM FORMAT ON DISK.
3 - READ DATA FROM DISK
4 - ANALYZE NETWORK
5 - PRINT SCHEDULE
6 - PRINT GANTT CHART
7 - RESEQUENCE TASKS
8 - READ WORKDATE/CALENDARDATE CONVERSION DATA
9 - UPDATE SCHEDULE
10 - END EXECUTION
SELECT OPTION?? 1
```

Screen 1 - CPM Main Menu After Reading Network Data From Disk

```
SEQ TASK# I-# J-# DUR DESCRIPTION                   AS       AF      PS      PF STAT

 1    10   10   20    5 CONSTRUCT FOOTINGS       850114 850118       0       0 100
 2    20   20   30    5 POUR FLOOR SLAB          850121 850125       0       0 100
 3    30   30   40   10 ERECT WALLS              850128      0       0 850208  40
 4    15   10   50   35 PROC INT FINISH MAT'LS   850121      0       0 850304  25
 5    40   40   50   10 ERECT ROOF                    0      0       0      0   0
 6    50   50   60   10 FINISH INTERIOR               0      0       0      0   0
ENTER R-REVISE, N-NEXT PAGE, X-EXIT?? R
CHANGE UPDATE DATA FOR SEQUENCE NBR?? 4
SEQ TASK# I-# J-# DUR DESCRIPTION                   AS       AF      PS      PF STAT

UPDATE: 850131
SEQ TASK# I-# J-# DUR DESCRIPTION                   AS       AF      PS      PF STAT

 4    15   10   50   35 PROC INT FINISH MAT'LS   850121      0       0 850304  25
CHANGE: 1-ACTUAL START       2-ACTUAL FINISH      3-PROJECTED START
        4-PROJECTED FINISH  5-PERCENT COMPLETE    6-DELETE ENTRY
        0-NO MORE CHANGES                         WHICH?? 4
BASED ON PROGRESS SINCE START,PROJECTED FINISH IS: 850311
BASED ON ESTIMATED DURATION, PROJECTED FINISH IS: 850308
ENTER PROJECTED FINISH DATE. M,D,Y?? 3,8,85
```

Screen 2 - Terminal Display During Update Routine, Programs CPM and AON

```
SET TERMINAL IN UPPERCASE MODE
YOU MAY: 1 - RECALL SAVED CALENDAR DATA FROM DISK
         2 - DEFINE A WORKDAY CALENDAR
WHICH?? 2
YOU MAY DESIGNATE ANY NUMBER OF DAYS OF THE WEEK AS NON-WORK
DAYS AND ANY CALENDAR DATE AS NON-WORK DATES. USE THE
M,D,Y FORMAT WHEN DESIGNATING CALENDAR DATES AS NON-WORK DATES.
PROJECT START DATE (M,D,Y EXAMPLE 2,3,86)?? 1,14,85
   1 14 85 IS A MON
OK- Y OR N?? Y
PLEASE WAIT ABOUT A MINUTE FOR CALENDAR CONSTRUCTION
SUN IS THIS A WORKDAY? Y OR N?? N
MON IS THIS A WORKDAY? Y OR N?? Y
TUE IS THIS A WORKDAY? Y OR N?? Y
WED IS THIS A WORKDAY? Y OR N?? Y
THU IS THIS A WORKDAY? Y OR N?? Y
FRI IS THIS A WORKDAY? Y OR N?? Y
SAT IS THIS A WORKDAY? Y OR N?? N
ENTER NON-WORK CALENDAR DATES (M,D,Y)?? 1,1,85
NO SUCH DATE IN THIS CALENDAR
ENTER NON-WORK CALENDAR DATES (M,D,Y)?? 1,1,86
ENTER NON-WORK CALENDAR DATES (M,D,Y)?? 1,1,87
ENTER NON-WORK CALENDAR DATES (M,D,Y)?? 1,1,88



ENTER NON-WORK CALENDAR DATES (M,D,Y)?? 7,4,85
ENTER NON-WORK CALENDAR DATES (M,D,Y)?? 7,4,86
ENTER NON-WORK CALENDAR DATES (M,D,Y)?? 7,4,87
ENTER NON-WORK CALENDAR DATES (M,D,Y)?? 12,25,85
ENTER NON-WORK CALENDAR DATES (M,D,Y)?? 12,25,86
ENTER NON-WORK CALENDAR DATES (M,D,Y)?? 12,25,87
ENTER NON-WORK CALENDAR DATES (M,D,Y)?? 0,0,0
PLEASE WAIT ABOUT A MINUTE
THERE ARE  777 WORKDATES IN THIS CALENDAR. LINE PRINT X WD/CD VALUES? X=? 0
Y TO SAVE ON DISK, N TO RETURN TO MAIN MENU?? Y
ENTER NAME OF CALENDAR FILE TO BE SAVED (8 CHARACTERS MAX)? C850114
SAVE ON DRIVE (A,B,C,ETC)?? B
```

Screen 3 — Use of Program REGIME to Specify Non-work Days and Dates

Page No. 1   UDATED 850131

PROJECT 1

TSK#	I-N#	J-N#	DUR	DESCRIPTION	ES/RVS	EF/RVS	LS/RVS	LF/RVS	TF	FF
10	10	20	5	CONSTRUCT FOOTINGS	850114	850118	850121	850125	5	0
			5	AS=850114 AF=850118	850114	850118	850128	850201	10	0
				SCH%= 100 ACT%= 100						
20	20	30	5	POUR FLOOR SLAB	850121	850125	850128	850201	5	0
			5	AS=850121 AF=850125	850121	850125	850204	850208	10	0
				SCH%= 100 ACT%= 100						
30	30	40	10	ERECT WALLS	850128	850208	850204	850215	5	0
			10	AS=850128 PF=850208	850128	850208	850211	850222	10	0
				SCH%= 40 ACT%= 40						
15	10	50	35	PROC INT FINISH MAT`LS	850114	850301	850114	850301	0	0
			40	AS=850121 PF=850308	850114	850308	850114	850308	0	0
				SCH%= 40 ACT%= 25						
40	40	50	10	ERECT ROOF	850211	850222	850218	850301	5	5
					850211	850222	850225	850308	10	10
50	50	60	10	FINISH INTERIOR	850304	850315	850304	850315	0	0
					850311	850322	850311	850322	0	0

Output 1 — Schedule by Program CPM With Calendardating and Update Data Reflected

PAGE NO. 1 SHEET NO. 1 UPDATED   850131

```
JAN85      JAN85     FEB85     FEB85     FEB85     MAR85     MAR85     MAR85
111111222222222233000000000011111111112222222222000000000011111111112222222222
45678901234567890112345678901234567890123456781234567890123456789012345678  9
             --        --        --        --        --        --        --        --
eeeee  .....
aaaaa  .....  .....
       --        --        --        --        --        --        --        --
       eeeee  .....
       aaaaa  .....  .....
       --        --        --        --        --        --        --        --
              eeeee eeeee  .....
              aaaap ppppp  .....  .....
       --        --        --        --        --        --        --        --
CCCCC CCCCC CCCCC CCCCC CCCCC CCCCC CCCCC
DDDDD AAAAA AAAAP PPPPP PPPPP PPPPP PPPPP PPPPP
       --        --        --        --        --        --        --        --
                           eeeee eeeee  .....
                           rrrrr rrrrr  .....  .....
       --        --        --        --        --        --        --        --
                                                  CCCCC CCCCC
                                                        RRRRR RRRRR
       --        --        --        --        --        --        --        --
00000 00000 00000 00000 00000 00000 00000 00000 00000 00000 00000
00000 00001 11111 11112 22222 22223 33333 33334 44444 44445 55555
12345 67890 12345 67890 12345 67890 12345 67890 12345 67890 12345
```

Output 2 — Bar Chart To Be Taped Aside Output 1

```
Page No.  1        UDATED 850131

PROJECT 1

TSK# DUR DESCRIPTION              ES/RVS EF/RVS LS/RVS LF/RVS  TF
  -   -   -   -   -   -   -   -    -      -      -      -      -   -   -
  10   5 CONSTRUCT FOOTINGS        850114 850118 850121 850125  5
       5 AS=850114 AF=850118
         SCH%= 100 ACT%= 100 -     -      -      -      -      -   -   -
  15  35 PROC INT FINISH MAT'LS    850114 850301 850114 850301  0
         AS=850121 PF=850308
         SCH%=  40 ACT%=  25 -     -      -      -      -      -   -   -
  20   5 POUR FLOOR SLAB           850121 850125 850128 850201  5
       5 AS=850121 AF=850125
         SCH%= 100 ACT%= 100 -     -      -      -      -      -   -   -
  30  10 ERECT WALLS               850128 850208 850204 850215  5
         AS=850128 PF=850208
         SCH%=  40 ACT%=  40 -     -      -      -      -      -   -   -
  40  10 ERECT ROOF                850211 850222 850218 850301  5
                                   850211 850222 850225 850308 10
  -   -   -   -   -   -   -   -    -      -      -      -      -   -   -
  50  10 FINISH INTERIOR           850304 850315 850304 850315  0
                                   850311 850322 850311 850322  0
  -   -   -   -   -   -   -   -    -      -      -      -      -   -   -
```

Output 3 — Schedule by Program AON With Calendardating and Update Data Reflected

LOGICAL RELATIONSHIPS

SEQ	RLTSHP#	LAG	I-N#	J-N#	TYPE	AF	SEQ	RLTSHP#	LAG	I-N#	J-N#	TYPE	AF
1	10	0	10	20	ES	5	4	40	0	40	50	ES	5
2	20	0	20	30	ES	5	5	15	0	15	50	ES	0
3	30	0	30	40	ES	5	6	0	0	0	0		0

Output 4 — Logical Relationships Used For Schedule Shown in Output 3

Page No.   1
PROJECT 1

| TSK# | DURATIONS | | | | DESCRIPTION | ES(ED) | EF(ED) | LS(ED) | LF(ED) | TF |
	OPT	MED	PESS	EFF						
	—	—	—	—	—	—	—	—	—	—
10	4	5	6	5	CONSTRUCT FOOTINGS	0	5	5	10	5
	—	—	—	—	—	—	—	—	—	—
15	30	35	40	35	PROC INT FINISH MAT'LS	0	35	0	35	0
	—	—	—	—	—	—	—	—	—	—
20	4	5	6	5	POUR FLOOR SLAB	5	10	10	15	5
	—	—	—	—	—	—	—	—	—	—
30	8	10	12	10	ERECT WALLS	10	20	15	25	5
	—	—	—	—	—	—	—	—	—	—
40	8	10	12	10	ERECT ROOF	20	30	25	35	5
	—	—	—	—	—	—	—	—	—	—
50	8	10	12	10	FINISH INTERIOR	35	45	35	45	0
	—	—	—	—	—	—	—	—	—	—

Output 5 - PERT Schedule by Program AON-PERT

| SEQ | RLN# | LAGS | | | I-N# | J-N# | TYPE | AF | SEQ | RLN# | LAGS | | | I-N# | J-N# | TYPE | AF |
		OPT	MED	PES							OPT	MED	PES				
1	10	0	0	0	10	20	ES	5	4	40	0	0	0	40	50	ES	5
2	20	0	0	0	20	30	ES	5	5	15	0	0	0	15	50	ES	0
3	30	0	0	0	30	40	ES	5	6	0	0	0	0	0	0		0

Output 6 - Logical Relationships for Project 1

PAGE NO.   1 SHEET NO.   1

```
0000000000000000000000000000000000000000000000000000000000000000000000000000
0000000000111111111122222222223333333333444444444455555555556666666666777777
12345678901234567890123456789012345678901234567890123456789012345678901234567890123456789012345
  +    +    +    +    +    +    +    +    +    +    +    +    +    +    +    +
eeeee.....
  +    +    +    +    +    +    +    +    +    +    +    +    +    +    +    +
CCCCCCCCCCCCCCCCCCCCCCCCCCCCCCCCCCCCC
  +    +    +    +    +    +    +    +    +    +    +    +    +    +    +    +
    eeeee.....
  +    +    +    +    +    +    +    +    +    +    +    +    +    +    +    +
      eeeeeeeeee.....
  +    +    +    +    +    +    +    +    +    +    +    +    +    +    +    +
        eeeeeeeeee.....
  +    +    +    +    +    +    +    +    +    +    +    +    +    +    +    +
                    CCCCCCCCCC
  +    +    +    +    +    +    +    +    +    +    +    +    +    +    +    +
```

Output 7 - PERT Bar Chart To Be Taped Aside Output 5

TABLE OF RANDOM NUMBERS

25	31	31	52	6	79	50	36	98	90	73	1	97	0	96
4	90	66	55	82	91	86	87	51	58	45	87	3	60	78
29	78	14	23	22	88	86	57	36	3	88	76	20	61	37
23	75	26	93	45	4	89	0	4	28	50	75	38	73	13
38	88	2	20	70	4	58	71	89	23	13	30	12	71	79
55	29	81	48	99	13	86	13	10	77	43	76	98	80	99
15	63	4	43	22	54	2	0	48	95	34	59	35	29	4
66	30	47	12	71	42	66	37	91	43	1	11	29	4	5
15	6	51	77	68	22	1	63	73	64	42	85	5	30	57
68	10	27	36	61	9	3	54	32	57	29	16	50	87	26
45	96	38	13	66	95	97	79	94	33	100	8	73	80	40
82	53	21	5	30	55	6	45	48	62	16	22	92	1	45
86	96	31	51	55	85	24	94	62	9	3	1	84	24	44
66	30	57	84	42	52	36	67	78	36	7	82	79	43	82
53	31	21	71	73	9	88	71	12	65	5	55	9	43	32
45	22	2	56	59	96	37	35	82	5	21	14	27	88	16
13	70	15	64	43	78	5	33	78	68	88	89	51	66	71
42	0	74	76	99	56	26	56	46	27	70	67	18	1	57
95	72	93	84	96	23	20	3	97	99	39	8	19	60	58
48	75	75	67	30	61	59	56	70	71	94	98	72	33	30
4	70	37	94	6	91	89	15	2	41	68	29	73	33	29
21	52	13	20	63	77	41	40	62	5	21	6	68	37	13
45	63	75	84	0	28	86	87	24	9	63	33	92	14	40
81	59	84	60	3	41	91	97	89	48	68	20	80	13	49
83	11	70	95	34	45	92	70	80	32	34	32	14	25	84
3	96	76	93	17	28	51	12	4	52	80	100	86	36	40
43	2	9	65	94	44	82	42	74	22	98	54	85	8	21
82	65	93	78	3	35	21	80	24	60	64	38	5	84	11
43	14	11	81	0	75	91	68	53	19	29	62	16	18	41
81	80	92	18	82	6	16	78	34	39	71	77	27	97	73
75	71	99	63	5	70	12	74	14	18	80	50	91	12	92
92	5	14	14	84	16	55	92	23	36	57	55	56	1	64
52	58	25	51	98	40	89	24	98	23	64	37	67	67	39
20	40	56	2	72	94	77	70	86	76	49	14	19	1	81
4	95	39	100	70	6	45	34	9	88	58	8	28	8	46
21	59	16	84	11	43	60	21	32	22	23	41	8	49	43
99	76	56	75	17	100	21	15	41	64	24	46	77	61	81
51	58	72	15	53	49	74	96	55	47	25	98	57	40	6
92	85	54	8	56	60	99	44	60	61	32	30	46	96	6
61	18	63	56	56	32	15	47	55	22	28	85	22	10	7
63	56	90	91	17	43	99	22	72	11	57	14	76	88	6
16	21	16	70	84	38	1	66	64	87	98	29	88	24	14
26	32	8	16	12	9	66	43	26	80	39	89	62	49	7
38	49	78	71	63	89	57	33	43	6	5	45	83	80	90
17	3	84	29	8	14	1	12	48	71	19	88	90	7	73
72	97	24	19	1	39	97	50	55	92	17	36	91	48	35
71	3	33	66	66	29	57	84	32	68	68	2	19	43	70
81	71	89	5	15	86	93	81	50	99	52	86	98	63	54

INDEX